HOW TO grill

HOW TO grill

BY STEVEN RAICHLEN

Photography by Greg Schneider

Styling by Rebecca Flast

WORKMAN PUBLISHING ▪ NEW YORK

In 1975, a young man fresh out of college had grand dreams of becoming a food writer. He applied for—and to his great astonishment received—a fellowship to study medieval cooking in Europe. This book is dedicated with appreciation to the Thomas J. Watson Foundation, which helped turn a dream into a life's work.

· ·

Library of Congress Cataloging-in-Publication Data

Raichlen, Steven
How to Grill / by Steven Raichlen ; photos by Greg Schneider
p. cm.
Includes index.
ISBN 0-7611-2014-9 (alk. paper)—ISBN 0-7611-2482-9
1. Barbecue cookery. I. Title.
TX840.B3 R357 2001
641.7'6—dc21

Cover design by Lisa Hollander and Paul Hanson
Book design by Lisa Hollander with Janet Parker and Susan Macleod
Typesetting by BPE

Workman books are available at special discounts when purchased in bulk for premiums and sales promotions as well as for fund-raising or educational use. Special editions or book excerpts can be created to specification. For details, contact the Special Sales Director at the address below.

Workman Publishing Company, Inc.
708 Broadway
New York, NY 10003-9555
www.workman.com

Printed in the U.S.A.

First Printing May 2001
10 9 8 7

ACKNOWLEDGMENTS

This book began with a simple idea, but it took the hard work of a small army of incredibly dedicated people to bring it to fruition.

My first thanks go to the extraordinary team who spent an incredible amount of time sequestered in a photo studio near the Orange Bowl in Miami to help me show how to grill through literally more than 1,000 color photographs: photographer Greg Schneider; food stylist Rebecca "Beck" Flaste; photographic assistant Maria Jose "Chichi" Mari; Tamara Bigelow (who joined us in the ninth inning, but played a terrific game); Greek grill meister Peter Arvanitakes; and Miami pit master Jack Cooper.

Equally warm thanks go to my friends at Workman Publishing: Suzanne Rafer, the most sensitive, capable, and hard-working editor in the business (in a thousand years I could never thank her enough for her friendship and for all she's contributed to this book); Lisa Hollander, the incredibly gifted art director who transformed a chaotic collection of photographs and text into the handsome book you hold in your hands; creative directors Paul Hanson and Paul Gamarello, who created the look of the *Barbecue! Bible* series; copy editor Barbara Mateer, who put so much productive time and effort into this book, and who gently helped me mind my p's and q's; Patty Bozza, who coordinated all the pieces; publicists Jim Eber and Kate Tyler, who help me spread the barbecue gospel; the diligent assistant editor Beth Doty; the astute Pat Upton; and the energetic Jenny Mandel and Bruce Harris. And, of course, the one and only Peter Workman, whose business it is to turn wild dreams into books that actually sell. There aren't many publishing houses like Workman, and I'm lucky to be a part of it.

A huge round of thanks to my family—especially my wife, Barbara (a partner in all my endeavors), who kept the home fires burning and proved extraordinarily understanding about my crazy work schedule; superkids Jake and Betsy; not to mention my mother-in-law, Miriam Seldin.

My agent, Angela Miller, is such a constant presence in my life, I consider her

Left: Stylist Rebecca Flaste (left) with assistant "Chichi" Mari. Right: Photographer Greg Schneider.

family, too. And Heather Short, as well, who kept the office running smoothly with and without me.

I'd also like to thank some of my many barbecue and food friends for their expertise and support, including Donna Myers of the DHM Group, Elizabeth Karmel of BSMG, Don Hysco at Peoples Woods, Jerry Lawson at W W Wood, Diane Jackson and Mary Huff at Fleishman Hillard, Laura Fleming of the Alaska Seafood Marketing Institute, Roger Berkowitz of Legal Sea Foods, Burt Culver at Culver Duck Farms, Inc., John and Sukey Jamison of Jamison Farm, Brian Maynard at KitchenAid, Karen Adler at Pig Out Publications, Nancy Eisman at Melissa's, Sonja Torres-Weisberg at Cookworks, Alan Milam at Milam's Market, and Carl Johnson at Scotty's Market.

And last but not least, thanks to Jeff Piccoli and Eastman Kodak Company for E100VS films supplied for the book, David Ramchal and Bobby Ramnath and LIB Color Labs for all the E-6 processing, and Manuel Revuelta and Modernage for plates and other photo assistance.

Many grill and accessory manufacturers and food purveyors provided support for this project. They're good people and I encourage you to check out their Web sites.

Alaska Seafood Marketing Institute
www.alaskaseafood.org

Brugger Brothers
www.talamancapepper.com

Calphalon Corporation
www.cooking.com

Carlisle FoodService Products
www.carlislefsp.com

Char-Broil
www.charbroil.com

Charcoal Companion
www.companiongroup.com

Cookworks
www.cookworks.com

Culver Duck Farms
www.culverduck.com

Cutco Cutlery Corporation
www.cutco.com

DCS
www.dcs-range.com

Ducane Gas Grills
www.ducane.com

Grilla Gear
www.grillagear.com

Jamison Farm
www.jamisonfarm.com

KitchenAid
www.kitchenaid.com

Legal Sea Foods
www.sendlegal.com

Melissa's
www.melissas.com

Mushroom Council
www.mushroomcouncil.com

National Cattlemen's Beef Association
www.beef.org

National Pork Producers Council
www.otherwhitemeat.com

OXO International
www.oxo.com

Perdue Farms
www.perdue.com

Peoples Woods
www.peopleswoods.com

Pig Out Publications
www.pigoutpublications.com

Pottery Barn
www.potterybarn.com

Viking Range Corporation
www.vikingrange.com

Weber-Stephen Products
www.weberbbq.com

Williams-Sonoma
www.williams-sonoma.com

Zwilling J. A. Henckels
www.j-a-henckels.com

CONTENTS

LAMB

CHICKEN AND MORE

CONTENTS

DESSERTS

RUBS, SAUCES, AND CONDIMENTS

GRILLS AND GEAR

WHY I WROTE THIS BOOK

This book was born under a giant sycamore tree on a warm summer night in Pittsboro, North Carolina. The place was an elegant country inn called the Fearrington House. I'd been invited there to do what I love best: talk about barbecue and demonstrate grilling. As I do whenever I teach, I opened the floor to questions. For a moment, I feared I was bringing coals to Newcastle. Here I was in the heart of North Carolina barbecue country. What could I possibly teach people who'd been pit roasting pigs and savoring pulled pork since they were old enough to eat solid food?

Perhaps it was the singular setting—a grassy lawn with elegantly set tables—or perhaps it was the leisurely pace of the class and meal that followed. The flowing wine certainly helped. Whatever the reason, the students opened up in a way they rarely do, posing a wide range of questions that aspiring grill masters everywhere would like to ask, but seldom get the opportunity to.

They inquired about the difference between barbecuing and grilling, between direct and indirect grilling. They asked how to tell when a steak was done and how to cook chicken through without burning it. They wanted to know if there was a difference in cooking over charcoal, gas, or wood, and which way was best. They asked how to tell when the coals are ready and whether you really can smoke on a gas grill. They wanted to know how to grill everything from asparagus to zucchini, from lobster to lamb, from pork chops to whole hogs.

It was fascinating for me to see who asked the questions and how. Women were initially more forthcoming than men. Their questions reflected a basic discomfort with lighting and operating a grill. The men posed their questions more tentatively. "This is what I do and it comes out great, but I'm not sure I'm doing it right" was the typical way of framing a query. It wasn't until after the class that one man after another took me aside to confide his grilling uncertainties. "My steaks are always tough," confessed one. "Do I have to boil my ribs before smoking them?" asked another. "How do I keep my salmon from sticking to the grill?" "Can you really grill pizza?" And so on.

The men seemed to have more ego involvement in barbecue. They felt as if they were expected to be experts and were reluctant to admit gaps in their knowledge. Both sexes raised legitimate questions but had no easy mechanism for getting them answered.

After all, cooking is taught in numerous adult education programs, on television, and even in high school, but there are relatively few grilling instructors and even fewer classes on grilling.

In the months following my evening at the Fearrington House, I began to write down the questions I was asked at cooking demonstrations and on call-in radio shows. I did online chats for popular Internet forums and started an "Ask the Grilling Guru" section on my own Web site (www.barbecuebible.com)—again with the goal of learning what people needed to know about grilling.

The more I listened, the more I became convinced that my next book on grilling would actually teach you how to grill, not just offer recipes. And because a picture speaks a thousand words, I decided the book would need photographs. Hundreds of them, showing step-by-step techniques for preparing foods for grilling and how to cook them on the grill.

How to Grill addresses the questions you always had about grilling, but didn't know who to ask. It walks you through every step of live-fire cooking: from choosing and buying a grill to lighting it safely to using it for direct and indirect grilling and smoking. The book covers basic dishes *everyone* should know how to grill: a perfect chicken breast; a fish fillet that doesn't stick; a tender, juicy T-bone. It also covers the theatrical dishes that make you the star of a cookout: beer-can chicken, grilled pizza, even a whole spit-roasted lamb.

How I Wrote This Book

Like many of my brainstorms,

the idea for this book came a lot easier than the execution. I began to make a list of the dishes people habitually have trouble grilling (this list included whole chickens, steaks, briskets, ribs, pork shoulders, and fish of any sort). To this list, I added items I personally wished people would grill more of: vegetables, breads, vegetarian dishes, even desserts. I drafted a second list of essential techniques—direct grilling, indirect grilling, rotisserie grilling, grilling in leaves and in the embers. I began to create recipes that would illustrate these fundamental techniques.

As the book started to take shape, I called my photographer-friend, Greg Schneider, a fellow grilling enthusiast whose expertise in food photography is surpassed only by his insistence on perfection and his willingness to work fourteen hours a day to get it. The third musketeer of the grill would be food stylist Rebecca Flast.

Our team assembled, I next focused on the set-up. I knew I wanted to show how to use a wide variety of grills and cookers, so we brought in tiny hibachis and Volkswagen-size gas grills, smokers, ceramic *kamado* cookers, kettle and electric grills. We also acquired every imaginable type of grilling utensil and accessory, not to mention a dazzling array of charcoals, woods, and smoking chips. The studio began to look like a patio shop showroom, and we hadn't even started grilling!

As we grilled, we tried to break each process into logical steps: how to cut, bone, or fillet; how to rub or marinate; how to place the food on the grate and grill it; and how to recognize when it's done. We cooked each and every dish from start to finish on the spot. Greg created two sets: a how-to set, where we photographed the process, and a beauty set, where we photographed the finished dishes. It was important to all of us to show not only the step-by-step techniques of grilling but how beautiful a finished grilled dish could look.

Everything you see in this book was prepared from scratch and grilled on the sort of grills you or your neighbors have in the backyard. The hands in the photos are mine and while I tried to keep them presentable, you'll see some inevitable burns and scratches. By the way, just because I'm not wearing mitts in a grilling photo doesn't mean you shouldn't. I have hands that have been hardened by years of live-fire cooking, meaning, I don't always wear barbecue mitts when I should. If I thought a photo would be clearer without a mitt on, I left it off.

Two lessons required the help of outside experts and I'd like to acknowledge them here. When it came time to grill a whole lamb on a rotisserie, I called my Greek friend, Peter Arvanitakes. Peter grew up grilling lamb in Athens and there probably isn't a better Greek pit master anywhere on the East Coast. Peter helped cook the lamb on page 195. Jack

Cooper has been barbecuing pork for the neighborhood every Saturday for longer than I've lived in Miami. He was the only person I trusted to help me cook the whole pig on page 154.

How to Use This Book
Writing an instruction book of
this sort poses several challenges. I wanted to make it basic enough for the person who has never grilled in his or her life. (So basic that, after reading it, you can walk into a store, buy a grill, light it, cook on it safely and confidently, and turn out a basic barbecue repertory that includes steaks, ribs, chicken, brisket, and pork shoulder.) But I also wanted a book that would fire the interest of seasoned grill jockeys—and give them new recipes and dishes to show off with for years to come.

Of course, I planned to show *all* the basic live-fire cooking techniques (direct and indirect grilling, rotisserie grilling, smoking, and so on) using both gas and charcoal grills. But I also wanted to cover the basic cooking and butchering skills you need to be a great griller: how to spatchcock a chicken or trim a beef tenderloin, for example; how to peel shrimp or assemble satés; and how to make and use rubs, mops, and barbecue sauces.

To achieve these goals, I divided *How to Grill* into three sections. The first covers the basic techniques of grilling: You'll see how to light grills (both charcoal and gas) and how to set them up for direct and indirect grilling, rotisserie grilling, and smoking. You'll learn how to replenish the coals of a charcoal grill and how to smoke on a gas grill; how to operate a rotisserie and a smoker.

The second and larger part of *How to Grill* consists of more than 100 individual lessons, each focusing on a particular technique. In the beef chapter, for example, you'll learn how to grill everything from a whole prime rib to a tiny saté, including a succulent steak, an opulent whole beef tenderloin, smoky ribs, and perfect burgers. Most of the chapters focus on the foods you'd expect to find in a grill book—beef, pork, poultry, fish, shellfish, and vegetables—but you'll also find oddball items that will earn you the amazement of your family and friends, including grilled pizza, quesadillas, salads, tofu, and even a few desserts.

Each lesson includes a brief description of the technique and a photograph of how a finished dish using that technique can look. The **Tips** are designed to make the execution of the technique easier and warn you about how to avoid potential pitfalls. The **Method** listing tells you how to set up your grill, while **Cooking Time** and **Advance Preparation** give you a rough guideline as to how long the preparation, marinating, and grilling will take (this is a *rough* guide, as everyone works at a different pace). **You'll Need** alerts you to a nonfood item you may not already have in your kitchen—butcher's string and bamboo skewers, for example.

Next come the **technique photos** and **captions,** followed by a representative **recipe** (which illustrates the technique). **Variations** and **Also Good For** tell you about other interesting ways to use the basic recipe and technique. Each photograph of a finished dish has a caption naming the principle dish and its accompaniments. When an accompaniment is capitalized, the recipe or technique for preparing it will be found elsewhere in the book.

Obviously, the technique photos refer to specific dishes (the ones described in the recipes), but they also should be viewed as general how-to guides. On page 204, for example, you'll learn how to truss a chicken, but the same technique applies to a turkey, duck, or game hen. On page 354, you'll find how to grill a "raft" of asparagus, but any long, slender vegetable, from okra to green

I wanted to show how to use a wide variety of grills and cookers, so we brought in **tiny hibachis and Volkswagen-size gas grills,** smokers, ceramic kamado cookers, kettle and electric grills.

beans, can be cooked in this fashion. And just because I use a particular spice blend on ribs doesn't mean you have to. The instructions let you know when to spice the ribs; they're not meant to lock you into a particular blend.

The recipes have been chosen as exemplars of particular grilling or barbecuing techniques. Many are classics of American or world barbecue: Texas-style barbecued brisket (see page 44), North Carolina pulled pork (see page 109), smoked salmon (see page 313), shish kebabs (see page 188), yakitori (see page 252), and even s'mores (see page 438). Other recipes are personal favorites of mine that illustrate specific techniques. The Sichuan-Spiced Lamb Chops on page 180, for example, will teach you how to triple rub and grill loin lamb chops. The Rosemary-Grilled Scallops on page 345 will show you how to use a fresh rosemary sprig as a skewer for grilling.

As with all my books, I hope you'll use these recipes as a springboard for your imagination. Perhaps you want to use the tandoori marinade on page 182 with chicken instead of lamb. Or maybe you want to "beer can" a game hen or duck instead of a chicken (see page 219). The jerk pork on page 115 could just as easily be prepared with a pork shoulder or tenderloin as with the shoulder ham shown in the photos. In other words, I invite you to experiment with these recipes and make my specialties your own.

The last part of the book covers basic equipment and includes the different types of grills and the various utensils, accessories, and fuels you'll need or find handy.

I've said it before and I'll say it again, grilling isn't brain surgery. The most important thing is to have fun. Remember: There's no such thing as a mistake in the kitchen — just a new recipe waiting to be discovered! Your chicken caught fire? Scrape off the burnt part and dust the bird with chopped parsley, garlic, and lemon zest. ("That's how they do it in Tuscany," you'll proudly tell your guests.) Your rack of lamb comes off the grill still raw in the center? Declare with confidence that you're using a new technique called double grilling, cut it in half, and put it back on the fire. I've been in this business for 25 years and I still learn something new every day.

By all means, let me know how your grilling's going. I'd love to hear from you on my Web site: www.barbecuebible.com. Use the "Ask the Grilling Guru" bulletin board to tout your successes and troubleshoot your mistakes. I try to answer every serious query (although it may take me a few weeks to do so).

Grilling is the world's oldest and most widespread cooking method. I hope this book will add to your knowledge and help you eat a lot of good food in the process.

Steven Raichlen

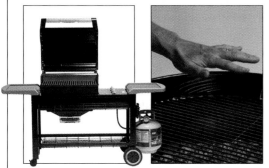

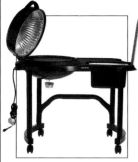

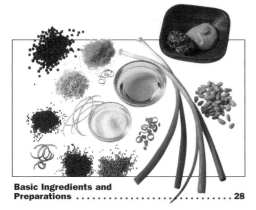

GETTING STARTED

Nothing brings out flavor like grilling: the sanguine taste of beef, the briny succulence of seafood, the natural sweetness of vegetables. The smoke and charring associated with grilling add a depth of flavor unattainable by any other cooking method.

Perhaps that's why interest in grilling is skyrocketing, fueled by innovative new grills, ingenious new accessories, and our continuing lust for bold flavors. Grilling is healthy; grilling is theatrical; and it's a magnet for people when you entertain. Show me a man or woman who is comfortable behind a grill and I'll show you a seasoned showman, a consummate host, and a cook who has the guts to put his or her money where his or her mouth is.

This book is designed to take the uncertainty out of grilling. In the following pages you'll learn how to light a fire safely—with any luck on the first try. You'll learn how to control any fire—charcoal, wood, or gas—so that it will give you a steady, reliable source of heat. You'll learn how

to master the basics—direct and indirect grilling—as well as specialized techniques, such as smoking, rotisserie grilling, and roasting in the embers. And you'll learn about the various grills, accessories, fuels, rubs, and seasonings you need to make perfect grilled, barbecued, and smoked food every time.

Setting the Stage

Most Americans know something about barbecuing and grilling (according to Barbecue Industry Association figures, 85 percent of American families own grills and fire them up more than 3 billion times a year). But everyone has to start somewhere, so imagine for a moment that you've never used a grill or even owned one before.

Before I begin grilling, I make sure my grill is on level ground and all the fuel and utensils I'll need are close at hand.

Grills are available in every imaginable size, shape, style, and price range. Before you can choose a grill, however, you need to consider your cooking habits. Do you usually just cook for yourself and perhaps a companion or do you like to share your culinary prowess with large numbers of friends? This will help you decide what size grill to buy. Do you tend to cook the same three dishes over and over or are you an adventurer? (I hope you will be after reading this book!) This will tell you whether to buy a basic no-frills model or a grill with all the latest bells and whistles. Are you convenience and result oriented, focusing on the outcome over the process? Or is the journey of live-fire cooking just as exciting to you as the ultimate destination? (And what's your tolerance for uncer-

tainty?) This will help you make the most important decision facing the fledgling griller: whether to buy a gas grill or a charcoal grill.

I'd like to share one tip with you here: If you're mechanically minded, few things are more satisfying than assembling a grill out of the box. If you're all thumbs, most hardware stores will assemble the grill for you for a modest fee, or you may even be able to save time and money by buying a floor model.

The Perfect Spot

Once you have your grill assembled, the next thing to decide is where to put it. A patio or deck makes a logical choice—preferably near a door off your kitchen. (Most of your prep work will take place in the

kitchen and that's where you'll find that basting brush or bottle of barbecue sauce you should have remembered to bring outdoors but didn't.)

A grill puts out a lot of heat, so you should position it several feet away from the side of the house (especially one with wooden shingles) or any plants or shrubbery. You'll have an easier time with heat and smoke control if you choose a spot with good ventilation, but that's sheltered from the wind. (However, it's axiomatic that wherever you place the grill, the smoke will blow in your face.)

The grill should rest securely on level ground—even if it's on the grass in your backyard. When positioning a grill on a wooden deck, remember that sparks and live embers can fall from a charcoal grill (and fat can drip from a gas grill). Place a large, heavy sheet of metal under the grill or use a patio protector, like the one manufactured by DiversiTech (see page 474). Never operate a grill indoors, in a garage, or in a carport. Grills put out carbon monoxide, which is toxic. For that matter, it's not a good idea to grill under a trellis, arbor, or low-canopied tree.

It helps to have a counter or table near your grill (it's my experience you can never have enough workspace when grilling). An outdoor sink, garden hose, or bowl of water is always useful for washing your hands during grilling. Don't underestimate the importance of a good light source after sundown. It can make all the difference between recognizing when food is cooked or when it's still raw or burned beyond redemption. Try to position your grill to take advantage of the best light on your patio or invest in a grill light (see page 474). It's handy also to have an electric outlet nearby to plug in the light or your rotisserie.

As grill mania sweeps the country, the simple backyard barbecue grill is being replaced by elaborate outdoor kitchens, complete with sinks and built-in refrigerators. The latter are handy for keeping meats and drinks cold, but you can also use a large cooler filled with ice. You may want to invest in a couple of large new plastic garbage bins with tight-fitting lids for storing your charcoal, wood chips, and even grill accessories (I currently have three). For that matter, a clean garbage can can be converted into an outdoor refrigerator for large quantities of meat or even a whole lamb or salmon simply by filling it with ice.

An Important Note About Safety

Most important of all, of course, is to never, *ever* leave a lit grill unattended. Second in importance is to have a dry chemical fire extinguisher on hand (see page 472). Make sure it's fully charged and current (someone at your local fire department will be able to check this for you) and make sure you know how to use it. Also handy are a bucket of sand (for dumping over

a ground fire) and a box of coarse salt (for sprinkling over a grease fire in your grill). When shutting down a gas grill, shut off the gas at the tank as well as the burner. At the start of every season you should run a little fire drill. I hope you never need it, but at least you'll be prepared if you do.

Let me also say a few words about what you shouldn't have close to your grill: The short list includes small children, pets, and flammables. You don't want a hyperactive four-year-old or golden retriever knocking over your fire. If you use lighter fluid to ignite your coals (on page 8 I'll show you some great alternatives to petroleum starters), store the can far away from the fire.

I also have some thoughts on what to wear—and I'm not just talking about your "Kiss the Chef" apron. Always wear closed shoes, not sandals, to protect your feet from dripping grease or falling cinders. If you have long hair, it's a good idea to tie it back. When grilling during the daytime, wear a hat and sunscreen to protect your skin from the sun. I won't tell you not to wear shorts and a T-shirt (after all, this is barbecue), but I will observe that many serious grill jockeys I know wear long-sleeve shirts and long pants—again for protection from heat and sparks. You should have on hand some thick grill gloves, oven mitts, or pot holders. Finally, that apron will help you stay clean. If you want to look like a pro, tie the apron around your waist with the bib

portion folded down and inside so it covers your legs (professional chefs *never* wear bib aprons). I like to tuck one or two clean dish towels into the apron ties—these are handy for wiping your fingers or mopping up spills.

The Mise en Place

While we're on the subject of chefs, there are three words used in every professional kitchen that are essential for master grilling: *mise en place.* The *mise* (as it's affectionately referred to in American kitchens) refers to the basic setup of ingredients and equipment you need at grillside before you start cooking.

A typical *mise en place* for a barbecue would include your fuel (extra charcoal or propane and soaked wood chips); your tools (grill brush, tongs, spatula, basting brush or mop, grill gloves or pot holders, a cutting board and knives for carving, platters or plates for serving); and your ingredients (salt, pepper, and seasonings in shakers; bastes and butters in bowls; sauces in bowls or squirt bottles; and, of course, the food to be grilled—on ice if necessary). You might want to have a bowl or bucket of sudsy water nearby for hand washing.

Use a grill brush on a hot grate to dislodge burnt-on food.

A WORD ABOUT CLEANLINESS

A certain editor I know (bless her) used to scrub her grill grate with Brillo until it shone like silver. More than one bubba I've seen on the barbecue circuit cooks in a smoker so encrusted with grease and grime, it's a wonder it's not condemned by the local health department. So how clean should your grill be? I suggest a happy medium.

THE GRATE: The grate is the part of the grill that comes in direct contact with the food, so it should be clean. Fortunately, this is as simple as bringing it up to grilling temperature when you preheat the grill and then scrubbing it with a dry stiff wire brush before adding the food. The heat loosens any burnt-on scraps and sterilizes the grate, while the brush removes the debris. There's no need to scrub the metal with abrasives or soap. On the contrary: You season a grate, by using it and brushing it clean (washing is unnecessary).

I clean my grill grate twice: once before putting the food on and again after grilling. The latter is especially important when you grill fish. Run the grill until any cooked-on bits of food or oils are burnt off, and then clean the grate with your wire brush. With a gas grill simply let it continue burning for 15 to 30 minutes. With a charcoal grill, you may need to rake the partially depleted coals into a pile to concentrate the heat. (Never extinguish used coals with water. Simply cover the grill and close all the vents or uncover the grill and open all the vents and let the coals burn out.) Should the coals burn out before the grill grate is clean, hose it down with water and scrub off any burnt-on pieces with a wire brush. Dry it with paper towels to prevent rusting.

THE FIREBOX: In general, the firebox (the metal bowl of a kettle grill or rectangular box of a gas grill) will clean itself in the process of grilling. Of course, any bits of food that have fallen through the bars of the grate or pools of congealed fat should be shoveled out with a garden trowel. One thing you *should* clean often is the catch pan, or drip pan, for grease. In terms of more long-term maintenance, barbecue shops sell heavy-duty grill cleaners you can use for removing a season's worth of soot.

The Countdown

More than with virtually any other type of cooking, time management is key to successful barbecuing and grilling. This is especially true when working with charcoal: You need to budget time to light the coals and let them burn down to the proper temperature before you start cooking. That doesn't include the time you need for rubbing and marinating, smoking, or letting the meat rest before carving or pulling. And because you're cooking, and often serving, outdoors, allow extra time for setting up your cooking and dining area.

Here's a basic timetable that will help you get your grill lit, your food rubbed, marinated, and cooked, and your guests served—without having a nervous breakdown.

AT THE BEGINNING OF BARBECUE SEASON (if you're not a year-round griller): Take the grill out of your garage or basement. If you are using a gas grill, make sure there are no spiders or cobwebs under the burner knobs or in the grill manifolds (dislodge any you may find with a slender bamboo skewer). If any of the tiny pinholes on the burner tubes are clogged, unclog them with a pin. Make sure the burner valves turn freely: If any feel stuck, spray in a little WD-40. Check that all connections are tight and that there are no holes or worn spots in any of the hoses. And most important: Follow all of the manufacturer's maintenance instructions.

THE DAY BEFORE YOUR BARBECUE: Rub or marinate large cuts of meat, like briskets and pork shoulders. Marinate them overnight in a nonreactive (glass or stainless steel) pan or bowl or even in a clean garbage bag in the refrigerator. Turn the meat several times to ensure even marinating. If using a gas grill, fill the propane tank and one or two backup tanks. If using a charcoal grill, buy a few extra bags of charcoal. Prepare side dishes that aren't time sensitive, such as baked beans or coleslaw.

THE MORNING BEFORE YOUR BARBECUE: Rub or marinate medium-size cuts of meat, such as chickens or whole fish. Make your sauces. If you're smoking large cuts of meat, you may need as many as 6 to 8 hours for smoking. Soak the wood chips an hour before you plan to start and light your grill or smoker accordingly.

THE AFTERNOON BEFORE YOUR BARBECUE: Indoors, rub or marinate small cuts of meat, like steaks or chicken breasts. Skewer kebab ingredients; slather the garlic butter on corn and bread; prep vegetables and side dishes. Prepare the salad (have your dressing ready, but don't toss it in the salad). Set up your bar or prepare drinks but don't add ice until the last minute. Ice down the beer or soft drinks.

Ready nonperishables in advance.

Outdoors, set up tables and get out your plates, glasses, and cutlery. Clean and ready your grill. Lay out your grilling utensils.

ONE HOUR BEFORE YOU PLAN TO START GRILLING: Soak wood chips or chunks in cold water to cover. If you are using a charcoal grill, set up your chimney starter. Light it 20 to 40 minutes before you actually plan to start grilling. One chimney starter's worth of coals (40 to 50 briquettes) is enough to fuel a 22½-inch kettle grill for 1 hour. When working on a large grill, like a table grill, you may need two or three chimney starters in order to light enough charcoals at one time. When the coals blaze orange, dump them out of the chimney starter and rake them over the bottom of the grill. Place the grate on the grill over the fire. Let the coals burn until lightly ashed over, 5 to 10 minutes.

If you are using a gas grill, preheat it 15 to 20 minutes before grilling. If you're smoking, start the grill on high and add wood chips to the smoker box or put on a smoker pouch (see page 17) and preheat until you see smoke. Then reduce the heat to the desired temperature.

JUST BEFORE PUTTING THE FOOD ON THE GRILL: Clean the hot grill grate with a wire brush and oil the grate as shown on pages 26 and 27. Add the wood chips, if called for and if you are using a charcoal grill. You'll need two handfuls of chips (about 1 cup) for each hour of grilling. Put the food on the grill. If what you're cooking will take more than 1 hour, have backup charcoal in a chimney

starter ready to light 15 minutes before you need it.

WHILE YOU GRILL: First, grill items that can be prepared ahead, served at room temperature, or that hold well. This includes vegetables, pulled pork, brisket, and ribs. Grill smaller items that must be served hot off the grill—steaks, hamburgers, chicken breasts—when people are ready to eat them. Don't forget to let meats stand for a few minutes before carving and serving them. This allows them to regain their juiciness.

RIGHT AFTER GRILLING: Run the grill on high to burn off any bits of food. Brush the grate with a wire brush to remove what debris is left.

FOUR TO SIX HOURS AFTER THE BARBECUE OR THE NEXT DAY: Drain or discard the fat in the catch or drip pan. If you used a charcoal grill, scoop or empty the ashes and burnt wood chips into the trash, using a garden trowel or small shovel. Make sure the ashes are stone cold before discarding them. In fact, to play it safe, put them in a small metal trash can first.

AT THE END OF THE BARBECUE SEASON (again, for those folks who don't grill all year round): Scrub down your grill. Remove any ash from a charcoal grill or from the smoker box of a gas grill. Oil any parts of the grill that seem prone to rusting. If you have a gas grill, disconnect the tank. If you are leaving your grill outdoors, cover it with a tarp or cover. Even indoors, it doesn't hurt to cover it.

THE DIFFERENT WAYS TO GRILL

Before we start, a word about nomenclature. The word *barbecue* means different things to different people, depending on where you live. On the East and West Coasts of the United States and in the Frost Belt and Canada, it describes any sort of live-fire cooking outdoors. In Texas, the South, and parts of the Midwest, it refers to a specific kind of meat that's slow cooked and heavily smoked, usually via the indirect method. Thus, to a North Carolinian, barbecue means pulled pork; to a Texan, beef brisket. Elsewhere, barbecue may refer to a piece of cooking equipment (the barbecue grill), a social gathering (for example, a church barbecue), or simply a meal outdoors.

Being an ecumenical sort of guy, I use the word in all these senses in this book. But here are the precise technical terms for the various types of live-fire cooking.

GRILLING: Cooking food directly over glowing coals or a fire. In general, grilling involves small or thin pieces of meat (like steaks, chicken breasts, and fish fillets) cooked quickly and directly over a hot fire. When I say hot, I mean it: Most grilling is done at 450° to 650°F.

DIRECT GRILLING: Another name for the process just described .

MODIFIED DIRECT GRILLING: A variation of direct grilling done on a grill with a very deep firebox so that the grate rests relatively high above the coals. This enables you to grill large cuts of meat, like pork shoulders and even whole pigs, without burning them.

INDIRECT GRILLING: A hybrid process that bridges the techniques of grilling and barbecuing. In indirect grilling, the grill is set up in such a way that the fire is on one side or opposite sides of the grill and the food is cooked away from it, over the unlit portion. The virtue of this method is that it turns your grill into a sort of outdoor oven. Indirect grilling enables you to cook through a large piece of meat, like a whole chicken or pork shoulder, without burning the exterior. It also allows you to smoke the food by adding wood chips or chunks to the fire. With indirect grilling, you don't need to turn the food. Indirect grilling is generally done at a medium temperature, 325° to 350°F. It's always done with the grill covered.

BARBECUING: True barbecue (as practiced in Texas and the American South) is a low-heat, indirect method that uses lots of wood smoke to cook and flavor the food. The traditional cooker is a horizontal barrel smoker, or pit, which has a firebox at one end and a cooking or smoking chamber at the other. The food cooks at a low (225° to 250°F) to medium-low (300°F) temperature and slowly (as long as 18 hours for a brisket), with a generous amount of wood smoke (usually oak or hickory). The resulting food has an intense smoky flavor and is generally tender enough to pull apart with your fingers. A growing number of cooks have recreational-size pits at home, but in this book, I'll tell you how to barbecue on a gas or charcoal grill.

SMOKING: A variation on true barbecue. Smoking can be done in a horizontal barrel smoker (see above) or in a vertical water smoker (see page 25). There are two types of smoking: **hot smoking** and **cold smoking**. Hot smoking, really another name for barbecuing, is generally done at 225° to 250°F and I have included techniques for it in this book. In cold smoking, the food is located so far away from the fire that it smokes without cooking. It is used to make Scottish- or Norwegian-style salmon and sometimes beef jerky. It's beyond the scope of this book.

Basting a duck as it rotisserie grills makes for a crisp, flavorful skin.

ROTISSERIE GRILLING (SPIT ROASTING): Cooking meats on a slowly rotating spit. When cooking larger pieces of meat (a whole lamb, for example—see page 195), the fire may be under the food. More often, it's next to the food, as you'd find on your average backyard grill with a rotisserie. The slow turning bastes the meat inter-

Sweet potatoes and white potatoes are particularly flavorful when roasted in the embers.

nally and externally, making rotisserie grilling ideal for roasts and chickens.

ROASTING IN THE EMBERS: This is, perhaps, the oldest method of grilling. The food (often a tuber, like a yam or potato) is cooked right in the coals. You scrape off the burnt exterior to reveal the soft, smoky flesh inside.

Banana leaves make perfect wrappers for grilling fragile pieces of fish.

GRILLING IN LEAVES: Another ancient method of grilling. Pieces of fish, chicken, or pork—or even whole quail—are wrapped in leaves and cooked on the grill or in the embers. One good example of the use of this technique is the Bluefish in Banana Leaves on page 307. The New England clambake, with its seaweed-lined fire pit, combines the techniques of grilling in leaves and roasting in embers.

GRILLING ON A CHARCOAL GRILL

Are you process or result oriented? Adventuresome or safety minded? What's important to you when you travel: the journey or the destination? These are some pretty philosophical questions, but the answers will help you choose the right barbecue grill. I'm referring, of course, to the great debate that has divided grill jockeys for decades: charcoal versus gas.

Most professional grill jockeys prefer charcoal and with good reason. Charcoal generally burns hotter than gas, so you get a more truly grilled taste. Charcoal grills are more versatile than gas grills: It's easier to toss wood chips or herbs on the coals and you get a better smoke flavor. Not to mention the fact that they give you something to do during the barbecue (in other words, they require constant attention), which will make you feel like a real pit master, not a cook whose stove happens to be outdoors. Charcoal grills cost a lot less than gas grills and you can use them to burn both charcoal and wood. Visit a barbecue festival, like Memphis in May or the Kansas City Royal, and you won't find a gas grill around for miles.

So why doesn't everyone grill on charcoal? First of all, it's messy.

It's also relatively unpredictable (every fire burns differently) and it's harder to control the heat. A charcoal fire invariably has hot spots and cool spots and doesn't burn the same way 30 minutes or an hour into the cooking process as it does when you first put the food on the grill. And if you are cooking for longer than an hour, the coals must be replenished. So charcoal grills require more supervision than gas grills. Of course, that's what makes using them so much fun.

Once you master grilling over charcoal, you can pretty much cook on any type of grill, which is another reason to make your first one a charcoal grill. And, with that in mind, the photographs illustrating the techniques in the book feature charcoal grills. Every serious grill master should have at least one charcoal grill on his or her patio.

Lighting a Charcoal Grill

In the old days you doused the charcoal with lighter fluid and tossed on a match. Maybe it lit and maybe it didn't. To solve this problem, manufacturers created self-lighting charcoal, which has the lighter fluid built into it. As you'd imagine, self-lighting charcoal burns easily and evenly, and it's available in most supermarkets. But many people still don't like the idea of grilling food over charcoal that's been laced with petroleum products. Today, there are two cleaner, safer, more ecologically sound ways to light charcoal.

THE ELECTRIC STARTER: An electric starter is a looped heating element you place beneath a pile of charcoal.

To use an electric starter, nestle its metal end in a pile of charcoal in your grill and plug the starter in. It will glow red and begin igniting the charcoal after 2 or 3 minutes. Pull it out after a good portion of the coals are blazing—10 to 15 minutes.

Plug the device in and the coals will be blazing in 15 minutes. The electric starter is clean and easy to work with, but it doesn't light the charcoal quite as evenly as does a chimney starter (see below). Another drawback is that you need a power outlet near your grill. I like to use an electric starter to light a deep or small grill, like a ceramic cooker or hibachi.

THE CHIMNEY STARTER: The more popular method for lighting charcoal is to use a chimney starter, a large, upright, hollow metal cylinder with a wire partition in the center. The charcoal briquettes or lump charcoal go in the top and a crumpled piece of newspaper goes in the bottom. As an alternative to newspaper, you can use paraffin starters (see page 478). You light the paper and in 15 to 25 minutes you have blazing coals. The beauty of a chimney starter is that its cylindrical shape helps ignite the coals evenly. Also, it allows you to light additional coals to replenish those in a smoker or grill used for indirect grilling in advance of when you'll need them. Chimney starters are widely available at grill shops and hardware stores.

SETTING UP A CHIMNEY STARTER

1 Place one or two loosely crumpled sheets of newspaper in the bottom of the chimney starter.

2 Place the chimney starter on the bottom grate of your grill. Place the charcoal briquettes, lump charcoal (seen here), or even chunks of wood in the top of the starter, filling the cylinder to the top.

3 Light the newspaper using a gas lighter (a lighter with a long metal snout) or a long kitchen match. At first, you'll see a thick column of smoke. This is normal. Then, the charcoal or wood will ignite.

4 The coals are ready when all glow orange-red, a process that takes 15 to 25 minutes.

How to Set Up a Charcoal Grill for Direct Grilling

It takes 15 to 25 minutes for the charcoal in a chimney starter to light and another 5 to 10 for it to start to ash over so you can begin cooking. For everyday grilling when you're only cooking a few small items (a couple of chops, hamburgers, or steaks, for example, or boneless chicken breasts or fish fillets), a simple **single-zone** fire will do just fine. To make a single-zone fire, first light the charcoal in a chimney starter. When the coals glow bright orange, dump them out and spread or rake them into a single layer across the bottom of the grill. Leave one corner of the grill without coals as a safety

GAUGING THE HEAT OF A CHARCOAL FIRE

To gauge the heat, hold your hand about 4 inches above the grate and start counting "one Mississippi, two Mississippi, three Mississippi." Soon the intensity of the heat will force you to remove your hand.

- A high fire is a two to three Mississippi fire.
- A medium-high fire is a four to five Mississippi fire.
- A medium fire is a six to eight Mississippi fire.
- A medium-low fire is a nine to ten Mississippi fire.
- A low fire is an eleven to fourteen Mississippi fire.

zone over which you can move the food if it starts to burn. Start grilling when the coals are just beginning to ash over.

Over the years I've experimented with a lot of charcoal configurations for grilling larger items, and I've finally settled on a setup I call a **three-zone** fire. Some of the coals are piled in a double layer on

one side of the grill, which gives you a very hot zone for searing. The remaining coals are arranged in a single layer in the center of the grill, which gives you a moderately hot zone for cooking. The remaining area of the grill is left without coals, which gives you a cool zone where you can move the food if it starts to burn. A garden hoe makes

SETTING UP A CHARCOAL GRILL FOR DIRECT GRILLING

Dump the lit coals from the chimney starter into the bottom of the grill. Wear a heavy glove to protect your hand.

Using a garden hoe, or other long-handled implement, rake the burning coals to form either a single-zone or three-zone fire.

A three-zone fire: The coals are in a double layer on the left side (for a strong blast of heat for searing) and in a single layer in the center (for a steady, moderate heat for cooking). The right side of the grill is left free of coals to give you a cool zone for keeping food warm without overcooking.

When grilling chicken directly over a three-zone fire, to increase the heat, move the chicken toward the hot zone. To decrease the heat or prevent burning, move the chicken over the cool zone.

a handy tool for spreading out the coals to make a three-zone fire. Once the coals are arranged, wait until they start to ash over before grilling.

....

Replenishing the Coals

....

Once your fire begins to ash over, you have about 1 hour cooking time before it becomes too weak to continue the cooking. For prolonged grilling, you'll need to replenish the coals. The easiest way to do this is simply to toss fresh charcoal on the fire. The problem with this method is that it takes 10 to 15 minutes for the new charcoal to light and the process generates an acrid smoke, although lump charcoal ignites more quickly and generates less

smoke than charcoal briquettes.

The alternative method is to light a fresh batch of charcoal in a

WHEN IS CHARCOAL HOT ENOUGH?

Once you've dumped the lit coals into the grill, it will take time for them to achieve the temperature you need for direct grilling. Here's a rough guide to how long you'll need to wait, but remember coals behave differently in every grill. For indirect grilling, control the temperature by opening and closing the vents.

TEMPERATURE	TIME	APPEARANCE
High (450° to 650°F)	5 to 10 minutes	Glowing bright orange
Medium-High (400°F)	10 to 15 minutes	Glowing bright orange with a faint layer of ash
Medium (325° to 350°F)	15 to 25 minutes	Glowing orange with a light layer of ash
Medium-Low (300°F)	25 to 30 minutes	Pale orange with a medium layer of ash
Low (225° to 250°F)	30 to 40 minutes	Faint orange with a thick layer of ash

chimney starter 15 to 20 minutes before you need it. Light the starter on brick or a concrete slab or on bare ground away from grass or anything flammable. Never light a chimney starter on a wood deck. Add the hot coals to the hot zone of your fire. (If using an electric starter, you'll have to light the charcoal in a second grill, then transfer the coals to the first grill with a shovel.)

All this sounds a good deal more complicated than it really is. With a little practice, you'll instinctively know how your grill heats and when to add fresh coals. When it comes down to it, controlling the heat is as simple as moving food closer to or farther away from the fire.

ADDING COALS

When the coals have mostly turned to ash, after about 1 hour, it's time to replenish them.

If using unlit charcoal, first rake the remaining embers into a pile and place fresh fuel on top of them. Leave the grill uncovered until the charcoal lights.

Or, light a fresh batch of charcoal in a chimney starter on the side. Don't place the chimney starter on or near anything flammable. Add the hot coals to your fire and rake them out into the desired configuration.

Light hardwood chunks in a chimney starter exactly as you would charcoal.

You can buy wood chunks in an Instant Light Cookout Bag sold by W W Wood of Texas (see Mail-Order Sources, page 481). To light, simply touch a match to the corners of the bag. You'll have blazing wood in 15 minutes.

You can toss a hardwood log on a conventional charcoal fire. The blazing log will give your food the delectable taste of wood smoke.

How to Set Up a Charcoal Grill for Indirect Grilling

As noted earlier, when grilling using the indirect method, the food is cooked next to, not directly over, the fire. You position the coals on either side of the grill, leaving the center bare.

When grilling food that requires several hours of cooking using the indirect method, you'll need to replenish the coals and wood chips (if you are using them) every hour. The easiest way to do this is to add twelve unlit pieces of charcoal to each side. Leave the grill uncovered until they light (they will light in a covered grill, but you may get an acrid-tasting smoke on the food). The drawback of this method is that you lose heat when you uncover the grill, lengthening the cooking time, and letting out flavorful smoke, if you're using wood. I prefer to light a fresh batch of charcoal in a chimney starter on the side and add the coals to the side basket.

Direct Grilling Over Wood

Charcoal gives you a clean, high, dry heat for grilling, but it doesn't impart much flavor. The flavor-producing components are burnt out of the wood when it's kilned to make charcoal. Wood, on the other hand, gives you a great flavor—a fact appreciated by grill jockeys from Florence to Buenos Aires. (I'm talking here about grilling over wood, not using wood for smoking.) In order to enjoy wood-grilled food, you used to have to go to a restaurant. New fuels and technologies have made it easy to grill over wood at home, and you'll be astonished by the flavor. If you have a kettle-style charcoal grill, it's easy to cook with wood. Just remember: *Always grill over hardwood,* such as oak, hickory, apple, cherry, and mesquite. Softwoods, like pine and fir, produce too much soot and

unpleasant, even dangerous, residues.

There are two basic ways to grill with wood. The first is to use hardwood chunks in place of charcoal. (Look for wood chunks at grill shops or hardware stores, or see the Mail-Order Sources on page 481.) The second is to toss a log or two on a charcoal fire to achieve that fragrant wood flavor.

The best way to gauge the temperature of meat is by using an instant-read meat thermometer. Insert it into the thickest part of the meat or poultry but not so that it touches a bone. Ground beef should always be cooked to at least 160°F. Pork should be cooked to at least 150°F. Pork for pulling should be cooked to at least 190°F. Chicken and turkey breasts should be cooked to at least 170°F; thighs should be cooked to 180°F.

DEGREE OF DONENESS	INTERNAL TEMPERATURE FOR BEEF AND LAMB	INTERNAL TEMPERATURE FOR PORK, CHICKEN, AND TURKEY
Rare	125° to 130°F	Not applicable
Medium-Rare	140° to 145°F	Not applicable
Medium	150° to 160°F	160° to 165°F (pork only)
Medium-Well	165° to 170°F	170° to 175°F
Well	170° to 190°F	180° to 195°F

SETTING UP A CHARCOAL GRILL FOR INDIRECT GRILLING

Light your charcoal in a chimney starter, as described on page 9. If your grill lacks side baskets, rake the coals into two piles at opposite sides of the grill, using a long-handled implement, like a garden hoe. Place a drip pan in the center.

If your grill comes with side baskets, fill them with lit coals. Place an aluminum foil drip pan in the center.

Most indirect grilling is done at a moderate heat. To adjust the temperature, partially open the vents on the bottom. Closed vents will extinguish the fire. Wide-open vents, like these pictured here on a Weber kettle grill, will give you a hot fire.

Adjust the vents on the top of the grill lid. Again, closed vents (top) will extinguish the fire. Wide-open vents (bottom) will give you a hot fire.

The vent is partially open on this Big Green Egg charcoal grill to control air flow and, thus, the heat.

When the vents are adjusted properly, the temperature of the grill will be between 325° and 350°F, depending on the recipe.

To smoke on a charcoal grill, first add the lit coals to the side baskets or rake them out into two piles on opposite sides of the grill.

You'll generate smoke by adding soaked, drained wood chips to the hot coals.

How to Smoke on a Charcoal Grill

One of the advantages of grilling is that it allows you to add the old-fashioned flavor of wood smoke. Throughout this book, for the most part, you'll be instructed to use wood chips for smoking, but you could use chunks or even whole logs to generate wood smoke. Wood chips are available in an intriguing array of "flavors" (a basic "larder" would include hickory, oak, apple, cherry, and mesquite).

To get good smoke flavor out of the chips, soak them in water to cover for an hour or so, then drain the chips well before placing them on the fire. I usually soak my chips in a disposable aluminum foil pan, adding cool water to cover. Sometimes, for extra flavor, I'll soak the chips in beer, wine, or apple cider.

To turn your charcoal grill into a smoker, set it up for indirect grilling. When you're ready to cook, toss a handful of soaked, drained wood chips (about one-half cup) or some wood chunks on the mound of coals on each side of the grill (for a total of one cup of chips). With small quantities, I simply shake the water off before adding them. The smoke should start rising almost at once. Cover the grill and adjust the vents to obtain the desired temperature. When smoking large cuts of meat, you generally need to add an additional handful of drained chips to each side when you replenish the coals every hour.

GRILLING ON A GAS GRILL

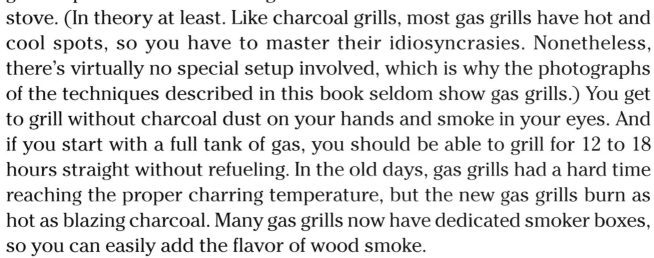

So why doesn't everyone grill over charcoal? One simple word: *convenience*. Most gas grills start with the push of a button. You control the heat with the twist of a knob, which makes cooking on a gas grill as predictable as cooking on the stove. (In theory at least. Like charcoal grills, most gas grills have hot and cool spots, so you have to master their idiosyncrasies. Nonetheless, there's virtually no special setup involved, which is why the photographs of the techniques described in this book seldom show gas grills.) You get to grill without charcoal dust on your hands and smoke in your eyes. And if you start with a full tank of gas, you should be able to grill for 12 to 18 hours straight without refueling. In the old days, gas grills had a hard time reaching the proper charring temperature, but the new gas grills burn as hot as blazing charcoal. Many gas grills now have dedicated smoker boxes, so you can easily add the flavor of wood smoke.

Lighting a Gas Grill

Nothing could be easier than lighting a gas grill, but here, too, there's a science. First and foremost, always open the lid of the grill before you turn on the gas. Failure to do so can result in a gas buildup and subsequent explosion. I have seen this happen, so please, *please*, unless the manufacturer's instructions specifically indicate otherwise, always open the grill before turning on the gas.

On some models, the igniter is keyed to a specific burner tube. You must light that tube first, before lighting the rest of the grill. Again, follow the manufacturer's instructions. Then preheat your grill to the desired temperature, generally high for direct grilling and medium for indirect grilling. Some gas grills have a hard time getting hot enough for proper searing. To ensure maximum heat, I always preheat a gas grill until hot (15 to 20 minutes), then let it burn an additional 10 minutes to get really good and hot.

SETTING UP A GAS GRILL

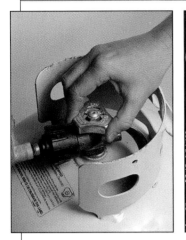

1 After opening the lid of the grill, open the valve at the top of the tank to start the flow of gas.

2 Turn the burner knob to start the flow of gas to the burner designated for lighting.

3 Press or turn the ignition switch and keep pressing or turning until you hear the gas light (if this fails, light the gas with a match).

4 Make sure the grill is on. Hold your hand about 4 inches above the grate. You should feel heat rising. If the gas fails to ignite within 1 minute, shut off the burner. Wait a few minutes for the gas to dissipate before trying Steps 2 through 4 again.

If your grill fails to light, you may be out of gas, the valve on your gas tank may be closed, or the holes of the burner may be clogged with water or dirt. Use a straight pin to unclog them. If all seems to be in order but your grill still fails to light, it's best to call the manufacturer.

Grilling Using Gas

DIRECT GRILLING: Set all the burners on high. You can control the heat by turning the burner knobs.

Or you can build a three-zone fire on a three- or four-burner gas grill. Set one burner on high, one or two burners on medium, and leave one burner off. Move the food back and forth from the hot section of the grate to cooler sections to find the optimum temperature for grilling.

INDIRECT GRILLING is easy on a gas grill, but you must have a grill with at least two burners. For a two-burner grill, preheat only one. When it gets hot, place the food over the unlit burner. With a three-burner gas grill, you light the front and rear or right and left burners and cook the food in the center. With a four-burner gas grill, light the outside burners; put the food in the center. Most gas grills have built-in catch pans (grease collectors) under the firebox, so generally you don't need a drip pan.

Smoking Using Gas

In the past, smoking was not something gas grills did well. Many grills didn't get quite hot enough to make the wood chips smolder. Even if they did, it was difficult to place the chips near the fire. Even worse, many grills had to be run at full bore to generate smoke, and that's too hot for indirect grilling or smoking most food.

This problem has been resolved recently by the advent of a slide-out smoker box with a dedicated burner. The box is a long slender drawer you open and fill with wood

A pull-out smoker box ready for loading with wood chips.

chips. The dedicated burner makes smoking a snap, because you can run a high heat under the chips to make smoke—even while you're maintaining the low to moderate heat on the rest of the grill needed for low and slow smoking. From the consumer's point of view, the best position for the smoker box is on one side of the grill, not in the center. When the smoker box is in the center, the heat it produces can interfere with indirect grilling.

If your grill has a smoker box, follow the manufacturer's instructions and add soaked wood chips. If your grill has no smoker box, you'll need to make a smoker pouch.

Smoking large cuts of meat, like pork shoulders or whole turkeys, requires a prolonged cooking time and can present special challenges on a gas grill—depending on the model. If your grill has a dedicated smoker box that loads from the exterior, simply replenish it with wood chips every hour without uncovering the grill.

If your grill has a smoker box that loads from the interior or if you are using smoker pouches, you don't want to have to remove the food and the grate every hour just to add wood chips. Not only is that a pain, but you'd

have to preheat the grill to high again, lower the heat, add the food, and resume smoking. Instead, put all the wood chips in the smoker box at once or double, triple, or even quadruple up on the smoker pouches, adding all the smoke flavor during the first hour. Then simply finish cooking the meat with gas but without additional smoke.

Using a Smoker Pouch

In order to smoke on a gas grill that doesn't have a smoker box, I like to make a smoker pouch. This is easy

HOW TO MAKE A SMOKER POUCH

1 Place soaked wood chips in the center of a sheet of heavy-duty aluminum foil.

2 Bring the short sides of the foil up over the center of the chips.

3 Fold over the edges twice to make a seal.

4 Fold in the sides of the pouch, also folding them over twice to make a seal.

5 Poke holes in the top of the pouch with a knife tip or pencil to allow the smoke to escape.

6 When heated, the pouch will produce smoke.

S M O K I N G   O N   A   G A S   G R I L L

If you are using a smoker pouch, position it under the grate directly over one of the burners.

Run the grill on high until you see smoke, then reduce the heat to the desired temperature.

Alternatively, position one or two soaked wood chunks under the grate directly over one of the burners. Again, run the grill on high until you see smoke, then reduce the heat to the desired temperature.

to do with a piece of heavy-duty aluminum foil. Once the chip-filled pouch is made, you place it under the grate over one of the burners as shown at left. When the smoker pouch is in place, run the grill until a thick plume of smoke emerges. With many gas grills, you have to preheat the grill to high to get the chips smoking, then reduce the heat to the desired temperature when you're ready to start cooking.

You can use a couple of soaked wood chunks the same way you use a smoker pouch.

HEAT CONTROL

The biggest challenge in grilling is controlling the heat. This is especially true for charcoal and wood-burning grills, but even gas grills have their idiosyncrasies. The reason heat control is so tricky is that every fuel and fire burns differently. The heat of a single charcoal or wood fire will vary, depending on how long it's been burning (a charcoal fire loses 50° to 100°F every hour it burns). Grilling—especially charcoal grilling—is not like turning on the burner on your stove, which is why a mastery of heat control is so important.

HEAT CONTROL ON A CHARCOAL OR WOOD-BURNING GRILL: There are four ways to control the heat on a charcoal or wood-burning grill:

■ *By varying the amount of time between igniting the charcoal and putting the food on the grill.* When you light charcoal in a chimney starter, it takes 15 to 20 minutes for all of it to ignite (it will glow orange when it's all lit). Once you've raked the coals over the bottom of the grill, it takes another 5 minutes for them to start ashing over. From that point on, the heat of the fire will gradually diminish. (As I've said, an hour after ignition, the fire will be 50 to 100 degrees cooler than at the start.) To work over a hot fire,

you need to place the food on the grill the moment the coals begin to ash over (20 to 30 minutes after ignition). To work over a cooler fire, let the coals burn longer before putting on the food.

■ *By raking the coals into a pile or spreading them in a thin layer.* Coals piled in a double or triple layer burn hotter than coals in a single layer. This is the principle behind a three-zone fire, wherein some of the coals are piled in a double layer, the rest in a single layer, and one section of the grill is left coal free. To control the heat, you simply move the food back and forth from the hot zone to the medium zone to the cool zone. Use the hot zone for searing and

When raking the coals, leave a portion of the grate bare for a cool zone.

crisping, the medium zone for cooking, and the coal-free zone for warming (or letting food cool off if it starts to burn).

GRILLING TEMPERATURES

HEAT	TEMPERATURE	WHERE TO PLACE FOOD ON A CHARCOAL GRILL	HOW TO TELL WHEN A CHARCOAL GRILL IS READY*	BURNER SETTING FOR A GAS GRILL	HOW TO TELL WHEN A GAS GRILL IS READY	USE FOR
High	450° to 650°F	Over a hot single-zone fire or over the hot zone of a three-zone fire.	The coals will glow bright orange; and you can hold your hand about 4 inches above the grate for 2 to 3 seconds (count "1 Mississippi, 2 Mississippi").	Set burners on high.	450° to 650°F on the grill's thermometer; you can hold your hand about 4 inches above the grate for a count of 2 to 3 Mississippi.	Direct grilling small or thin cuts of meat, seafood, and vegetables. Searing larger pieces of meat.
Medium-High	400°F	Between the hot and medium zones of a three-zone fire or over a medium-hot single-zone fire.	Coals will glow orange while starting to ash over; count 4 to 5 Mississippi.	Set burners on medium-high.	400°F on the grill's thermometer; count 4 to 5 Mississippi.	Direct grilling thin pieces of meat, seafood, and vegetables. More gentle searing of larger cuts of meat.
Medium	325° to 350°F	Over the medium zone of a three-zone fire or over a medium single-zone fire.	Coals will be lightly ashed over, but still glowing orange; count 6 to 8 Mississippi.	Set burners on medium.	325° to 350°F on the grill's thermometer; count 6 to 8 Mississippi.	Direct grilling thicker pieces of meat, like half or spatchcocked chickens; most indirect grilling.
Medium-Low	300°F	Between the medium and cool zones of a three-zone fire or over a medium-low single-zone fire.	Coals will be ashed over and have a faint orange glow; count 9 to 10 Mississippi.	Set burners on medium-low.	300°F on the grill's thermometer; count 9 to 10 Mississippi.	Indirect grilling and smoking. Warming direct-grilled foods.
Low	225° to 250°F	Between the medium and cool zones of a three-zone fire, but mostly over cool zone, or over a low single-zone fire.	Coals will be thickly ashed over with a very faint orange glow; count 11 to 14 Mississippi.	Set burners on low.	225° to 250°F on the grill's thermometer; count 11 to 14 Mississippi.	Smoking and indirect grilling of large or delicate foods. Warming direct-grilled foods.

*NOTE: The color of the coals is approximate. You could conceivably indirect grill over orange glowing coals, adjusting the vents to lower the temperature.

■ *By adjusting the vents on the top and bottom of the grill.* Oxygen makes coals burn hotter; absence of oxygen extinguishes them. When grilling using the indirect method (or using a vented hibachi for direct grilling), open or close the vents to raise or lower the heat. When direct grilling, the bottom vents should be open.

■ *By raising or lowering the grate.* The closer the food is to the coals, the hotter and faster it will cook; the farther away, the cooler and slower. Some charcoal grills (notably hibachis, table grills, and the Barbecook grill on page 466) have grates you can raise and lower to control the heat.

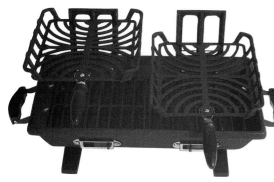

There are two ways to control the heat on this hibachi: adjust the bottom vents and raise or lower the grill grates.

HEAT CONTROL ON A GAS GRILL: Controlling heat on a gas grill is easier—at least in theory. All you do is adjust the burner thermostat. However, the desired heat is not achieved instantaneously. So on a

On a gas grill you can set the level of heat by turning the knobs of the burners.

three- or four-burner grill, I often recommend setting one burner on high, one or two on medium, and one on low. In effect, this creates a three-zone fire. You control the heat by moving the food back and forth from the hottest zone to the coolest zone.

Some gas grills, particularly inexpensive grills, have a hard time reaching a high enough temperature for proper searing.

Preheat the grill to high for the length of time recommended by the manufacturer (generally 15 minutes), then let it burn an additional 5 to 10 minutes. This should bring the heat up to the temperature needed for searing. I don't bother with the three-zone configuration on a low-power grill—it's hard enough to get one zone to burn sufficiently hot.

ON ANY GRILL: You can generally shorten the cooking time by cover-

ing the grill. If you do this on a charcoal grill, all vents should be wide open. Covering the grill is useful for grilling a thick steak, spatchcocked chicken, or small whole fish using the direct method.

One final rule of thumb: The small or thinner the food you're grilling, the higher the heat you can use. Cook thin steaks, chicken breasts, fish fillets, and sliced vegetables directly over a hot fire. Cook thicker steaks, chicken pieces or half chickens, whole fish, or thick vegetables over more moderate heat. You can sear them first over high heat, then finish cooking them over the lower heat. If you try to cook a thick piece of meat solely over a hot fire, you'll burn the exterior before the center is cooked through.

Grill thin pieces of food, like sliced zucchini, directly over high heat.

OTHER GRILLS

This brings us to smokers, rotisseries, and what I call the pseudo-grills. Smokers, logically, are used for smoking. While most (but not all) models are charcoal or wood fired, the food does not cook directly over the flames. In fact, in a traditional American smoker (sometimes referred to as a horizontal barrel smoker—see page 25), the food cooks in a chamber separate from the fire.

Electric smokers are also available, and if you're not embarrassed by the convenience of electricity (and some purists are), electric smokers produce an excellent smoke flavor with a lot less fuss than their charcoal counterparts.

Speaking of electricity, electric "grills" are becoming more and more popular—especially with condo and apartment dwellers whose building associations often prohibit the use of gas or charcoal grills. A good electric grill will produce the same sort of high dry heat you get on a gas grill, and the hot grate leaves convincing grill marks. Purists would deny that these devices are grills at all, but I say they're better than nothing. The same is true of grill pans and grill skillets, which have raised ridges to make grill marks on burgers, steaks, and chicken breasts.

And then there are rotisseries. These offer a unique rotary grilling process in which the food turns slowly in front of or next to the fire. They can be fueled by charcoal, gas, or an electric burner. The gentle turning of the spit is particularly well suited to cylindrical roasts and poultry. The slow rotation promotes a natural external and internal basting. Foods come out dark and crusty on the outside and plump and moist inside, which makes the rotisserie a winner in my book.

How to Grill on an Electric Grill

Electric grills are primarily used for direct (*not* indirect) grilling. They are best suited to cooking small or thin pieces of meat, seafood, or vegetables, such as steaks, pork and lamb chops, chicken breasts, fish fillets, fish steaks, shrimp, or sliced vegetables.

To grill, preheat to high, then position the food directly over the heating element. You want an electric grill to be as hot as it can get.

How to Grill Using a Rotisserie

Some of the world's best live-fire-cooked food comes not off the grill but off a rotisserie. As I've said, the food cooks next to or in front of the fire, so it roasts rather than grills. But it's close enough to the flame to acquire a smoke flavor and a dark, savory, crackling-crisp crust. Since rotisserie cooked chickens baste themselves as they turn, they are the most succulent birds you'll ever sink a fork into. Rotisserie cooking has another advantage: Because it's a long, slow cooking method, there's plenty of time to melt off fat. The melting fat keeps the food from drying out, while conveniently disappearing by the time you're ready to eat.

So what foods should you cook on a rotisserie? Chicken, duck, and game hens are the most obvious candidates. Cylindrical roasts, like rib roasts and leg of lamb (both whole or butterflied and rolled) do well, too. But don't stop there. Pork ribs are delectable cooked on the rotisserie, as you'll find from the surprising recipe on page 147.

The classic French setup for rotisserie cooking is to have the heat source behind the turning food. Visit a poultry shop in Paris and you'll find multiple spits of golden chickens turning in front of a wall of heat (rows of gas jets provide the heat). This is the setup used by many gas grill manufacturers in the United States, from affordable grills like the

Weber makes a handy rotisserie attachment for its kettle grill. The ring raises the spit to the proper height for rotisserie grilling.

SETTING UP A ROTISSERIE

1 If you are using a kettle grill, position the rotisserie ring on the grill. Don't attach the spit yet.

2 For charcoal, mound the coals on one side of the grill, parallel to where the spit will be, and place drip pans in the center under the spit. Here the spit is in place to show you the relationship of the coals and drip pans to it.

3 Whether using charcoal or gas, you need to attach what you plan to grill on the spit. Insert one pair of prongs on the spit, points facing inward. Skewer the food, here a chicken.

4 Slide the remaining pair of prongs onto the spit, making sure the food is held snugly in place. Tighten the screw, gripping it between the tines of a fork.

5 Insert the pointed end of the spit into the rotisserie motor socket.

6 If your grill has one, set the counterweight on the handle end to balance the weight of the meat on the spit.

Ducane to high-priced supergrills like the Viking. To use them, all you do is fire up the burner, spit the food, and turn on the rotisserie motor.

To rotisserie grill on a gas grill with three front-to-back burners, light the rear burner and position the spit and food over the unlit center burner.

SETTING UP A VERTICAL WATER SMOKER

Smoking in a water smoker will take 3 to 8 hours, depending on the food being smoked and the temperature at which you smoke it. For true barbecue, smoke at a low temperature—around 225°F. Replenish the coals and wood chips every hour. Lift the lid to check for doneness.

1 For a charcoal smoker, light the charcoal in a chimney starter, as described on page 9. You just plug in an electric smoker.

2 Dump the coals on the bottom grate of the firebox.

3 Position the center section of the smoker over the firebox and place the water pan in the center. Add at least 2 inches of water or a flavorful liquid, like beer, wine, or cider.

4 Put on the top grate and place the food in the center over the water pan. Add wood chips to the coals or the smoker pan through the door. Cover the smoker.

The heavy-duty motor on a DCS gas grill enables you to use it to spit roast as many as four chickens or two heavy roasts at one time.

You can also do a sort of rotisserie grilling on a gas grill with three or four side-by-side burners. Light the outside burners and position the food over the unlit center burners. To the purist, this isn't really true rotisserie grilling because the food doesn't face the flame. But you'll still get tasty results, even if the exterior won't be quite as crisp and brown.

How to Cook in a Smoker

For many people, especially those who live in Texas, Memphis, Kansas City, or North Carolina, grilling is a mere footnote to the glory of true barbecue. The real star of the show is the smoker.

Smoking is a uniquely American form of live-fire cooking—the *only* real barbecue, some would argue—the ultimate indirect method whereby whole hogs, Boston butts, and beef shoulders and briskets are reduced into morsels of smoky perfection, cooked tender enough to pull apart and eat with your fingers.

There are two basic types of backyard smokers: water smokers and barrel smokers. Both are easy to use and produce exquisite down-home barbecue every time.

Using a Vertical Water Smoker

The vertical water smoker looks like a giant upright bullet, with a firebox at the bottom, water pan in the center, and cooking chamber under the domed lid. The genius of this type of smoker lies in the water pan. Smoking tends to dry foods out, so by placing a pan of water (or beer, wine, cider, or other flavorful liquid) in the center of the smoker, you keep the food moist and succulent.

The traditional water smoker burns charcoal. But more and more people are using electric water smokers, which maintain an even heat and output of smoke and don't require hourly refueling.

Using a Horizontal Barrel Smoker

The horizontal barrel smoker is modeled on the giant cookers used by the pros at barbecue competitions. The smoker consists of a cylindrical or boxlike smoke chamber set off from the firebox. The smoke chamber can run horizontally, as pictured here and on page 471, or vertically. The offset firebox allows you to burn whole logs or charcoal while maintaining the requisite low temperature in the smoke chamber. Most home models burn charcoal; you add soaked wood chunks to generate smoke.

SETTING UP A HORIZONTAL BARREL SMOKER

1 Light the charcoal in a chimney starter placed in the firebox (see page 9).

2 Dump the coals into the firebox.

3 Add soaked hardwood chunks or chips to the firebox.

4 Regulate the heat by opening or closing the vent on the firebox. Further adjustment is made by opening or closing the vent on the chimney. Open the vents to raise the temperature. Close the vents to lower the heat. Completely closing the vents will put out the fire.

5 Place the food in the smoke chamber. If you are smoking for longer than 1 hour, you'll need to replenish the coals and wood hourly.

6 Smoke has a drying effect on food. Sometimes, I'll wrap ribs or brisket in aluminum foil for the last hour or so of cooking to seal in the juices.

SOME FINAL TIPS

Grill jockeys can be a pretty grubby lot, but they're quite fastidious when it comes to their grill grates. That's because this is the part of the grill that actually comes in contact with the food. Besides being disgusting, a dirty grate causes food to stick, and it won't give you well-delineated grill marks. So savvy grill jockeys keep their grates clean and always oil them before putting on any food that may stick.

How to Clean a Grill

The tool of choice for cleaning the grate is a long-handled, stiff wire brush. Use it twice and brush vigorously: first, when the grate is preheated but before the food goes on (heating the grill sterilizes the grate and loosens any burnt-on debris). Brush the grate a second time after you are done cooking—again, while the grill is still hot. Many wire brushes come with scrapers on the end; use these to dislodge any particularly stubborn debris.

I don't generally bother with cleaning the firebox, unless it gets really disgusting. Should this happen, a scrub brush and a grill cleaner or soapy water will do the trick.

How to Oil a Grill Grate

The other secret to keeping food from sticking to the grate is to oil or grease it first (a well-oiled grill grate also gives you better grill marks). You have a choice of three greasing techniques: using an oil-soaked paper towel or rag, a piece of bacon or beef fat, or a can of spray oil. When you oil the grate with a paper towel or rag, you give it one last cleaning. If you are working on a large industrial-size grill, tie a tightly folded clean dish towel or washcloth to the end of a pole and use it for oiling. Be sure the grate is very hot before oiling it.

Oiling a grill grate with a piece of bacon or beef fat may give you a little extra flavor. It certainly looks expert. Spray oil is the quickest way to oil a grill grate, but be sure to remove the grate from the fire when spraying. The grate should always be oiled when grilling fish, chicken breasts, steaks, and other foods that tend to stick. Oiling is optional when grilling fatty cuts, like ribs, and vegetables with smooth skins, like corn.

CLEANING A GRILL GRATE

Preheat the grill. When the grate is hot, brush it vigorously with a long-handled wire brush to remove any debris.

This wire pad brush gets the grate extra clean, but its short handle is a problem. Your arm will get mighty hot using it. Unlike me, you'd be wise to wear a grill glove.

OILING A GRILL GRATE

AVOID THIS!

Fold a paper towel into a small pad and grip it with long-handled tongs. Dip it in a small bowl of vegetable oil.

Rub the oiled paper towel over the bars of the grate. In addition to oiling the grate, the paper towel cleans off fine debris.

One cool way to oil the grate is to use a folded-up piece of bacon (as here) or a chunk of steak fat. Rub it over the bars of the grate, using tongs to hold it.

You can also spray oil on a grill grate. The proper way to do this is to hold the grate well away from the fire when you spray.

The wrong way to oil a grate: Never spray the oil onto the grate over the fire. The tiny droplets of oil can catch fire, causing a conflagration.

How to Empty an Ash Catcher

Many charcoal grills come with an ash catcher, a saucepan-shaped metal receptacle attached to the bottom that's designed to hold the ashes that accumulate as the charcoal burns out. To use the ash catcher on a Weber kettle grill, open and close the bottom vent several times to knock the ashes into the catcher. When the catcher is full, unfasten it from the base of the grill and discard the ashes. *Warning:* Never discard hot ashes in a paper bag or plastic trash pail. Be sure ashes are stone cold before transferring them to the trash. I usually wait until the day after I've used the grill to discard the ashes. The last thing you want to do is to combine hot ashes with other potentially flammable rubbish.

How to Empty a Drip Pan or Catch Pan

Grilling a chicken or pork shoulder using the indirect method generates a lot of drippings. If you've set up your charcoal grill properly, with the drip pan under the food, it will be full of fat at the end of your grill session. Let the grill and drip pan cool completely before discarding the fat (this will take a couple of hours). Remove the grate and carefully lift out the drip pan. Drain it into an empty milk carton or other resealable container, or place a dis-

posable pan, drippings and all, in a sturdy plastic garbage bag. Some people are tempted to save the drippings for another use. If you're of this school, strain them through a fine-mesh strainer into a clean jar. The strainer must have a very fine mesh to remove any ash.

On gas grills the catch pan or grease pan takes the place of the drip pan. It's positioned under the firebox. Empty it after the grill has cooled off.

So, now you know everything there is to know about building a fire, the various grilling and smoking techniques, and keeping the grill clean and lubricated. After a quick review of a few of the ingredients I use throughout the book, it'll be time to get down to some live-fire cooking.

BASIC INGREDIENTS AND PREPARATIONS

A word about some basic ingredients. As you cook your way through the recipes that illustrate the techniques in this book, you'll be asked to reach for salt, pepper, butter, brown sugar, sesame seeds, and other familiar flavorings. As you probably expect by now, I have strong opinions about even the most commonplace of these ingredients. But I also believe in common sense and I'd hate to see you make a special shopping trip to get unsalted butter or light brown sugar, when you have salted butter in your refrigerator or dark brown sugar in your cupboard. So here are my thoughts on some of the basic seasonings, as well as instructions on toasting pine nuts and sesame seeds.

BROWN SUGAR: Many rub and sauce recipes in this book call for brown sugar. Dark brown sugar has a richer flavor than light. But for most recipes (especially when you need only 1 or 2 tablespoons), you can use either light or dark brown sugar—whichever you have on hand. It's not worth buying a new box for small quantities. There are instances, however, when the rich molasses flavor of dark brown sugar works best.

BUTTER: When I attended cooking school in Paris, I was taught to cook with unsalted butter. In my travels on the world's barbecue trail, I've seen grill jockeys reach for both salted and unsalted.

Salted butter adds a bit more flavor when brushed on grilled vegetables or seafood, but unsalted butter will give you a fine taste, too. The difference isn't worth making a run to the grocery store. For most recipes use whatever type of butter you have in your refrigerator. However, if a recipe specifically calls for salted butter, try to use it.

FRUIT JUICES AND CITRUS ZEST: Many recipes in this book call for lemon, lime, or orange juice. You should always squeeze it fresh—the flavor is far superior to bottled. The zest is the oil-rich outer skin of a citrus fruit. The easiest way to remove it from the fruit is to use a vegetable peeler. Take only the outer rind, not the bitter white pith beneath it.

MUSTARD: Prepared mustard is a mainstay of great barbecuing and grilling. Two main types are called for in this book. By Dijon-style, I mean a smooth, tart, French-style mustard typified by Grey Poupon (this is not a sweet mustard). By grainy, or Meaux-style, I mean a coarsely ground French-style mustard—again without sweetness. Honey mustard is a dulcet American-style mustard sweetened with honey and sometimes thickened with eggs. Ballpark mustard is a traditional sharp American mustard colored with turmeric—think of French's.

MUSTARD SEEDS: Mustard seeds add a peppery crunch to rubs, glazes, and barbecue sauces. There are three varieties—in ascending order of spiciness: yellow, brown,

and black. Several recipes in this book call for the mustard seeds to be toasted, which makes them softer and more aromatic. To toast yellow mustard seeds, place them in a heavy, dry skillet and cook over medium heat until the seeds begin to brown, shaking the pan to ensure even cooking. This will take 2 to 4 minutes. Immediately transfer the seeds to a shallow heatproof bowl to cool. Toast brown and black mustard seeds the same way, but you'll have to check doneness by smell, rather than color (the toasted seeds will smell fragrant and aromatic).

OIL: Oil is the lifeblood of barbecue. A generous basting of olive oil or sesame oil can make all the difference between succulent grilled chicken or seafood and food that's as dried out as jerky. I like an oil that has an inherent flavor, so in most recipes I call for olive oil, sesame oil, or in rarer instances walnut or hazelnut oil. The olive oil should be extra virgin (the highest, most flavorful grade); the sesame oil should be dark (made with toasted sesame seeds)—look for Japanese and Korean sesame oils. Occasionally, you'll be asked to use vegetable oil, because the flavor of a costlier oil would be lost among the other ingredients in a recipe.

PEPPER: When recipes in this book call for pepper, I generally mean freshly ground black pepper. Fresh grinding gives you an intense aromatic flavor you simply don't find in preground pepper. You can use a peppercorn grinder, of course, but you may find it easier and more con-

venient to grind a large batch of peppercorns in a spice mill or coffee grinder every couple of weeks, so that you always have freshly ground pepper on hand. In the interest of objective reporting, let me say that most of the world's grill jockeys use preground black pepper and produce excellent barbecue in the process. If this is easier for you, by all means use it. By the way, white pepper is black pepper with the dark skin removed. It's less flavorful, but a little hotter, than black pepper. Cayenne pepper and hot red pepper flakes aren't true peppercorns at all but ground or flaked cayenne chile peppers.

PINE NUTS: These small, buttery nuts (a.k.a., pignoli) are used as a flavoring by Italian, Mexican, and Southwestern American grill jockeys. To bolster the flavor, the nuts are often toasted. To toast pine nuts, place them in a heavy, dry skillet and cook over medium heat until the nuts begin to brown, shaking the pan to ensure even cooking. This will take 3 to 5 minutes. Immediately transfer the nuts to a shallow heatproof bowl to cool.

SALT: Salt is the most important ingredient in barbecue and your choice of salt can go a long way in determining the taste of your end product. I like to use coarse salt: The crystals take longer to dissolve than those of regular table salt, so you get little bursts of salty flavor (coarse salt also feels nifty between your fingers). My favorites are kosher salt (which I like for its purity) and sea salt (which I prize for its flavor-enhancing minerals). Sea salt goes especially well with seafood.

SCALLIONS: Scallions are a popular flavoring throughout the world of barbecue. There are two parts to a scallion: the white and the green. Scallion whites are milder and more oniony; scallion greens taste more like beefed-up chives. Often, I'll use the white and light green parts of a scallion in a marinade, while chopping the darker green part to use as a garnish. To trim a scallion, cut off the root and remove any browned tips on the greens.

SESAME SEEDS: Many recipes in this book call for toasted sesame seeds. The reason is simple: Toasting intensifies the seeds' flavor, imparting a pleasing nutty fragrance to boot. To toast sesame seeds, place them in a heavy, dry skillet and cook over medium heat until the seeds begin to brown, shaking the pan to ensure even cooking. This will take 2 to 4 minutes; don't let them burn. Immediately transfer the seeds to a shallow heatproof bowl to cool.

TURBINADO SUGAR: Turbinado sugar is a pale brown granulated sugar. It's made by adding molasses to granulated sugar. This gives it a deeper color and flavor. One good brand is Sugar In The Raw.

BEEF
A N D
VEAL

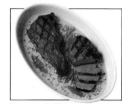

METHOD:
Indirect grilling

COOKING TIME:
2½ to 3 hours

HOW TO GRILL A PRIME RIB

Grilling is the easiest and best way I know to cook prime rib. The high dry heat forms a delectable, crisp crust (with just the right amount of fat), while the beef inside remains tender and juicy. And nothing brings out the sanguine flavor of beef like a fragrant blast of wood smoke. Few sights make eyes pop and jaws drop like a whole prime rib on the grill. The only downside is the formidable cost of the meat, so make this dish when price is no object and you want to impress a crowd.

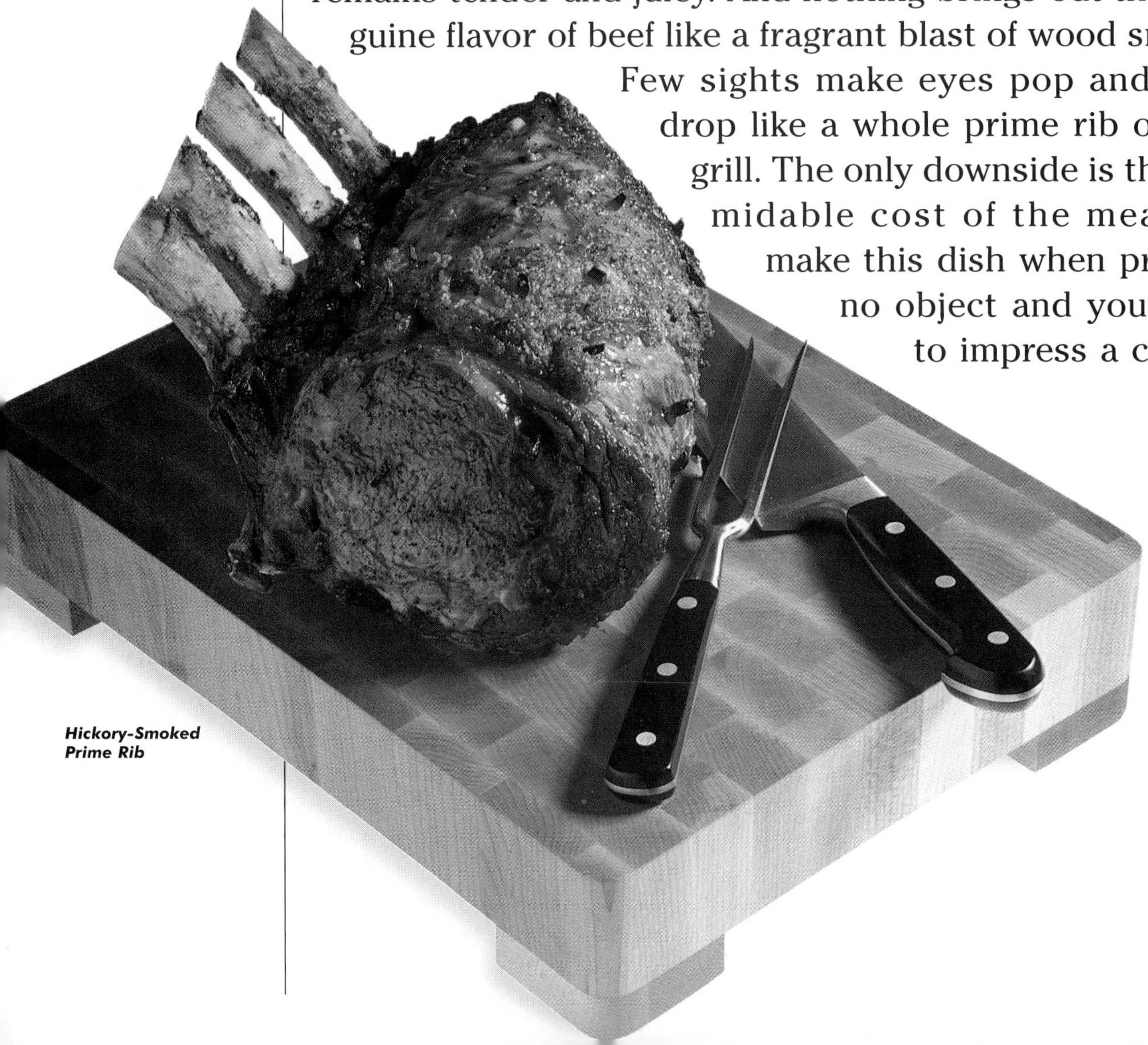

Hickory-Smoked Prime Rib

SETTING UP THE GRILL

1 To set up a charcoal grill for indirect grilling, first light the charcoal in a chimney starter (see page 9).

2 Form two heat zones by raking the coals into two piles at opposite sides of the grill, using a long-handled implement, like a garden hoe.

3 If your grill has side baskets, divide the coals evenly between them. Note the drip pan in the center of the grill.

TIPS

■ Soak all the wood chips you need at once. Then they'll be ready to add as you need them.

■ Prime rib roasts come in varying sizes, a 7-rib roast (16 to 18 pounds) being the largest. Each rib section will feed two to three people.

■ Look for a roast with a thick layer of fat (¼ to ½ inch). As the fat melts, it bastes the meat, keeping it moist and tender. The fat also cooks into an incredibly flavorful crust.

PREPARING THE MEAT

1 French the ribs or have your butcher do this for you. To French, cut through the cap of fat that covers the ends of the rib bones. Cut straight to the bone.

2 Once you reach the bone, turn your knife toward the ends of the ribs. Lift and remove the cap of fat.

3 Cut out the pieces of meat between the ends of the ribs.

4 Trim off any excess fat covering the roast. Leave about ¼ inch of fat intact.

5 Using the tip of a sharp, slender knife, make slits in the prime rib all over, about ½ inch deep and 1 inch apart. Insert slivers of garlic in each slit.

6 Sprinkle the rub over the entire roast, patting it onto the meat with your fingers.

GRILL THE PRIME RIB: If the bones start to brown too much before the meat is cooked, protect them with a strip of aluminum foil.

TEST FOR DONENESS: Insert an instant-read meat thermometer into the center of the roast, away from the bones. Alternatively, press the roast with your fingers. It should feel gently yielding.

THE RECIPE

HICKORY-SMOKED PRIME RIB

FOR THE BEEF:
1 prime rib roast (4 ribs;
    9 to 11 pounds)
3 large cloves garlic, each clove
    cut lengthwise into 6 or 8
    slivers

FOR THE RUB:
2 teaspoons garlic salt
2 teaspoons onion salt
2 teaspoons hickory-smoked salt
2 teaspoons dried rosemary
1 teaspoon black pepper

Herbed Horseradish Sauce (page 455),
    for serving

1. French the prime ribs as shown in Preparing the Meat, Steps 1 through 4 on pages 33 and 34 or have your butcher do this for you.

Using the tip of a knife, make slits in the prime rib as shown in Step 5 on the facing page and insert the slivers of garlic into these slits.

SERVES 8 TO 12

YOU'LL NEED:
3 cups wood chips (optional, preferably hickory or oak), soaked for 1 hour in cold water to cover, then drained; roast rack (optional)

VARIATION: *If you have a very large grill with a very heavy-duty rotisserie, you can spit roast the prime rib. You'll need 2½ to 3 hours for a roast this size.*

ALSO GOOD FOR:
You can also use this method to cook a boneless rib roast, and it makes a terrific rack of pork or veal.

2. Combine all the ingredients for the rub in a small bowl and stir to mix. Sprinkle the rub over the roast on all sides, patting it onto the meat with your fingertips.

3. Set up the grill for indirect grilling (see page 12 for charcoal or page 16 for gas) and preheat to medium. If using a charcoal grill, place a large drip pan in the center. If using a gas grill, place all the wood chips, if desired, in the smoker box or in a smoker pouch (see page 17) and preheat on high until you see smoke, then reduce the heat to medium.

4. When ready to cook, if using a charcoal grill, toss half of the wood chips, if desired, on the coals. Place the roast on a rack, if using, fat-side up, in the center of the hot grate, away from the heat. If not using a rack, place the roast, fat-side up, directly in the center of the hot grate, away from the heat. Cover the grill.

5. Grill the roast until done to taste: 2 hours for rare (about 125°F on an instant-read meat thermometer), 2 to 2½ hours for medium-rare (about 145°F), or 2½ to 3 hours for medium (about 160°F); remember, the roast will continue cooking even after it comes off the grill. If using a charcoal grill, you'll need to add 12 fresh coals per side every hour, and toss the remaining wood chips, if desired, on the coals after the first hour of grilling.

6. Transfer the roast to a platter or carving board and cover loosely with aluminum foil. Let the roast rest for 15 minutes before carving and serving. To carve, run a sharp, slender carving knife between the ribs and the meat to release the meat from the bones. Thinly slice the roast, then cut the ribs apart and serve them on the side. Alternatively, leave the ribs attached and carve the roast with them (the slices will be much thicker in this case). Serve the horseradish sauce on the side.

HOW TO GRILL A STUFFED RIB ROAST

METHOD:
Indirect grilling

COOKING TIME:
About 1½ hours

In the world of grilled meats, barbecued boneless rib roast is a world-class contender. Its generous marbling makes the meat ideal for indirect grilling. You wind up with a roast that's crusty and brown on the outside and tender and succulent on the inside. And that's before you add any seasonings! The recipe that accompanies this technique takes its inspiration from the *boliches* (stuffed pot roasts) of the Spanish Caribbean. I've larded the roast with strips of chorizo (spicy Spanish sausage), cheese, and carrot: When you slice the meat, you get an attractive mosaic of color. As for the flavor, well, I've never been to a barbecue that a perfect chorizo could not improve.

Rib Roast Stuffed with Chorizo and Cheese with Grilled Asparagus (page 354) and sweet potatoes

SETTING UP THE GRILL

1 To set up a charcoal grill for indirect grilling, first light the charcoal in a chimney starter (see page 9).

2 Form two heat zones by raking the coals into two piles at opposite sides of the grill, using a long-handled implement, like a garden hoe.

3 If your grill has side baskets, divide the coals evenly between them. Note the drip pan in the center of the grill.

PREPARING THE MEAT

1 Using a long, slender carving knife, make a 1-inch width slit lengthwise through the center of the roast for the chorizo. Cut the chorizos so that the squared-off ends will butt up snugly against each other inside the roast.

2 Push the chorizo pieces through the slit, starting with the uncut end of one chorizo.

3 Using a sharpening steel, make three lengthwise tunnels in the roast around the chorizo.

4 Push the carrot pieces through the tunnels.

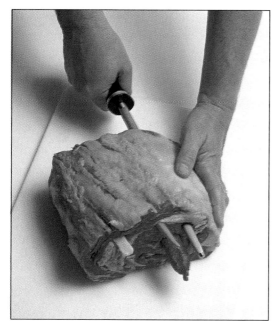

5 Using the steel, make three more lengthwise tunnels in the roast around the chorizo and between the carrots. Push the strips of cheese through these tunnels. Note how one end of each strip has been cut to a point to facilitate insertion.

6 Cut off the ends of the chorizos, carrots, and cheese leaving ½ inch protruding.

7 Tightly tie the roast into a cylindrical shape with butcher's string.

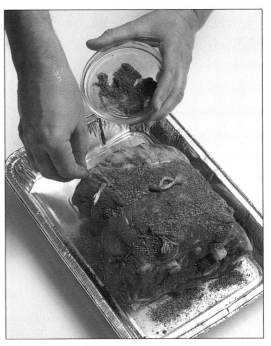

8 Season the roast on all sides with the rub.

ON THE GRILL

Place the roast on a roast rack, if using, in the center of the grill grate, away from the heat. Use the finger poke test to test for doneness; when fully cooked, the roast will feel firm yet yielding to the touch. The internal temperature on an instant-read meat thermometer should be about 145°F for medium-rare.

CARVING THE ROAST: Remove the butcher's string and carve the roast crosswise into ¼-inch slices.

RIB ROAST STUFFED WITH CHORIZO AND CHEESE

FOR THE BEEF:
1 rib roast (4 to 4½ pounds)
3 links (each about 2 ounces) cooked
    chorizo sausage
3 long slender carrots, trimmed and
    peeled
2 slices (each ¼ inch thick;
    about 4 ounces total)
    Romano, aged Provolone, or
    other firm white cheese, cut into strips

FOR THE RUB:
2 tablespoons sweet paprika
2 teaspoons coarse salt
1 teaspoon ground cumin
1 teaspoon dried oregano
1 teaspoon garlic powder
1 teaspoon black pepper

1. Using a long, slender carving knife, make a lengthwise cut through the center of the roast. Cut one end off two of the chorizos. Cut both ends off the third chorizo. Insert the chorizos through the roast as shown in Preparing the Meat, Steps 1 and 2 on page 38.

2. Using a sharpening steel (wipe it clean with a paper towel), make lengthwise tunnels through the roast around the sausage and insert the carrots and cheese strips as shown in Steps 3 through 5. You may need to insert more than 1 strip of cheese per tunnel. Cut off the ends of the sausages, carrots, and cheese, leaving ½ inch protruding.

3. Make the rub: Combine the paprika, salt, cumin, oregano, garlic powder, and pepper in a small bowl and stir to mix. Sprinkle this mixture all over the roast, rubbing it onto the meat with your fingers. Let the roast sit while you preheat the grill.

4. Set up the grill for indirect grilling (see page 12 for charcoal or page 16 for

gas) and preheat to medium. If using a charcoal grill, place a large drip pan in the center.

5. When ready to cook, place the roast on a roast rack, if using, in the center of the grate, away from the heat. If not using a rack, place the roast directly in the center of the hot grate, away from the heat. Cover the grill.

6. Grill the roast until crusty and handsomely browned, and cooked to taste, about 1½ hours for medium-rare. To test for doneness, press the ends of the roast with your fingers: It should be gently yielding. Or, use an instant-read meat thermometer: The internal temperature should be about 145°F for medium-rare. If using charcoal, add 12 fresh coals per side after 1 hour.

7. Transfer the roast to a carving board and let rest for 10 minutes. Remove the string and thinly slice the roast crosswise using a sharp carving knife. Sometimes pieces of chorizo come loose. Make sure each slice includes one.

SERVES 8

YOU'LL NEED:
Sharpening steel or larding iron; butcher's string; roast rack (optional)

ALSO GOOD FOR:
A pork or veal loin can be larded and indirect grilled the same way.

TIPS

■ The grilling time of an unstuffed boneless roast is the same as a stuffed one.

■ Chorizo comes both cooked and uncooked. This recipe calls for the already-cooked kind.

METHOD:
Indirect grilling

COOKING TIME:
About 6 hours

ADVANCE
PREPARATION:
4 to 6 hours for
curing the meat
(optional)

HOW TO SMOKE A BRISKET

O n the professional barbecue circuit, brisket is the true test of a pit boss's mettle. Each has his own secret formula. For me, the essentials boil down to this: a long, slow cooking over low heat. You're looking for an internal temperature of about 190°F, but you must achieve this temperature gradually. Rush it and you'll wind up with what chews like a mouthful of shoe leather.

So how slowly should you cook a brisket? In Texas, it's not uncommon for pit masters to smoke brisket for 15 to 20 hours. The home cook should count on at least 6 hours, which makes brisket something you need to plan ahead for. The good news is that once you've mastered the art of smoking a brisket—and you can do it equally well on a gas grill, charcoal grill, or smoker—you'll be turning out tender slabs of succulent, smoky, spicy beef every time.

Lean and Mean Texas Barbecued Brisket with Sweet-and-Smoky Baked Beans and barbecue sauce

SETTING UP THE GRILL

1 To set up a charcoal grill for smoking, first light the charcoal in a chimney starter (see page 9).

2 Place a drip pan in the center of the grill and divide the coals evenly on either side of it.

3 Place ½ cup of drained wood chips on each mound of coals.

PREPARING THE MEAT

1 A trimmed brisket ready for smoking. Note the layer of fat covering the brisket. This will keep the meat moist during smoking.

2 Sprinkle the rub over the meat, patting it on with your fingers.

3 Turn the meat and sprinkle the bottom with rub, too.

TIPS

■ A whole brisket weighs 16 to 18 pounds and has three separate parts: the cap, the point, and the flat. In this technique, I suggest cooking only the center portion of the flat. This rectangular muscle is lean and compact, producing handsome slices when you carve it. Order brisket at most supermarkets and butcher shops, and this is the cut you'll get.

■ Cook the brisket in an open aluminum foil pan. The pan keeps the bottom of the meat from drying out, first by shielding it from direct heat, then by collecting the melting fat, which bastes the meat. It's especially important to use a foil pan when smoking a brisket on a gas or charcoal grill (these tend to dry meats out). You can omit the pan when using a barrel or water smoker (see page 24).

1 When smoking a brisket on a charcoal grill, add soaked wood chips every hour. Place them on the coals.

2 Mop the brisket with the mop sauce every hour.

3 To test for doneness, insert an instant-read meat thermometer in the side of the brisket as deeply as possible. The internal temperature should be about 190°F. You should be able to pull the meat apart with your fingers.

SERVES 10 TO 12

YOU'LL NEED:
6 cups wood chips or chunks (preferably hickory or oak), soaked for 1 hour in cold water or beer to cover, then drained

THE RECIPE

LEAN AND MEAN TEXAS BARBECUED BRISKET

FOR THE BRISKET AND RUB:
1 trimmed brisket (5 to 6 pounds), with a
    layer of fat at least ¼ inch thick
3 tablespoons chili powder
1 tablespoon coarse salt
2 teaspoons black pepper
1½ teaspoons brown sugar
1½ teaspoons garlic salt
1½ teaspoons onion powder
1 teaspoon ground cumin
1 teaspoon dried oregano
½ to 1 teaspoon cayenne pepper

FOR THE VINEGAR-BEER MOP SAUCE:
1 cup distilled white vinegar
1 cup beer
1 tablespoon garlic salt
1 tablespoon brown sugar
1 teaspoon hot red pepper flakes
1 teaspoon black pepper

Sweet and Smoky Baked Beans
    (recipe follows), for serving

1. Rinse the brisket under cold running water and blot dry with paper towels. Combine all the ingredients for the rub in a small bowl and stir to mix. Rub this mixture onto the brisket on all sides. If you have the time, let the brisket stand in the refrigerator, covered, for 4 to 6 hours. But you can certainly cook it right away.

2. Combine all the ingredients for the mop sauce in a nonreactive bowl and stir until the salt and brown sugar are dissolved.

3. Set up the grill for indirect grilling (see page 12 for charcoal or page 16 for gas) and preheat to low. If using a gas grill, place all the wood chips in the smoker box or in a smoker pouch (see page 17) and preheat on high until you see smoke, then reduce the heat to low.

4. When ready to cook, if using a charcoal grill, toss 1 cup wood chips on the coals. Place the brisket, fat-side up, in an aluminum foil pan and place in the center of the hot grate, away from the heat and cover the grill. Grill the brisket until tender, about 6 hours (the cooking time will depend on the size of the brisket and the heat of the grill). Baste or mop the brisket with the mop sauce once an hour for the first 4 hours. If using a charcoal grill, you'll need to add 12 fresh coals and ½ cup wood chips per side every hour. To test for doneness, use an instant-read meat thermometer: The internal temperature should be about 190°F.

5. Transfer the brisket to a cutting board and let rest for 10 minutes. Thinly slice across the grain, using an electric knife or sharp carving knife. Transfer the sliced meat to plates or a platter and pour the pan juices on top.

Sweet and Smoky Baked Beans

SERVES 10 TO 12

6 ounces bacon, cut crosswise into ¼-inch slices
1 large onion, finely chopped
3 cans (15.5 ounces each) cooked navy or great
   Northern beans
3 tablespoons brown sugar
3 tablespoons molasses
3 tablespoons maple syrup
3 tablespoons Basic Barbecue Sauce
   (page 447) or your favorite
   commercial brand or ketchup
1½ tablespoons dry mustard
1½ tablespoons Worcestershire sauce
1½ tablespoons cider vinegar
½ teaspoon liquid smoke
Coarse salt and black pepper
2 to 3 jalapeño peppers, thinly sliced
   (optional)

1. Place the bacon and onion in a large nonreactive saucepan over medium heat and cook until the bacon fat renders and the onion is golden brown, about 5 minutes. Pour off any excess fat.

2. Stir in the beans, brown sugar, molasses, maple syrup, barbecue sauce, mustard, Worcestershire sauce, vinegar, and liquid smoke. Gently simmer the beans until thick and richly flavored, 10 minutes, adding 2 or 3 tablespoons water if necessary to keep the beans from burning. Taste for seasoning, adding salt and pepper as necessary. Stir in the jalapeños during the last 5 minutes of cooking, if desired.

Note: If you have the time, you can simmer the beans for 5 minutes, then spoon them into an aluminum foil pan and bake in a 350°F oven or in a covered grill set up for indirect grilling and preheated to medium, until thick and richly flavored, about 30 minutes. Add salt and pepper to taste and jalapeños, if desired.

TIPS

■ For extra flavor and tenderness, I like to mop a brisket with a vinegar-beer mop sauce as it cooks.

■ If the brisket starts to dry out before the meat is fully cooked and tender, wrap it in aluminum foil to finish cooking.

ON THE SIDE: *Texans don't much go for sweet sauces with their brisket (the traditional sauce is meat drippings mixed with a little ketchup).*

ALSO GOOD FOR: *You can also smoke a clod (shoulder) or baron (haunch) of beef using this rub and mop sauce. Of course, the cooking time will be longer.*

METHOD:
Direct grilling

COOKING TIME:
About 30 minutes

**ADVANCE
PREPARATION:**
1 to 2 hours for
marinating the
meat (optional)

HOW TO GRILL A WHOLE BEEF TENDERLOIN

This is the sort of technique I call millionaire grilling. You spend 15 minutes of preparation time and you wind up with a dish that looks and tastes like a million bucks. Whole grilled beef tenderloin makes a spectacular center-piece for a party, yet it's not much more difficult to cook than steak. It's simple and regal, and anyone who has priced beef tenderloin recently will appreciate your largesse. To this add the visual allure of a veritable painter's palette of barbecue and steak sauces served with the beef, and you wind up with a dish that makes you look like you're rolling in dough.

Herb-Crusted Grilled Beef Tenderloin with, clockwise from the top, Béarnaise Mayonnaise, Shallot Marmalade, Three-Herb Chimichurri, Mustard Sauce, and Cucumber Relish

SETTING UP THE GRILL

1 To set up a charcoal grill for direct grilling, first light the charcoal in a chimney starter (see page 9).

2 Using a garden hoe or other long-handled implement, rake the burning coals into an even layer.

3 To see if the grill is preheated to medium-high, use the test on page 10.

PREPARING THE MEAT

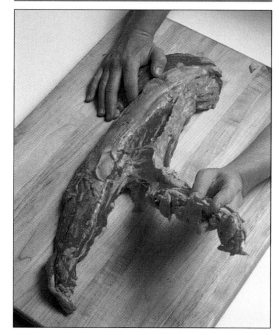

1 Starting at the tail end of the tenderloin, remove the chain. You should be able to pry it off with your fingers. Save it for kebabs (see page 50).

2 Trim the head to give your tenderloin a uniform diameter (save this meat for making kebabs, too). Cut out the pocket of fat that connects the head to the center of the tenderloin.

TIP

■ A whole beef tenderloin has a ropelike strip of meat running its length called the chain. This is perfectly tasty, but the meat is fattier than the heart of the tenderloin and it doesn't look so terrific either. I remove it and save it for shish kebab or grind it for burgers.

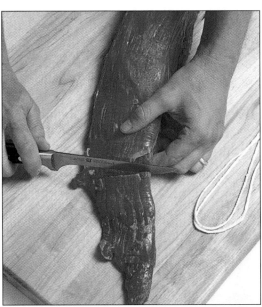

3 Trim off all the fat and pull off the silver-skin (the sheath of sinew covering the tenderloin) with your fingers. Slide the knife under the latter to loosen it from the meat and pull it off in inch-wide strips. If you pull it toward the head, it will come off without tearing the meat.

4 Cut halfway through the tail about 4 inches above the end of the tenderloin.

5 Tie the head to give the meat a cylindrical shape. Fold the tail under and tie it with butcher's string. This helps to give you a piece of meat of uniform thickness.

6 Working on a baking sheet, drizzle the tenderloin with olive oil, rubbing the oil onto the meat. Tenderloin is a lean cut of beef, so you want to use plenty of oil.

7 Sprinkle the tenderloin first with salt, pepper, and garlic, then with the chopped herbs.

8 Pat these ingredients onto the meat with your fingertips. Let marinate 30 minutes to 2 hours.

ON THE GRILL

1 Gently lay the beef tenderloin on the grill as shown here.

2 Grill the tenderloin until nicely browned all over. Here the bottom is being checked for browning before rotating the meat 90 degrees to get crosshatch grill marks. (This meat needs more time.)

TIP

■ I like to grill the tenderloin directly over the coals, which gives you a crisp, smoky crust. You could also use the indirect method, which requires no skill other than pulling the tenderloin off the grill when the meat is cooked.

SERVES 8

YOU'LL NEED:
Butcher's string

ALSO GOOD FOR:
Grilling in an herb crust is a great way to cook whole pork loins and pork tenderloins.

HERB-CRUSTED GRILLED BEEF TENDERLOIN

FOR THE TENDERLOIN:
1 whole beef tenderloin (about 5 pounds)
3 to 4 tablespoons extra-virgin olive oil
Coarse salt and black pepper
4 cloves garlic, minced
2 cups chopped mixed fresh herbs, including
  tarragon, basil, rosemary, oregano,
  marjoram, and/or flat-leaf parsley

FOR SERVING (any or all of the following):
Béarnaise Mayonnaise (page 452)
Mustard Sauce (page 454)
Three-Herb Chimichurri (page 457)
Cucumber Relish (page 460)
Shallot Marmalade (page 461)

1. Prepare the tenderloin as shown in Preparing the Meat, Steps 1 through 5 on pages 47 and 48.

2. Transfer the tenderloin to a baking sheet and generously drizzle oil on it. Sprinkle the meat with salt and pepper and thickly coat it with the garlic and chopped herbs, patting these onto the meat with your fingertips. You can cook the tenderloin right away, but it will be more flavorful if you let it sit in the refrigerator, covered, for 1 to 2 hours.

3. Set up the grill for direct grilling (see page 10 for charcoal or page 16 for gas) and preheat to medium-high.

4. When ready to cook, brush and oil the grill grate. Place the tenderloin on the hot grate. Grill the tenderloin, turning with tongs, until crusty and darkly seared on the outside and cooked to medium-rare, 6 to 8 minutes per side, cooking the tenderloin on all 4 sides (about 30 minutes in all). To test for doneness, insert an instant-read meat thermometer into the thickest part of the tenderloin: The internal temperature should be about 145°F for medium-rare.

5. Transfer the tenderloin to a cutting board, cover loosely with aluminum foil, and let rest for 5 minutes. Remove the string, carve the tenderloin into crosswise slices, and serve with the sauces.

Beef Kebabs

Turn a piece of beef tenderloin into tender kebabs: Cut the meat into 1-inch cubes and marinate them in the oil, garlic, and herbs as suggested in Step 2, this page. Thread 6 cubes of meat per skewer and direct grill over high heat, 2 to 3 minutes per side, 8 to 12 minutes total.

HOW TO MAKE CHURRASCO (Sliced Beef Tenderloin)

METHOD:
Direct grilling

COOKING TIME:
4 to 6 minutes

ADVANCE PREPARATION:
30 minutes to 1 hour for marinating the meat

If you love the rich flavor of beef tenderloin and you're looking for a different way to prepare it, you need go no further than *churrasco,* Latin America's popular grilled-beef dish. Here I feature a Nicaraguan version, using broad, thin sheets of tenderloin sliced along the grain, not against it, to maximize the surface area of the beef exposed to the fire. What results is a steak with a remarkable flame-charred flavor, and it's tender enough to cut with your fork. The sauce— a variation on Argentinean *chimichurri,* a garlic-parsley-vinegar sauce— does double duty, first as a marinade and then as a serving sauce.

Churrasco with Three-Herb Chimichurri

SETTING UP THE GRILL

1 To set up a charcoal grill for direct grilling, first light the charcoal in a chimney starter (see page 9).

2 Using a garden hoe or other long-handled implement, rake the burning coals into an even layer.

3 To see if the grill is preheated to high, use the test on page 10.

PREPARING THE MEAT

1 Using the palm of your hand, hold the meat flat. Hold a sharp, slender carving knife parallel to the cutting board, and cut the tenderloin into four even, flat slices.

2 Place each slice between two sheets of plastic wrap and gently pound with the side of a cleaver or a scallopini pounder to a thickness of ¼ inch.

3 Arrange the beef slices on top of a quarter of the *chimichurri*. Pour another quarter of the *chimichurri* on top.

ON THE GRILL: Use tongs to rotate the steaks for attractive grill marks.

T H E   R E C I P E

CHURRASCO WITH THREE-HERB CHIMICHURRI

SERVES 4

*2 cups Three-Herb Chimichurri
(page 457)*

*1 piece center-cut beef tenderloin (5 to 6
inches long; about 1½ pounds)*

1. Pour a quarter of the *chimichurri* into a baking dish that is just large enough to hold the meat.

2. Prepare the tenderloin as shown in Preparing the Meat on the facing page. Arrange the beef slices on top of the *chimichurri* in the baking dish. Pour another quarter of the *chimichurri* on top. Marinate the beef, covered, in the refrigerator for 30 minutes to 1 hour. Reserve the rest of the *chimichurri* for serving.

3. Set up the grill for direct grilling (see page 10 for charcoal or page 16 for gas) and preheat to high.

4. When ready to cook, remove the beef slices from the marinade and drain well. Arrange them on the hot grate at a 45 degree angle to the bars of the grate and grill until cooked to taste, 2 to 3 minutes per side for medium-rare, another 1 minute per side for medium, rotating the slices 90 degrees after 1 minute to create an attractive crosshatch of grill marks. Spoon the reserved *chimichurri* sauce onto plates or a platter, place the *churrasco* on top, and serve.

ALSO GOOD FOR:
This is a wonderful way to cook pork loin, pork tenderloin, and chicken breasts. You could even prepare a salmon fillet in this fashion.

KNOW YOUR STEAK

Not every cut of beef is good for grilling. Some, like blade steak or chuck, require the slow, moist, gentle heat of braising to make them palatable. But most steaks positively triumph when exposed to the searing heat of the grill. Choosing the right steak is the first step toward mastering grillsmanship. Here are photo IDs to help you recognize the players. Grill all over high heat.

porterhouse will serve two to three people.

T-BONE STEAK: Similar to a porterhouse, but cut closer to the center of the steer. This makes the strip sirloin portion of a T-bone steak more tender than that of a porter-

T-BONE STEAK

house, but the tenderloin section will be smaller. (The tenderloin tapers as it runs toward the center of the steer.) T-bone steaks are generally cut thinner than porter-houses, so you can serve one per person.

RIB EYE STEAK

RIB EYE STEAK (also known as **DELMONICO STEAK**): This is my favorite steak—and with good reason. The rib eye is cut from the small end of the rib roast and it's about the juiciest steak money can buy. Thanks to a generous marbling, it's almost impossible to ruin a rib eye by overcooking. You do need to watch for fat fires when grilling a rib eye, however. Should flare-ups occur, simply move the steaks to a cooler section of the grill.

STRIP STEAK: The sheer multiplicity of names for this steak indicates its popularity: Depending on where you are, it will be called strip steak, New York strip, Kansas City strip, or top loin, among other names. Strip steak is basically the top loin without the tenderloin. New York and Kansas City strips are typically boneless; when called shell, club, or strip, the steak will generally have a piece of the bone. Lean, meaty, and firm textured, it's the sort of steak carni-vores love to sink their

STRIP STEAK

teeth into. Strip steaks should be cut at least ¾ to 1 inch thick.

PORTERHOUSE STEAK: This two-fisted cut is actually two steaks in one: a firm meaty strip and a soft, succulent tenderloin, both attached to a T-shaped bone.

PORTERHOUSE STEAK

Porterhouses are thick steaks—1 to 2 inches. Sear them over a high heat, but be ready to turn down the heat on a gas grill (or move them to a cooler section of a char-coal grill) if they start to scorch. A good size

FILET MIGNON

FILET MIGNON (also known as a **TENDERLOIN STEAK**): A handsome, rel-atively small, thick steak, round in shape, cut from a beef tenderloin. Its enthusiasts praise its leanness and tenderness. Depending on your perspective, the flavor is subtle or downright bland.

SIRLOIN STEAK

SIRLOIN STEAK: This is a beef lover's steak—rich,

red, and meaty. Sirloin is probably the most flavorful steak you can buy, but it can be tougher than a strip or rib eye. For this reason, grill jockeys will often serve sirloin London broil style—thinly sliced on the diagonal—to make the meat seem more tender.

FLANK STEAK: The flank steak is a broad flat muscle from the underbelly of the steer. It's a highly flavorful cut, but tough and stringy. However, by thinly slicing the steak across the grain, you produce meltingly tender slices of beef that are richly flavored. It's best served medium-rare.

FLANK STEAK

SKIRT STEAK: Latin Americans have long prized this long, thin, fibrous steak cut from the steer's underbelly. The flavor is rich and beefy; the meat, moist; and the stringiness can be moderated by thinly slicing the

SKIRT STEAK

steak across the grain. Skirt steak can cost less than half of what a strip steak costs—which makes it a winner in my book.

THE DONENESS POKE TEST

Buying a great steak can be a costly proposition. But, no matter how much you spend, it won't taste great unless you know how long to cook it. The pros use the poke test to gauge the desired degree of doneness: A quick poke of the meat with your finger will tell you whether it's rare, medium, or (heaven forbid) well-done. If you're concerned about the heat of the grill, slide the steak off before testing. Once you become a seasoned grill meister, a poke over the heat won't bother you.

Use the following guide to help you, but remember: A steak will continue cooking even after it comes off the grill.

VERY RARE STEAK (a.k.a. still mooing): *The meat is bloodred in the center and barely warm. The steak will feel soft and squishy to the touch.*

RARE STEAK: *The meat is red in the center and warmish hot. The steak will feel soft to the touch.*

MEDIUM-RARE STEAK: *The meat is pinkish red in the center and hot. The steak will be gently yielding to the touch.*

MEDIUM STEAK: *The meat will be pink in the center and quite hot. The steak will yield only slightly to the touch.*

MEDIUM-WELL STEAK: *The meat will be mostly gray-brown in the center, with only a trace of pink. The steak will feel firm to the touch.*

WELL-DONE STEAK: *The meat will be uniformly gray-brown and will feel almost hard to the touch.*

METHOD:
Direct grilling

COOKING TIME:
14 to 20 minutes

HOW TO GRILL A PORTERHOUSE STEAK

*Tuscan-Style
Porterhouse
Steak*

The porterhouse is a steak lover's steak, a slab of beef that includes both a top strip loin and a tenderloin. All self-respecting grill masters should have a good porterhouse recipe in their repertoires, and the best one I know of is the way it's prepared in Florence, Italy. Tuscan grill masters start with a thick slab of dark, rich Chianina beef, grill it over a superhot bed of blazing oak embers, and douse it with the most fragrant olive oil money can buy.

Beef from the United States isn't quite as tasty as Chianina, so I've added a few additional flavorings to the traditional Tuscan recipe, namely garlic, rosemary, and sage. When the hot steak comes in contact with these ingredients, the herb oils perfume the meat.

SETTING UP THE GRILL

1 To set up a charcoal grill for direct grilling, first light the charcoal in a chimney starter (see page 9).

2 Using a garden hoe or other long-handled implement, rake the burning coals into an even layer.

3 To see if the grill is preheated to high, use the test on page 10.

TIP

■ You can certainly cook over charcoal or gas, but to experience porterhouse at the height of its glory, grill it over oak. Instructions for grilling over wood are found on page 12.

OILING THE GRATE: Oil the bars of the grate with a piece of steak fat before placing the steak on the grill.

TESTING FOR DONENESS

Sear the seasoned steak on the outside, rotating it 45 degrees to create a crosshatch of grill marks. If you like your meat quite rare in the center, when done it will feel soft when poked with your finger.

Another way to test for doneness is to insert an instant-read meat thermometer in the side of the steak but not touching the bone. Rare meat will take 7 to 10 minutes per side and register about 125°F.

FINISHING THE STEAK

1 Transfer the steak to a baking dish strewn with chopped garlic, fresh sage, and fresh rosemary.

2 Drizzle olive oil over the steak.

3 Turn the steak a couple of times to coat both sides with olive oil.

4 After the steak has marinated for 3 to 5 minutes, cut the tenderloin off the bone.

5 Cut the strip portion off the bone.

6 Cut both pieces crosswise into ¼-inch-thick slices. Use a spoon to baste the meat with the olive oil and meat juices right before serving.

THE RECIPE

TUSCAN-STYLE PORTERHOUSE STEAK

1 porterhouse steak (1½ to 2 inches thick; 1¾ pounds)
Coarse salt and black pepper
2 cloves garlic, finely chopped

1 tablespoon coarsely chopped fresh rosemary leaves
6 whole fresh sage leaves
½ cup cold-pressed, extra-virgin olive oil

SERVES 2 TO 3

1. Set up the grill for direct grilling (see page 10 for charcoal, page 12 for wood, or page 16 for gas; ideally you'll be using wood or charcoal) and preheat to high.

2. Generously season the steak with salt and pepper. When ready to cook, brush and oil the grill grate. Arrange the steak on the hot grate at a 45 degree angle to the bars of the grate and grill until cooked to taste, 7 to 10 minutes per side for rare (about 125°F on an instant-read meat thermometer), rotating the steak after 3 to 4 minutes to create crosshatch grill marks.

3. Scatter the garlic, rosemary, and sage leaves over the bottom of a deep dish or platter. Arrange the grilled steak on top and pour the oil over it. Turn the steak a few times to coat with the garlic, herbs, and oil. Spoon the oil that gathers in the bottom of the dish over the steak. Let the steak marinate for 3 to 5 minutes.

4. To carve and serve, cut the tenderloin and top loin strip off the bone and slice, as shown in Steps 4 through 6. Spoon the herbed oil and meat juices over the meat one final time and serve at once.

ALSO GOOD FOR:
You could certainly grill a veal chop or pork chop in this fashion. For that matter, it's a good way to prepare a spatchcocked chicken (see page 220).

HOW TO GRILL T-BONE STEAKS

Steak au poivre (pepper steak) is one of the glories of the French bistro. Too bad it's traditionally cooked in a frying pan, not on the grill. That set me thinking: Why not put the coarsely ground pepper on a mustard-slathered steak and char it on the grill? I tried it. I liked it. Especially made with a cut of beef that can really stand up to the spices and heat—a T-bone steak. Of course, *no* Frenchman would ever douse a steak with Tabasco sauce, but I like the way it pumps up the heat.

Hellfire Steak with pepper-corn relish

SETTING UP THE GRILL

1 To set up a charcoal grill for direct grilling, first light the charcoal in a chimney starter (see page 9).

2 Using a garden hoe or other long-handled implement, rake the burning coals into an even layer.

3 To see if the grill is preheated to high, use the test on page 10.

PREPARING THE MEAT

1 The T-bone is one of the tastiest steaks ever to come off the grill, offering the best of two worlds—the rich flavor of the strip (the larger side of the T-bone) and the tenderness of beef tenderloin (the smaller side of the bone).

2 Season well with salt and plenty of pepper. Dust the steak with dry mustard, patting it onto the meat with a fork.

TIPS

■ I tend to like my food hot, so I use a heavy hand with the mustard and Tabasco sauce. Use plenty of salt to offset the acidity in the hot sauce.

■ I like to apply the pepper twice—at the beginning, and again when the steaks are on the grill.

■ Set your grinder to grind as coarsely as possible. To vary the flavor, you could use a blend of black, white, green, and pink peppercorns.

TIP

■ For tableside drama, flambé the steaks with a pepper vodka, like Absolut Peppar. Warm 3 or 4 tablespoons of vodka in a saucepan but do not let it boil. Off the burner, touch a lit match or lighter to the vodka to ignite it, then pour it over the steaks.

3 Sprinkle the steak with hot sauce to make a fiery crust.

ON THE GRILL: Grind lots of pepper onto the steaks. I like coarsely ground pepper for this. The steaks will be done in 8 to 12 minutes.

SERVES 4

ALSO GOOD FOR:
Of course, you can make pepper steak with any sort of steak—sirloin, strip, or rib eye. The preparation is equally great for tuna and salmon steaks.

THE RECIPE

HELLFIRE STEAKS

4 T-bone steaks (1 inch thick; about 12 ounces each)
Coarse salt and black pepper

2 to 3 tablespoons dry mustard
2 to 3 tablespoons Tabasco or other hot sauce, or to taste

1. Place the steaks on a plate and sprinkle on both sides with salt and plenty of pepper and the dry mustard, patting the spices onto the meat with a fork. Drizzle the Tabasco sauce over the steaks, again patting it on with a fork. Let the meat sit while you preheat the grill.

2. Set up the grill for direct grilling (see page 10 for charcoal or page 16 for gas) and preheat to high.

3. When ready to cook, brush and oil the grill grate. Arrange the steaks on the hot grate at a 45 degree angle to the bars of the grate. Grill for 4 to 6 minutes per side for medium-rare (about 145°F on an instant-read meat thermometer), rotating the steaks after 3 minutes to create an attractive crosshatch of grill marks. Coarsely grind as much pepper as you can bear over the steaks as they grill. Transfer the steaks to plates or a platter and let rest for 3 minutes, then serve.

HOW TO GRILL STRIP STEAKS

METHOD:
Direct grilling

COOKING TIME:
8 to 12 minutes

S teak. One simple word that spells a heap of pleasure. Steak is the measure of a grill jockey's mettle, and the ability to grill one to the perfect degree of doneness is the mark of a master. Fortunately, by following three simple procedures, it's easy to produce a perfect steak every time.

First is the choice of steak. The high, dry heat of grilling requires a tender cut of beef. Second is the heat of the grill. Steak needs a high heat to sear the outside. Finally, you need to give the steak a rest before serving. The high heat of the grill forces the juices deep into the meat. When you let the steak rest for a few minutes, the juices flow back throughout the meat.

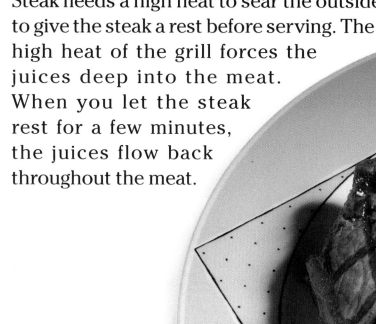

*Strip Steak
with Tarragon Butter
and grilled yellow
and red beets*

SETTING UP THE GRILL

1 To set up a charcoal grill for direct grilling, first light the charcoal in a chimney starter (see page 9).

2 Using a garden hoe or other long-handled implement, rake the burning coals into an even layer.

3 To see if the grill is preheated to high, use the test on page 10.

ON THE GRILL

1 To create a handsome crosshatch of grill marks, arrange the steak on a 45 degree angle to the bars of the grate.

2 Rotate the steak 90 degrees after 2 to 3 minutes.

3 Turn the steak over with tongs and cook on the other side the same way. The steak will take a total of 8 to 12 minutes to cook to medium-rare.

STRIP STEAKS WITH TARRAGON BUTTER

4 boneless strip steaks
(8 to 10 ounces each)
Coarse salt and black pepper

4 tablespoons Tarragon Butter
(page 450)

1. Set up the grill for direct grilling (see page 10 for charcoal or page 16 for gas) and preheat to high. If using a gas grill, place the wood chips, if desired, in the smoker box or in a smoker pouch (see page 17) and preheat until you see smoke. Generously season the steaks on both sides with salt and pepper.

2. When ready to cook, if using a charcoal grill, toss the wood chips on the coals, if desired.

3. Brush and oil the grill grate. Arrange the steaks on the hot grate at a 45 degree angle to the bars of the grate. Grill for 4 to 6 minutes, pressing on the steaks with a spat-

ula for a few seconds. Rotate the steaks 90 degrees after 2 to 3 minutes to create an attractive crosshatch of grill marks. Turn the steaks over with tongs and grill the second side the same way for medium-rare. Test for doneness, using the poke method (see page 55). Or insert an instant-read meat thermometer in the thickest portion of the meat. The internal temperature will be about 145°F for medium-rare.

4. Transfer the steaks to plates or a platter. Top each steak with a round of the Tarragon Butter, rubbing it over the meat with a fork. Let the steaks rest for 2 to 3 minutes before serving.

SERVES 4

YOU'LL NEED:
2 cups wood chips (optional; preferably mesquite or oak), unsoaked

---

ALSO GOOD FOR:
Any beefsteak can be grilled this way and topped with any type of flavored butter you fancy (see recipes on pages 450 and 451). You can also use this basic method for grilling pork and veal chops, chicken breasts, and fish steaks and fillets.

METHOD:
Direct grilling

COOKING TIME:
12 to 15 minutes

**ADVANCE
PREPARATION:**
2 to 4 hours for
marinating the
meat

HOW TO GRILL FILET MIGNON

For many people, filet mignon is the ultimate steak. It's certainly the most expensive. Curiously, the very qualities that make filet mignon so expensive and desirable—it is lean, tender, and mildly flavored—pose a challenge for the cook. Fat is what gives meat its flavor, and a fillet's relative leanness makes its taste somewhat bland. The lack of marbling also gives it a tendency to dry out. To combat these tendencies, I like to marinate filet mignon before grilling (the marinade adds flavor and moistness). I also like to wrap the fillets in bacon to keep them from drying out.

*Juniper-Flavored
Filets Mignons*

SETTING UP THE GRILL

1 To set up a charcoal grill for direct grilling, first light the charcoal in a chimney starter (see page 9).

2 Using a garden hoe or other long-handled implement, rake the burning coals into an even layer.

3 To see if the grill is preheated to high, use the test on page 10.

PREPARING THE MEAT

1 First cut the beef tenderloin crosswise into 2-inch filet mignon steaks. Save the tenderloin "tail" (at bottom) for kebabs or satés.

2 Wrap the filets mignons in bacon.

TIP

■ **You can use any marinade in this book in place of the wine marinade here. The teriyaki marinade from Tangerine Teriyaki Tofu, Step 2, on page 417 goes especially well with filet mignon. You can even skip the marinade, but do wrap the fillets in bacon to keep them moist.**

TIP

■ Because filet
mignon is such a thick
steak, grill the sides
as well as the top and
bottom.

3 Tie the bacon in place with butcher's string. Transfer the fillets to a baking dish.

4 Adding red wine and diced vegetables and herbs gives the filets mignons a wild game flavor.

5 Juniper berries give the beef a distinctive woodsy aroma and flavor. For a stronger flavor, crush the berries before adding them.

ON THE GRILL: Grill the filets mignons on their sides as well as the top and bottom, for a total of 12 to 15 minutes.

JUNIPER-FLAVORED FILETS MIGNONS

SERVES 6

YOU'LL NEED:
Butcher's string

1 piece beef tenderloin, trimmed
    (about 2½ pounds), or
    6 filet mignon steaks
    (about 6 ounces each)
6 strips bacon or pancetta
    (Italian bacon)
2 cups dry red wine
2 shallots, thinly sliced
1 rib celery, finely chopped
1 carrot, finely chopped

2 cloves garlic, crushed with
    the side of a cleaver
2 bay leaves
2 sprigs fresh thyme or 1 teaspoon dried
¼ cup extra-virgin olive oil
2 teaspoons juniper berries or
    1 tablespoon gin
Coarse salt and black pepper
1 piece (1 inch) butter (2 tablespoons)
Shallot Marmalade (optional; page 461)

ALSO GOOD FOR:
The marinade in this recipe will give any type of grilled meat the flavor of its analog in wild game. Thus, grilled pork acquires the flavor of wild boar; grilled lamb, mountain goat; grilled chicken, partridge; and so on.

1. If using tenderloin, cut into filet mignon steaks, as shown in Preparing the Meat, Step 1 on page 67. Wrap each filet mignon with a strip of bacon, as shown in Steps 2 and 3, securing it with butcher's string.

2. Place the wine in a nonreactive bowl or measuring cup and stir in the shallots, celery, carrot, garlic, bay leaves, and thyme. Generously rub the steaks on both sides with some of the oil and place in a baking dish. Pour the wine mixture over the meat and add the juniper berries on top. Pour any remaining oil over the meat and let marinate in the refrigerator, covered, for 2 to 4 hours, turning the fillets 2 or 3 times.

3. Set up the grill for direct grilling (see page 10 for charcoal or page 16 for gas) and preheat to high. When ready to cook, brush and oil the grill grate.

4. Remove the meat from the marinade and drain well. Season the steaks on both sides with salt and pepper and arrange them on the hot grate. Grill until cooked to taste, 4 to 6 minutes each for the top and bottom for medium-rare (about 145°F on an instant-read meat thermometer inserted in the center of the meat). Turn the steaks on their sides with tongs for 2 to 3 minutes to crisp the bacon. Transfer the steaks to a platter, rub the tops with the butter, and let rest for 3 to 5 minutes before serving. Remove and discard the strings. Serve the beef with the Shallot Marmalade, if desired.

METHOD:
Direct grilling

COOKING TIME:
12 to 16 minutes

**ADVANCE
PREPARATION:**
4 to 12 hours for
marinating the
meat

HOW TO MAKE LONDON BROIL

London broil lives in our collective imagination, but there's really no such thing on a steer. That is to say that *London broil* refers to a method of grilling and carving a thick steak, not to a particular cut of meat. The steaks used tend to be tough and flavorful, such as thick cuts like top round or bottom round, or even the thinner cut, flank steak. The genius of the London broil lies in the way you carve it: sharply on the diagonal to minimize the length of the tough meat fibers. This makes a tough cut tender, and it gives you broad meaty slices that are charred on the outside, delectably rare on the inside, and that look drop-dead delicious carpeting your plate. Top London broil with grilled scallions and mushrooms.

*Ginger-Soy
London Broil with
Grilled Mushrooms
(page 373)
and Scallions
(page 380)*

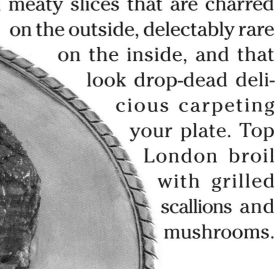

1 To set up a charcoal grill for direct grilling, first light the charcoal in a chimney starter (see page 9).

2 Using a garden hoe or other long-handled implement, rake the burning coals into an even layer.

3 To see if the grill is preheated to high, use the test on page 10.

MAKING LONDON BROIL

PREPARING THE MEAT: Spread the marinade on the steak, here cut from the top of the round. Marinate the meat for 4 to 6 hours, covered, in the refrigerator, or even overnight.

ON THE GRILL: Use tongs to move the steak away from flare-ups and the finger poke test to check for doneness.

CARVING THE MEAT: Carve the London broil by holding your knife at a 45 degree angle to the top of the meat to obtain the broad thin slices that are its hallmark.

TIPS

■ Three cuts of meat are commonly used for London broil: top round, bottom round, and flank steak. The first two give you the broadest slices and a rich beefy flavor, but they can be a little tough—even when sliced on the diagonal. Flank steak has the most marbling, giving you a crusty, succulent London broil.

■ Feel free to season the London broil with another marinade or rub from this book. Particularly recommended are the Chinese Five-Spice Rub (page 442), Mucho Macho Pepper Rub (page 443), and Cajun Rub (page 441).

ALSO GOOD FOR:
My local butcher sells a turkey "London broil" for health-conscious grillers. To make it, marinate and grill a boneless turkey breast as described in the recipe. When working with poultry, however, you must cook it through, to at least 170°F, which will take 15 to 20 minutes per side.

THE RECIPE

GINGER-SOY LONDON BROIL

1 piece (2 inches) fresh ginger,
    peeled and thinly sliced
½ red onion, cut into 1-inch chunks
4 cloves garlic, coarsely chopped
½ cup chopped fresh cilantro or
    flat-leaf parsley
¼ cup dry red wine
¼ cup soy sauce

¼ cup vegetable oil
½ teaspoon black pepper
1 beefsteak (1¼ to 1½ inches thick;
    1½ to 2 pounds) cut from
    the top or bottom round or
    1 flank steak (1½ to 2 pounds)

1. Prepare the marinade: Place the ginger, onion, garlic, and cilantro in a food processor and process until a smooth paste forms. Add the wine, soy sauce, oil, and pepper and process to combine.

2. Place the steak in a baking dish just large enough to hold it and spread the marinade over it. Let marinate in the refrigerator, covered, for at least 4 hours, ideally 6 hours, or even overnight (12 hours) if time permits, turning the steak a few times.

3. Set up the grill for direct grilling (see page 10 for charcoal or page 16 for gas) and preheat to high. When ready to cook, brush and oil the grill grate. Remove the steak from the marinade and drain well. Place the steak on the hot grate and grill until cooked to taste, 6 to 8 minutes per side for medium-rare, 2 minutes more per side for medium, rotating the steak 90 degrees after 3 minutes if a crosshatch of grill marks is desired. (This isn't absolutely essential, as the steak will be carved for serving, but the perfectionist in you may want to do it anyway.)

4. Transfer the steak to a cutting board and let rest for 5 minutes. Using a sharp knife, carve it into broad thin slices, holding the knife blade at a 45 degree angle to the top of the meat. Serve at once.

HOW TO STUFF AND GRILL FLANK STEAK

METHOD:
Direct grilling

COOKING TIME:
1½ to 2 hours

In South America, a butterflied, stuffed, rolled, grilled flank steak is called *matambre:* hunger killer. And, indeed, it will lay your hunger to rest. I'm always on the lookout for theatrical dishes that take a short time to make yet look and taste like something you've labored over for hours, and *matambre* is a perfect example. Its preparation looks complicated—especially when you serve a slice of this savory meat with its colorful pinwheel of vegetables, sausage, and cheese. Just don't let on that this show-stopper took only 20 minutes to assemble.

Classic Matambre

SETTING UP THE GRILL

1 To set up a charcoal grill for direct grilling, first light the charcoal in a chimney starter (see page 9).

2 Using a garden hoe or other long-handled implement, rake the burning coals into an even layer.

3 To see if the grill is preheated to medium, use the test on page 10.

PREPARING THE MEAT

1 Position the flank steak lengthwise at the edge of the cutting board. Place one hand on top to hold it flat. Using a sharp, slender knife, cut through the side of the steak to butterfly it (open it up). As you cut, fold open the top to help you see what you're doing. Open the meat up like a book.

2 Arrange the strips of bacon on a sheet of aluminum foil, running parallel to an edge and leaving 1-inch spaces between slices.

TIPS

■ If you're not comfortable with your knifesmanship skills, ask your butcher to butterfly the flank steak.

■ Don't worry if you make a few holes in the flank steak as you're cutting it open. The meat is rolled, so you won't even see them.

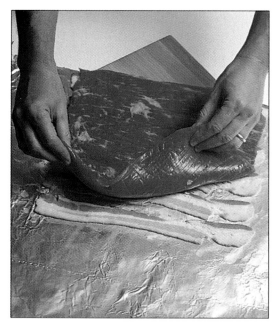

3 Lay the butterflied flank steak on top of the bacon, with the grain running parallel to the bacon and season with salt, pepper, oregano, and vinegar.

4 Starting at the edge of the meat closest to you, arrange kielbasa, celery, carrot, ham, cheese, and bell pepper on top of the steak in neat parallel rows, alternating colors.

5 Starting at the edge of the meat closest to you, and using the aluminum foil to help you, roll up the flank steak, like a jelly roll.

6 Twist the ends of the foil to seal the roll. Make shallow holes in the foil all over and to ensure a perfectly cylindrical shape, tie the roll in a few places with butcher's string.

TIPS

■ If necessary pound the butterflied meat flat with the side of a meat cleaver (do this only if there is a bump in the center).

■ I call for grilling the *matambre* directly over a medium heat here. I like the way direct grilling gives you a crisp, caramelized crust.

■ The traditional sauce for *matambre* is *chimichurri* (parsley-garlic sauce—see the recipe on page 457).

TESTING FOR DONENESS: Grill the roll over medium heat, turning it every 20 minutes. Use an instant-read meat thermometer to test for doneness. When fully cooked (1½ to 2 hours), the internal temperature will be 180°F.

SLICING THE MEAT: Let rest for 10 minutes. Unwrap the *matambre* and cut it crosswise into ½-inch slices. Note the beautiful mosaic of vegetables and meat you get in each slice.

SERVES 8 TO 12 AS AN APPETIZER, 4 AS A MAIN COURSE

YOU'LL NEED: Butcher's string

ALSO GOOD FOR:
To make a pork matambre, use a roll-cut pork loin (see page 117) in place of the flank steak. You can also make a veal matambre, using boneless breast of veal. Both will take 1¼ to 1½ hours to cook.

THE RECIPE

CLASSIC MATAMBRE

FOR THE BEEF:
1 flank steak (1½ to 1¾ pounds)
6 thin slices bacon
Coarse salt and black pepper
1 teaspoon dried oregano
1 tablespoon red wine vinegar

FOR THE FILLING:
1 piece (6 to 8 ounces) kielbasa, or other cooked smoked sausage, cut lengthwise in thin strips

4 ribs celery, cut lengthwise in thin strips
2 large carrots, cut lengthwise in thin strips
6 ounces smoked cooked ham (sliced ¼ inch thick), cut lengthwise into ¼-inch strips
6 ounces Romano cheese (sliced ¼ inch thick), cut lengthwise into ¼-inch strips
1 red bell pepper, stemmed, seeded, and cut lengthwise into ¼-inch strips

1. Butterfly the flank steak as shown in Preparing the Meat, Step 1 on page 74.
2. Place a large piece of heavy-duty

aluminum foil, 24 inches long, on your work surface, shiny side down. (It's okay to double up two smaller pieces of aluminum foil.) Arrange the bacon slices on the foil in a row parallel to an edge of the foil and place the flank steak on top, as shown in Steps 2 and 3 on pages 74 and 75. Season with salt and pepper and sprinkle with the oregano and vinegar.

3. Place a row of kielbasa strips at the edge of the meat closest to you. Place a row of celery strips next to it, followed by rows of carrot, ham, cheese, and bell pepper strips, as shown in Step 4. Repeat this sequence until all the filling ingredients are used up. Leave the last 2 inches of meat uncovered.

4. Starting at the edge closest to you and using the aluminum foil to help you, roll up the meat with the filling to make a tight roll. Wrap the foil around the meat, twisting the ends of the foil. Using the tip of a paring knife, poke holes in the aluminum foil at 1-inch intervals. Tie the meat in several places with butcher's string. The *matambre* can be prepared up to this stage several hours ahead. Store, covered, in the refrigerator.

5. Set up the grill for direct grilling (see page 10 for charcoal or page 16 for gas) and preheat to medium. When ready to cook, place the roll on the hot grate and grill until cooked through and the meat is very tender, 1½ to 2 hours, turning with tongs every 15 or 20 minutes. If using a charcoal grill, you'll need to add 24 to 30 fresh coals after 1 hour. To test for doneness, use an instant-read meat thermometer: The internal temperature should be about 180°F. Transfer the *matambre* to a cutting board and let rest for 10 minutes. Remove the string and foil and cut the roll crosswise into ½-inch slices. Serve hot or at room temperature.

VARIATION:
You can also cook the matambre using the indirect method. It's absolutely no fuss, but the exterior of the meat won't be quite as crusty. You'll need to cook it for 1½ to 2 hours at medium. You can crisp up the crust by grilling the roll directly for the last 20 minutes.

METHOD:
Direct grilling

COOKING TIME:
2 to 4 minutes

ADVANCE PREPARATION:
30 minutes for marinating the satés

HOW TO MAKE BEEF SATES

Let the Turks have their shish kebab, the French, their brochettes. I raise my skewer to saté. This tiny kebab is the meat-on-a-stick of choice throughout Southeast Asia, and its explosive flavor and diminutive single-bite size make it a perfect hors d'oeuvre for a cookout. Satés are fun to eat—in part because they're so small (it takes a lot of them to fill you up) and in part because the flavorings are so varied and intense. Here's a beef saté seasoned with an explosive mixture of lemongrass, garlic, chiles, and Asian fish sauce and sprinkled with cilantro and chopped toasted peanuts.

Lemongrass Beef Satés with Cucumber Relish

SETTING UP THE GRILL

1 To set up a charcoal grill for direct grilling, first light the charcoal in a chimney starter (see page 9).

2 Using a garden hoe or other long-handled implement, rake the burning coals into an even layer.

3 To see if the grill is preheated to high, use the test on page 10.

PREPARING THE LEMONGRASS

1 Trim the leaves (the green flexible part) off the lemongrass and reserve.

2 Trim the root end off the lemongrass.

3 Remove the outside layer from the lemongrass core.

4 Finely chop the lemongrass core. The leaves have been trimmed and tied together to make a basting brush (see Tips at right).

TIPS

■ When you buy lemongrass, be sure you're getting the bulbous base (the part you use), not just the leafy tops.

■ To make a basting brush from lemongrass leaves, gather them together, trim the tops evenly, and wrap a piece of butcher's string tightly around the bottom.

TIPS

■ To make a great saté you need to think small. Most of the Asian varieties are intended to be consumed in one or two bites.

■ Soak the bamboo skewers in water to prevent them from catching fire.

PREPARING THE MEAT

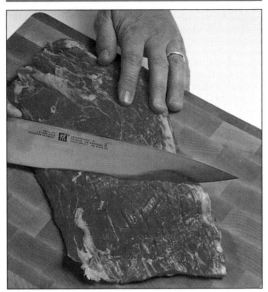

1 Lay the flank steak flat on a cutting board and lightly score it in a crosshatch pattern on both sides. This speeds up the absorption of the marinade.

2 Thinly slice the flank steak crosswise into long thin strips with the knife blade held at a 45 degree angle to the meat. Each strip should be about 5 inches long, ¾ inch wide, and ⅛ inch thick.

SKEWERING THE SATES

1 Weave the flank steak slices onto bamboo skewers.

2 The meat will bunch up as it goes on the skewer. Gently spread it open with your fingers.

ON THE GRILL: Baste the satés with oil as they cook, using the lemongrass brush.

LEMONGRASS BEEF SATES

FOR THE BEEF AND MARINADE:
*2 to 3 stalks lemongrass, trimmed and
    finely chopped (⅓ cup), leaves
    reserved*
3 cloves garlic, coarsely chopped
*1 to 3 Thai chiles or jalapeño peppers,
    seeded and chopped (for hotter satés,
    leave the seeds in)*
¼ cup chopped fresh cilantro
3 tablespoons brown sugar
2 teaspoons ground coriander
⅓ cup fish sauce or soy sauce

¼ cup lime juice
4 tablespoons vegetable oil
1½ pounds flank steak

FOR SERVING:
*¼ cup coarsely chopped dry-roasted
    peanuts*
¼ cup chopped fresh cilantro
*Cucumber Relish (optional;
    page 460)*
*Asian Peanut Sauce (optional;
    page 456)*

1. Prepare the marinade: Combine the lemongrass, garlic, chiles, cilantro, and brown sugar in a mortar or food processor and pound with the pestle or process to a coarse paste. Work in the coriander, fish sauce, lime juice, and 2 tablespoons of oil.

2. Score and then slice the flank steak crosswise into long thin strips and thread the strips onto skewers as shown in the steps on the facing page. Arrange the skewers in a shallow dish. Pour the marinade over the beef and let marinate for 30 minutes, turning the skewers to ensure even seasoning.

3. Make a basting brush from the reserved lemongrass leaves (see Tips, page 79).

4. Set up the grill for direct grilling (see page 10 for charcoal or page 16 for gas) and preheat to high. When ready to cook, brush and oil the grill grate. Arrange the satés on the grill so that the meat is over the fire and the exposed skewers are away from the heat. Grill the beef, basting with the remaining oil, using the lemongrass brush, until cooked, 1 to 2 minutes per side. Arrange the satés on a platter or banana leaf and sprinkle with the peanuts and cilantro. If desired, serve the Cucumber Relish and/or the Asian Peanut Sauce as accompaniments.

**MAKES ABOUT
36 SATES;
SERVES 6 TO 8 AS
AN APPETIZER,
4 AS A LIGHT MAIN
COURSE**

YOU'LL NEED:
About 36 long,
slender bamboo
skewers, soaked
for 1 hour in cold
water to cover,
then drained;
butcher's string,
for tying the
lemongrass brush

ALSO GOOD FOR:
*Pork, lamb, chicken,
and even seafood
satés can be
prepared the same
way.*

COOKING METHOD:
Direct grilling

COOKING TIME:
8 to 12 minutes

**ADVANCE
PREPARATION:**
1 to 2 hours for
marinating the
beef and soaking
the noodles

HOW TO MAKE A GRILLED BEEF SALAD

To millions of Thais, the world would be an infinitely less lovely place without *yam nua yang,* an electrifying salad of grilled beef, cooling lettuces, fiery chiles, and fresh herbs. You don't have to be Thai to enjoy the summery contrast of grilled beef and fresh, crisp salad greens. The recipe with this technique is ecumenical in its approach, incorporating flavorings from grill jockeys all over Asia. The sesame oil and soy sauce marinade will remind you of Korean cooking, while the rice noodles are the traditional accompaniment to grilled beef in Vietnam. The trio of fragrant herbs—fresh cilantro, mint, and basil—are straight out of Bangkok. Put them together and you get a salad that's eminently refreshing and long on flavor but short on fuss and preparation time.

*Asian Grilled
Beef Salad*

SETTING UP THE GRILL

1 To set up a charcoal grill for direct grilling, first light the charcoal in a chimney starter (see page 9).

2 Using a garden hoe or other long-handled implement, rake the burning coals into an even layer.

3 To see if the grill is preheated to high, use the test on page 10.

PREPARING THE MEAT

1 Lightly score the flank steak on both sides in a crosshatch pattern.

2 Spoon the marinade over the steak.

TIPS

■ This recipe calls for flank steak that's cooked and cut like London broil. I particularly like flank steak, because it gives you thin, even slices. But you could certainly use sirloin, strip steak, or even a luscious rib eye.

■ Flank steak has a tendency to curl when cooking. To keep it flat, I lightly score the steak in a crosshatch pattern on the top and bottom. This also speeds up the absorption of the marinade.

TIP

■ Rice noodles are available at Asian markets, gourmet shops, and most supermarkets. Some varieties need only soaking, others soaking and a brief boiling. Taste the noodles after they've soaked for 1 hour; if they're tender, you don't need to boil them. If you do boil the noodles, keep the cooking time brief, just 1 to 3 minutes.

ON THE GRILL: Grill the marinated flank steak until cooked to taste: 145°F for medium-rare. Insert the meat thermometer into the steak sideways. This gives you an accurate reading in the center.

CARVING THE FLANK STEAK: Carve the steak to obtain broad thin slices by holding the knife blade at a 45 degree angle to the top of the meat.

SERVES 4

THE RECIPE

ASIAN GRILLED BEEF SALAD

*FOR THE FLANK STEAK AND
    MARINADE/DRESSING:*
1 flank steak (about 1¼ pounds)
4 cloves garlic, minced
1 tablespoon peeled, minced
    fresh ginger
3 scallions, white part only, sliced
2 to 4 Thai chiles or jalapeño
    peppers, seeded and minced
3 tablespoons sugar
⅓ cup soy sauce
⅓ cup lime juice
2 tablespoons Asian (dark)
    sesame oil

TO FINISH THE SALAD:
1 ounce Asian rice noodles
1 head Boston, Bibb, or red leaf lettuce,
    or a mixture of lettuces, broken into
    leaves, washed, and spun dry
1 cucumber, seeded (optional) and
    thinly sliced
1 small sweet onion, thinly sliced and
    broken into rings
1 pint cherry tomatoes, halved
⅓ cup fresh mint leaves
⅓ cup fresh cilantro leaves
⅓ cup fresh basil leaves
¼ cup chopped dry-roasted peanuts
Small mint sprigs for garnish

1. Score the flank steak on both sides as shown in Preparing the Meat, Step 1 on page 83. Arrange in a nonreactive baking dish just large enough to hold it.

2. Place the garlic, ginger, scallion whites, chiles, and sugar in a large nonreactive mixing bowl and mash to a paste with the back of a spoon. Add the soy sauce, lime juice, sesame oil, and 3 tablespoons of water and stir or whisk until the sugar is dissolved. Pour half the marinade over the steak and let marinate for 1 to 2 hours in the refrigerator, covered, turning several times to ensure even marinating. Reserve the rest of the marinade for dressing the salad.

3. Soak the rice noodles in cold water to cover in a large bowl for 1 hour. Taste a noodle. If tender as is, drain well. If the rice noodles are still tough, cook in 3 quarts rapidly boiling water until tender, 1 to 3 minutes. Drain in a colander, rinse with cold water, and drain well.

4. Set up the grill for direct grilling (see page 10 for charcoal or page 16 for gas) and preheat to high.

5. Line salad plates with large lettuce leaves. Tear the smaller leaves into 2-inch pieces. Place the lettuce pieces, cucumber, onion, tomatoes, mint, cilantro, and basil in the mixing bowl with the reserved dressing, but do not mix.

6. When ready to cook, brush and oil the grill grate. Place the flank steak on the hot grate and grill until cooked to taste, 4 to 6 minutes per side for medium-rare (about 145°F on an instant-read meat thermometer). Transfer to a cutting board and let rest for 3 minutes. Cut the steak into paper-thin slices by holding the knife blade at a 45 degree angle to the top of the meat.

7. Toss the salad and loosely mound it on the lettuce-lined plates. Place a mound of rice noodles in the center of each. Arrange the beef slices on top of the salad and sprinkle with the peanuts. Place a mint sprig on each salad and serve at once.

VARIATIONS:
To give the salad a Thai or Vietnamese accent, use fish sauce instead of soy sauce and omit the sesame oil. Another variation is to replace the sugar with an equal amount of honey.

ALSO GOOD FOR:
This salad can be made with any sort of meat—pork tenderloin, lamb loin, chicken breast—or even tuna or tofu.

METHOD:
Direct grilling

COOKING TIME:
About 25 minutes
for grilling both
the vegetables and
the beef

**ADVANCE
PREPARATION:**
40 minutes to
1 hour for
marinating the
meat

HOW TO MAKE BEEF FAJITAS

It's hard to remember when cuisine in the United States didn't include fajitas, but there was a time when this Tex-Mex classic would have seemed positively exotic. Who knew that an inexpensive cut of beef—the skirt steak—would become one of America's most popular party foods? Well, what skirt steak may lack in refinement (it's a narrow, stringy piece of meat), it certainly makes up for in flavor.

The genius of the fajita is its interactivity. You lay out platters of grilled beef and vegetables, tortillas, salsas, and Tex-Mex garnishes. Guests get to assemble their own fajitas, customizing the ingredients to suit their tastes.

*Beef Fajitas with
Salsa Verde,
sour cream, and
Pico de Gallo*

SETTING UP THE GRILL

1 To set up a charcoal grill for direct grilling, first light the charcoal in a chimney starter (see page 9).

2 Using a garden hoe or other long-handled implement, rake the burning coals into an even layer.

3 To see if the grill is preheated to high, use the test on page 10.

PREPARING THE MEAT

1 Sprinkle the skirt steaks with the spice mixture.

2 Rub the spices onto the meat, then squeeze fresh lime juice over the skirt steaks to marinate them.

GRILLING THE VEGETABLES

1 Grill the poblano peppers until the skins are darkened and shriveled.

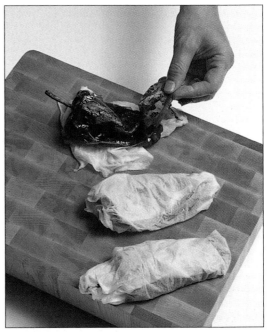

2 Wrap the peppers in wet paper towels to steam off the skin. Remove the skin with your fingers or scrape it off with a knife.

3 Cut the peppers in half, scrape out the seeds, and cut the pepper flesh into long thin strips, which are called *rajas* (pronounced ra-has).

4 Grill the scallions until nicely browned. Trim after grilling.

TIP

■ Lay the scallions on the grill grate at a diagonal to the bars. This keeps the individual scallions from falling through the spaces in the grate.

TESTING FOR DONENESS: Grill the meat for 3 to 4 minutes on each side for medium-rare. Use the finger poke method to test for doneness.

GRILLING THE TORTILLAS: Grill briefly; just until soft and pliable.

CARVING THE STEAKS

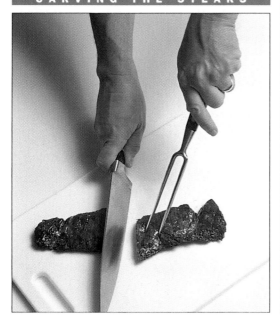

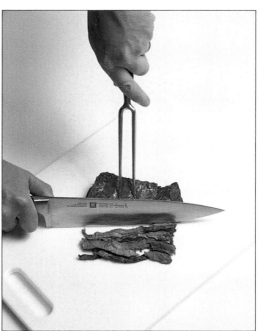

1 Cut each skirt steak in half crosswise.

2 Place one half on top of the other and thinly slice the steaks across the grain.

BEEF FAJITAS

FOR THE BEEF:
1½ pounds skirt steaks
1 tablespoon pure chili powder
1 teaspoon ground coriander
1 teaspoon coarse salt
½ teaspoon ground cumin
½ teaspoon garlic powder
½ teaspoon onion powder
½ teaspoon black pepper
2 limes

FOR THE GRILLED VEGETABLES:
3 poblano peppers or
    1 green bell pepper

1 red bell pepper
1 yellow bell pepper
3 bunches scallions

FOR SERVING:
1 bunch chopped fresh cilantro leaves
3 jalapeño peppers, thinly sliced
1 avocado, peeled, diced, and tossed with
    lime juice
2 cups sour cream
2 cups Pico de Gallo (page 458)
2 cups Salsa Verde (page 459)
3 limes, cut into wedges
18 small (7-inch) flour tortillas

1. Place the skirt steaks in a nonreactive baking dish in a single layer. Combine the chili powder, coriander, salt, cumin, garlic and onion powders, and black pepper in a small bowl and mix well. Sprinkle this mixture over the meat, patting it on with your fingertips. Let stand for 10 minutes. Squeeze the limes over the meat. Let marinate in the refrigerator for 30 minutes to 1 hour, covered.

2. Set up the grill for direct grilling (see page 10 for charcoal or page 16 for gas) and preheat to high.

3. Place the poblano and bell peppers on the hot grate and grill until charred on all sides, turning with tongs, 15 to 20 minutes. Transfer peppers to a cutting board, wrap in wet paper towels, and let cool. Meanwhile, grill the scallions until nicely browned, 3 to 5 minutes per side, turning with tongs.

4. Unwrap the peppers, pull off the burnt skin with your fingers (or scrape it off with a knife), cut the flesh off the core, scrape out the seeds, and cut into ¼-inch strips. Cut the scallions into 2-inch pieces or keep whole.

Arrange the pepper strips and scallions on a platter. Place the cilantro, jalapeños, avocado, sour cream, salsas, and lime wedges in attractive bowls.

5. Place the skirt steaks on the hot grate and grill until cooked to taste, 3 to 4 minutes per side for medium-rare. Use the poke test (see page 55) to test for doneness. Transfer the steaks to a cutting board and let rest for 3 minutes. Using a sharp knife, cut each steak in half crosswise and thinly slice across the grain, as shown in Steps 1 and 2 on page 89. Arrange the sliced steaks on the platter with the grilled vegetables.

6. Place the tortillas on the hot grate and grill until soft and pliable, 15 seconds per side. Place them in a basket.

7. To serve, have each guest place sliced beef and grilled vegetables on a tortilla and spoon some of the cilantro, jalapeños, avocado, sour cream, and/or salsas on top. After a squeeze of lime juice is added, the tortilla can be rolled into a neat bundle for eating. Tying the tortilla with a whole grilled scallion makes an elegant touch.

HOW TO GRILL CROSSCUT SHORT RIBS

METHOD:
Direct grilling

COOKING TIME:
8 to 12 minutes

**ADVANCE
PREPARATION:**
30 minutes to
2 hours for
marinating
the meat

N orth Americans tend to enjoy their ribs cut lengthwise, but Argentinean grill masters have developed a crosswise cut that gives you the meaty succulence of steak with the gnawable pleasure of ribs. Called *tira de asado* in Spanish, this ingenious cut consists of a long, thin (½ to 1 inch), crosswise section of beef short ribs. And thanks to the increasing Latinization of the American diet, you can find this delectable cut not only at Argentinean or Latino markets but at a growing number of supermarkets.

Because this cut of beef is so tasty, I've kept the seasoning straightforward: a simple salt, oregano, and hot pepper flake rub for the beef and a fresh salsa made with tomatoes and bell pepper, by way of an accompaniment.

*Argentinean
Rib Steaks with
Tomato-Pepper
Salsa*

SETTING UP THE GRILL

1 To set up a charcoal grill for direct grilling, first light the charcoal in a chimney starter (see page 9).

2 Using a garden hoe or other long-handled implement, rake the burning coals into an even layer.

3 To see if the grill is preheated to high, use the test on page 10.

TIPS

■ If short rib steaks aren't available in your area, ask your butcher to cut you some steaks from the short rib section. Or if you go to a kosher butcher, ask him to cut the steaks from flanken.

■ If you want a sauce for these rib steaks, try the Three-Herb Chimichurri on page 457.

PREPARING THE MEAT

1 Crosscut short ribs. Note how the ribs have plenty of meat between them.

2 Sprinkle the spices onto both sides of the ribs, patting them onto the meat with your fingertips. Then drizzle oil and sprinkle garlic over all.

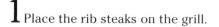

ON THE GRILL

1 Place the rib steaks on the grill.

2 Use the finger poke test to check for doneness. For medium, the meat should be firm but slightly yielding after 4 to 6 minutes per side.

THE RECIPE

ARGENTINEAN RIB STEAKS

SERVES 6

4 pounds short rib steaks
1½ teaspoons coarse salt
1½ teaspoons black pepper
1½ teaspoons dried oregano

1½ teaspoons hot red pepper flakes
3 to 4 tablespoons extra-virgin olive oil
3 cloves garlic, finely chopped
Tomato-Pepper Salsa (page 458), for serving

ALSO GOOD FOR:
If you can't find crosscut short ribs, prepare the recipe with skirt steak. It won't be the same but it will still be highly tasty.

1. Place the steaks in a baking dish and sprinkle both sides with the salt, pepper, oregano, and hot pepper flakes. Pat the seasonings onto the meat with your fingertips. Drizzle the meat on both sides with oil and sprinkle with the garlic. Let marinate in the refrigerator, covered, for as briefly as 30 minutes or as long as 2 hours—the longer, the better.

2. Set up the grill for direct grilling (see page 10 for charcoal or page 16 for gas) and preheat to high.

3. When ready to cook, place the steaks on the hot grate and grill until cooked to taste, 4 to 6 minutes per side for medium. (I like this cut better medium than medium-rare.) Poke the meat between the ribs to test for doneness (see page 55). Transfer the steaks to plates or a platter and serve the Tomato-Pepper Salsa on the side.

METHOD:
Indirect grilling

COOKING TIME:
1½ to 2 hours

ADVANCE
PREPARATION:
30 minutes for
curing the ribs

HOW TO SMOKE BEEF RIBS

Memphis-Style Beef Ribs with North Carolina Vinegar Sauce and cabbage slaw

Wet or dry? Say these simple words to a barbecue buff and you'll unleash a whole polemic. *Wet* refers to sweet, sticky, sauce-slathered ribs in the style of Kansas City, while *dry* refers to the spice-crusted ribs of Memphis, Tennessee. I'm not about to join the debate as to which is superior—I love barbecue much too much to choose sides. But since wet ribs are covered in the pork chapter, I thought beef would be a good place to discuss dry.

The rib in question here comes from the steer, specifically from one of the most prized cuts of beef—the prime rib. When the butcher cuts a rib roast, the by-product is a rack of ribs. It's not only the formidable size of these meaty staves that makes them so good. No, it's their generous marbling that turns the meat crusty and moist, without the greasiness associated with pork ribs.

SETTING UP THE GRILL

1 To set up a charcoal grill for smoking, first light the charcoal in a chimney starter (see page 9).

2 Place a drip pan in the center of the grill and divide the coals evenly on either side of it.

3 Place ½ cup of drained wood chips on each mound of coals.

PREPARING THE MEAT

1 A full rack of beef ribs has 7 ribs, which will comfortably feed two.

2 Sprinkle the rub on the meat. Note that I have placed the rub in a large shaker for sprinkling ease.

TIP

■ Look for beef ribs at your local butcher shop or in the meat section of your local supermarket. (Try the latter first: the price is apt to be more reasonable.)

ON THE GRILL: Note that the ribs are grilled in the center of the grate, away from the heat. Add more wood chips after 1 hour to generate more smoke.

TESTING FOR DONENESS: When fully cooked, the meat will shrink back from the bones. You should be able to pull the ribs apart with your fingers or a fork.

FINISHING THE RIBS

1 Once the ribs are grilled, use a clean barbecue mop to apply the sauce to them.

2 Give the ribs a final coating of rub just before serving.

T H E   R E C I P E

MEMPHIS-STYLE BEEF RIBS

2 racks of beef ribs (2½ to 3 pounds each)
3 tablespoons sweet paprika
2 teaspoons hot red pepper flakes
2 teaspoons mustard seeds
3 teaspoons coarse salt
2 teaspoons black pepper
2 teaspoons brown sugar
1 teaspoon celery salt

1 teaspoon garlic powder
1 teaspoon onion powder
1 teaspoon dried oregano
1 teaspoon cumin
1 cup distilled white vinegar
North Carolina Vinegar Sauce (optional; page 448)

1. Rinse the ribs under cold running water and blot dry with paper towels. Combine the paprika, hot pepper flakes, mustard seeds, 2 teaspoons coarse salt, pepper, brown sugar, celery salt, garlic powder, onion powder, dried oregano, and cumin in a small bowl or spice shaker. Set aside 2 tablespoons for the mop sauce. Sprinkle about 1 tablespoon of the rub on the meat side and ½ tablespoon on the bone side of each rack of ribs, rubbing the spices on with your fingers. Set the remaining rub aside for serving. Let the ribs sit for 30 minutes while you make the vinegar mop sauce and preheat the grill.

2. Combine the vinegar and remaining 1 teaspoon salt with the 2 tablespoons reserved rub in a small bowl and stir until the salt is dissolved.

3. Set up the grill for indirect grilling (see page 12 for charcoal or page 16 for gas) and preheat to medium. If using charcoal, place a large drip pan in the center. If using a gas grill, place all the wood chips or chunks in the smoker box or in a smoker pouch (see page 17) and preheat the grill on high until you see smoke, then reduce the heat to medium.

4. When ready to cook, if using a charcoal grill, toss half the wood chips or chunks on the coals. Place the ribs in the center of the hot grate away from and cover the grill. Cook for 1½ to 2 hours. When the ribs are cooked, they will be mahogany brown and tender enough to pull apart with your fingers; the meat will have shrunk back from the ends of the bones. If using charcoal, add 12 fresh coals per side and toss on the remaining wood chips after 1 hour.

5. Transfer the ribs to a clean cutting board. Mop on both sides with mop sauce and sprinkle with the remaining rub. Cut the rack into individual ribs and serve at once with any remaining mop sauce or the North Carolina Vinegar Sauce, if desired.

SERVES 4

YOU'LL NEED:
2 cups wood chips or chunks (preferably hickory), soaked for 1 hour in cold water to cover, then drained

VARIATIONS:
Beef ribs can also be prepared wet, like the Kansas City Sweet-and-Smoky Ribs on page 139 or even the Asian-style ribs on page 143.

ALSO GOOD FOR:
You could certainly prepare spare ribs or baby rack pork ribs in the Memphis dry rub style.

METHOD:
Direct grilling

COOKING TIME:
10 to 14 minutes

HOW TO GRILL THE PERFECT HAMBURGER

*Hamburger with
Herb Butter*

Chances are, if you're like most Americans, you dream of serving up smoky briskets and competition-quality ribs. But most of the time, when you fire up your grill, it's to cook a humble hamburger. Cooking a great burger has gotten harder in recent years, even though grills have become more sophisticated. The problem lies with the beef. When I was growing up, salmonella poisoning was a freak occurrence. Now, science and prudence dictate that you cook a hamburger to an internal temperature that is at least 160°F—in other words, until it's medium to medium-well done.

Desperate times require desperate measures. Here's a burger quite unlike any you've probably ever tasted. In order to keep succulence in a fully cooked burger, I place a disk of herb butter in the center. The melting butter moistens the meat from the inside, so you can cook it through without drying it out.

SETTING UP THE GRILL

1 To set up a charcoal grill for direct grilling, first light the charcoal in a chimney starter (see page 9).

2 Using a garden hoe or other long-handled implement, rake the burning coals into an even layer.

3 To see if the grill is preheated to high, use the test on page 10.

PREPARING THE MEAT

1 To make a hamburger, working quickly and with a light touch, form the ground beef into a flat ball and make a depression in the center with your thumb.

2 Place a slice of herb butter in the depression.

TIPS

■ The first secret to a great burger is to use a flavorful cut of meat. Ground chuck is perfect. So is ground round—or for a classy touch, ground sirloin.

■ The second secret to a great burger is fat. There, I've said it. Forget about calorie counting when you make burgers. A succulent burger requires a fat content of 15 to 20 percent.

3 Mold the ground beef around the butter to encase it. Keep the seasonings for the burger simple: Sprinkle with salt and pepper.

1 Arrange the burgers on the grill grate. Reseason with salt and pepper as they cook.

2 Testing for doneness: Use an instant-read meat thermometer. The meat should be at least 160°F to kill any potentially harmful bacteria.

3 Toast the buns on the grill.

HAMBURGERS WITH HERB BUTTER

SERVES 4

FOR THE HAMBURGERS:
1½ pounds ground sirloin, round, or chuck
4 tablespoons Garlic-Herb Butter (page 450),
    cut into 4 half-inch-thick slices
Coarse salt and black pepper
4 slices (2 to 3 ounces) pancetta
    (Italian bacon; optional)
4 slices white Cheddar cheese (optional)
4 hamburger buns or kaiser rolls
2 tablespoons melted butter

**FOR THE TOPPINGS (any or all of
    the following):**
Bibb or red leaf lettuce leaves
Thin slices of raw or grilled sweet
    onion (page 380)
Sliced ripe red tomato
Mustard, ketchup, mayonnaise,
    relish, or whatever other
    condiment you may fancy

1. Wet your hands with cold water and divide the ground beef into 4 portions. Pat each portion into a thick patty filled with a slice of herb butter, as shown in Preparing the Meat, Steps 1 through 3 on pages 99 and 100. Season with salt and pepper and refrigerate the burgers, covered, on a plate lined with plastic wrap while you preheat the grill.

2. Set up the grill for direct grilling (see page 10 for charcoal or page 16 for gas) and preheat to high. When ready to cook, brush and oil the grill grate.

3. Grill the pancetta, if using, until golden brown, 2 to 3 minutes per side. Transfer to a plate lined with paper towels to drain.

4. Place the burgers on the hot grate and season again with salt and pepper. Grill the burgers until cooked through, 5 to 7 minutes per side for medium. (If you like, rotate the burgers 90 degrees halfway through cooking to create an attractive crosshatch of grill marks.) If using cheese and/or pancetta, place a slice of each on each burger after you've turned it (pancetta first). To test for doneness, insert an instant-read meat thermometer through the side of the burger into the center. The internal temperature should be at least 160°F for medium.

5. Brush the buns with the melted butter and toast them on the grill, 30 seconds to 1 minute.

6. Assemble the burgers: On the bottom half of each bun, place a lettuce leaf followed by a slice of onion and tomato. Top with the burger, the condiments of your choice, and the top half of the bun.

VARIATIONS:
In the Balkans, burgers are made with a mixture of ground beef, veal, pork, and sometimes lamb. The spicing in the meat is a little more extravagant too: diced onion, chopped parsley, cumin, paprika, and fresh dill.

ALSO GOOD FOR:
To make lamb burgers, use ground lamb in place of the beef. To make lamb cheeseburgers, substitute goat cheese for the Cheddar.

METHOD:
Direct grilling

COOKING TIME:
10 to 12 minutes

HOW TO GRILL VEAL CHOPS

*Marinated
Veal Chop with
salad greens*

Whenever my wife and I crave a little luxury, we head for our local butcher and purchase some veal chops. We marinate them in a simple mixture of olive oil, lemon juice, and thyme, then grill them over wood.

There are two ways to approach a veal chop. One is to grill it just as you bought it: a bible-thick chop you can sink your knife and fork into. But sometimes, when I'm feeling ambitious, I'll pound the chop with the side of a cleaver to broaden it to plate-burying dimensions. This makes the meat more tender, although toughness is rarely a problem with a veal chop. Most of all, it puts a little drama on the plate. It's always nice to show off when you're grilling. But know that the following veal chops are delectable even without the pounding.

SETTING UP THE GRILL

1 To set up a charcoal grill for direct grilling, first light the charcoal in a chimney starter (see page 9).

2 Using a garden hoe or other long-handled implement, rake the burning coals into an even layer.

3 To see if the grill is preheated to high, use the test on page 10.

PREPARING THE MEAT

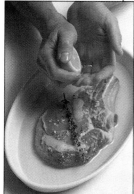

1 Place a veal chop between two sheets of plastic wrap and pound with the side of a heavy cleaver, or with a scallopini pounder, to a thickness of about ½ inch.

2 Marinate the chops in olive oil, thyme, lemon zest, and lemon juice. Note how I squeeze the lemon between my fingers to catch any seeds.

ON THE GRILL: To test for doneness, poke the meat with your finger; it should be slightly yielding. Rotating the chop gives you handsome grill marks.

TIPS

■ I know it sounds obvious, but try to buy chops that are all the same thickness. This way, they'll cook at the same rate.

■ The easiest way to get a great wood flavor is to build your fire with oak, cherry, or apple chunks instead of charcoal. Light them in your chimney starter, following the instructions on page 12. When working on a gas grill, use wood chips, but don't soak them (you want a light, Tuscan-style wood flavor, not a heavy Kansas City smoke).

SERVES 4

YOU'LL NEED:
Wood chunks for
building a fire, or
2 cups wood chips
(preferably oak,
cherry, or apple),
unsoaked

VARIATIONS:
You can certainly grill the veal chops without pounding (this is how I'm apt to do it when I'm not trying to show off). For extra pizzazz, drizzle the chops with more extra-virgin olive oil before serving and serve with lemon wedges.

THE RECIPE

MARINATED VEAL CHOPS

1 lemon
4 veal chops (1 inch thick;
        about 12 ounces each)
Coarse salt and black pepper

3 to 4 tablespoons extra-virgin
        olive oil
8 sprigs of fresh thyme

1. Remove 8 strips of zest (the oil-rich outer rind) from the lemon with a vegetable peeler. Cut the lemon in half.

2. Pound the veal chops as shown in Preparing the Meat, Step 1 on page 103. Generously season the veal chops on both sides with salt and pepper. Arrange them in a nonreactive baking dish and drizzle oil over them, turning the chops several times to coat evenly. Place a strip of lemon zest and sprig of thyme under and on top of each chop and squeeze the lemon over all. Let marinate for 20 to 30 minutes, while you light the grill.

3. Set up the grill for direct grilling (see page 10 for charcoal or page 16 for gas) and preheat to high. If possible, build your fire with wood chunks. If using a gas grill, place the wood chips in the smoker box or in a smoker pouch (see page 17) and preheat until you see smoke. When ready to cook, if using a charcoal grill and wood chips, toss the wood chips on the coals. Place the chops on the hot grill grate and grill until cooked to taste, 5 to 6 minutes per side for medium, rotating the chops 90 degrees after 3 minutes to obtain an attractive crosshatch of grill marks. Place a strip of lemon zest on each chop after turning them. Use the finger poke method to test for doneness (see page 55).

4. Transfer the chops to plates or a platter and let rest for 3 minutes, then serve.

**How to Make
Pulled Pork** 106

**How to Make
Jerk Pork** 111

**How to Grill a Stuffed
Pork Loin** 117

**How to Grill
Pork Tenderloin** 122

**How to Brine and Grill
Pork Chops** 127

**How to Grill Stuffed
Pork Chops** 131

**How to Smoke
Spareribs** 135

**How to Indirect Grill
Baby Back Ribs** 140

**How to Rotisserie
Grill Ribs** 144

**How to Grill
Sausages** 148

**How to Grill
Hot Dogs** 151

**How to Barbecue a
Whole Pig** 154

METHOD:
Indirect grilling

COOKING TIME:
4 to 6 hours

ADVANCE PREPARATION:
Up to 24 hours for curing the meat

HOW TO MAKE PULLED PORK

Pulled pork is part one of the Holy Trinity of American barbecue (the other two members are smoked brisket, see page 42, and barbecued ribs, see page 135). Its birthplace is the Carolinas, where pork shoulders are slow roasted over smoky hickory or oak embers until they're so tender you can pull them apart with your fingers—which is precisely what you do. Wood smoke is the soul of pulled pork; its beneficent presence is recognizable by the smoke ring, a reddish layer just below the surface of the meat. This smoke ring is the signature of a master pit boss. Follow the technique here and you'll achieve it, too.

North Carolina Pulled Pork with North Carolina Vinegar Sauce

1 To set up a charcoal grill for smoking, first light the charcoal in a chimney starter (see page 9).

2 Place a drip pan in the center of the grill and divide the coals evenly on either side of it.

3 Place ½ cup of drained wood chips on each mound of coals.

TIPS

■ Pulled pork is traditionally made with Boston butt—an odd name for a roast that's actually cut from the pork shoulder. It contains a blade-shaped bone and weighs in at 5 to 8 pounds. It's also known as a bone-in pork shoulder roast.

■ You'll find that pork pulls easiest when it's hot. To protect your hands, wear insulated rubber gloves for pulling.

PREPARING THE MEAT: Sprinkle the rub over the pork and massage it onto the meat with your fingers. Place it on the grill now or let it cure for up to 24 hours.

ON THE GRILL: After 4 hours the pork will develop a crusty exterior. If using charcoal, be sure to add fresh chips every hour.

MOPPING THE PORK

Mop the pork with the mop sauce every hour while it's on the grill to keep it moist. Remember that the more you baste, the better the pork will taste.

TESTING FOR DONENESS: The pork is done when it reaches an internal temperature of about 195°F on an instant-read meat thermometer, 4 to 6 hours. Another way to see if it is done is to try to wiggle the blade bone; it should move easily.

PULLING THE PORK

TIP

■ **The traditional way to serve pulled pork in the Carolinas is mounded on a bun or on a slice of white bread and crowned with coleslaw. This divine sandwich is anointed with vinegar sauce— clear if you're in eastern North Carolina, red (with a touch of ketchup) if you're in western North Carolina, or mustard-based if you're in South Carolina.**

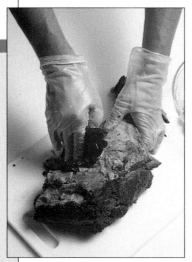

1 Transfer the pork to a cutting board and, wearing rubber gloves, pull off the burnt skin and fat.

2 Rest one hand on the meat; use the other to pull out and discard the bones.

3 With your fingers tear the meat into thin, tender shreds, about 2 inches long, working along the grain.

CHOPPING THE PORK: If pulling seems too time consuming, you can finely chop the pork with a cleaver.

SAUCING THE PORK: Pile the pulled pork into roasting pans and spoon some of the vinegar sauce over it.

THE RECIPE

NORTH CAROLINA PULLED PORK

1 Boston butt (bone-in pork shoulder roast;
5 to 7 pounds)
3 to 4 tablespoons Basic Barbecue Rub
(page 441)

FOR THE MOP SAUCE:
1 cup cider vinegar
1 small onion, thinly sliced
1 to 2 jalapeño peppers, thinly sliced
1 tablespoon coarse salt

1 tablespoon brown sugar
1 teaspoon black pepper
1 teaspoon hot red pepper flakes

FOR SERVING:
3 cups North Carolina Vinegar Sauce
(page 448)
10 to 12 hamburger buns
North Carolina Coleslaw
(recipe follows)

SERVES 10 TO 12

YOU'LL NEED:
4 to 6 cups wood
chips (preferably
hickory), soaked
for 1 hour in cold
water to cover,
then drained;
rubber gloves

1. Sprinkle the pork shoulder on all sides with the rub, patting it onto the meat with your fingers. Grill right away or let stand in the refrigerator, covered, for up to 24 hours. The longer you cure it, the richer the flavor will be.

2. Set up the grill for indirect grilling (see page 12 for charcoal or page 16 for gas) and preheat to medium-low. If using charcoal, place a large drip pan in the center. If using a gas grill, place all the wood chips in the smoker box or in a smoker pouch (see page 17) and preheat to high until you see smoke, then reduce the heat to medium-low.

3. Combine all the ingredients for the mop sauce with ½ cup water in a nonreactive bowl and stir until the salt and brown sugar dissolve. When ready to cook, if using charcoal, toss 1 cup wood chips on the coals. Place the pork, fat-side up, in the center of the hot grate, away from the heat. Cover the grill and cook the pork until very tender, 4 to 6 hours (about 195°F on an instant-read meat thermometer). If using charcoal, add 12 fresh coals and ½ cup wood chips per side every hour. After 1 hour, baste the pork with the mop sauce; repeat every hour.

4. Transfer the cooked pork to a cutting board, cover loosely with aluminum foil, and let rest for 15 minutes. When ready to serve, wearing rubber gloves pull off the skin and fat. Finely chop the crisp skin with a cleaver to add to the pulled pork or discard. Discard the fat. Pull the pork into pieces, as shown in Step 3 on page 108, or chop it, as shown on page 109. Transfer the shredded pork to a roasting pan and stir in 1 to 1½ cups of the vinegar sauce, enough to keep the pork moist. Cover with aluminum foil and keep warm.

5. To serve, mound the pork on hamburger buns and top with coleslaw. Serve any remaining vinegar sauce on the side.

North Carolina Coleslaw

**MAKES 6 TO 8 CUPS;
SERVES 10 TO 12**

1 small head green or savoy cabbage (about 2 pounds)
1 cup North Carolina Vinegar Sauce (page 448), or more to taste

1. Core the cabbage and remove the outside leaves. Cut the cabbage into chunks and finely chop it in a food processor.

2. Transfer the cabbage to a nonreactive mixing bowl and toss with the vinegar sauce. Taste for seasoning, adding vinegar sauce as necessary.

HOW TO MAKE JERK PORK

Jamaica's contribution to the world of barbecue is jerk pork roasted over what may be the most incredibly fragrant fuel in the world, smoldering allspice wood. What makes jerk pork "jerk" is the seasoning, a fragrant, fiery paste of Scotch bonnet chiles, allspice berries, escallions (the Caribbean version of chives), fresh thyme, and perhaps a dozen other flavorings. Tradition calls for the meat to be "jooked," that is poked with a pointed stick, to allow the seasoning to penetrate the meat. Jooking, in fact, may be how jerk got its name.

In Jamaica jerk would be made with an entire pig; I make it with a fresh shoulder ham that I butterfly and bone before marinating and grilling. Shoulder ham is a fatty cut, with plenty of skin to protect the meat from the fire. As the fat melts, it bastes and crisps the meat, giving the jerk its flavorful crust.

METHOD:
Direct grilling

COOKING TIME:
30 to 40 minutes

ADVANCE PREPARATION:
6 to 12 hours for marinating the meat

*Jamaican Jerk Pork served with corn bread
(The raw Scotch bonnets are for admiring, not eating.)*

SETTING UP THE GRILL

1 To set up a charcoal grill for direct grilling, first light the charcoal in a chimney starter (see page 9).

2 Using a garden hoe or other long-handled implement, rake the burning coals into an even layer.

3 To see if the grill is preheated to medium, use the test on page 10.

(see page 9). use the test on page 10.

TIP

■ True jerk is smoked over allspice wood—a fuel that would be prohibitively expensive in this country, if you could find it, which you can't. To hint at the fragrance of smoldering allspice wood, I suggest adding a handful of allspice berries to the wood chips. And even though you are grilling directly, cover the grill to hold in the smoke.

PREPARING THE SEASONING

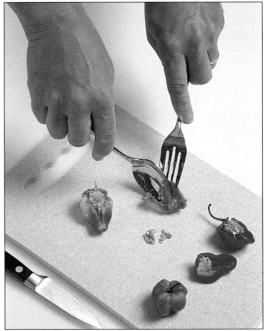

1 Here are some of the defining flavors of jerk seasoning (clockwise from the top): Scotch bonnet chiles, cinnamon, fresh thyme, allspice berries, and nutmeg. For the freshest taste of spice, grate the latter on a nutmeg or cheese grater.

2 Whole Scotch bonnet chiles are too hot to handle for most people. Hold the chiles with a fork and seed with a spoon to keep the virulent juices off your fingers.

3 First, purée the solid ingredients for the jerk seasoning in a food processor.

4 Add the liquid ingredients with the processor running to make a thick paste.

PREPARING THE MEAT

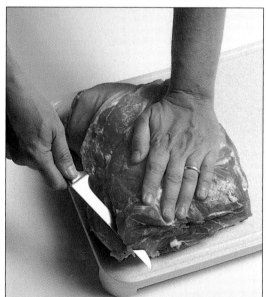

1 To butterfly a shoulder ham, make a cut in the side of the ham to the bone, holding the knife parallel to the cutting board.

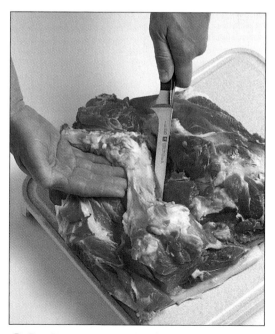

2 Cut first on one side of the bone, then on the other, using the tip of a sharp knife.

TIP

■ Don't be disconcerted by the seemingly large quantity of salt in this recipe. In the days before refrigeration, it helped to preserve the meat. Jerk is supposed to be salty—that's part of what makes it jerk.

3 Cut under the bone and then lift it out and discard it.

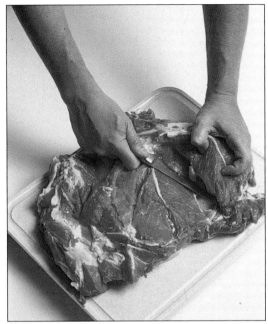

4 Cut through the thick part of the ham almost to the edge. Unfold it to obtain a broad, flat slab of meat.

5 Make a series of small holes (½ inch deep and wide) in the meat and the skin side, with 2 inches between holes. Jamaicans call this "jooking" the pork and it allows the seasoning to penetrate the meat.

6 Pour the jerk seasoning over the pork, forcing it into the holes with your fingertips. I have asbestos fingers, so I'm using my bare hands. If you have sensitive skin, wear rubber gloves.

ON THE GRILL: Grill the jerk pork until dark brown and very tender, 15 to 20 minutes per side. The internal temperature should be about 190°F.

CUTTING THE MEAT: Using a cleaver, thinly slice or chop the pork.

THE RECIPE

JAMAICAN JERK PORK

6 to 12 Scotch bonnet chiles, stemmed and seeded

2 bunches scallions, trimmed and roughly chopped

1 small onion, roughly chopped

6 cloves garlic, peeled

½ cup chopped fresh cilantro leaves

½ cup chopped fresh flat-leaf parsley leaves

2 tablespoons coarsely chopped peeled fresh ginger

1 tablespoon fresh thyme or 1½ teaspoons dried

1 tablespoon chopped fresh marjoram or 1½ teaspoons dried

2 teaspoons ground allspice

½ teaspoon black pepper

½ teaspoon freshly grated nutmeg

¼ teaspoon ground cinnamon

3 tablespoons lime juice

3 tablespoons soy sauce

3 tablespoons dark rum

3 tablespoons vegetable oil

2 tablespoons coarse salt

2 tablespoons distilled white vinegar

2 tablespoons brown sugar

1 fresh shoulder ham (5 to 7 pounds)

SERVES 8 TO 10

YOU'LL NEED:
2 cups wood chips (preferably hickory or oak), plus 2 tablespoons allspice berries, soaked for 1 hour in cold water to cover, then drained; rubber gloves (optional)

VARIATION:
You can cook the pork using the indirect method, in which case, preheat the grill to medium. You'll need to let it grill for about 1 hour, adding wood chips as you normally would for smoking. But move the pork directly over the flame for the last 10 minutes to sear the crust.

ALSO GOOD FOR:
The distinctive blast of smoke and spice that characterizes jerk goes great with just about any cut of pork—ribs, chops, loin, tenderloin—and for that matter, with other meats, like lamb and chicken. I've also had jerk fish and I can easily imagine jerk tofu.

1. Prepare the jerk seasoning: Place the chiles, scallions, onion, garlic, cilantro, parsley, ginger, thyme, and marjoram in a food processor and finely chop. Add all the remaining ingredients, except the ham.

2. Butterfly the shoulder ham, as shown in Steps 1 through 4 on pages 113 and 114 or have your butcher do this for you. Using the tip of a paring knife, make tiny holes all over the pork on both sides, each about ½ inch deep and 2 inches apart. Place the pork in a large nonreactive baking dish.

3. Spread the jerk seasoning over the pork on both sides with a rubber spatula or with your hands, wearing rubber gloves, and stuff it into the knife holes. Let the pork marinate, covered, in the refrigerator for at least 6 hours or as long as overnight, turning it once or twice.

4. Set up the grill for direct grilling (see page 10 for charcoal or page 16 for gas) and preheat to medium. If using a gas grill, place all the wood chips and allspice berries in the smoker box or in a smoker pouch (see page 17) and preheat to high until you see smoke, then reduce the heat to medium.

5. When ready to cook, if using a charcoal grill, toss all the wood chips and allspice berries on the coals. Place the pork on the hot grate, skin side down, cover the grill, and cook until the meat is well-done, 15 to 20 minutes per side. To test for doneness, use an instant-read meat thermometer: The internal temperature should be about 190°F.

6. Transfer the pork to a cutting board and let rest for 5 minutes. Slice or chop it crosswise and serve at once. To be authentic, serve it on sheets of waxed paper.

HOW TO GRILL A STUFFED PORK LOIN

METHOD:
Indirect grilling

COOKING TIME:
About 1 hour

The pork loin is one of the handiest cuts of meat on the planet, a handsome hunk of pure protein. However, its relative lack of fat presents a formidable challenge to barbecuers: how to grill it without having the meat dry out?

Here's one strategy for grilling a pork loin: a technique called roll-cutting. The roast is cut and unrolled, almost the way you would unroll a roll of paper towels. Once it's unrolled, I spread the meat with tapenade (a tangy olive paste), which bastes and flavors the meat from the inside. (You can stuff pork loin with anything, from chopped, sautéed mushrooms to sliced pepperoni and cheese.) Best of all, when you roll the roast back up, grill it, and cut it for serving, you get slices with a handsome pinwheel of white pork and dark tapenade—which is about one of the most visually stunning presentations ever to turn up at a barbecue.

Tapenade Pork Loin with Grilled Zucchini (page 397)

SETTING UP THE GRILL

1 To set up a charcoal grill for indirect grilling, first light the charcoal in a chimney starter (see page 9).

2 Form two heat zones by raking the coals into two piles at opposite sides of the grill, using a long-handled implement, like a garden hoe.

3 If your grill has side baskets, divide the coals evenly between them. Note the drip pan in the center of the grill.

TIP

■ Tapenade is a Mediterranean olive spread. For the sake of simplicity, I call for canned California olives that have been pitted, but to make a tapenade everything that it can be, use some or even all high-class olives, like Moroccan oil-cured olives or Greek kala-matas. You can also make a green tape-nade by using green olives.

PREPARING THE MEAT

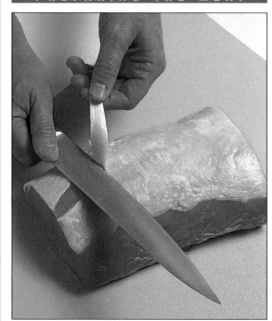

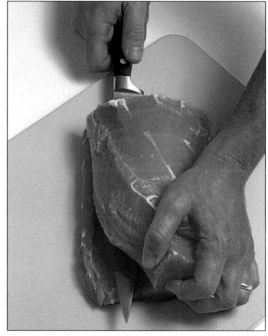

1 Trim off the sheath of fat and sinew that covers the roast.

2 Hold a long, sharp, slender knife parallel to the cutting board, and starting at the bottom of the roast, about ½ inch above the cutting board, make a lengthwise cut in the roast. Cut almost to the other side.

3 Unfold the top of the roast (it's a bit like unrolling a roll of paper towels that's lying on its side).

4 Continue cutting and unrolling the roast in a lengthwise fashion, knife parallel to and about ½ inch above the cutting board to obtain a broad, flat rectangle of pork that's about ½ inch thick.

ROLLING THE PORK

1 Spread the pork rectangle all over with the tapenade.

2 Beginning at the end you cut last, gently roll the pork back into a roast.

TIP

■ This recipe may make more tapenade than you actually need. The leftover tapenade makes a great topping for grilled bread.

TYING THE ROAST

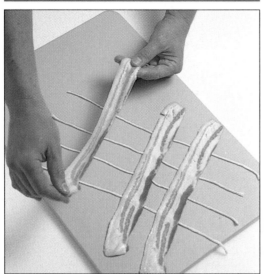

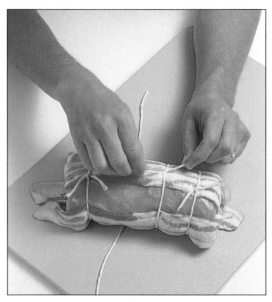

1 Lay four 12-inch lengths of butcher's string on the work surface, each an inch or so apart. If you like, lay three strips of bacon on the string, perpendicular to it, 1 to 2 inches apart. (Try to position them so the middle strip will be on the bottom of the roast and the other two strips on the side.)

2 Place the roast on the bacon, parallel to the strips. Lay a fourth strip of bacon on top of the roast. Loop the ends of the string over the roast and tie as pictured. Start tying at the ends (this keeps the stuffing from oozing out) and work toward the center.

ON THE GRILL: Place the roast in the center of the grill, away from the fire.

TESTING FOR DONENESS: When fully cooked, the roast will feel firm yet gently yielding to the touch after about 1 hour. The internal temperature should be at least 160°F.

TAPENADE PORK LOIN

SERVES 6

YOU'LL NEED:
Butcher's string

FOR THE TAPENADE:
2 cups drained, pitted black olives
    (two 6-ounce cans) or 1½ cups
    pitted kalamata and/or
    oil-cured olives
2 cloves garlic, coarsely chopped
2 tablespoons drained capers
1 tablespoon Dijon-style mustard
1 teaspoon dried oregano

Black pepper
1 tablespoon extra-virgin olive oil

FOR THE PORK:
1 pork loin roast (2½ to 3 pounds)
Coarse salt and black pepper
4 strips bacon or pancetta
    (Italian bacon), optional

ALSO GOOD FOR:
Sometimes I use a butterflied leg of lamb instead of pork (I roll it and tie it like the pork loin).

Tapenade is one of those preparations that taste great with just about everything. Use it as a stuffing for the chicken breasts on page 239. Smear it on grilled veal chops. Serve it as a dip for grilled vegetables. The possibilities are endless.

1. Prepare the tapenade: Place the olives, garlic, capers, mustard, and oregano in a food processor and process to a smooth paste. Add pepper to taste and the oil and process until blended.

2. Roll-cut the pork roast, as shown in Preparing the Meat, Steps 1 through 4 on pages 118 and 119. Season the top of the meat with salt and pepper (go easy on the salt—the olives are quite salty). Spread the tapenade on the meat and roll it back into a roast, as shown in Rolling the Pork, Steps 1 and 2 on page 119. Cut four 12-inch pieces of butcher's string and lay them out on a cutting board, as shown in Step 1 on the facing page. If using the bacon strips, place them on the string as shown in Step 1. Tie the roast as shown in

Step 2. Season the roast on the outside with salt (if not using bacon) and pepper.

3. Set up the grill for indirect grilling (see page 12 for charcoal or page 16 for gas) and preheat to medium.

4. When ready to cook, place the roast in the center of the hot grate, away from the heat, and cover the grill. Grill the roast until cooked through, about 1 hour. To test for doneness, insert an instant-read meat thermometer into the side of the roast: The internal temperature should be at least 160°F.

5. Transfer the roast to a cutting board and let rest for 5 minutes. Remove the strings. Using a sharp knife, cut the roast crosswise into ½-inch slices.

METHOD:
Direct grilling

COOKING TIME:
12 to 16 minutes

ADVANCE PREPARATION:
3 to 12 hours for marinating the meat

HOW TO GRILL PORK TENDERLOIN

One of the best-kept secrets of barbecue, pork tenderloin is as tender and tasty as beef tenderloin—at a fraction of the price. It looks great. It readily absorbs the flavors of rubs and marinades. And its large ratio of surface area to meat guarantees a scrumptious crust. Serve it whole or sliced—just make sure it is part of your repertory.

I particularly like to prepare pork tenderloin in the style of Miami's Cuban-Americans. You marinate the pork in a tangy sauce of fried garlic, fresh lime juice, and cumin called *mojo*. Serve this bad boy with grilled plantains and black beans.

Mojo-Marinated Pork Tenderloin, with black beans and grilled plantains

SETTING UP THE GRILL

1 To set up a charcoal grill for direct grilling, first light the charcoal in a chimney starter (see page 9).

2 Using a garden hoe or other long-handled implement, rake the burning coals into an even layer.

3 To see if the grill is preheated to high, use the test on page 10.

PREPARING THE MOJO

1 Fry the garlic for the *mojo* until it is lightly browned.

2 Add the orange juice and lime juice and bring the *mojo* to a boil.

TIP

■ The traditional souring agent for *mojo* is *naranja agria* (sour orange). To approximate the flavor of this tropical fruit, I mix fresh lime juice and orange juice. To make a grapefruit *mojo*, use fresh grapefruit juice; for a tangerine *mojo*, mix lime juice and tangerine juice.

TIPS

■ Pork tenderloin comes sheathed in a silvery skin of sinew. Trim it off with a sharp knife, as shown in Steps 1 and 2, beginning at right.

■ Like beef tenderloin, a pork tenderloin tapers to a long, slender tail. To ensure even cooking, I like to fold this tail over and tie it to the center of the tenderloin (a strategically placed cut facilitates folding; see Preparing the Meat, Steps 2 through 5 at right). This gives you a neat, cylindrical roast that cooks up evenly on the grill.

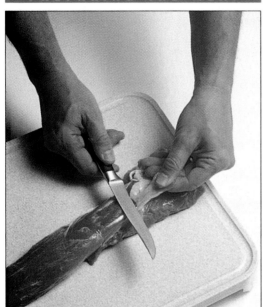

1 Pull off the silverskin, working toward the head of the tenderloin. Use a knife to ease it away from the meat.

2 Make a ½-inch-deep cut in the tail of the tenderloin, about 3 inches from the end.

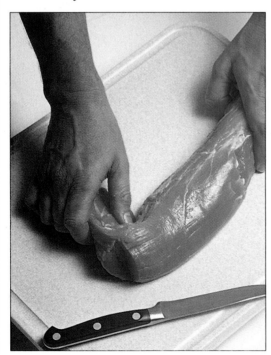

3 Fold the tail over to give the tenderloin a cylindrical shape.

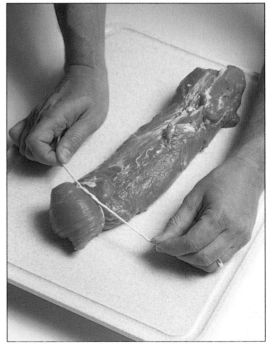

4 Tie the tail to the tenderloin with butcher's string.

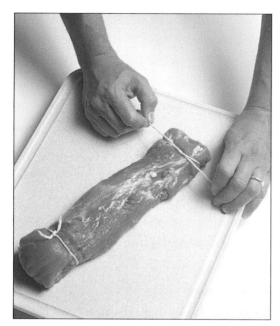

5 Tie the head of the tenderloin with butcher's string.

6 Spoon half of the *mojo* over the pork tenderloin as a marinade. Reserve the remainder to serve as a sauce.

GRILLING THE ONION SLICES: Note how the slender bamboo skewers hold the rings together.

TESTING FOR DONENESS: Use the finger poke test to check for doneness, steadying the pork with tongs. Pork cooked to medium will be just slightly yielding to the touch and take 3 to 4 minutes on each of its four sides.

TIP

■ To keep the onions from falling apart during grilling, skewer them crossways with slender bamboo skewers or wooden toothpicks.

MOJO-MARINATED PORK TENDERLOIN

SERVES 4

YOU'LL NEED:
Butcher's string;
8 to 10 slender
bamboo skewers
or wooden
toothpicks, soaked
for 1 hour in cold
water to cover,
then drained,
for skewering
the onions

VARIATION:
*For absolutely care-
free cooking, grill the
tenderloin using the
indirect method. You'll
need to allow 30 to 40
minutes of grilling
time at medium heat.*

ALSO GOOD FOR:
*Any sort of meat or
fish can be grilled
with mojo. For pork
chops, steak, chicken
breasts, fish fillets, or
shrimp marinate for
30 minutes to 1 hour
in half the mojo, then
direct grill. For pork
shoulder, marinate for
12 hours, then indirect
grill or use a smoker.*

½ cup olive oil
8 large cloves garlic, thinly sliced crosswise
1 teaspoon ground cumin, or more to taste
⅓ cup lime juice
⅓ cup orange juice
1½ teaspoons coarse salt, or more to taste
½ teaspoon black pepper

½ teaspoon ground oregano
¼ cup chopped fresh cilantro or mint
2 to 3 pork tenderloins (1½ pounds total)
2 large sweet onions, cut into ½-inch-thick
   slices
1 navel orange, peeled and sectioned with
   membranes removed, for serving

1. Prepare the *mojo:* Heat the oil in a deep saucepan over medium heat. Add the garlic and cumin and cook until the garlic is fragrant and a pale golden brown, 1 to 2 minutes. Do not let the garlic brown too much, or it will become bitter. Stir in the lime and orange juices, salt, pepper, and oregano and ⅓ cup water. Stand back: The sauce may sputter. Bring the sauce to a rolling boil. Taste for seasoning, adding salt or cumin as necessary. Let cool to room temperature, then stir in the cilantro.

2. Trim, fold, and tie the pork tenderloins, as shown in Preparing the Meat, Steps 1 through 5 on pages 124 and 125. Arrange the tenderloins in a nonreactive baking dish just large enough to hold them. Pour half the *mojo* over the pork and let marinate, covered, in the refrigerator for at least 3 hours, preferably overnight, turning to ensure even marinating. Refrigerate the remaining *mojo* to serve as a sauce.

3. Set up the grill for direct grilling (see page 10 for charcoal or page 16 for gas) and preheat to high.

4. When ready to cook, brush and oil the grill grate. Arrange the tenderloins on the grill. Brush the onion slices with any excess marinade, skewer them crosswise on skewers or toothpicks, and place on the grill. Grill the pork and onions until cooked to taste. The meat will take 3 to 4 minutes on each of its four sides, 12 to 16 minutes in all for medium. To test for doneness, insert an instant-read meat thermometer in the thickest part of the meat. The internal temperature should be about 160°F. Rotate the tenderloins 90 degrees after 2 minutes on each side to create an attractive crosshatch of grill marks. The onions should be nicely charred after 4 to 6 minutes per side.

5. Transfer the tenderloins to a cutting board and let rest for 3 minutes. Slice the tenderloins crosswise on the diagonal. Fan out the slices on plates or a platter and top with the unskewered grilled onions. Spoon the reserved *mojo* over them, garnish with the orange sections, and serve at once.

HOW TO BRINE AND GRILL PORK CHOPS

A quarter century ago, in an effort to eat more healthily, consumers in the United States began demanding leaner cuts of pork. The industry obliged, but in the process of slashing the fat, we've sacrificed flavor. Grill your average pork chop and you'll wonder how it became so dry.

There is a simple way to put the flavor and succulence back into a pork chop—brine it before grilling. Brining consists of marinating a meat in a salty liquid. Thanks to the miracle of osmosis, the brine flows into the meat, making for a tastier, juicier pork chop.

Pork has a natural affinity with apples, as you know if you grew up in the South. Wait until you taste these chops with the electrifying fresh horseradish applesauce that accompanies them.

METHOD:
Indirect grilling to start, followed by direct grilling

COOKING TIME:
20 minutes for indirect grilling, plus 8 to 14 minutes for direct grilling

ADVANCE PREPARATION:
2 to 4 hours for brining the meat

Bourbon-Brined Pork Chops with Volcanic Applesauce and grilled okra

SETTING UP THE GRILL

1 To set up a charcoal grill for indirect grilling, first light the charcoal in a chimney starter (see page 9).

2 Form two heat zones by raking the coals into two piles at opposite sides of the grill, using a long-handled implement, like a garden hoe.

3 If your grill has side baskets, divide the coals evenly between them. Note the drip pan in the center of the grill.

BRINING THE CHOPS

1 Arrange the pork chops in a baking dish with sliced onions, bay leaves, a cinnamon stick, and peppercorns. Whisk hot water into the sugar and salt (these ingredients dissolve more quickly in hot water than cold). Then whisk in the cold water.

2 Pour the brine over the pork chops to marinate them. Alternatively, you can brine the chops in a resealable plastic bag.

ON THE GRILL

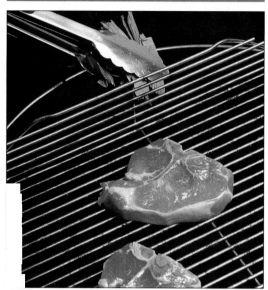

1 Place the brined chops in the center of the grill grate, away from the heat. Add wood chips to the coals.

2 Once the chops are smoked, after 20 minutes, move them directly over the fire to sear in grill marks. This will take 4 to 7 minutes per side.

THE RECIPE

BOURBON-BRINED PORK CHOPS

4 loin pork chops (each 1 inch thick and
*   10 to 12 ounces)*
1 small onion, thinly sliced
2 bay leaves
1 cinnamon stick
10 black peppercorns
5 allspice berries
3 cloves
3 tablespoons brown sugar

3 tablespoons coarse salt
1 cup hot water
2 cups cold water
3 tablespoons bourbon
2 tablespoons walnut, hazelnut, or
*   vegetable oil, plus 1 to 2 tablespoons*
*   for basting*
Volcanic Applesauce (recipe follows),
*   for serving*

1. Rinse the pork chops under cold running water and blot dry with paper towels. Arrange the chops in a baking dish just large enough to hold them or in a resealable plastic bag. Arrange the onion, bay leaves, cinnamon stick, peppercorns, allspice, and cloves over the meat.

2. Make the brine: Combine the brown sugar and salt in a large bowl. Add the hot

water and whisk until the brown sugar and salt are dissolved. Stir in the cold water, bourbon, and 2 tablespoons of oil. Pour this mixture over the chops, turning the chops a couple of times to coat evenly. Brine the chops, covered, in the refrigerator for 2 to 4 hours, turning once or twice to ensure even brining.

3. Set up the grill for indirect grilling

SERVES 4

YOU'LL NEED:
2 cups wood chips
(preferably
hickory), soaked
for 1 hour in cold
water to cover,
then drained

ALSO GOOD FOR:
Once you've mastered the technique of brining, you can use it for any type of meat that has the tendency to dry out during grilling, including chicken breasts (see page 236), turkey, and even brisket (prepared this way, brisket is known as corned beef).

VARIATIONS:
You could cook the chops by the direct grilling method for the whole time, tossing the wood chips on the coals under the pork or, if using gas, placing them in the smoker box or a smoker pouch (see page 17). In this instance, you'll need to grill the chops 6 to 8 minutes per side.

The maple-cinnamon butter on page 392 would make a luscious topping for the chops.

(see page 12 for charcoal or page 16 for gas) and preheat to high. If using a gas grill, place the wood chips in the smoker box or in a smoker pouch (see page 17) and preheat until you see smoke.

4. When ready to cook, brush and oil the grill grate. Drain the pork chops and blot dry with paper towels, dusting off any loose spices. Brush the chops on both sides with the remaining oil. Arrange the chops in the center of the hot grate away from the heat. If using a charcoal grill, toss the wood chips on the coals. Cover the grill and smoke the chops for 20 minutes. Then move the chops directly over the heat: If using a charcoal grill, place 2 chops on each side over the mounds of coals. If using a gas grill, place all 4 chops over the lit portion of the grill. Grill the chops, uncovered, until cooked through (about 160°F on an instant-read meat thermometer), 4 to 7 minutes per side, rotating the chops 90 degrees after 2 minutes to create an attractive crosshatch of grill marks. Transfer the chops to plates or a platter and let rest for 3 minutes, then serve at once with the applesauce.

Volcanic Applesauce

MAKES 1 CUP; SERVES 4

1 piece (1 to 2 inches long and 1 to 1½ inches across; about 2 ounces) fresh horseradish
1 cup applesauce (preferably homemade)
¼ teaspoon ground cinnamon

Peel the horseradish and finely grate it into a mixing bowl or chop it in a food processor fitted with a metal blade. (If using the food processor, cut the horseradish into ¼-inch-thick slices before processing.) Whichever method you use, take care not to breathe the potent horseradish fumes. Stir in the applesauce and cinnamon. The applesauce can be made up to 12 hours ahead. Store it in the refrigerator, covered.

HOW TO GRILL STUFFED PORK CHOPS

METHOD:
Direct grilling

COOKING TIME:
8 to 14 minutes

Wherever you find people grilling, you'll find stuffed meats, from the *matambres*—hunger killers—of South America (see page 73) to the stuffed chicken breasts of the Mediterranean (see page 239). If ever there was a cut of meat ripe for stuffing, it's the pork chop. A stuffing—even a simple one—does much to dignify this simple, straightforward cut. The following recipe was inspired by a pizza shop favorite, the calzone. If you like Italian cold cuts and cheese cooked in dough, just wait until you taste them grilled in a pork chop. As with all the recipes in this book, please view this one as a basic guide; you can customize the flavors and fillings to suit your taste.

Grilled Pork Chop "Calzone" with grilled broccolini

SETTING UP THE GRILL

1 To set up a charcoal grill for direct grilling, first light the charcoal in a chimney starter (see page 9).

2 Using a garden hoe or other long-handled implement, rake the burning coals into an even layer.

3 To see if the grill is preheated to high, use the test on page 10.

see page 9).
use the test on page 10.

TIPS

■ Any sort of pork chop can be stuffed (obviously, the thicker the chop, the better). The easiest one to make a pocket in and stuff is a boneless loin chop. You don't have to worry about the rib.

■ Hold the chop flat with one hand when you cut a pocket in it— this helps you keep the knife straight and even.

PREPARING THE MEAT

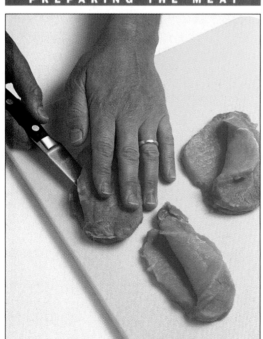

1 Place the chop on a cutting board, rounded side facing out. Holding a sharp, slender knife parallel to the board and holding the chop flat with your free hand, insert the knife in the side and cut a deep pocket.

2 Have the stuffing ingredients arranged on a plate or in bowls, to ease the stuffing process.

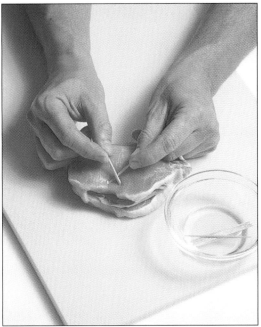

T I P

■ Oil the toothpicks before inserting them in the chops. This makes it easier to remove them when the chops are cooked.

3 Holding the pocket open with your fingers, insert the stuffing. Tuck these ingredients in as deeply as you can, leaving the front edge of the chop clear.

4 Pin the chops shut with two oiled toothpicks. Note how the toothpicks are inserted in an X fashion. This enables you to close the chop without pinching the meat.

5 Before pouring the oil over the chops, arrange them in a baking dish, placing a sage leaf underneath and on top of each.

ON THE GRILL: Rotate the chops 90 degrees after 2 minutes. They will be done after 4 to 7 minutes on each side.

SERVES 4

YOU'LL NEED:
8 wooden
toothpicks, oiled
with 1 teaspoon
vegetable oil,
for skewering
the meat

ALSO GOOD FOR:
*You can pretty much
stuff and grill any flat
piece of meat—from
chicken breasts to
veal chops to strip
steaks. The stuffing is
limited only by your
imagination. Some-
times I make a grilled
veal saltimbocca by
stuffing a veal chop
with sliced prosciutto,
smoked mozzarella,
and sage leaves. OK,
the mozzarella isn't
traditional, but it
tastes good.*

THE RECIPE

GRILLED PORK CHOP "CALZONES"

*4 thick boneless loin pork chops
(each ¾ to 1 inch thick;
about 8 ounces each)*
8 fresh basil leaves
2 ounces thinly sliced pepperoni
*2 ounces thinly sliced smoked ham
or prosciutto*

*2 ounces thinly sliced Provolone
cheese*
Coarse salt and black pepper
8 fresh sage leaves
*2 tablespoons olive or
walnut oil*

1. Cut a deep pocket in the side of a pork chop, as shown in Preparing the Meat, Steps 1 and 2 on page 132. Stuff the chop with 2 basil leaves and a quarter of the pepperoni, smoked ham, and cheese. Pin the pocket shut with 2 oiled toothpicks, as shown in Step 4. Prepare and stuff the remaining chops the same way.

2. Set up the grill for direct grilling (see page 10 for charcoal or page 16 for gas) and preheat to high.

3. Meanwhile, season the stuffed chops on both sides with salt and pepper. Arrange the chops in a baking dish, placing a sage leaf underneath and another on top of each one. Drizzle the oil over the chops, patting it on with your fingertips. Let marinate until the grill is ready.

4. When ready to cook, brush and oil the grill grate. Arrange the pork chops on the hot grate and grill until cooked through (160°F on an instant-read meat thermometer), 4 to 7 minutes per side, rotating the chops 90 degrees after 2 minutes to create an attractive crosshatch of grill marks. Transfer the chops to plates or a platter and let rest for 3 minutes, then remove the toothpicks and serve at once.

HOW TO SMOKE SPARERIBS

Ribs are the ultimate barbecue. And mastering the perfect rib is how grill meisters earn the title. So what constitutes perfection? First, the ribs should be tender without being soft or mushy. The perfect ribs will be sweet and smoky, but there should also be an undertaste of acidity and spice. Great ribs will be messy to eat, but they shouldn't be slimy with barbecue sauce.

Spareribs are a challenge—they're larger and tougher than baby backs (but more flavorful), requiring long, slow smoking to reduce them to a meaty perfection. That's why they're the rib of choice for people who compete on the professional barbecue circuit.

Kansas City Sweet-and-Smoky Ribs with Basic Barbecue Sauce (page 447)

METHOD:
Indirect grilling

COOKING TIME:
2¼ to 3 hours

ADVANCE PREPARATION:
2 hours for marinating the meat

1 To set up a charcoal grill for smoking, first light the charcoal in a chimney starter (see page 9).

2 Place a drip pan in the center of the grill and divide the coals evenly on either side of it.

3 Place ½ cup of drained wood chips on each mound of coals.

(see page 9)

PREPARING THE MEAT

TIP

■ Ribs (both spare and baby back) come with a papery membrane on the bone side. The membrane is harder to remove from spareribs than baby backs. The trick is to use a slender, blunt instrument, like a meat thermometer or a clean Phillips head screwdriver, to loosen the membrane from the bones; wiggle it under the membrane. Then use a dishcloth to grab a corner of the membrane, which is too slippery to hold with your fingers, and pull it off.

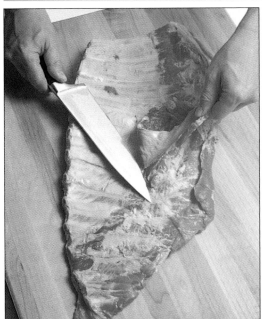

1 Cut off the flap of meat on the inside of the ribs. You can barbecue this—sprinkle it with rub, smoke cook it for a couple of hours, and serve it diced, on toothpicks.

2 Turn the ribs meat side up. Following the line of fat at the base of the ribs, cut off the cartilaginous rib tips. These, too, can be barbecued. The piece of meat to the right of the ribs is the flap removed in Step 1.

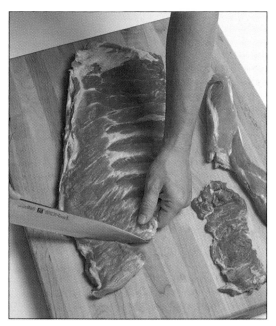

3 Cut the pointed end off the ribs. You'll be left with a handsome rectangular rack (this step is optional). Turn the rack bone-side up.

4 Worm a sharp implement under the membrane covering the bone side of the ribs. Insert it right next to a rib bone and loosen the membrane from the ribs.

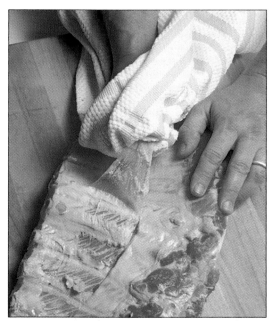

5 Using a dishcloth to secure a good grip, pull off the membrane.

6 You can marinate the ribs in apple cider and lemon juice for 4 to 6 hours. Squeezing the lemons so the juice runs through your fingers will enable you to catch the seeds.

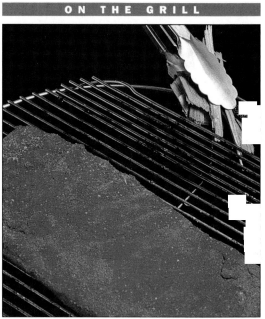

RUBBING THE RIBS: Sprinkle the ribs with rub, massaging it on with your fingers. Let the rubbed ribs stand in the refrigerator, covered, for up to 2 hours.

1 Place the ribs on the grill, membrane-side down, and add wood chips to the coals.

2 Every half hour or so, spray the ribs with apple cider. The ribs will be done in 2 to 3 hours.

3 Start brushing the ribs with barbecue sauce about 20 minutes before they are fully cooked. Brush them one final time before serving.

THE RECIPE

KANSAS CITY SWEET-AND-SMOKY RIBS

4 racks of spareribs (4 to 6 pounds total)
6 cups apple cider, plus additional for
    spraying the ribs
4 whole lemons (optional), halved
⅔ cup Basic Barbecue Rub (page 441) or
    your favorite commercial brand

3 cups of your favorite homemade
    barbecue sauce (for some ideas,
    see pages 447 and 448) or your favorite
    commercial brand

1. Trim each rack of ribs as shown in Preparing the Meat, Steps 1 through 5 on pages 136 and 137, or have your butcher do this for you.

2. Place the ribs in a large nonreactive roasting pan. Pour the cider over the ribs. Squeeze the juice from the lemons over the ribs, catching the seeds with your fingers. Turn the ribs a couple of times to coat all over with marinade. If desired, let the ribs marinate in the refrigerator, covered, for 4 to 6 hours, turning several times.

3. Drain the ribs and blot dry with paper towels. Sprinkle ½ cup of the rub on both sides of the ribs, patting it onto the meat with your fingers. Let the ribs stand in the refrigerator, covered, for 1 to 2 hours.

4. Set up the grill for indirect grilling (see page 12 for charcoal or page 16 for gas) and preheat to medium. If using a charcoal grill, place a large drip pan in the center. If using a gas grill, place all the wood chips in the smoker box or in a smoker pouch (see page 17) and preheat to high until you see smoke, then reduce the heat to medium.

5. When ready to cook, if using charcoal, toss 1 cup of wood chips on the coals. Place the ribs in the center of the hot grate, away from the heat. Cover the grill and cook the ribs for 2 to 3 hours. After 30 minutes, spray the ribs with apple cider and continue to spray every half hour until ready to brush with the sauce. If using a charcoal grill, you'll need to add 12 fresh coals and ½ cup wood chips per side after each hour.

6. Lightly brush the ribs with 1 cup of the sauce 20 minutes before the ribs are done. When the ribs are fully cooked, the meat will have shrunk back from the bones about ¼ inch, and the meat will be tender enough to tear apart with your fingers. But don't overcook; the ribs should have some chew to them. If the ribs start to dry out, wrap them in aluminum foil for the last hour of cooking.

7. Transfer the ribs to plates or a platter. Sprinkle the ribs with the remaining rub and lightly brush again with barbecue sauce. Let the ribs rest for a few minutes, then serve with the remaining barbecue sauce on the side.

SERVES 4 TO 8

YOU'LL NEED:
3 cups wood chips (preferably hickory), soaked for 1 hour in apple cider to cover, then drained; spray bottle; rib rack (optional)

VARIATION:
You can also cook the ribs in a smoker. Smoke them for 4 to 5 hours at 225°F.

ALSO GOOD FOR:
This is a wonderful way to prepare baby back ribs. In this case, you'll need to allow 1 to 1½ hours for indirect grilling or 2 to 3 hours for cooking in a smoker.

METHOD:
Indirect grilling

COOKING TIME:
1¼ to 1½ hours

**ADVANCE
PREPARATION:**
6 to 12 hours
for marinating
the meat

HOW TO INDIRECT GRILL BABY BACK RIBS

Some of the best ribs I have ever tasted were in Vietnam, where they season the Southeast Asian version of baby backs with a fragrant paste of lemongrass, ginger, garlic, chiles, and fish sauce. Grilled until sizzling crisp, the ribs are served with chopped peanuts for a touch of nutty sweetness and crunch.

Grill jockeys in Vietnam use what I call modified direct grilling. The ribs are positioned over the coals as in conventional direct grilling, but the grate is a foot or more above the fire so the ribs cook slowly, as in indirect grilling. The easiest way to achieve this effect in your backyard is to use the indirect grilling method.

*Asian Flavor
Baby Back Ribs
with Vietnamese
Dipping Sauce*

SETTING UP THE GRILL

1 To set up a charcoal grill for indirect grilling, first light the charcoal in a chimney starter (see page 9).

2 Form two heat zones by raking the coals into two piles at opposite sides of the grill, using a long-handled implement, like a garden hoe.

3 If your grill has side baskets, divide the coals evenly between them. Note the drip pan in the center of the grill.

PREPARING THE MEAT

1 A rack of baby back ribs ready for trimming.

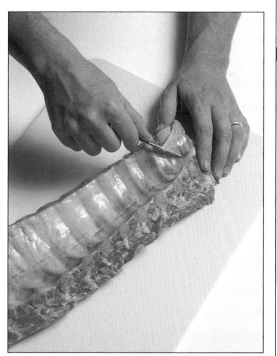

2 Worm a sharp implement, like the tip of a meat thermometer, under the membrane covering the ribs. The best place to insert it is right next to a rib.

TIP

■ Lemongrass is a scallion-shaped herb with pale green stalks that have a haunting herbal lemon flavor but none of the acidity associated with lemons (for instructions on trimming lemongrass, see page 79). If lemongrass is unavailable, substitute the zest (the oil-rich outer rind) of 1 lemon.

TIPS

■ Fish sauce is a malodorous but tasty condiment made from pickled anchovies. Look for it at Asian markets. If unavailable, use soy sauce.

■ Use a rib rack (see page 475) to stand the baby backs upright. That way, you'll be able to fit four racks of ribs on a conventional-size grill.

■ You may be surprised that no wood chips are used in this recipe. Smoking is a North American phenomenon. When Asians cook ribs, they use fire, not smoke.

3 Using a dishcloth to secure a good grip, pull off the membrane.

4 Place the ribs on a baking sheet or in a baking dish and spread the seasonings on both sides, patting it on with your fingers.

ON THE GRILL

1 Arrange the ribs in a rib rack. Stand the racks upright, as shown here. The ribs will be done after 1¼ to 1½ hours.

2 When the ribs are cooked, the meat will shrink back from the ends of the bones by about ¼ inch. The ribs will be tender enough to pull apart with your fingers.

ASIAN FLAVOR BABY BACK RIBS

FOR THE RIBS AND MARINADE:
4 racks baby back pork ribs (about
    4 pounds total)
4 stalks lemongrass, trimmed and
    finely chopped
4 cloves garlic, finely chopped
2 shallots, finely chopped
1 piece (2 inches) fresh ginger, peeled
    and finely chopped
2 to 6 jalapeño peppers or Thai chiles,
    thinly sliced
1 cup chopped fresh cilantro
3 tablespoons sugar

2 teaspoons ground coriander
1 teaspoon black pepper
¼ cup soy sauce
3 tablespoons Asian fish sauce
    or an equal amount soy sauce
3 tablespoons lemon juice
⅓ cup vegetable oil

FOR SERVING:
¾ cup chopped fresh cilantro
¾ cup chopped dry-roasted peanuts
Vietnamese Dipping Sauce
    (page 457)

**SERVES 8
AS AN APPETIZER,
4 AS A MAIN
COURSE**

YOU'LL NEED:
Rib rack (optional)

1. Remove the thin membrane from the back of each rack of ribs as shown in Preparing the Meat, Steps 2 and 3 on pages 141 and 142, or have your butcher do this for you. Arrange the ribs in a large nonreactive roasting pan.

2. Make the marinade: Place the lemongrass, garlic, shallots, ginger, jalapeños, and cilantro in a nonreactive mixing bowl. Stir in the sugar, coriander, pepper, soy sauce, fish sauce, lemon juice, and oil. Pour this mixture over the ribs, rubbing it onto the meat on both sides. Marinate, covered, in the refrigerator for at least 6 hours or as long as 12. Turn the ribs two or three times while marinating.

3. Set up the grill for indirect grilling (see page 12 for charcoal or page 16 for gas) and preheat to medium. If using a charcoal grill, place a drip pan in the center.

4. When ready to cook, place the ribs, preferably in a rib rack, in the center of the hot grate, away from the heat, and cover the grill. Grill until cooked, 1¼ to 1½ hours. If using a charcoal grill, you'll need to add 12 fresh coals per side after 1 hour. When the ribs are cooked, the meat will have shrunk back from the bones about ¼ inch and will be tender enough to tear apart with your fingers. But don't overcook; the ribs should have some chew to them.

5. Transfer the ribs to a cutting board. Let rest for a few minutes, then, using a chef's knife, cut the racks into individual ribs and place on plates or a platter. Sprinkle with the cilantro and peanuts and serve at once.

ALSO GOOD FOR:
Pork chops would be delicious prepared in this fashion. For that matter, so would chicken (cut it into pieces for marinating) and steak.

HOW TO ROTISSERIE GRILL RIBS

Ribs grilled on a rotisserie have a flavor that is completely different from what you're probably used to. Gone is the heavy smoke taste so prized by pit bosses in the United States. In its stead is the crusty succulence you get when you cook a fatty meat in front of a fire. The flames create a dark, crisp crust, while the slow, gentle turning bastes the meat with the melting fat. What results is a rib with a little more chew to it than a traditional American baby back. And instead of the sweet taste of barbecue sauce, you get to enjoy the natural flavor of the pork.

*Rotisseried
Baby Back Ribs with
Grilled Peppers
(page 383)*

SETTING UP THE GRILL

1 To set up a rotisserie on a charcoal grill, first light the charcoal in a chimney starter (see page 9).

2 Position the rotisserie ring on the grill.

3 Mound the coals on one side of the grill, parallel to where the spit will be, and place drip pans in front of them.

TIP

■ You want to use a fairly short rib on the rotisserie—baby backs are perfect (the tips of long spareribs come uncomfortably close to the fire).

PREPARING THE MEAT

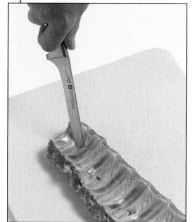

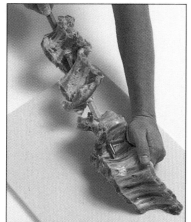

1 Using a sharp, slender knife and starting on the bone side, make starter holes in the meat between every two ribs. Twist the knife blade to widen the holes. This makes it easier to insert the spit. Note that the membrane has already been removed from these ribs.

2 Use an over and under weaving motion to thread the ribs, through the holes, onto the spit.

3 Brush the ribs with olive oil and then sprinkle them with *herbes de Provence*.

TIP

■ This recipe makes
enough to feed two
people generously.
That's because most
rotisseries can accom-
modate only two racks
of ribs.

ATTACHING THE SPIT

1 Insert the end of the spit into the rotisserie motor socket.

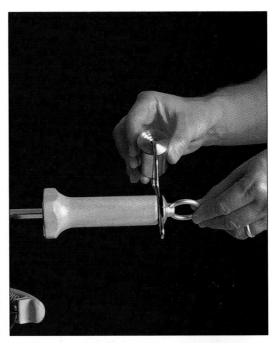

2 If your rotisserie spit has a counterweight, position it so that it counterbalances the meat.

ON THE GRILL

1 As the ribs cook, baste them with lemon
oil. Note the drip pans under the turning
ribs on this gas grill. The ribs will be done
after 40 minutes to 1 hour.

2 When the ribs are cooked, the meat will
shrink back about ¼ inch from the ends
of the bones. Another test for doneness is
to wiggle a bone. It should feel a little loose.

ROTISSERIED BABY BACK RIBS

2 racks baby back pork ribs
**   (about 2 pounds total)**
¼ cup extra-virgin olive oil
1 or 2 lemon wedges

1 bunch fresh rosemary
Coarse salt and black pepper
2 tablespoons herbes de Provence
**   (page 163) or a commercial mix**

1. Remove the thin papery membrane on the back of each rack of ribs (as shown in Steps 2 and 3 on pages 141 and 142) or have your butcher do this for you.

2. Thread the ribs onto the rotisserie spit as shown in Preparing the Meat, Steps 1 and 2 on page 145.

3. Place the oil in a bowl and squeeze in a wedge or two of lemon. Using the rosemary as a basting brush, lightly brush the ribs on both sides with some of the lemon oil. Generously season the ribs on both sides with salt and pepper, then the *herbes de Provence.* You can grill the ribs right away, but they'll be even more flavorful if you let them marinate for 15 to 20 minutes.

4. Set up the grill for rotisserie grilling (see page 22) and preheat to high.

5. When ready to cook, attach the spit to the rotisserie mechanism and turn on the motor. Grill the ribs, covered, until golden brown and cooked through, 40 minutes to 1 hour, depending on their size. Baste the ribs with lemon oil as they cook, using the rosemary as a brush. The ribs are done when the meat has shrunk back about ¼ inch from the ends of the bones. Serve at once.

SERVES 2 VERY HUNGRY PEOPLE

YOU'LL NEED:
Rotisserie

ALSO GOOD FOR:
Lamb riblets (the rib-bone part of a rack of lamb) are great spit roasted this way. Make friends with a butcher and ask him to procure this delectable cut of lamb for you.

METHOD:
**Poaching and
direct grilling**

COOKING TIME:
12 to 18 minutes

HOW TO GRILL SAUSAGES

Sausages are particularly delicious grilled. The blast furnace heat of the fire crisps the casings, melts out the fat, and generally adds a rich smoky flavor to the meat.

There are two basic types of sausages: raw and cooked. Uncooked sausages, whether pork, beef, or poultry, pose the greater challenge for grilling. First, there's the issue of dripping fat, which can turn your grill into a conflagration. Then, there's the problem of steam buildup in the casings. If not properly vented, sausages can literally explode on the grill. Finally, there's the challenge of cooking a sausage through without burning the casing. Fortunately, all three problems are easy to remedy, as you'll see here.

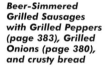

*Beer-Simmered
Grilled Sausages
with Grilled Peppers
(page 383), Grilled
Onions (page 380),
and crusty bread*

SETTING UP THE GRILL

1 To set up a charcoal grill for direct grilling, first light the charcoal in a chimney starter (see page 9).

2 Using a garden hoe or other long-handled implement, rake the burning coals into an even layer.

3 To see if the grill is preheated to medium-high, use the test on page 10.

PREPARING THE SAUSAGES

1 Sausages must be pricked before grilling to allow the steam to escape without rupturing the skins. Insert a needle or pin in a cork to minimize the risk of losing it.

2 Prick each sausage in several places with the needle or pin.

TIPS

■ Today's grill jockey has a myriad of sausages to choose from: Italian sweet or hot sausages, German bratwurst, Spanish chorizo, Portuguese *linguica*, South African *boerewors*—the list is virtually endless. Cooked sausages need only be heated on the grill. Uncooked sausages must be cooked all the way through.

■ When dripping fat causes flare-ups, you'll need to move the sausage to another section of the grill. For this reason, it's important not to crowd the grill when cooking sausages.

■ To guarantee complete cooking, partially poach the sausages before grilling. This has the added advantage of melting out some of the excess fat.

TIP

■ Another way to control flare-ups is with a few quick squirts from a water pistol. Do not overuse this technique, however, or you risk putting out the fire.

POACHING THE SAUSAGES: Simmering the sausages with beer, water, and onions shortens the grilling time and adds extra flavor.

ON THE GRILL: Grill the separated sausage links until nicely browned on both sides, 4 to 6 minutes per side.

SERVES 6 TO 8

YOU'LL NEED:
A needle or pin and a cork

VARIATIONS:
Poaching is optional and not every grill jockey does it. If you omit the poaching, you'll need to grill the sausages 7 to 10 minutes per side.

For absolutely foolproof sausage grilling, use the indirect method. The sausages will be fully cooked in about 30 minutes.

THE RECIPE

BEER-SIMMERED GRILLED SAUSAGES

3 pounds uncooked sausages, such as sweet or hot Italian sausages, bratwurst, chorizo, linguica, or any other sausages you prefer

1 onion, thinly sliced
3 cups beer, as needed
About 1 tablespoon vegetable oil
Mustard, for serving

1. Prick each sausage a half-dozen times with a needle or pin stuck in a cork. Arrange the onion slices on the bottom of a sauté pan just large enough to hold all the sausages. Place the sausages on top and add beer and water to cover (the ratio should be about 3 parts beer to 1 part water). Place the pan over medium heat and gradually bring the liquid to a simmer, not a rapid boil. Poach the sausages until half-cooked, 4 to 5 minutes. Transfer the sausages to a rack on a baking sheet to drain or drain in a colander. Separate the sausages into links.

2. Set up the grill for direct grilling (see page 10 for charcoal or page 16 for gas) and preheat to medium-high.

3. When ready to cook, brush and oil the grill grate. Lightly brush the sausages on all sides with oil and place on the hot grate. Grill until the casings are crisp and nicely browned and the sausages are cooked through, 4 to 6 minutes per side. You may want to rotate the sausages 90 degrees after 2 minutes on each side to create an attractive crosshatch of grill marks. Should flare-ups arise, move the sausages to a different section of the grill. Use a slender metal skewer to test for doneness. Insert it into the center of one of the sausages: It should come out hot to the touch.

4. Transfer the sausages to plates or a platter and let rest for 3 minutes. Serve with plenty of mustard.

HOW TO GRILL HOT DOGS

METHOD:
Direct grilling

COOKING TIME:
8 to 10 minutes

You may be surprised, even a little insulted, to find a technique for grilling hot dogs here. After all, what could be easier than popping a tube steak on the grill? Even if you're a total neophyte and you've never grilled anything else, you've probably grilled a hot dog.

Well, that's what I thought until I went to Brazil. Grill jockeys in Rio de Janeiro elevate grilling the humble hot dog to the level of art. Their secret is simple: They cut a series of small notches in the wiener and fill them with an aromatic mince of onions, peppers, and garlic. That set me thinking about other stuffings and soon I was making my hot dogs hot and cheesy with the addition of sliced jalapeños and Monterey Jack.

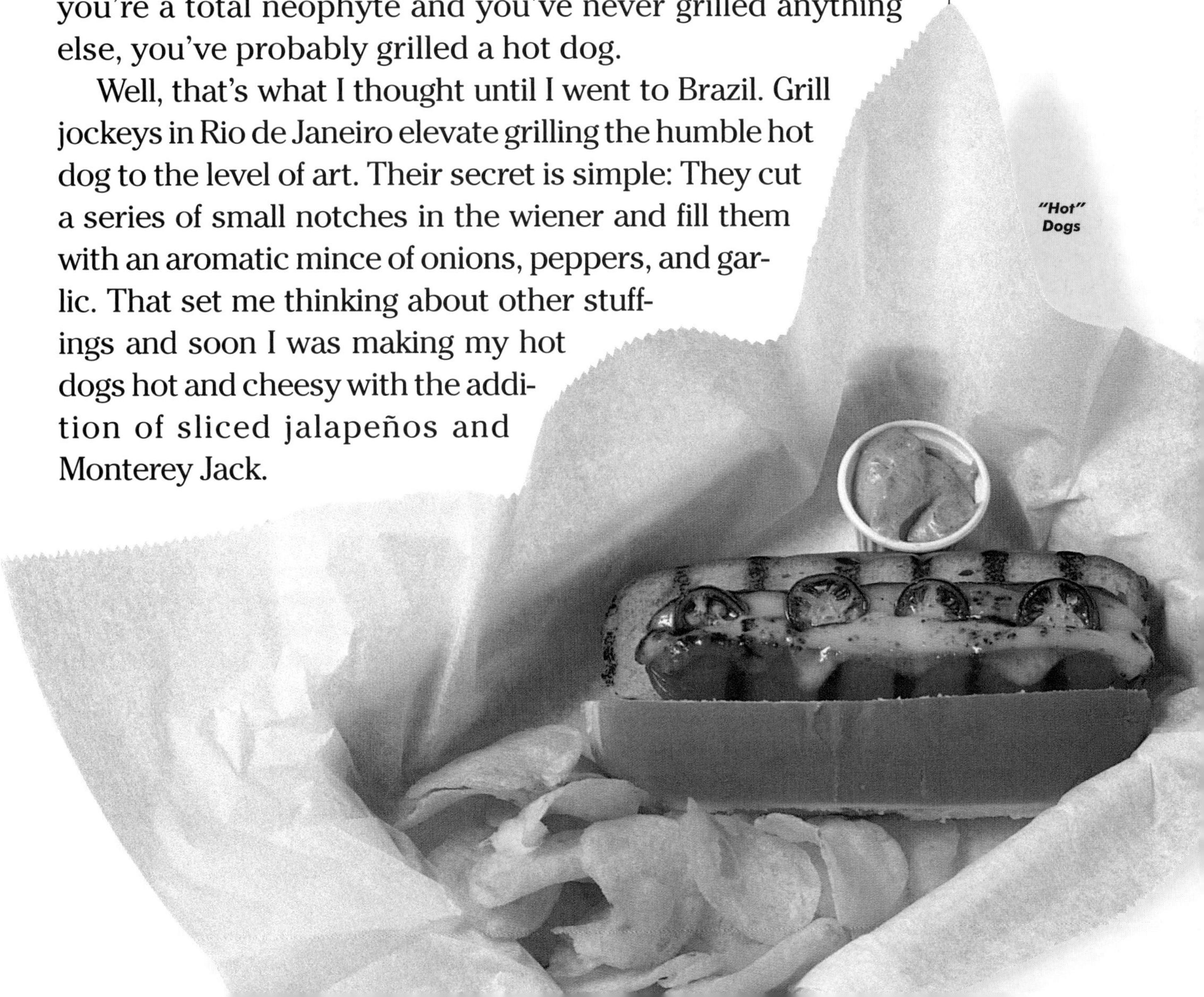

"Hot"
Dogs

SETTING UP THE GRILL

1 To set up a charcoal grill for direct grilling, first light the charcoal in a chimney starter (see page 9).

2 Using a garden hoe or other long-handled implement, rake the burning coals into an even layer.

3 To see if the grill is preheated to high, use the test on page 10.

PREPARING THE HOT DOGS

TIPS

■ For ease in slitting and stuffing, choose a thick hot dog.

■ You might think fresh jalapeños will be too fiery, but the peppers mellow during grilling. For milder "hot" dogs, seed the peppers. Or use sliced pickled jalapeño peppers, which are milder still.

1 Make two lengthwise cuts in each hot dog to remove a slender V-shaped strip from the center. The idea is to cut the hot dog almost in half lengthwise but leave the halves attached at the bottom.

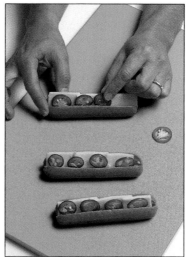

2 Insert the cheese and four jalapeño slices in the slit.

3 Tie each hot dog crosswise in two places with butcher's string.

ON THE GRILL

1 Place the hot dogs on the grill parallel to the bars of the grate, so the bars hold the hot dogs upright.

2 Grill the bottoms until crisp, then roll the hot dogs slightly to grill each side.

THE RECIPE

"HOT" DOGS

8 thick hot dogs or knockwursts
4 to 6 jalapeño peppers, sliced crosswise
   (32 slices)
4 to 5 ounces Monterey Jack, Cheddar,
   Munster, or Gruyère cheese, cut into strips

8 hot dog buns
2 tablespoons melted butter
Mustard, ketchup, relish, and/or diced onions,
   for serving

1. Slit and stuff each hot dog with jalapeños and cheese as shown in Preparing the Hot Dogs, Steps 1 through 3 on the facing page. Tie each hot dog in two places with butcher's string to hold in the filling.

2. Set up the grill for direct grilling (see page 10 for charcoal or page 16 for gas) and preheat to high.

3. When ready to cook, place the hot dogs on the hot grate so they are supported by the bars of the grate. Grill until nicely

browned on the bottom and both sides, slightly tilting the hot dogs on their sides with tongs to brown them, 8 to 10 minutes. Turn the hot dogs perpendicular to the grate for the last 2 minutes of grilling for attractive grill marks. Transfer to a platter and snip off and discard the strings.

4. Brush the inside of the buns with the melted butter and grill them on the grill for 1 minute. Serve the "hot" dogs with the toppings of your choice.

SERVES 4

YOU'LL NEED:
Butcher's string

ALSO GOOD FOR:
Any sort of cooked sausage can be stuffed and grilled in this manner.

METHOD:
Modified
direct grilling

COOKING TIME:
4 to 5 hours for a
50-pound pig

HOW TO BARBECUE A WHOLE PIG

A whole hog is the ultimate test of a pit master's skill—a test of logistical and organizational skills, culinary prowess, even endurance. Cooking a whole hog isn't as difficult as you might think, especially if you start with a small one. A 50-pound pig is light enough to handle by a couple of people and will still feed twenty-five. And you can cook it in an afternoon, which won't interfere with your beauty rest.

Once you've mastered a small pig, you can graduate up to larger ones, until you're smoking hundred-pounders to feed the whole neighborhood. Your spouse will become your sous-chef—or divorce you. Here are basic instructions for cooking a small whole hog, but the principle is the same for a large one.

Barbecued Pig

PREPARING THE PIG

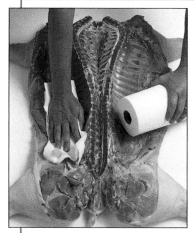

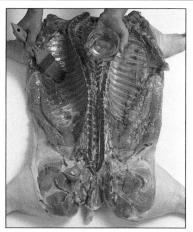

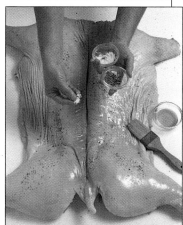

1 Have your butcher prepare the pig so that it will lie flat on the grill (he'll need to partially cut through the backbone). Blot the cavity dry with paper towels.

2 Brush the inside of the pig with oil and then generously season with salt and pepper.

3 Invert the pig, brush the skin with oil, and season with salt and pepper.

SETTING UP THE GRILL

1 Light the charcoal and place the grate on top. The leaping flames will clean it.

2 When the coals are completely lit and ashed over, shovel them into two piles, one where the pig's shoulders will be, one where the thighs will be.

3 Place a couple of hickory or oak logs on the coals. If logs aren't available, use soaked wood chunks. (Chips would be too small.) These will be your source of smoke.

TIPS

■ The first challenge is locating a whole hog, which will be easy if you live in barbecue country or in a city with a large Hispanic population. Ask your local butcher if he can order one for you. You'll need to give him several days' notice. I try to leave the pig at the butcher's until I'm ready to cook it. The refrigerator there is a lot larger than mine.

■ To cook a whole small pig, you'll need a smoker the size of a 55-gallon drum. You can probably rent one from a party supply house.

■ If you have to get the pig a day ahead of time, you can make a temporary refrigerator by filling a very large cooler with ice.

TIP

■ If a whole pig is
too large for your
smoker, have your
butcher cut off the
backbone. This gives
you two whole hog
halves, which are
easier to maneuver
on the grill.

ON THE GRILL

1 Lay the pig flat on the grate, bone-side
down.

2 The pig is ready for turning when the
underside is a dark golden brown and
the skin is dark from wood smoke.

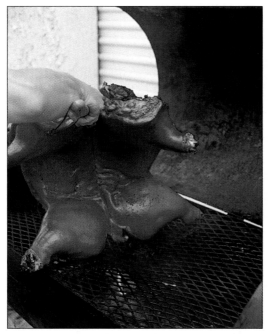

3 Using tongs or grill mitts to hold it, invert
the pig. With a large pig, you may need a
friend to help you. Continue cooking the pig
until the skin is crisp and a dark golden brown.

4 Every half hour, mop the pig with the
vinegar sauce.

5 Turn the pig one last time to crisp the meat. Notice how the skin has become crackling crisp.

6 Don't forget to mop the skin side, too. The pig will be done after 4 to 6 hours.

THE RECIPE

BARBECUED PIG

1 small whole pig, dressed
    (gutted and butterflied),
    about 50 pounds
3 tablespoons olive oil
Coarse salt and black pepper

FOR THE MOP SAUCE:
1 quart cider vinegar
1 medium onion, thinly sliced
2 to 4 red or green jalapeño peppers,
    thinly sliced

3 tablespoons coarse salt
1 tablespoon hot red pepper flakes
1 tablespoon black pepper

TO SERVE:
North Carolina Vinegar Sauce
    (page 448) or Mustard Barbecue Sauce
    (page 448) or the barbecue sauce
    of your choice

SERVES 20 TO 25

YOU'LL NEED:
55-gallon, drum-style smoker; 30 to 50 pounds charcoal, plus 4 small hardwood logs (hickory or oak) or 3 to 4 pounds oak or hickory chunks (if using wood chunks, soak for 1 hour in cold water to cover, then drain); one 3-foot-square piece of plywood; heavy-duty rubber gloves

1. Blot the cavity of the pig dry with paper towels. Brush the pig on both sides with oil and season generously with salt and pepper.

2. Set up the grill for modified direct grilling, using 20 pounds of charcoal and following Setting Up the Grill, Steps 1 through 3 on page 155. Let the coals burn until lightly ashed over (medium heat), then rake them into two mounds: one where the pig's shoulders will be, one where the thighs will be. Toss a couple of hardwood logs or a handful of wood chunks on each mound. Place the grate over the fire.

3. Place the pig on the grate, bone-side down, and tightly cover the smoker. Smoke until the underside of the pig is nicely browned, 1 to 2 hours.

4. Meanwhile, make the mop sauce: Combine all the ingredients in a large nonreactive bowl and stir until the salt dissolves. Turn the pig, as shown in Step 3 on page 156, and mop it with the vinegar mop sauce.

5. Continue grilling, mopping every 30 minutes, until the skin side is crackling crisp and a dark golden brown, about 2 hours more. You'll need to add 3 to 5 pounds of fresh charcoal per side each hour, plus another couple of logs or some wood chunks. Leave the grill uncovered for 10 minutes or so to let the charcoal light. Try to maintain the temperature of the grill at medium.

6. When the skin is crisp and dark brown, rake a pile of coals into the center of grill, then turn the pig again to finish cooking the underside, about 1 hour more. The pig is ready when you can pull the meat off the bones. To test for doneness, insert an instant-read meat thermometer into the thickest part of one of the legs or shoulders (do not touch the bones); it should read about 190°F. Your total cooking time will be 4 to 5 hours.

7. Wrap a 3-foot-square sheet of plywood in aluminum foil. Transfer the pig to the wrapped plywood. You'll need some help doing this. Present the pig to the admiring crowd in all its porcine glory. Wearing heavy-duty rubber gloves, pull off the skin and cut it into tasty shards with a meat cleaver. Shred the pork with your fingers (see Pulling the Pork on page 108), chop it with a cleaver, or slice it with a knife. Serve the pork with shards of crisp skin and vinegar sauce or mustard sauce spooned over it.

LAMB

METHOD:
Indirect grilling

COOKING TIME:
1½ to 2 hours

HOW TO GRILL A WHOLE LEG OF LAMB

The robust flavor of lamb is perfectly suited to the searing heat and smoke of live fire. Yet a large cut, like a whole leg, presents a challenge to the griller. How to achieve a crisp, golden crust, while cooking the meat through to the bone? The secret is to use the indirect method of grilling. I promise the results will make you want to throw stones at oven-roasted lamb.

Roast Leg of Lamb Provençal with grilled eggplant and tomatoes

SETTING UP THE GRILL

1 To set up a charcoal grill for indirect grilling, first light the charcoal in a chimney starter (see page 9).

2 Form two heat zones by raking the coals into two piles at opposite sides of the grill, using a long-handled implement, like a garden hoe.

3 If your grill has side baskets, divide the coals evenly between them. Note the drip pan in the center of the grill.

PREPARING THE MEAT

1 Using the tip of a sharp, slender knife, make tiny holes in the leg of lamb, all over, about ½ inch deep and 1 inch apart. Insert garlic slivers in some of the holes, olive slivers in others, and rosemary leaves in the rest. It's okay for the ends of these ingredients to stick out.

2 Spray the lamb on all sides with olive oil.

3 Sprinkle the lamb on all sides with the *herbes de Provence.*

TIP

■ The common size for a whole leg of lamb is 8 to 10 pounds. When photographing this technique, I used a baby leg of lamb—ordered from Jamison Farms in Pennsylvania (see Mail-Order Sources on page 481). The recipe on page 162 calls for a small leg of lamb or a half leg (4 to 5 pounds). Cooking time for a baby leg is given in the Variations on page 163.

TIPS

■ *Herbes de Provence* is a mix of dried herbs that you can buy at any gourmet shop. But it's easy to make your own, so I've included a recipe here.

■ Freezing the olive slivers makes them stiff enough to insert in the meat easily.

ON THE GRILL

1 Baste the lamb with olive oil from time to time, using a bunch of rosemary as a brush. The lamb will be done after 1½ to 2 hours.

2 To test for doneness use an instant-read meat thermometer inserted into the deepest part of the meat, but don't touch the bone.

SERVES 6 TO 8

YOU'LL NEED:
2 cups wood chips (optional; preferably oak), soaked for 1 hour in cold water to cover, then drained; spray bottle

---

THE RECIPE

ROAST LEG OF LAMB PROVENÇAL

1 bunch fresh rosemary
1 small or ½ large bone-in leg of lamb (4 to 5 pounds)
6 cloves garlic, cut into slivers
6 kalamata olives, cut into slivers and frozen
Extra-virgin olive oil in a spray bottle, plus 3 to 4 tablespoons for basting

1 tablespoon coarse salt
1 tablespoon Homemade Herbes de Provence (recipe follows) or a commercial brand
1 teaspoon cracked black peppercorns

1. Strip the leaves off 2 rosemary sprigs. Finely chop the leaves of 1 sprig. Set aside the remainder of the bunch of rosemary.

2. Using the tip of a sharp, slender knife, make a series of ½-inch-deep holes in the lamb, mostly in the sheath of fat on top, but also on the sides and bottom. The holes should be about 1 inch apart. Insert the garlic, olives, and whole rosemary leaves in the holes, one flavoring per hole.

3. Spray the leg of lamb on all sides with

oil. Combine the salt, *herbes de Provence,* peppercorns, and chopped rosemary leaves and sprinkle them all over the lamb, patting them on with your fingertips.

4. Set up the grill for indirect grilling (see page 12 for charcoal or page 16 for gas) and preheat to medium. If using a charcoal grill, place a drip pan in the center. If using a gas grill, place all the wood chips, if desired, in the smoker box or in a smoker pouch (see page 17) and preheat on high until you see smoke, then reduce the heat to medium.

5. When ready to cook, if using a charcoal grill, toss half of the wood chips, if desired, on the coals. Place the lamb on the hot grate, away from the heat, and cover the grill. Grill until cooked to taste, 1½ to 2 hours for medium-rare. Every 30 minutes, baste the leg of lamb with oil, using the remaining rosemary sprigs as a basting brush. To test for doneness, insert an instant-read meat thermometer into the thickest part of the leg but not touching the bone: The internal temperature will be about 125°F for rare; 145°F for medium-rare; and 160°F for medium. If using a charcoal grill, you'll need to add 12 fresh coals and ½ cup wood chips to each side after 1 hour of grilling.

6. Transfer the lamb to a cutting board, let rest for 10 minutes, then carve and serve.

Homemade Herbes de Provence

MAKES ABOUT 1 CUP

3 tablespoons dried rosemary
3 tablespoons dried basil
3 tablespoons dried marjoram
3 tablespoons dried oregano
2 tablespoons dried summer savory (optional)
1 tablespoon dried thyme
2 teaspoons fennel seeds
2 teaspoons dried lavender
1 teaspoon black pepper
1 teaspoon ground coriander
½ teaspoon ground bay leaves

In a small mixing bowl crumble the rosemary between your fingers to break the needles into small pieces. Add the remaining ingredients and toss with your fingers to mix. Store the *herbes de Provence* in an airtight container away from light; it will keep for as long as 6 months.

Note: This recipe makes more *herbes de Provence* than you'll need. The seasoning is great sprinkled on virtually any grilled meat, poultry, seafood, or vegetables.

VARIATIONS:

A baby leg of lamb weighs about 3 pounds. If you use one, shorten the cooking time by 30 minutes. This is also a great way to fix a pork loin roast or pork shoulder.

If you have a heavy-duty rotisserie, you can use it to grill the lamb. Run the spit through the leg so the meat is centered as evenly as possible. Leg of lamb is even more crusty and succulent when rotisserie grilled.

METHOD:
Direct grilling

COOKING TIME:
20 to 30 minutes

**ADVANCE
PREPARATION:**
4 to 12 hours
for marinating
the meat

HOW TO GRILL A BUTTERFLIED LEG OF LAMB

*Sesame-Ginger
Leg of Lamb with
Asian Pear
Dipping Sauce*

Butterflying turns a cumbersome leg of lamb into a piece of meat thin enough to grill using the direct method. You get all the taste benefits—the flavor-seared exterior, moist interior, and smoky flavor—and it melts out extra fat. The recipe used to demonstrate this technique was inspired by a Korean beef dish called *bool kogi.* The sweet, nutty sesame oil marinade goes great with lamb, as does the unexpected crunch and sweetness of the grilled pear accompaniment.

SETTING UP THE GRILL

1 To set up a charcoal grill for direct grilling, first light the charcoal in a chimney starter (see page 9).

2 Using a garden hoe or other long-handled implement, rake the burning coals into an even layer.

3 To see if the grill is preheated to medium-high, use the test on page 10.

PREPARING THE MEAT

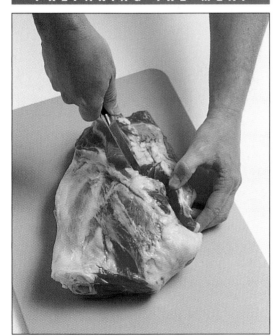

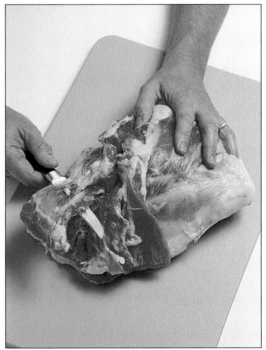

1 Locate the hip or "haich" bone at the top end of the leg. Using the tip of a sharp, slender knife cut along the line of the bone.

2 Cut the meat away from the hip bone on both sides, following it with the tip of your knife. When you get to the socket of the leg bone, cut around it and remove the hip bone.

TIP

■ Butterflying a leg of lamb isn't difficult, but, if you'd rather not do it yourself, ask your butcher to do it for you.

TIP

■ The best part of the leg for butterflying and grilling is the butt end, not the shank end (the latter contains more sinews). The butt end requires a little more knife work, but the results are worth it.

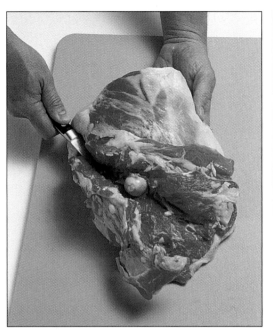

3 Cut through the side of the leg to the leg bone, cutting along the side closest to the bone. Open the leg as you cut to expose the bone.

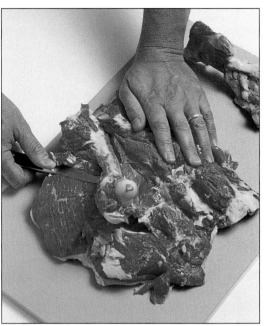

4 Cut the meat away from the bone on both sides and the bottom.

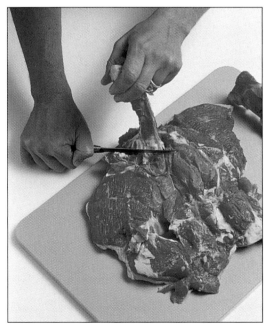

5 Remove the leg bone.

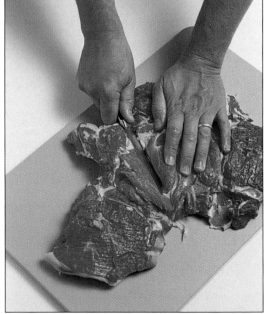

6 Holding your knife parallel to the cutting board, continue cutting through the leg almost but not quite to the other side. Open the leg of lamb like a book and lay it flat.

7 Pour one third of the marinade in a baking dish. Arrange the butterflied leg of lamb on top. Pour the remaining marinade on top of it.

ON THE GRILL: Grill the butterflied leg of lamb over medium-high heat. If it starts to burn, lower the heat on a gas grill or use tongs to move it to a cooler section of the grill.

TIP

■ Boiling the marinade for 3 minutes sterilizes it and makes it a good glaze and basting sauce for the lamb.

GLAZING THE LAMB: Brush the glaze on each side during the last 5 minutes of grilling.

GRILLING THE PEARS: While the lamb rests, grill the pears.

T H E   R E C I P E

SESAME-GINGER LEG OF LAMB

VARIATIONS:
*You could marinate
the lamb in one of the
other marinades in
this book. For a Near
East accent, use the
yogurt saffron mari-
nade from Saffron-
Grilled Chicken on
page 234. For a
Japanese accent, use
the teriyaki marinade
from Tangerine
Teriyaki Tofu Step 2,
on page 417. The
Brazilian coconut
marinade from Step 2
of the shrimp kebabs
on page 320 and
lemongrass marinade
from Chicken Satés
Step 2 on page 257
are other good possi-
bilities.*

ALSO GOOD FOR:
*Almost any type of
meat can be mari-
nated, grilled, and
served in this fashion,
especially beef and
chicken. The gingery
marinade also goes
great with seafood
and even tofu. In fact,
I'd be hard-pressed
to think of food that
wouldn't taste great
prepared this way.*

FOR THE LAMB AND MARINADE:
Butt end of a leg of lamb (4 to 5 pounds
    bone-in; 3 to 4 pounds butterflied)
2 tablespoons peeled, chopped fresh ginger
4 cloves garlic, chopped
1 bunch scallions, trimmed and
    finely chopped
¾ cup soy sauce
¾ cup sake, Chinese rice wine, or dry sherry
½ cup Asian (dark) sesame oil
1 tablespoon sugar
½ teaspoon black pepper

FOR THE GLAZE:
3 tablespoons butter
1 tablespoon sugar

FOR SERVING:
2 Asian or Bosc pears, cut into thin
    wedges and seeded
1 head romaine lettuce, separated
    into leaves and washed
Asian Pear Dipping Sauce
    (page 456)

1. Butterfly the lamb, as shown in Preparing the Meat, Steps 1 through 6 on pages 165 and 166, or have your butcher do this for you.

2. Prepare the marinade: Combine the ginger, garlic, and scallions in a food processor and process to mix. Add the soy sauce, sake, sesame oil, sugar, and pepper and process to mix. Pour one third of this mixture over the bottom of a nonreactive baking dish just large enough to hold the lamb. Arrange the butterflied lamb on top and pour the remaining marinade over it. Let the lamb marinate in the refrigerator, covered, for 4 hours (or even overnight—the longer the better), turning the lamb once or twice to ensure even marinating.

3. Set up the grill for direct grilling (see page 10 for charcoal or page 16 for gas) and preheat to medium-high.

4. Drain the lamb, pouring the leftover marinade into a saucepan. Add the butter and sugar to the marinade and boil the mixture until thick and syrupy, 3 to 5 minutes. You'll use this glaze for basting.

5. When ready to cook, brush and oil the grill grate. Spread out the lamb on the hot grate, fat-side down. Grill until the lamb is cooked to taste, 10 to 15 minutes per side for medium-rare (about 145°F on an instant-read meat thermometer inserted in the thickest part). If the lamb starts to burn, lower the heat to medium or move the lamb to a cooler section of the grill. During the last 5 minutes of grilling on each side, brush the lamb with the glaze. Transfer the lamb to a cutting board and let rest for 10 minutes.

6. Meanwhile, grill the pear wedges over the hottest section of the grill, 2 to 4 minutes per side, turning the slices 90 degrees after a minute or so to create a handsome crosshatch of grill marks.

7. Using a sharp carving knife, thinly slice the lamb across the grain. Arrange the slices on plates or a platter. Arrange the grilled pears, lettuce leaves, and a bowl of the dipping sauce alongside.

8. To eat, wrap a piece of lamb and a wedge of pear in a lettuce leaf, dip it into the sauce, and pop it into your mouth.

HOW TO DIRECT GRILL A RACK OF LAMB

METHOD:
Direct grilling

COOKING TIME:
16 to 24 minutes

ADVANCE PREPARATION:
2 to 4 hours for marinating the meat

A rack of lamb is a regal cut and there's no better way to cook this luxury than on the grill. I usually grill it directly over the fire—a process that requires constant attention, as the dripping fat can cause Vesuvian flare-ups. A little vigilance rewards you with meltingly moist, tender lamb nicely charred on the outside.

Moroccans are masters of grilling lamb and the recipe accompanying the technique takes its inspiration from a pit boss in Marrakech. The cumin, cardamom, paprika, and ginger recall the fragrant Berber spice mixes of the Atlas Mountains.

Rack of Lamb Marrakech with couscous and turnips

SETTING UP THE GRILL

1 To set up a charcoal grill for direct grilling, first light the charcoal in a chimney starter (see page 9).

2 Using a garden hoe or other long-handled implement, rake the burning coals into an even layer.

3 To see if the grill is preheated to medium-high, use the test on page 10.

MIXING THE SPICE PASTE

1 Mash the garlic and salt into a paste with the back of a spoon.

2 Grate the onion over the bowl with the garlic paste. You'll add the spices to this mixture.

PREPARING THE MEAT

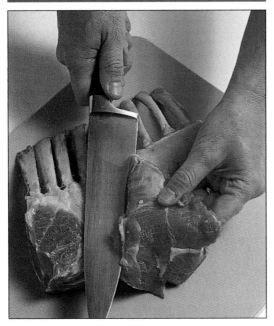

1 Trim off the flap of fat covering the outside of each Frenched rack of lamb.

2 Spread the spice paste over the racks of lamb. They'll marinate for 2 to 4 hours.

ON THE GRILL

1 Grill the racks meat-side down for 8 to 12 minutes before turning.

2 Turn the rack over and grill the bone side for the same length of time for medium-rare.

TIPS

■ Racks of lamb come covered with a flat layer of stringy but tasty meat and fat. Depending on how flush you're feeling, you'll want to remove some or all of it. Pull it off in a sheet, using a chef's knife to help you. I like to season and grill this piece of scrap, then cut it into small squares to be served on toothpicks as an appetizer.

■ If the bones start to burn, slide a folded sheet of aluminum foil underneath to protect them.

TIP

■ In Morocco, lamb would traditionally be served with a fiery pepper relish called *harissa*. You can buy *harissa* canned or in jars at Middle Eastern and North African markets or gourmet shops, or you can make your own. You'll find recipes in *The Barbecue! Bible*. In the West, we like to pair lamb with mint jelly. Sometimes I combine *harissa* and mint jelly to make a condiment with a North African kick.

3 Don't forget to stand the rack upright to grill the ends for a minute or two.

4 When the rack is cooked to medium-rare, the ends will feel gently yielding to the touch. The foil protects the lamb ribs from burning.

SERVES 4

THE RECIPE

RACK OF LAMB MARRAKECH

2 racks of lamb (1½ pounds each)
2 cloves garlic, minced
Coarse salt
1 small onion, peeled and cut
   in half lengthwise
1 teaspoon ground cumin, plus
   1 tablespoon, for serving

1 teaspoon ground coriander
1 teaspoon ground paprika
1 teaspoon ground white pepper
½ teaspoon ground cardamom
½ teaspoon ground ginger
¼ cup extra-virgin olive oil
Lemon wedges, for serving (optional)

1. French the racks of lamb following the instructions for prime rib on pages 33 and 34, or have your butcher do this for you. Trim the layer of fat off each rack as shown in Preparing the Meat, Step 1 on page 171. Place the racks in a baking dish.

2. Place the garlic and 1 teaspoon salt in a mixing bowl and mash to a smooth paste with the back of a wooden spoon. Coarsely grate the onion into the bowl. Stir in the 1 teaspoon cumin, and the coriander, paprika, pepper, cardamom, ginger, and oil. Spread this spice paste all over the meaty parts of the racks of lamb but not on the rib bones. Let the lamb marinate in the refrigerator, covered, for 2 to 4 hours.

3. Set up the grill for direct grilling (see page 10 for charcoal or page 16 for gas) and preheat to medium-high. When ready to cook, place the lamb on the hot grate, meat-side down, and grill until cooked to taste, 8 to 12 minutes per side for medium-rare, about 145°F on an instant-read meat thermometer (the cooking time will depend on the size of the racks). Rotate the racks 90 degrees after 4 minutes to create an attractive cross-hatch of grill marks and stand the racks upright for 1 to 2 minutes to grill each end. You'll probably get flare-ups, so be ready to move the lamb to a cooler part of the grill. If the ends of the bones start to burn, protect them with folded aluminum foil.

4. Transfer the racks to a platter and let rest for 3 minutes. Carve the lamb into chops. To serve, place 1 tablespoon each of coarse salt and cumin in tiny bowls. Arrange the lemon wedges around the lamb, if desired. Have everyone sprinkle the lamb with a little coarse salt and cumin and season it with lemon juice, if using.

ALSO GOOD FOR:
This Moroccan seasoning is good for any cut of lamb: whole or butterflied leg, loin or rib chops, even cubes of lamb for shish kebabs. For that matter, it's not half bad for beef.

METHOD:
Indirect grilling

COOKING TIME:
25 to 35 minutes

HOW TO INDIRECT GRILL A RACK OF LAMB

Rack of lamb in a mustard crust was one of the first dishes I learned to make at cooking school in Paris. It's certainly one of the easiest: All you do is paint the lamb with mustard, dredge it in bread crumbs, and roast it in the oven. Now, I'm of the school of thought that if something tastes great baked, it most likely tastes even better grilled. So one day, I decided to try cooking this French classic on the grill. The French never knew what they were missing.

Using the indirect grilling method has another advantage. Flare-ups are not an issue when you grill lamb this way, because the fat drips clear of the flames. So the next time you want to look like a genius while doing hardly any work at all, unscrew a jar of mustard and make this savory rack of lamb.

Rack of Lamb in a Mustard Crust with Grilled Onions (page 380)

SETTING UP THE GRILL

1 To set up a charcoal grill for indirect grilling, first light the charcoal in a chimney starter (see page 9).

2 Form two heat zones by raking the coals into two piles at opposite sides of the grill, using a long-handled implement, like a garden hoe.

3 If your grill has side baskets, divide the coals evenly between them. Note the drip pan in the center of the grill.

PREPARING THE MEAT

1 Trim the flap of stringy meat and fat off the top of each Frenched rack.

2 Spread the meat with mustard on all sides. Here I'm using a grainy, Meaux-style mustard.

3 Dredge the racks of lamb in the herbed bread crumbs.

TIP

■ Any recipe this simple lives or dies by the quality of the ingredients. Use the best mustard you can buy—an imported smooth mustard from Dijon or a grainy one from Meaux. Steer clear of sweet honey mustards.

ON THE GRILL: Grill the rack meat-side up for 25 to 35 minutes for medium-rare. Tent the ribs with aluminum foil to keep them from burning.

TESTING FOR DONENESS: Insert an instant-read thermometer into the thickest part, but don't touch the bone. It should read about 145°F for medium-rare. Or press the ends with your fingers. The meat should feel gently yielding.

SERVES 4

YOU'LL NEED:
Spray bottle

THE RECIPE

RACK OF LAMB IN A MUSTARD CRUST

2 racks of lamb (about 1½ pounds each)
Coarse salt and black pepper
3 cups dried bread crumbs
   (preferably homemade)
¼ cup minced fresh parsley
   (preferably flat-leaf)

1 tablespoon chopped fresh rosemary
3 cloves garlic, minced
1 tablespoon paprika
1 teaspoon dried oregano
1½ cups grainy or Dijon-style mustard
Extra-virgin olive oil in a spray bottle

1. Set up the grill for indirect grilling (see page 12 for charcoal or page 16 for gas) and preheat to medium-high. If using a charcoal grill, place a drip pan in the center.

2. French the racks of lamb following the instructions for prime rib on pages 33 and 34, or have your butcher do this for you. Trim the layer of fat off the meat of each rack of lamb as shown in Preparing the Meat, Step 1 on page 175. Generously season the lamb racks on all sides with salt and pepper.

3. Place the bread crumbs, parsley, rosemary, garlic, paprika, and oregano in a baking dish and stir to mix. Spread the mustard over the meaty parts of the racks of lamb, using a spatula. Dredge the racks in the crumb mixture to coat on all sides with crumbs. To be sure the meat is evenly covered, sprinkle some of the crumbs over the meat and pat them on with your fingers.

Spray the lamb on both sides with oil.

4. When ready to cook, place the racks of lamb in the center of the hot grate over the drip pan away from the heat and cover the grill. Grill the lamb until cooked to taste, 25 to 35 minutes, for medium-rare; when done it will register about 145°F on an instant-read thermometer.

5. Transfer the racks to a cutting board and let rest for 3 minutes, then cut each rack in half and serve.

ALSO GOOD FOR:
The French have a curious name for foods cooked in a mustard-crumb crust: à la diable (in the style of the devil). This is a great way to prepare a spatchcocked chicken (see page 220); it will take 40 minutes to 1 hour. A bone-in pork loin will take 1 to 1½ hours.

METHOD:
Direct grilling

COOKING TIME:
8 to 16 minutes

**ADVANCE
PREPARATION:**
30 minutes to
1 hour for
marinating
the meat

HOW TO GRILL LOIN LAMB CHOPS

The following lamb chops are Chinese in their inspiration—although I'm not sure this exact recipe has ever been served in China. The seasonings—Sichuan peppercorns, coriander, white pepper, cilantro, and sesame oil—are Chinese and so is the practice of cooking the lamb on the grill.

The seasoning technique is a three-stage process: first the lamb is rubbed with a dry rub, then with oil, finally with chopped fresh herbs and garlic. The spices adhere to the meat, the oil to the spices, and the herbs to the oil, so you get a more complex layering of flavors than if you'd simply combined the seasonings in a paste.

*Sichuan-Spiced Loin
Lamb Chops with
Chili-Mint Jelly*

SETTING UP THE GRILL

1 To set up a charcoal grill for direct grilling, first light the charcoal in a chimney starter (see page 9).

2 Using a garden hoe or other long-handled implement, rake the burning coals into an even layer.

3 To see if the grill is preheated to high, use the test on page 10.

PREPARING THE MEAT

1 Note how the T-bone of a lamb shoulder chop connects the loin and tenderloin. Trim some of the fat off the loin side of the chop.

2 Crush the Sichuan peppercorns in a mortar with a pestle or grind them in a spice mill or coffee grinder.

TIPS

■ Loin lamb chops are thicker and meatier than rib chops, so they take longer to cook. I like them bible thick (2 inches) and I cook them about 6 to 8 minutes per side for medium-rare.

■ Sichuan peppercorns aren't peppercorns at all but the small, dried, reddish berries of a plant that grows in China. Their clean, pungent, woodsy taste goes great with lamb.

TIP

■ Five-spice powder is a traditional Chinese seasoning commonly made from star anise, cinnamon, fennel seeds, cloves, white pepper, and/or Sichuan peppercorns. Buy it bottled at an Asian market or gourmet shop, or make your own, following the recipe on page 442.

3 After sprinkling the chops with the spice mix, brush them with sesame oil, then sprinkle them with a mixture of the cilantro and garlic. Pat the seasonings onto the meat with your fingertips.

ON THE GRILL: Grill the chops for 4 to 8 minutes per side for medium-rare, rotating them after 2 minutes to create a handsome crosshatch of grill marks. When grilling thick chops, like the ones pictured here, turn them to grill the edges, as I am doing.

SERVES 4

THE RECIPE

SICHUAN-SPICED LOIN LAMB CHOPS

8 loin lamb chops (2 inches thick;
    6 to 8 ounces each)
1 teaspoon ground Sichuan peppercorns
1 teaspoon ground coriander
1 teaspoon coarse salt
1 teaspoon white pepper

½ teaspoon Chinese five-spice powder
    (page 442)
2 tablespoons Asian (dark) sesame oil
3 cloves garlic, minced
¼ cup chopped fresh cilantro
Chili-Mint Jelly (recipe follows)

1. Trim the excess fat off the chops as shown in Preparing the Meat, Step 1 on page 179 (leave a little on), and arrange the chops in a baking dish. Combine the

Sichuan peppercorns, coriander, salt, pepper, and five-spice powder in a small bowl and stir to mix. Sprinkle this rub over the chops on both sides, patting it on with your fingertips.

2. Brush the chops on both sides with the sesame oil. Sprinkle with the garlic and cilantro, again patting it on with your fingertips. Let the lamb marinate in the refrigerator, covered, for 30 minutes to 1 hour.

3. Set up the grill for direct grilling (see page 10 for charcoal or page 16 for gas) and preheat to high.

4. When ready to cook, brush and oil the grill grate. Place the chops on the hot grate and grill until cooked to taste, 4 to 8 minutes per side for medium-rare (an instant-read meat thermometer will register about 145°F). Rotate the chops 90 degrees after 2 minutes to create an attractive crosshatch of grill marks. Turn the chops on their edges for 1 to 2 minutes to grill them.

5. Transfer the chops to plates or a platter and let rest for 3 minutes, then serve with the Chili-Mint Jelly.

Chili-Mint Jelly

MAKES ABOUT 1 CUP

¾ cup mint jelly
2 to 3 tablespoons sambal oelek
    (see Note)
1 tablespoon distilled white vinegar

Combine all the ingredients in a small nonreactive mixing bowl and whisk to mix.

Note: Sambal oelek, a fiery Indonesian chili paste, is available at Asian markets and many gourmet shops. You can substitute Vietnamese or Thai chili paste or even your favorite North American chili jelly or hot sauce.

ALSO GOOD FOR:
The three-level rubbing in this recipe lends itself well to grilling a wide variety of foods—steaks, pork chops, chicken breasts, seafood, tofu—you name it, I'll try it. Naturally it's delicious on rib lamb chops and lamb steaks (cut from the leg).

METHOD:
Direct grilling

COOKING TIME:
8 to 12 minutes

**ADVANCE
PREPARATION:**
4 to 12 hours for
draining the yogurt
(optional), plus
4 to 12 hours
for marinating
the meat

HOW TO GRILL RIB LAMB CHOPS TANDOORI STYLE

Tandoori is the barbecue of India and in the unlikely event you haven't tried it, you should run, not walk, to the nearest Indian restaurant. Born in the bakeries of northern India, tandoori takes its name from the tandoor, a charcoal-burning, urn-shaped clay pit or oven, the unique design of which raises the cooking temperature to 700° to 900°F. But the blistering heat is only part of what makes Indian tandoori unique. There's also the tandoori marinade, a pungent paste of yogurt, ginger, garlic, lemon juice, and as many as a dozen different spices. What results is some of the most delectable barbecue on the planet.

*Tandoori
Lamb
Chops*

SETTING UP THE GRILL

1 To set up a charcoal grill for direct grilling, first light the charcoal in a chimney starter (see page 9).

2 Using a garden hoe or other long-handled implement, rake the burning coals into an even layer.

3 To see if the grill is preheated to high, use the test on page 10.

DRAINING THE YOGURT

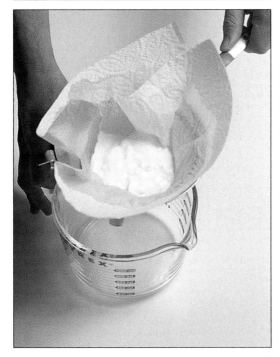

Use a yogurt strainer or metal strainer lined with a paper towel or cheesecloth. Refrigerate the yogurt during draining.

PREPARING THE MEAT

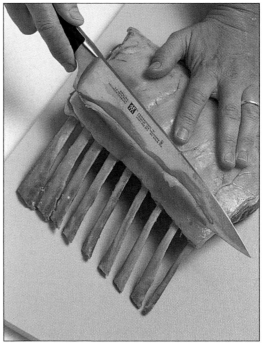

1 Trim off the thick sheath of fat covering each Frenched rack of lamb.

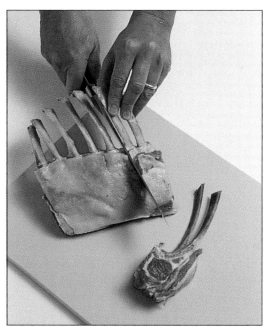

2 Cut each rack into five double chops, running the knife close along the bone of every second rib. The last chop will be double, but have only one rib bone.

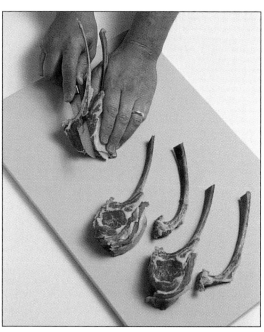

3 Remove one bone from each chop by running your knife on the inward side of one of the ribs. Cut through the meat, keeping the knife next to the bone. Cut through the cartilage attaching the rib and remove it.

4 Spoon the marinade over the lamb chops and let them marinate from 4 to 12 hours.

ON THE GRILL: Baste the grilled lamb chops with melted butter. Note how a sheet of aluminum foil has been placed under the ribs to prevent them from burning.

SERVES 4

TANDOORI LAMB CHOPS

1 quart whole-milk yogurt
2 racks of lamb (about 1½ pounds
    each), or 8 double-thick rib
    lamb chops, or 16 single
    rib lamb chops
½ teaspoon saffron threads
1 to 3 tablespoons warm water
6 cloves garlic, coarsely chopped
1 piece (2 inches) fresh ginger,
    peeled and coarsely
    chopped
3 tablespoons heavy cream
3 tablespoons lemon juice

1½ teaspoons coarse salt
1 teaspoon ground coriander
½ teaspoon ground cumin
½ teaspoon ground turmeric
½ teaspoon black pepper
½ teaspoon cayenne pepper
1 to 2 drops orange food coloring
    (optional)
3 tablespoons melted butter
Red onion rings, for serving
Lemon wedges
Cilantro leaves, for garnish

ALSO GOOD FOR:
*Almost anything you
can grill, you can
grill as tandoori—
especially chicken,
lobster, prawns, and
fish. Just marinate
it in the tandoori
marinade and cook
it over the hottest fire
you can muster.*

1. Drain the yogurt, if desired, in a yogurt strainer or strainer lined with a paper towel or cheesecloth and set over a bowl in the refrigerator for at least 4 hours or as long as overnight.

2. French the racks of lamb following the instructions for prime rib on pages 33 and 34, or have your butcher do this for you. Trim the layer of fat off the meat. Cut the racks of lamb into double-thick chops and trim, as shown in Steps 2 and 3 on the facing page. Arrange the lamb chops in a nonreactive baking dish.

3. Use your fingers to crumble the saffron into a small bowl. Add 1 tablespoon of warm water and let stand for 5 minutes. Grind the garlic and ginger to a fine paste in a minichopper or blender (you may need to add a spoonful or two of warm water). Place the soaked saffron, the garlic-and-ginger paste, the drained yogurt, and the cream, lemon juice, salt, coriander, cumin, turmeric, pepper, cayenne, and food coloring, if using, in a

nonreactive mixing bowl and stir to mix. Spoon the tandoori marinade over the lamb chops, turning the kebabs to coat both sides of the chops. Let the chops marinate, covered, in the refrigerator for at least 4 hours or as long as 12.

4. Set up the grill for direct grilling (see page 10 for charcoal or page 16 for gas) and preheat to high.

5. When ready to cook, place the chops on the hot grate and grill until cooked to taste, 4 to 6 minutes per side for medium (about 160°F on an instant-read meat thermometer; Indians tend to prefer their lamb well cooked), or to taste. Rotate the chops 90 degrees after 2 minutes to create an attractive crosshatch of grill marks. Baste the chops with melted butter after turning.

6. Transfer the chops to plates or a platter and let rest for 3 minutes, then serve with onion rings and lemon wedges and sprinkle with cilantro leaves.

METHOD:
Direct grilling

COOKING TIME:
8 to 12 minutes

**ADVANCE
PREPARATION:**
4 to 12 hours
for marinating
the meat

HOW TO GRILL SHISH KEBABS

Meat on a stick is the world's oldest form of grilling. Virtually every culture has a version: Peruvian *anticuchos,* Spanish *pinchos,* Indonesian saté, Japanese yakitori—the list is virtually endless. But none is quite so famous or beloved as the shish kebab of the Near East.

So what makes the perfect shish kebab? For starters, there's the meat. Lamb is the traditional kebab meat in central Asia and the Middle and Near East. A marinade is essential to flavor the meat. Slices of onion or bell pepper placed strategically between the cubes of meat add flavor, color, and visual excitement. A brisk fire sears the meat quickly, and a generous basting with olive oil or saffron butter keeps the kebab from drying out.

Saffron-Lemon Shish Kebabs with steamed rice

SETTING UP THE GRILL

1 To set up a charcoal grill for direct grilling, first light the charcoal in a chimney starter (see page 9).

2 Using a garden hoe or other long-handled implement, rake the burning coals into an even layer.

3 To see if the grill is preheated to high, use the test on page 10.

PREPARING THE KEBABS

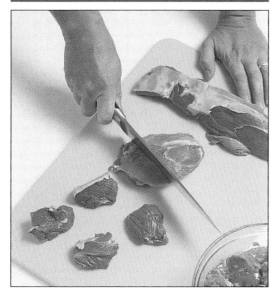

1 Cut the lamb into 1-inch pieces and place in the marinade.

2 Cut the onion into eight chunks: First, cut it from top to root into quarters; then cut each quarter in half crosswise. Cutting the flesh of the bell peppers off the core eliminates having to core and seed them. Cut the bell peppers into 1-inch squares. Using both red and green peppers will make the kebabs more attractive.

TIPS

■ Shish kebabs are generally made from one of two cuts of lamb: the leg or the shoulder. Leg of lamb has a more robust flavor and it's easier to cut, but it's also a little chewier. Shoulder contains more fat, so it tends to be moister and richer. I've used both and I like both. Whatever type of lamb you opt for, be sure to cut it into same-size cubes.

■ When buying saffron, look for threads rather than powder. They're less likely to have been adulterated.

TIP

■ Middle and Near Eastern grill jockeys use flat skewers for making shish kebabs. This keeps the lamb chunks from slipping when you turn the kebabs. Flat skewers are available at Middle Eastern markets (see Mail-Order Sources, page 481); or you can use two-pronged skewers (see page 475), which are available at grill shops and hardware stores.

ASSEMBLING THE SHISH KEBABS: Alternate bell pepper and onion pieces with the cubes of lamb.

BASTING THE KEBABS: Baste the kebabs with saffron butter at least once per side. The kebabs will be done after 2 to 3 minutes on each of their four sides.

SERVES 4

YOU'LL NEED:
4 long, flat or 8 two-pronged skewers

THE RECIPE

SAFFRON-LEMON SHISH KEBABS

FOR THE LAMB AND MARINADE:
1½ pounds boneless leg or shoulder of lamb
½ teaspoon saffron threads
1 tablespoon warm water
¼ cup lemon juice
2 strips lemon zest (½ by 1 inch each)
1 teaspoon coarse salt, plus more for
*   seasoning the kebabs*
½ teaspoon black pepper, plus more for
*   seasoning the kebabs*
1 medium onion, finely chopped
4 cloves garlic, finely chopped
½ cup extra-virgin olive oil

2 bay leaves

FOR THE VEGETABLES:
1 large onion
1 large red bell pepper
1 large green bell pepper

FOR THE BASTING MIXTURE:
¼ teaspoon saffron threads
1 tablespoon warm water
4 tablespoons (½ stick) butter, cut into
*   ½-inch slices*
2 tablespoons lemon juice
Black pepper

1. Rinse the lamb under cold running water and blot dry with paper towels. Cut the meat into 1-inch cubes. Don't trim away too much fat—it will help keep the kebabs moist while they grill.

2. Prepare the marinade: Use your fingers to crumble the saffron into a large nonreactive mixing bowl. Add the water and let stand for 5 minutes.

3. Add the lemon juice and zest, 1 teaspoon salt, ½ teaspoon pepper, the chopped onion, and garlic and stir until the salt is dissolved. Add the oil, bay leaves, and lamb cubes and toss to mix. Let the lamb marinate in this mixture, covered, in the refrigerator, for as few as 4 hours or as long as overnight—the longer you marinate, the richer the flavor will be. Stir the lamb every few hours to ensure even marinating.

4. Prepare the vegetables: Cut the onion into 8 chunks, as shown in Preparing the Kebabs, Step 2 on page 187. Break each chunk into individual layers. Cut the flesh of the bell peppers off the cores and then cut it into 1-inch cubes.

5. Set up the grill for direct grilling (see page 10 for charcoal or page 16 for gas) and preheat to high.

6. Prepare the basting mixture: Use your fingers to crumble the saffron into a small bowl. Add the water and let stand for 5 minutes. Place the butter and lemon juice in a small nonreactive saucepan. Add the saffron water and cook over medium-low heat until the butter is melted, about 3 minutes. Season with pepper to taste.

7. When ready to cook, thread one quarter of the lamb chunks onto each of the 4 skewers, placing pieces of onion and bell pepper between them. Place the kebabs on the hot grate and grill until cooked to taste, 2 to 3 minutes per side (8 to 12 minutes in all) for medium-rare. Generously season the kebabs with salt and pepper as they grill, and baste them with the saffron butter mixture.

8. Transfer the kebabs to a platter. Never try to eat the lamb and vegetables directly off a skewer, or you might burn your lips. Rather, slide them off the skewer onto your plate.

Grilled Pita Bread

SERVES 4

4 pita breads
2 to 3 tablespoons olive oil

1. Set up the grill for direct grilling (see page 10 for charcoal or page 16 for gas) and preheat to high. Lightly brush the pita breads on both sides with oil and cut into wedges.

2. When ready to cook, place the pita wedges on the hot grate and grill until lightly browned on both sides, 1 to 3 minutes per side. Transfer to a bread basket and serve at once.

VARIATIONS:
Vary the marinade, substituting yogurt for the olive oil, for example, or use the lemongrass marinade from the Chicken Satés, Step 2 on page 257.

Many Turkish grill jockeys group the onions and peppers each on their own skewers. The advantage of this system is that, because each vegetable—and the lamb—cooks at a different rate, you get to grill each to the perfect degree of doneness.

METHOD:
Direct grilling

COOKING TIME:
8 to 12 minutes

ADVANCE
PREPARATION:
1 hour for chilling
the seasoned lamb

HOW TO MAKE GROUND LAMB KEBABS

Ground lamb kebabs are the sausages of the Moslem and Hindu worlds and the sheer multiplicity of their names—*kofta* in Lebanon, *kubideh* in Iran, *lyulya* in Azerbaijan, *seekh kebab* in India, *saté buntel* in Indonesia—attests to their global popularity. By molding ground lamb on a flat metal skewer, you get the pleasure of a grilled sausage without the fuss of stuffing a sausage casing. This allows the fat to melt out and the meat to sizzle and smoke.

Ground lamb kebabs run from simple (flavored with chopped onion and parsley) to elaborate (enriched with ground split peas and aromatic root vegetables). Here's how they do it in India.

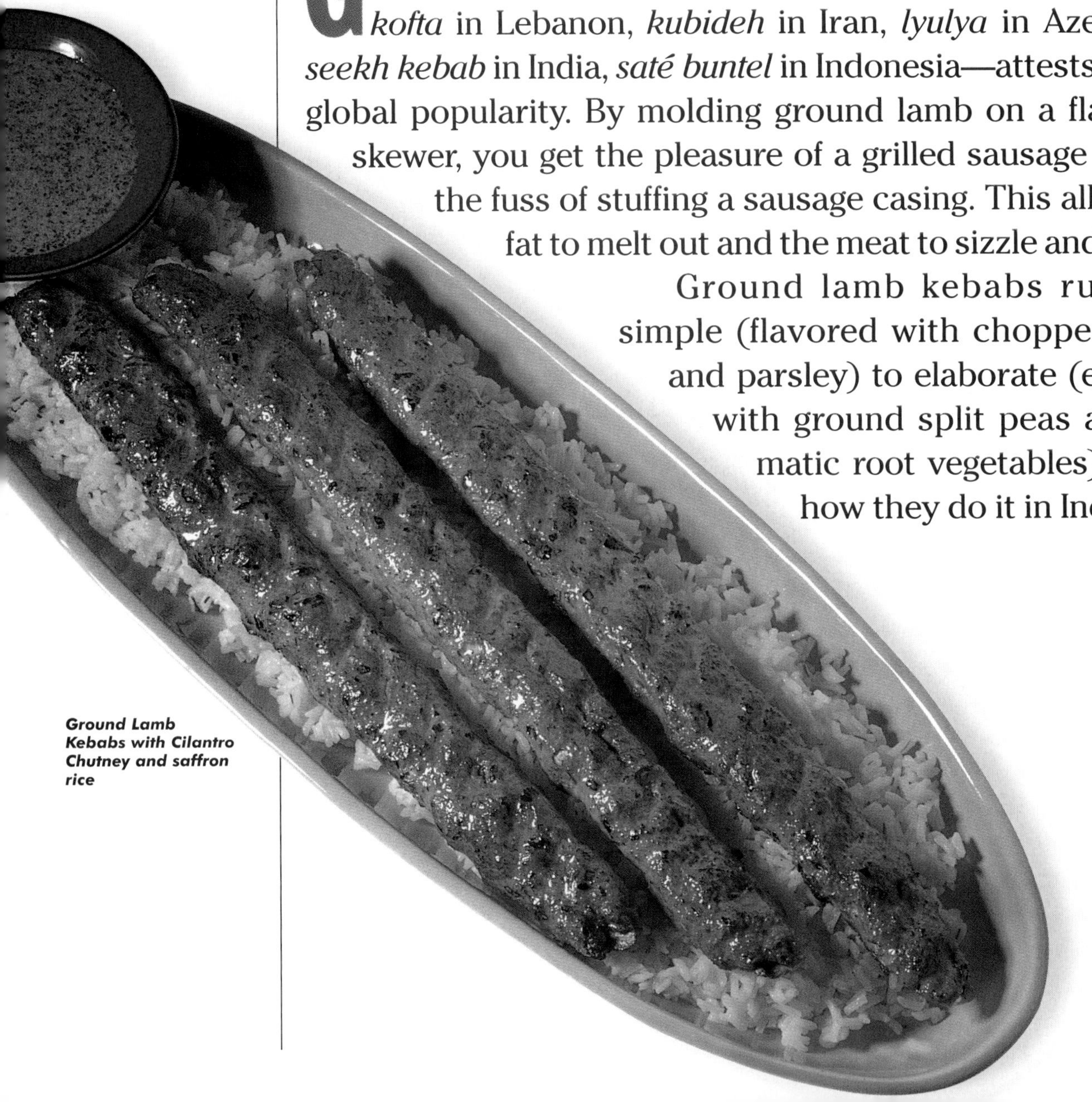

Ground Lamb Kebabs with Cilantro Chutney and saffron rice

SETTING UP THE GRILL

1 To set up a charcoal grill for direct grilling, first light the charcoal in a chimney starter (see page 9).

2 Using a garden hoe or other long-handled implement, rake the burning coals into an even layer.

3 To see if the grill is preheated to high, use the test on page 10.

PREPARING THE MEAT

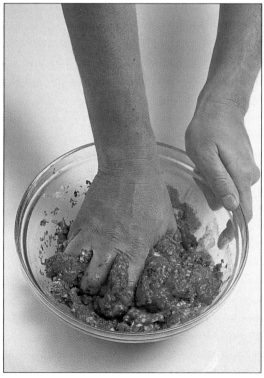

1 The best way to mix the ground lamb and seasonings is with your fingers.

2 To taste the mixture for seasoning, grill a small portion on the end of a skewer first.

TIPS

■ The only remotely challenging part about making ground lamb kebabs is molding the meat on the skewers. It helps to have the meat cold and to lightly wet your hand in cold water before molding the kebabs.

■ Because of the fragility of these kebabs, they're usually cooked over the fire on a grill without a grate. Suspending them from bricks serves the same purpose. You can grill the kebabs directly on the grate, just be sure it's very well brushed and oiled.

MOLDING THE KEBABS

1 Scoop up a handful of ground lamb and wrap it around the skewer.

2 Squeeze the meat down the skewer with your hand to form a long tube. Suspend the finished kebabs between two aluminum-foil-wrapped bricks to keep the ground lamb from flattening.

3 One way to put the signature "ripple" on the kebab is to scissor the meat with your fingers. Wet your hand in cold water to keep the meat from sticking.

4 If you wish to make the kebabs ahead of time, arrange them on a rimmed baking sheet lined with plastic wrap, cover them, and refrigerate until ready to cook.

ON THE GRILL: Place two foil-wrapped bricks on the grill so that you can suspend the kebabs between them. Grilling the kebabs this way keeps the meat above the grate. They'll be done after 4 to 6 minutes per side. Wear a grill mitt when turning the kebabs to keep from burning your fingers.

UNSKEWERING THE KEBAB

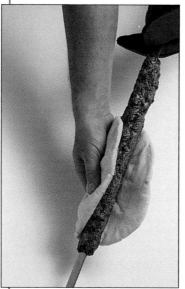

Wrap a pita bread around the grilled kebab and gently pull it toward you. Now, use the pita to push the meat away from you. It will slip off the skewer easily.

THE RECIPE

GROUND LAMB KEBABS

SERVES 4

YOU'LL NEED:
4 wide
(at least ⅜-inch),
flat metal
skewers; 2 flat,
aluminum-foil-
wrapped bricks

1½ pounds ground lamb
3 tablespoons minced fresh cilantro
2 scallions, trimmed and minced
1 to 2 jalapeño peppers, seeded
   and minced
2 teaspoons peeled, minced
   fresh ginger
2 cloves garlic, minced
½ teaspoon ground coriander
½ teaspoon ground cumin
½ teaspoon black pepper, or more to taste

¼ teaspoon ground nutmeg
Coarse salt, to taste
4 pita breads
1 small red onion or large shallot,
   very thinly sliced, for serving
   (optional)
Lemon wedges, for serving
   (optional)
Cilantro Chutney (page 460),
   for serving

VARIATIONS:

Using the procedure and rough proportions in Ground Lamb Kebabs, you can make myriad different versions. Here are some classic combinations. Start with ground meat and salt and pepper:

Kofta (Middle Eastern): To the lamb, add onion, chopped fresh parsley and mint, and ground cinnamon.

Kubideh kebabs (Iranian): Replace half the lamb with ground beef. Add chopped onion and a pinch of baking soda.

Kufteh (Bulgarian): Substitute ground veal and pork for the lamb. Flavor with chopped onion, fresh parsley, and cumin.

Lula (Afghan): To the lamb, add chopped onion, hot chiles, cumin, turmeric, and fresh cilantro and dill.

Mititei (Romanian): Replace half the ground lamb with beef. Add chopped onion and garlic, paprika, dried marjoram, caraway seeds, and ground allspice.

1. Combine the ground lamb, cilantro, scallions, jalapeño, ginger, garlic, coriander, cumin, pepper, nutmeg, and salt in a large mixing bowl and knead with your fingers to mix. Refrigerate the ground lamb mixture, covered, for 1 hour.

2. Set up the grill for direct grilling (see page 10 for charcoal or page 16 for gas) and preheat to high.

3. Grill a little portion of the meat mixture (as shown in Step 2, on page 191) to test for seasoning, adding salt and pepper if necessary.

4. Lightly wet your hand. Mold one quarter of the lamb mixture onto each of 4 skewers as shown in Steps 1 through 4 on page 192. Each tube will be 12 to 14 inches long. Suspend the finished kebabs between 2 foil-wrapped bricks until ready to grill or arrange on a rimmed baking sheet lined with plastic wrap.

5. When ready to cook, arrange the 2 aluminum-foil-wrapped bricks on the hot grill grate, as shown on page 193. Suspend the kebabs between the bricks and grill until sizzling and golden brown, 4 to 6 minutes per side. The meat will be nicely browned and firm to the touch. If you don't have bricks and you wish to grill directly on the grate, scrub the grate well with a wire brush and generously oil before placing the kebabs on it.

6. Unskewer the kebabs, using pita bread as shown on page 193. Serve with the pita bread, chutney, sliced onion, and lemon wedges, if desired.

METHOD:
Rotisserie grilling

COOKING TIME:
3 to 3½ hours

**ADVANCE
PREPARATION:**
4 to 12 hours
for marinating
the meat
(optional); 1 hour
for attaching lamb
to the turnspit

HOW TO GRILL A WHOLE LAMB

S pit-roasted lamb is found throughout the Mediterranean, but for my money, no one does it better than the Greeks. They've certainly had practice. Greeks have been roasting lamb this way since the time of Homer.

Spit-roasted lamb makes a terrific centerpiece to a cookout. It's not hard to do in your backyard, and few sights (or aromas or tastes) have more wow power. But where do you find a rotisserie large enough to handle the lamb? I go to my local party rental supply house. The technique here may seem complicated, but really it's just a series of simple steps. Remember, Greeks were spit roasting lamb long before the advent of high-tech grills and barbecue pits— for that matter, before there was electricity for the rotisserie or gas or even charcoal!

*Spit-Roasted Lamb with
Greek salad*

PREPARING THE LAMB

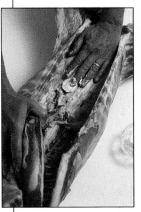

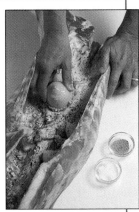

1 Smear the inside cavity of the lamb with butter.

2 Season the inside of the cavity with salt, pepper, and oregano.

3 Squeeze lemon juice in the cavity, catching any seeds with your fingers.

4 Rub the inside of the cavity with the squeezed lemon. Leave the lemon rinds in the cavity.

TIPS

■ Finding a whole lamb may be a bit of a challenge. I order mine by mail from Jamison Farm in Pennsylvania (see page 482). Alternatively, check with a Greek, Italian, or Middle Eastern market or specialty butcher shop and order it well ahead. Easter time is the easiest time to find one. A whole lamb probably won't fit in your refrigerator overnight, so try to time the delivery for the day of your cookout. Or you can store it in a large cooler filled with ice.

■ If you have a refrigerator large enough to hold the lamb, season and butter the chest cavity the day before you cook it. The meat will be even more flavorful.

SPITTING THE LAMB

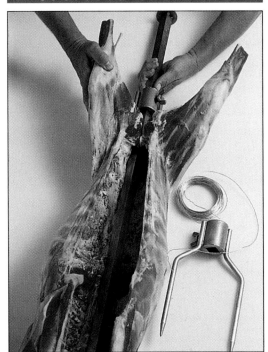

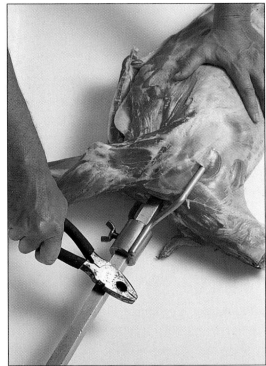

1 Run the turnspit through the lamb, starting from the rear.

2 After inserting the two-pronged skewers at each end, use your pliers to tap them snugly in place.

3 Use a piece of wire about 7 inches long to fashion a U-shape that is 1 inch wide with sides about 3 inches long. Push it through the lamb so the ends of the wire straddle both sides of the backbone and the turnspit.

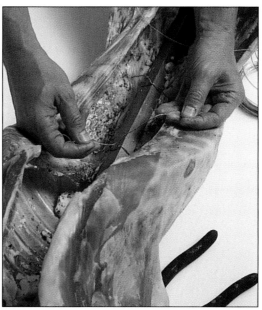

4 Twist the ends of the wire to fasten the lamb to the turnspit, tightening the wire with pliers.

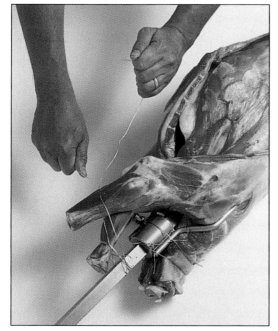

5 Wire first the hind legs and then the forelegs (seen here) to the spit.

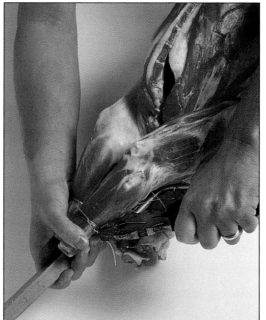

6 Twist the wire with pliers to firmly attach the legs.

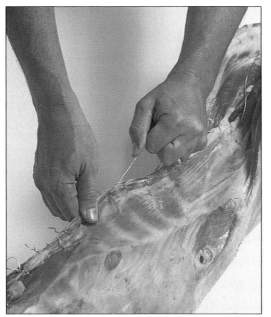

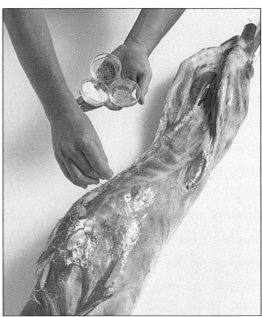

7 Starting at the neck end of the chest cavity, wire the cavity shut. As you get closer to the rear legs, you can use one long piece of wire to "sew" the cavity shut.

8 Once the lamb is on the spit, brush the outside all over with ¼ cup olive oil and season with salt, pepper, and oregano.

ON THE GRILL

1 Set up the grill: Light the charcoal, and when it is hot, rake it into two mounds, one below where the shoulders of the lamb will rotate, one below where the thighs will rotate.

2 Attach the spitted lamb to the rotisserie mechanism.

3 When the lamb starts to brown, after about 30 minutes, start basting it.

4 After 2 hours, rake a pile of coals under the belly of the lamb, so it cooks through, too.

FINISHING TOUCHES

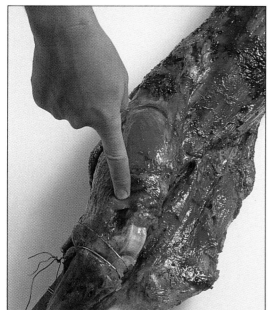

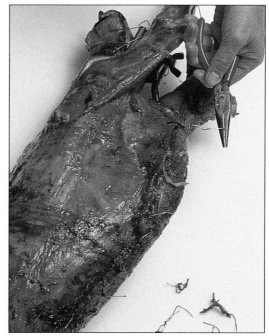

1 The lamb is cooked when the exterior is dark brown and crackling crisp and the meat starts to split.

2 Be sure to remove *all* the wire before serving the lamb. Snip it with wire cutters and use pliers to pull the pieces out.

YOU'LL NEED:
Commercial rotisserie; 40 to 50 pounds of charcoal; single strand picture wire (18 or 19 gauge); wire cutter; pliers; 3-foot-square piece of plywood

T H E   R E C I P E

SPIT-ROASTED LAMB

4 tablespoons (½ stick) butter,
   at room temperature
1 whole lamb, gutted and dressed
   (about 25 pounds)
3 to 4 tablespoons coarse salt
3 to 4 tablespoons white pepper

3 to 4 tablespoons dried oregano
1 lemon, cut in half
2¼ cups olive oil (preferably Greek)
½ cup lemon juice
½ cup dry white wine
6 cloves garlic, minced

1. Smear the butter in the chest cavity of the lamb. Sprinkle 1 tablespoon each of the salt, pepper, and oregano into the cavity. Squeeze the lemon into the cavity, spreading the juice with your fingers. Place the used lemon rinds in the cavity. If you have a very large refrigerator or cooler, wrap the lamb in plastic wrap and marinate for at least 4 hours and as long as 12. If not, continue with the recipe.

2. About 5 hours before you plan to serve the lamb, wire it to the turnspit and wire the cavity shut following Steps 1 through 7 on pages 196 through 198.

3. About 4 hours before you plan to serve the lamb, light 1 bag (20 pounds) of charcoal in the firebox of the rotisserie. For better heat reflection, line the firebox with aluminum foil, shiny-side up, before adding the charcoal. When the coals are covered with a thin layer of gray ash, rake them out so that there are high piles where the lamb's shoulders and legs will be and no coals in the center (this ensures even cooking). Rub the surface of the lamb with ¼ cup oil. Season the surface of the lamb with 1 to 2 tablespoons salt, pepper, and oregano. Combine the remaining 2 cups oil, the lemon juice, wine, garlic, and 1 tablespoon each of salt, pepper, and oregano in a large nonreactive bowl and whisk to mix.

4. When ready to cook, attach the spitted lamb to the rotisserie mechanism (it should be 2 to 2½ feet above the coals). You'll need some help doing this. Roast it without basting for 30 minutes. The spit should be turning slowly but continuously. Stir the basting mixture and baste the lamb all over. Continue basting every 30 minutes. Replenish the coals as needed, adding roughly 5 pounds of fresh charcoal per side after 1 hour. After 2 hours are up, add 5 pounds of charcoal per side and wait 15 minutes for it to light, then rake a pile of coals into the center of the grill to cook the center of the lamb. As the lamb fat melts, it may cause flare-ups. Snuff these out by flattening the coals with a metal spatula.

5. Rotisserie grill the lamb for 3 to 3½ hours. The lamb is done when the exterior is dark brown and the meat is deeply cracked and tender enough to pull off with a fork. Insert an instant-read meat thermometer into a thick part of the meat but not touching the bone; the internal temperature should be about 170°F. Greeks like their lamb well-done.

6. Wrap a 3-foot-square piece of plywood in heavy-duty aluminum foil. Transfer the lamb to the wrapped plywood. Let rest for 15 minutes, then remove from the spit, making sure to remove *all* the pieces of wire. Cut or pull the meat into chunks for serving.

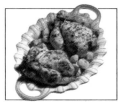

METHOD:
Indirect grilling

COOKING TIME:
1¼ to 1½ hours

HOW TO INDIRECT GRILL A WHOLE CHICKEN

There are at least three reasons you should roast a chicken on the grill, not in your oven. First, you can add a smoke flavor. Second, it's a lot less messy. And third, the meat will remain more succulent—in short, your chicken will just plain taste better. In fact, roast chicken is so essential to human happiness that I've devoted four separate techniques to grilling it whole. First comes the easiest: indirect grilling.

Lemon-Garlic Chicken with fingerling potatoes

SETTING UP THE GRILL

1 To set up a charcoal grill for indirect grilling, first light the charcoal in a chimney starter (see page 9).

2 Form two heat zones by raking the coals into two piles at opposite sides of the grill, using a long-handled implement, like a garden hoe.

3 If your grill has side baskets, divide the coals evenly between them. Note the drip pan in the center of the grill.

PREPARING THE CHICKEN

1 Remove the lumps of fat in the body and neck cavities of the chicken.

2 Rub the outside of the chicken all over with grilled lemon.

3 Rub the outside of the chicken all over with grilled garlic.

4 Place some seasoning plus a half lemon and a half garlic head in the body cavity of the chicken.

TIPS

■ Smoking the chicken is optional. If you do use smoke, go easy on it (don't soak the chips) so you can appreciate the delicate lemon herb flavor of the chicken.

■ Anytime you indirect grill over charcoal you'll need to place a drip pan under the bird. Most gas grills have a drip pan built in.

TRUSSING POULTRY

Trussing a chicken or any other bird may seem like a lot of work; however, once you get the hang of it, it takes maybe 3 minutes and there are compelling reasons for mastering this technique. A trussed bird looks better. And, it roasts more evenly. The method shown here can be used for turkey, duck, and game hen as well. Remember, remove the trussing string before serving.

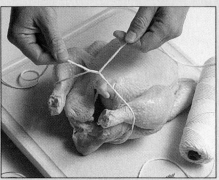

1. To truss the chicken, bring a piece of string (it should be about 30 inches long) under the tail end of the chicken and over the ends of the drumsticks and tie it tight.

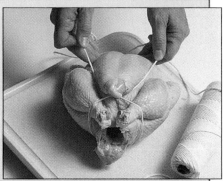

2. Hook the string under the tip of the breastbone and pull the ends up the front of the chicken between the legs and the body, then along the breast toward the neck. This will bring the ends of the drumsticks together.

3. Turn the chicken onto its breast. Draw the string over the "elbow" joints of the wings to the back of the chicken. Note how the wing tips have been folded under.

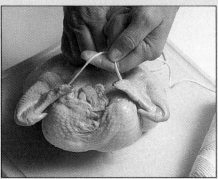

4. Cross one string under the other at the back of the chicken.

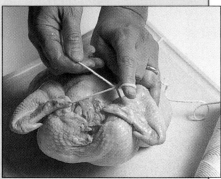

5. I like to make a slip knot here but you can simply make an ordinary tight knot. To make a slip knot, extend your left index finger and loop the right string over it (lefties reverse the hands). Roll your finger under and draw a piece of string through the loop to make a loose knot.

6. If making a slip knot, continue by bringing the right end of the string (now on the left) through the loop and pull gently.

7. Tuck any excess neck skin under the string. Pull the ends of the string tight and tie the skin in place.

8. Turn the chicken breast side up and tuck the "pope's nose" (the tail end) into the body cavity. The chicken is now trussed.

TESTING FOR DONENESS

Use an instant-read meat thermometer to test for doneness. Insert it into the thickest part of a thigh but not touching the bone. The internal temperature should be about 180°F.

Alternatively, insert a metal skewer into the thickest part of a thigh. It should be very hot to the touch when it comes out.

Or you can try wiggling a drumstick. When the chicken is fully cooked, the drumstick will move freely in the joint.

THE RECIPE

LEMON-GARLIC CHICKEN

1 chicken (3 ½ to 4 pounds)
Coarse salt and black pepper
1 tablespoon chopped fresh rosemary,
    plus 2 whole fresh sprigs

1 lemon, cut in half and seeded, direct grilled
    (optional; see Note)
1 head garlic, cut in half, direct grilled
    (optional; see Note)

1. Remove the packet of giblets from the body cavity of the chicken and set aside for another use. Remove and discard the fat just inside the body and neck cavities. Rinse the chicken, inside and out, under cold running water and then drain and blot dry, inside and out, with paper towels. Generously season the inside of the chicken with salt, pepper, and some of the chopped rosemary. Rub the outside with the cut lemon and garlic. Be sure to lift up the flap of skin over the neck cavity and rub the exposed flesh with the lemon and garlic. Place half of the garlic and lemon in the body cavity of the chicken. Truss the chicken as shown in Steps 1 through 8 on the facing page. Generously season the outside of the bird all over with salt, pepper, and the remaining chopped rosemary. Insert a rosemary sprig between each leg and the breast.

2. Set up the grill for indirect grilling (see page 12 for charcoal or page 16 for gas) and preheat to medium. If using a charcoal

SERVES 2 TO 4

YOU'LL NEED:
Butcher's string;
2 cups wood chips
(optional),
unsoaked

TIP

■ To boost the fire flavor, I like to grill the garlic and lemon before using them to rub and stuff the chicken. You can certainly skip this step if you're in a hurry.

VARIATIONS:
*Use this basic method
for grilling quail,
game hens, and duck.
Quail will take 30 to
40 minutes; game
hens, 40 minutes to
1 hour; and duck,
2 to 2½ hours.*

grill, place a drip pan in the center. If using a gas grill, place all the wood chips, if desired, in the smoker box or in a smoker pouch (see page 17) and preheat on high until you see smoke, then reduce the heat to medium.

3. When ready to cook, if using a charcoal grill, toss all the wood chips on the coals, if desired. Place the trussed chicken, breast-side up, in the center of the hot grate over the drip pan and away from the heat, and cover the grill. Grill the chicken until the skin is a deep golden brown and the meat is cooked through, 1¼ to 1½ hours (see page 205 for how to test for doneness).

If using a charcoal grill, you'll need to add 12 fresh coals per side after 1 hour.

4. Transfer the chicken to a platter and let rest for 5 minutes, then untruss. Quarter or carve the chicken and serve at once.

Note: It will take 4 to 6 minutes to get grill marks on the cut side of the lemon and garlic (note that neither will be cooked through, but the flavor will be enhanced); rotate each 45 degrees after 2 minutes.

HOW TO GRILL A WHOLE CHICKEN II

METHOD:
Indirect grilling

COOKING TIME:
1¼ to 1½ hours

If you've ever had a problem with your chicken being dry, this singular technique is for you. I'm talking about stuffing a chicken (or other bird) under the skin before grilling. You'll turn out some of the juiciest chicken you've ever tasted in the process. So what do you put under the skin of a chicken? How about butter creamed with fire-roasted garlic and freshly grated Parmesan cheese. As the chicken roasts, the herb butter sizzles the skin from the inside out, soaking and perfuming the meat.

Chicken Stuffed with
Flavored Butter

SETTING UP THE GRILL

1 To set up a charcoal grill for indirect grilling, first light the charcoal in a chimney starter (see page 9).

2 Form two heat zones by raking the coals into two piles at opposite sides of the grill, using a long-handled implement, like a garden hoe.

3 If your grill has side baskets, divide the coals evenly between them. Note the drip pan in the center of the grill.

PREPARING THE CHICKEN

1 To stuff a chicken under the skin, starting at the top of the neck cavity, tunnel your finger under the skin. Gently loosen the skin from the meat, taking care not to tear it.

2 Worm your whole hand under the skin, loosening it from the breast meat, then the thighs, and even the drumsticks.

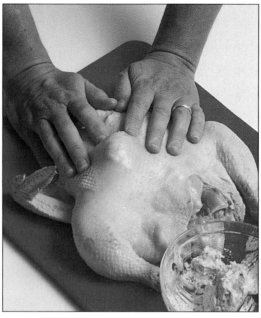

3 Spoon the flavored butter under the skin.

4 Spread the butter all over the chicken meat by rubbing the skin with your fingers. Truss the chicken as shown in Steps 1 through 8 on page 204.

TESTING FOR DONENESS

Use an instant-read meat thermometer. Insert it into the thickest part of a thigh but not so that it touches the bone. The internal temperature should be about 180°F.

You can also test for doneness by wiggling a drumstick. It should move easily in the joint.

TIPS

■ The finished dish will only be as good as the raw materials. Use real butter (not margarine) and freshly grated Parmigiano-Reggiano cheese. This latter is the original Parmesan, imported from the Parma region in northern Italy. It's expensive, but you won't find a tastier grating cheese anywhere.

■ I like to keep the focus on the roasted garlic and cheese in the butter, so I don't generally bother flavoring the chicken with wood smoke. You can if you want to.

SERVES 2 TO 4

YOU'LL NEED:
Butcher's string

VARIATIONS:
*There's no limit to the
possible flavorings
you can use in the
stuffing: any type of
herb or spice, a dif-
ferent type of cheese
(Roquefort is amaz-
ing), or other flavor-
ings, such as ground
roasted walnuts.*

T H E   R E C I P E

CHICKEN STUFFED WITH FLAVORED BUTTER

1 chicken (3½ to 4 pounds)

Roasted Garlic Butter (page 451)

1. Remove the packet of giblets from the body cavity of the chicken and set aside for another use. Remove and discard the fat just inside the body and neck cavities. Rinse the chicken, inside and out, under cold running water and then drain and blot dry, inside and out, with paper towels. Loosen the skin from the chicken and put the flavored butter between the skin and the meat as shown in Steps 1 through 4 on pages 208 and 209. Truss the chicken as shown in Steps 1 through 8 on page 204.

2. Set up the grill for indirect grilling (see page 12 for charcoal or page 16 for gas) and preheat to medium. If using a charcoal grill, place a drip pan in the center. When ready to cook, place the chicken, breast-side up, in the center of the hot grill grate over the drip pan and away from the heat, and cover the grill. Grill the chicken until the skin is a deep golden brown and the meat is cooked through, 1¼ to 1½ hours (see page 209 for how to test for doneness). If using a charcoal grill, you'll need to add 12 fresh coals per side after 1 hour.

3. Transfer the chicken to a platter, let rest for 5 minutes, then untruss. Quarter or carve the chicken and serve at once.

HOW TO ROTISSERIE GRILL A WHOLE CHICKEN

METHOD:
Rotisserie grilling

COOKING TIME:
1¼ to 1½ hours

T he truth is that there are few better ways to cook chicken than on a rotisserie. All types of poultry benefit from the slow, gentle rotation next to, not over, the fire—an action that bastes the meat internally and externally, even as it melts out the fat. If you have a rotisserie, dust off the cobwebs, and if you don't, by all means, get yourself to the nearest barbecue store and buy one.

Sesame Five-Spice Rotisserie Chicken with grilled bok choy

SETTING UP THE GRILL

1 To set up a rotisserie on a charcoal grill, first light the charcoal in a chimney starter (see page 9).

2 Position the rotisserie ring on the grill.

3 Mound the coals on one side of the grill, parallel to where the spit will be, and place drip pans in front of them.

PREPARING THE CHICKEN

1 Once you've removed the fat, sprinkle some of the spices in the cavity of the chicken. Stand the chicken upright in a bowl so you can add the spices without having to hold the bird.

2 Place pieces of ginger, scallion, and garlic in the cavity of the bird and truss the chicken (see Steps 1 through 8, page 204).

TIPS

■ Each grill has a different configuration for rotisserie grilling. Follow the basic guidelines on page 22 of this book or the manufacturer's instructions.

■ Trussing the chicken will give it an attractive appearance and will help it cook more evenly.

3 Brush the outside of the chicken with sesame oil and sprinkle with remaining spices.

4 Skewer the chicken on the turnspit from tail to neck (remember to place the tail end prong on the spit first).

ON THE GRILL

5 Slide the neck end prongs onto the spit and make sure the chicken is held snugly in place. Tighten the screw, gripping it between the tines of a fork for leverage.

1 Insert the pointed end of the spit into the rotisserie motor socket.

2 If your rotisserie spit has a counterweight, position it so that it counterbalances the chicken.

3 The chicken is now ready for grilling on the rotisserie (note the wood chips in the smoker box of this gas grill rotisserie). It should be deliciously done in 1¼ to 1½ hours.

SERVES 2 TO 4

YOU'LL NEED:
Rotisserie;
butcher's string;
2 cups wood chips
or wood chunks
(optional;
preferably
hickory or oak),
unsoaked

THE RECIPE

SESAME FIVE-SPICE ROTISSERIE CHICKEN

1 chicken (3½ to 4 pounds)
2 teaspoons coarse salt
2 teaspoons Chinese five-spice powder (page 442)
2 teaspoons turbinado or granulated sugar
½ teaspoon black pepper
2 slices fresh ginger (each ¼ inch thick), peeled and flattened with the side of a cleaver

2 cloves garlic, peeled and flattened with the side of a cleaver
2 scallions, trimmed, white part flattened with the side of a cleaver, green part finely chopped
1 tablespoon Asian sesame oil

1. Set up the grill for rotisserie grilling following the instructions on page 22 and preheat to medium-high. If using a char-

coal grill, place a large drip pan in the center. If using a gas grill, place all the wood chips or chunks, if desired, in the smoker box or in a smoker pouch (see page 17) and preheat on high until you see smoke, then reduce the heat to medium-high.

2. Remove the packet of giblets from the body cavity of the chicken and set aside for another use. Remove and discard the fat just inside the body and neck cavities. Rinse the chicken, inside and out, under cold running water and then drain and blot dry, inside and out, with paper towels. Combine the salt, five-spice powder, sugar, and pepper and sprinkle half of this mixture in the body and neck cavities of the chicken. Rub the outside of the bird with 1 slice of ginger and 1 clove of garlic. Be sure to lift up the flap of skin over the neck cavity and rub the exposed flesh with ginger and garlic. Place all the ginger and garlic and the scallion whites in the bird's body and neck cavities. Truss the chicken as shown in Steps 1 through 8 on page 204. Brush the outside of the chicken with the sesame oil and sprinkle the remaining rub over it. Secure the chicken on the spit as shown in Steps 4 and 5 on page 213.

3. If using a charcoal grill, toss all the wood chips on the coals, if desired. Attach the spit to the rotisserie mechanism as shown in Steps 1 and 2 on pages 213 and 214, and turn on the motor. Grill the chicken until the skin is a deep golden brown and the meat is cooked through, 1¼ to 1½ hours (see page 205 for how to test for doneness). If using a charcoal grill, you'll need to add 18 fresh coals after 1 hour.

4. Transfer the chicken to a platter, let rest for 5 minutes, then untruss. Garnish the whole chicken with the chopped scallion greens before quartering or carving. Serve at once.

ALSO GOOD FOR:
This recipe is great for quail, game hen, squab, and duck. Quail will take 30 to 40 minutes; game hens and squabs, 40 minutes to 1 hour; and duck, 1½ to 2 hours.

METHOD:
Indirect grilling

COOKING TIME:
1¼ to 1½ hours

HOW TO GRILL CHICKEN ON A BEER CAN

"Bizarre" and "outrageous" aren't necessarily words you expect to find in a cookbook. But how else would you describe roasting a chicken in a vertical position over an open beer can? I first encountered the method at the Memphis in May Barbecue Festival and described it in *The Barbecue! Bible*. Since then, I've prepared beer-can chicken hundreds of times, and each time this astounding technique produces an exquisite bird. The fact is, the upright position helps drain off the fat and crisp the skin, while the beer in the can steams and flavors the bird from the inside. Needless to say, the sight of a roasted chicken standing erect on an upright can of beer will astound your guests.

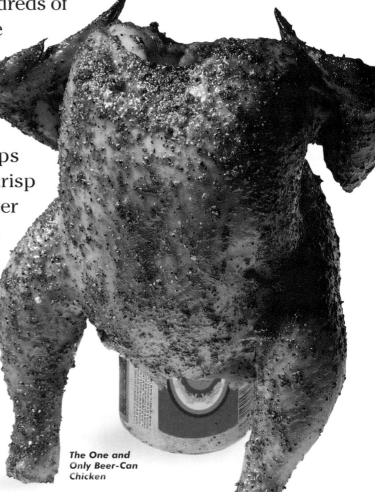

The One and Only Beer-Can Chicken

SETTING UP THE GRILL

1 To set up a charcoal grill for indirect grilling, first light the charcoal in a chimney starter (see page 9).

2 Form two heat zones by raking the coals into two piles at opposite sides of the grill, using a long-handled implement, like a garden hoe.

3 If your grill has side baskets, divide the coals evenly between them. Note the drip pan in the center of the grill.

TIPS

■ It's imperative to use an *open* can half drained of its beer (a sealed can will explode). Use the beer you pour out for soaking the wood chips (or you could drink it).

■ The recipe calls for the Basic Barbecue Rub on page 441, but you can use any rub you fancy to season the chicken.

PREPARING THE CHICKEN

1 Sprinkle the chicken inside and out with some of the rub.

2 Pop the top of the beer can and poke a few extra holes in it, using a church key-type can opener.

3 After pouring off half of the beer, sprinkle the remaining rub into the can.

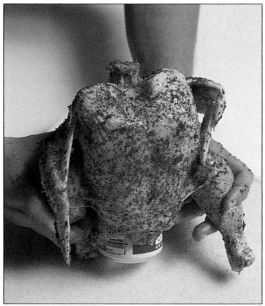

4 Holding the chicken with the opening of the body cavity at the bottom, lower it onto the beer can so the can fits into the cavity.

5 Pull the legs forward to form a sort of tripod so the bird stands upright (the rear leg of the tripod is the beer can).

■ Of course, you can cook beer-can chicken without smoke, but to me it just doesn't taste quite right. My favorite wood for smoking the bird is apple.

■ I always display the chicken upright on its beer can before serving. (Hey, I like theatrics as much as the next guy.) But I always remove the beer can (hold the bottom with tongs with one hand and lift the bird off it with tongs with the other) before serving the chicken, lest anyone get burned by hot beer.

6 Tuck the wing tips behind the chicken's back (obviously this is one chicken that needs no trussing).

ON THE GRILL: Here's a beer-can chicken smoking on a two-burner gas grill away from the heat. Note the chips smoking at the rear. The chicken will be ready to eat in 1¼ to 1½ hours.

THE ONE AND ONLY BEER-CAN CHICKEN

1 can (12 ounces) beer
1 chicken (3½ to 4 pounds)

2 tablespoons Basic Barbecue Rub (page 441)
or your favorite commercial rub

1. Pop the tab off the beer can. Using a church key-style can opener, make a few more holes in the top of the can. Pour out half the beer into the soaking water of the wood chips. Set the can of beer aside.

2. Set up the grill for indirect grilling (see page 12 for charcoal or page 16 for gas) and preheat to medium. If using a charcoal grill, place a large drip pan in the center. If using a gas grill, place all the wood chips or chunks in the smoker box or in a smoker pouch (see page 17) and preheat on high until you see smoke, then reduce the heat to medium.

3. Remove the packet of giblets from the body cavity of the chicken and set aside for another use. Remove and discard the fat just inside the body and neck cavities. Rinse the chicken, inside and out, under cold running water and then drain and blot dry, inside and out, with paper towels. Sprinkle 2 teaspoons of the rub inside the body and neck cavities of the chicken. Rub the bird all over on the outside with 2 teaspoons of the rub. If you have the patience, you can put some of the rub under the skin (see pages 208 and 209).

4. Spoon the remaining 2 teaspoons of rub through the holes into the beer in the can. Don't worry if it foams up: This is normal. Insert the beer can into the body cavity of the chicken and spread out the legs to form a sort of tripod, as shown in Steps 4 and 5 on the facing page. Tuck the wing tips behind the chicken's back.

5. When ready to cook, if using a charcoal grill, toss all the wood chips on the coals. Stand the chicken up in the center of the hot grate, over the drip pan and away from the heat. Cover the grill and cook the chicken until the skin is a dark golden brown and very crisp and the meat is cooked through (about 180°F on an instant-read meat thermometer inserted in the thigh), 1¼ to 1½ hours (see page 205 for how to test for doneness). If using a charcoal grill, you'll need to add 12 fresh coals per side after 1 hour.

6. Using tongs, carefully transfer the chicken in its upright position on the beer can to a platter and present it to your guests. Let rest 5 minutes, then carefully remove the chicken from the beer can. Take care not to spill the hot beer or otherwise burn yourself. (Normally I discard the beer, but some people like to save it for making barbecue sauce.) Quarter or carve the chicken and serve.

SERVES 2 TO 4

YOU'LL NEED:
2 cups wood chips or chunks (preferably apple or hickory), soaked for 1 hour in a half can of beer plus water to cover, then drained

VARIATIONS:
You can also barbecue a chicken on a can of cola, lemon-lime soda, or root beer.

ALSO GOOD FOR:
Use a "tall boy" (16 ounce) can of beer to barbecue a capon or duck. Use a "mini" (8 ounce) can of beer to barbecue a game hen.

METHOD:
Direct grilling

COOKING TIME:
24 to 30 minutes

ADVANCE PREPARATION:
2 to 12 hours for marinating the chickens

HOW TO GRILL A SPATCHCOCKED CHICKEN

Spatchcocked Chicken with Walnut-Dill Pesto and Grilled Zucchini (page 397)

While the indirect grill and rotisserie methods are great for roasting a whole chicken, nothing can beat the flame-charred smokiness of chicken pieces grilled directly over a fire. There is a way to do this and I learned it in one of the world's most unlikely barbecue destinations: Paris. The technique is spatchcocking and it looks as theatrical as it sounds. You cut out the backbone and open the bird flat, like a book. This makes the whole chicken thin enough to grill directly over the fire.

SETTING UP THE GRILL

1 To set up a charcoal grill for direct grilling, first light the charcoal in a chimney starter (see page 9).

2 Using a garden hoe or other long-handled implement, rake the burning coals into an even layer.

3 To see if the grill is preheated to medium, use the test on page 10.

PREPARING THE CHICKEN

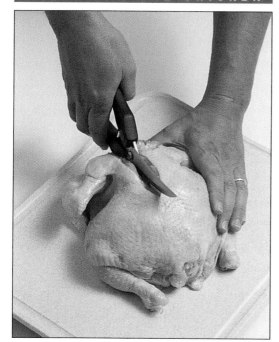

1 To spatchcock a chicken, place it on its breast. Using poultry shears and starting at the neck, make a lengthwise cut down one side of the backbone to the tail.

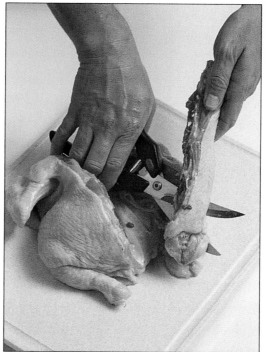

2 Make a lengthwise cut down the other side of the backbone. Remove and discard the backbone or save it for stock.

TIP

■ Poultry shears are the best tool for cutting out the backbone. Removing the breastbone is optional. The chicken will lie flatter if you take it out, but this adds another step. If you're not a great surgeon, simply removing the backbone is enough. The same is true for tucking the drumsticks through the body of the chicken. It looks better, but it adds a step. Skip it if you're so inclined.

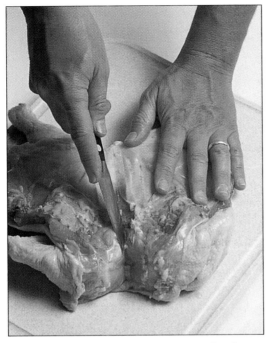

3 Fold the chicken open like a book, skin-side down. Use a paring knife to cut along each side of the breastbone.

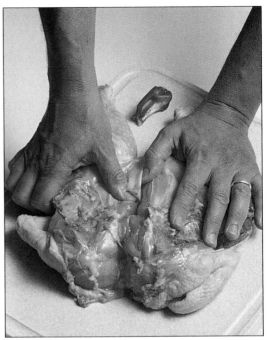

4 Run your thumbs along both sides of the breastbone and white cartilage, then pull them out.

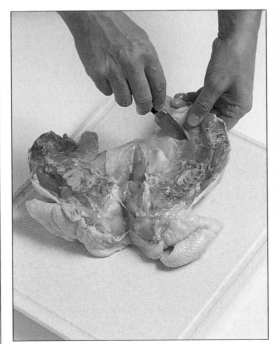

5 Using a paring knife, make a 1-inch slit in the rear portion of one side of the chicken. Repeat on the other side.

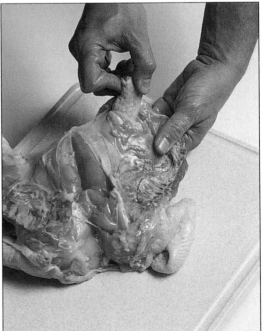

6 Reach under the bird and pull the end of the drumstick through this slit. Repeat on the other side.

7 Cut off the wing tips and trim off any loose skin. You can save the wing tips for stock. The chicken is now spatchcocked.

8 Spread the pesto evenly over the outside and inside of the spatchcocked chicken and let marinate, covered, in the refrigerator.

ON THE GRILL

1 Grill the chicken skin-side down for 12 to 15 minutes before turning it to complete the grilling. Use tongs and a spatula to turn the chicken.

2 Grill the chicken bone-side down 12 to 15 minutes more. Use an instant-read meat thermometer to test for doneness.

TIPS

■ I always start my chicken on the grill skin-side down to crisp the skin and cook out the fat. Then I turn it to finish cooking.

■ You'll have to be alert because the melting chicken fat can quickly turn your grill into a blaze. Be prepared to move the chicken away from those inevitable flare-ups. If you are using charcoal, leave a small area coal-free as a place to move the chicken.

SPATCHCOCKED CHICKEN WITH WALNUT-DILL PESTO

SERVES 4 TO 8

YOU'LL NEED:
Poultry shears

2 chickens (3½ to 4 pounds each)

FOR THE PESTO:
1 bunch fresh dill, washed, stemmed, and chopped (save a few dill sprigs for garnish)
1 bunch fresh basil, washed, stemmed, and chopped
5 cloves garlic, chopped
½ cup walnut pieces

¼ cup freshly grated Romano cheese
2 strips lemon zest (½ by 2 inches)
1 cup extra-virgin olive oil
¼ cup lemon juice
1 teaspoon coarse salt, or more to taste
1 teaspoon black pepper, or more to taste

Lemon wedges, for serving

ALSO GOOD FOR:
Any bird can be spatchcocked and grilled in this fashion, from quail to turkeys. Feel free to make the pesto with rosemary (1 cup of leaves) or another fresh herb.

1. Remove the packets of giblets from the body cavities of the chickens and set aside for another use. Remove and discard the fat just inside the body and neck cavities of the chickens. Rinse the chickens, inside and out, under cold running water and then drain and blot dry, inside and out, with paper towels. Spatchcock the chickens as shown in Steps 1 through 7 on pages 221 through 223. Place the chickens in a nonreactive roasting pan.

2. Prepare the pesto: Place the dill, basil, garlic, walnuts, cheese, and lemon zest in a food processor and process until very finely chopped. With the machine running, add the oil, lemon juice, salt, pepper, and ¾ cup water. Taste for seasoning, adding salt and pepper as necessary; the pesto should be highly seasoned. Set ½ cup pesto aside. Pour the remaining pesto over the chickens, spreading it on the meat with a rubber spatula. Turn the birds so you coat both sides. Let the chickens marinate in the refrigerator, covered, for as little as 2 hours or as long as overnight (12 hours), turning

once or twice to coat with marinade; the longer the chickens marinate, the richer the flavor will be.

3. Set up the grill for direct grilling (see page 10 for charcoal or page 16 for gas) and preheat to medium. When ready to cook, brush and oil the grill grate. Arrange the chickens on the grate, skin-side down. Grill for 12 to 15 minutes per side, turning once with tongs and a spatula. The chickens can be a little awkward to turn; you'll need to use both utensils. When you turn the chickens, spread the reserved ½ cup pesto on top. You'll probably get flare-ups as the melting fat hits the fire. Keep the birds moving to dodge the flames. If the skin browns too much, lower the heat or move the chickens to a cooler section of the grill. The chickens are done when an instant-read meat thermometer inserted into the thickest part of a thigh (but not touching the bone) registers about 180°F.

4. Transfer the chickens to a platter, let rest for a few minutes, garnish with the dill sprigs and lemon wedges, and serve.

HOW TO GRILL HALF CHICKENS

Most people grill chicken halves or pieces slathered in sugary barbecue sauce, but sugar burns with pro-longed exposure to heat, almost guaranteeing that the skin will char before the meat is cooked through. So what are the secrets to direct grilling chicken without burning it? First, season the bird with a rub rather than mar-inating it in a sugar-based barbecue sauce. This gives you plenty of flavor without the risk of burning. Next, if you must baste the bird (and basting is part of grilling chicken), use a vinegar-based mop, not a sweet barbecue sauce. Finally, apply the barbecue sauce at the end of cook-ing so that it sizzles without burning.

Good Old American Grilled Chicken with Basic Barbecue Sauce and Grilled Corn (page 361)

METHOD:
Direct grilling

COOKING TIME:
20 to 24 minutes

ADVANCE PREPARATION:
15 minutes to 4 hours for marinating the chickens

SETTING UP THE GRILL

1 To set up a charcoal grill for direct grilling, first light the charcoal in a chimney starter (see page 9).

2 Using a garden hoe or other long-handled implement, rake the burning coals into an even layer.

3 To see if the grill is preheated to medium, use the test on page 10.

PREPARING THE CHICKEN

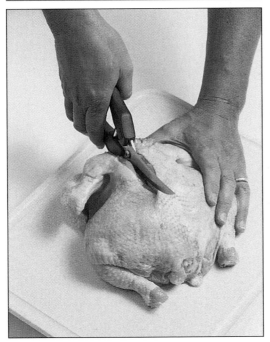

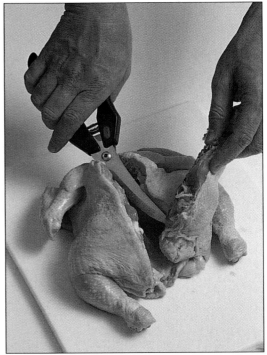

1 To cut a chicken in half, place it on its breast. Using poultry shears and starting at the neck, make a lengthwise cut down one side of the backbone to the tail.

2 Make a lengthwise cut down the other side of the backbone. Remove and discard the backbone or save it for stock.

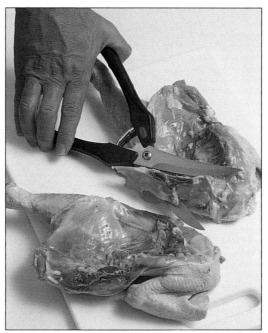

3 Fold the chicken open like a book and turn it over. Make a lengthwise cut along one side of the breastbone. The chicken will then be halved, with the breastbone attached to one of the halves.

4 Cut out the breastbone and white cartilage. Save the breastbone for stock.

5 Trim off any excess skin from both halves of the chicken. Cut off the wing tips and save them for stock.

6 Place the chicken halves in a baking dish just large enough to hold them. Sprinkle both sides with the barbecue rub.

ON THE GRILL

1 Grill the chicken halves skin-side down, basting often with mop sauce. Here the halves have been turned after grilling about 10 minutes. Note that I'm using a barbecue mop, but you can also use a basting brush.

2 Brush the chicken with the barbecue sauce during the last few minutes of cooking. The chicken will take a total of 20 to 24 minutes to grill.

SERVES 2 TO 4

**YOU'LL NEED:
Poultry shears;
barbecue mop
(optional)**

THE RECIPE

GOOD OLD AMERICAN GRILLED CHICKEN

2 chickens (3½ to 4 pounds each)
*3 tablespoons Basic Barbecue Rub
   (page 441) or your favorite
   commercial brand*

*1½ cups Basic Barbecue Mop Sauce
   (page 445)*
*2 cups Basic Barbecue Sauce
   (page 447)*

1. Remove the packets of giblets in the body cavities of the chickens and set aside for another use. Remove and discard the fat just inside the body and neck cavities. Rinse the chickens, inside and out, under cold running water and then drain and blot dry, inside and out, with paper towels. Cut the chickens in half as shown in Preparing the Chicken, Steps 1 through 5 on pages 226 and 227. Arrange the chicken halves in a baking dish and sprinkle on both sides with the rub. Pat the rub onto the chickens with your fingertips. Let the chickens sit in the refrigerator, covered, for as little as 15 minutes or as long as 4 hours; the longer they stand, the richer the flavor will be.

2. Set up the grill for direct grilling (see page 10 for charcoal or page 16 for gas) and preheat to medium. When ready to cook, brush and oil the grill grate. Arrange the chicken halves on the hot grate, all facing in the same direction, skin-side down. Baste the birds with mop sauce every 5 minutes or so. It's likely the melting fat from the skin will cause flare-ups. Move the chicken halves away from the flames to keep them from burning.

3. After 10 to 12 minutes, the skin side of the chickens should be crisp and golden brown. Turn the chicken halves, apply more mop sauce, and grill the bone side of the chickens the same way. Again, keep the chickens moving to prevent flare-ups. If the birds start to burn, move them to a cooler section of the grill.

4. Set aside 1 cup of barbecue sauce for serving. After the chickens have grilled about 8 minutes on the second side, brush the skin side with barbecue sauce and turn the halves. Grill for 2 minutes to sizzle the sauce, then brush the bone side with sauce and turn the chickens again.

Grill another couple of minutes before removing the chickens. The chickens are done when an instant-read meat thermometer inserted into the thickest part of a thigh (but not touching the bone) registers about 180°F.

5. Transfer the chicken halves to plates or a platter and let rest for 3 minutes before serving with the reserved sauce.

Using the Indirect Method

You can also grill chicken halves using the indirect method. In this case, arrange the chicken pieces on the grate skin-side up. Indirect grill for 40 to 50 minutes, mopping the chickens often. Brush the barbecue sauce on the birds at the end. It is not necessary to turn the chicken halves. Indirect grilling is safer and more predictable (it's virtually impossible to burn an indirect-grilled chicken if you follow the proper cooking time). But it lacks the theatrics of direct grilling and so should be avoided at a cookout where you want to show off. No guts, no glory.

ALSO GOOD FOR:
You can use this method to grill half game hens, chicken quarters, and whole chicken legs.

METHOD:
Direct grilling

COOKING TIME:
12 to 16 minutes

**ADVANCE
PREPARATION:**
4 to 8 hours
for marinating
the chickens

HOW TO GRILL CHICKEN PIECES

I f you're like most grillers, you've probably made a burnt offering or two to the God of Barbecue while trying to obtain chicken morsels that are golden brown and crisp on the outside, moist and cooked through on the inside, and smoky without being completely charred. You could take the easy way out, using the indirect method. Since I prefer the thrill of grilling chicken pieces directly over the coals, here's the way I like to do it.

*Saffron-Grilled
Chicken
with rice*

SETTING UP THE GRILL

1 To set up a charcoal grill for direct grilling, first light the charcoal in a chimney starter (see page 9).

2 Using a garden hoe or other long-handled implement, rake the burning coals into an even layer.

3 To see if the grill is preheated to medium, use the test on page 10.

PREPARING THE CHICKEN

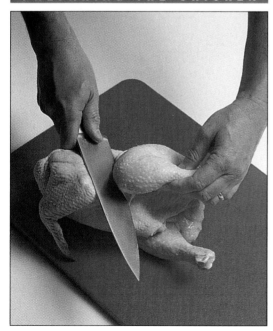

1 To cut a chicken into 10 equal pieces, first cut off a chicken leg. Run your knife under the thigh to the joint that attaches the leg to the body.

2 Holding the thigh, lift the leg and snap the thigh bone out of the joint. Continue cutting to the back of the chicken to remove the leg. Repeat with the other leg.

TIP

■ I'm an advocate of buying a whole chicken and cutting it up yourself. Why should you bother? Well, I use the French method, which is more equitable than a cut-up chicken from an American supermarket. (The wing has a portion of the breast meat attached, for example, so you get a more ample serving.)

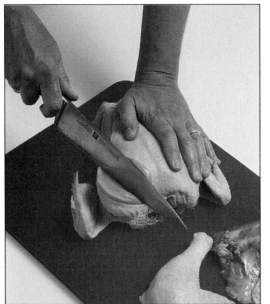

3 Place the chicken breast-side up. Holding the knife at an angle, cut off a wing, cutting straight down to include about 1 inch of breast meat.

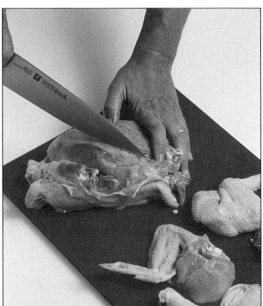

4 Turn the chicken on its side. Run your knife along the line of fat that separates the breast section from the back section of the chicken. Cut off and discard the back or save it for stock.

5 Lay the breast section skin-side down on the cutting board. Pull out the breast bone, following Steps 3 and 4 on page 222. Note here that I have already removed the cartilage.

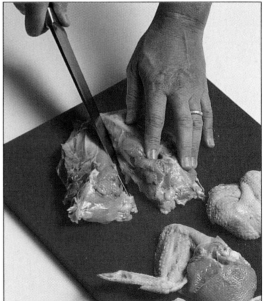

6 Cut the breast section in half lengthwise.

7 Cut each half breast in half crosswise through the ribs.

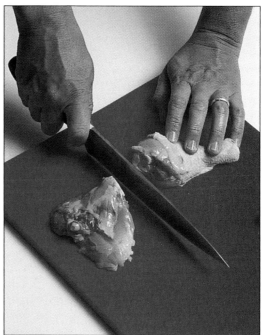

8 Cut each chicken leg into a thigh portion and drumstick portion, running the knife along the line of fat that separates them.

9 Cut off the wing tips.

10 Arrange the chicken pieces in a baking dish.

11 Spoon the sliced onions and marinade over the chicken and let marinate, covered, in the refrigerator.

ON THE GRILL: Grill the chicken pieces for 5 to 8 minutes per side, rotating each 45 degrees after 3 minutes to get a crosshatch of grill marks. Here I am basting the chicken with herb butter during the last couple minutes of grilling.

SERVES 4 TO 8

THE RECIPE

SAFFRON-GRILLED CHICKEN

FOR THE CHICKEN AND MARINADE:
2 chickens (3½ to 4 pounds each)
½ teaspoon saffron threads
1 tablespoon hot water
⅔ cup lemon juice
⅔ cup plain yogurt or sour cream
⅔ cup extra-virgin olive oil
¼ cup packed finely chopped fresh
    flat-leaf parsley
1 tablespoon peeled, finely chopped
    fresh ginger
1 tablespoon coarse salt
1½ teaspoons black pepper
½ teaspoon ground turmeric (optional)
1 large onion, thinly sliced crosswise

FOR THE SAFFRON-HERB BUTTER BASTE:
¼ teaspoon saffron threads
1 tablespoon hot water
4 tablespoons (½ stick) butter
2 tablespoons lemon juice
2 tablespoons chopped fresh
    flat-leaf parsley
Black pepper, to taste

FOR SERVING:
Parsley sprigs, for garnish
Lemon wedges
Sliced red onion

1. Remove the packets of giblets in the body cavities of the chickens and set aside for another use. Remove and discard the fat just inside the body and neck cavities of the chickens. Rinse the chickens, inside and out, under cold running water and then drain and blot dry, inside and out, with paper towels. Cut each chicken into 10 pieces as shown in Preparing the Chicken, Steps 1 through 9 on pages 231 through 233.

2. Make the marinade: Use your fingers to crumble the saffron into a large nonreactive mixing bowl. Add the water and let stand for 5 minutes. Add the lemon juice, yogurt, oil, parsley, ginger, salt, pepper, and turmeric, if using, and stir until the salt is dissolved.

3. Arrange the chicken pieces in a large nonreactive baking dish and top with the onion. Spoon the marinade over the chicken and let marinate in the refrigerator, covered, for at least 4 hours or as long as 8, turning several times.

4. Prepare the butter baste: Crush the saffron threads into a saucepan (tilt it slightly), add the water and let stand for 5 minutes. Add the butter, lemon juice, parsley, and pepper and cook over medium heat until the butter melts.

5. Set up the grill for direct grilling (see page 10 for charcoal or page 16 for gas) and preheat to medium. When ready to cook, brush and oil the grill grate. Place the chicken drumsticks and thighs skin-side down on the hot grate. Cook for 1 to 2 minutes, then add the breast pieces skin-side down. Cook all for 5 to 6 minutes, then turn all the pieces over. Continue grilling for 6 to 8 minutes more; you may need to turn the chicken pieces several times to keep them from burning. It's likely the melting fat from the skin will cause flare-ups; move the chicken pieces away from the flames to keep them from burning. The last 2 minutes or so, start basting the chicken with the saffron-herb butter.

6. Transfer the chicken pieces to plates or a platter and garnish with the parsley sprigs. Serve with lemon wedges and sliced red onion.

TIPS

■ When buying saffron, get threads, not powder. They have more flavor.

■ I start grilling the chicken skin-side down. This melts out the fat and crisps the skin, but it does tend to cause flare-ups. Be ready to move your chicken to a cooler part of the grill.

METHOD:
Direct grilling

COOKING TIME:
8 to 12 minutes

**ADVANCE
PREPARATION:**
2 hours for brining
the chicken

HOW TO GRILL BRINED CHICKEN BREASTS

D o your chicken breasts always come out dry on the grill? My friend the food scientist Shirley Corriher has a simple solution: soak them in brine before grilling. The salt in a brine enables chicken breasts to retain their moisture.

Chicken breasts aren't the only food to benefit from brining. Brine makes turkeys more succulent, pork chops less dry (see page 127), and fish steaks stay moist even after grilling.

Grilled Brined Chicken Breasts with Grilled Tomatoes (page 393) and julienned cabbage

SETTING UP THE GRILL

1 To set up a charcoal grill for direct grilling, first light the charcoal in a chimney starter (see page 9).

2 Using a garden hoe or other long-handled implement, rake the burning coals into an even layer.

3 To see if the grill is preheated to high, use the test on page 10.

PREPARING THE CHICKEN

1 Prepare the brine. Place the salt, brown sugar, peppercorns, chile, and bay leaves in a bowl. Add the hot water and whisk until the sugar and salt are dissolved. Add the cold water and let cool.

2 Place the skinless, boneless chicken breasts in a baking dish and cover with the brine. Add the lemon slices and other flavorings.

ON THE GRILL: Use the poke test to see if the chicken breasts are done. They'll take 4 to 6 minutes per side.

TIPS

■ The basic brine formula is salt and water. Try to use kosher salt or sea salt (the latter is loaded with flavorful minerals). Most barbecue brines also contain some sugar for sweetness. Brown sugar or even honey and/or molasses provide greater flavor than white sugar.

■ To speed up the brine mixing process, I dissolve the salt and sugar in some hot water, then stir in cold water to fill out the proportion. This maximizes the rate of dissolving, while minimizing the time you need to wait for the brine to cool.

■ You can brine the breasts in a baking dish, or you can use a resealable plastic bag, which takes up less room in the refrigerator.

■ Don't overbrine the chicken, or it will be rubbery. Just 2 hours will do it.

SERVES 4

GRILLED BRINED CHICKEN BREASTS

2 large, whole, boneless, skinless chicken
    breasts (each 12 to 16 ounces) or
    4 half breasts (each 6 to 8 ounces)
¼ cup coarse salt
¼ cup firmly packed dark brown sugar
20 whole black peppercorns
1 red chile pepper, thinly sliced

2 bay leaves
1 cup hot water, plus 3 cups cold water
1 lemon, thinly sliced
1 small onion, thinly sliced
2 cloves garlic, peeled and crushed
    with the side of a cleaver

1. If using whole breasts, cut each in half. Trim any sinews or excess fat off the breasts and discard. Rinse the breasts under cold running water, then drain and blot dry with paper towels and arrange in a nonreactive baking dish.

2. Make the brine: Place the salt, brown sugar, peppercorns, chile pepper, and bay leaves in a large nonreactive bowl and add the hot water. Whisk until the salt and brown sugar are dissolved. Stir in the cold water and let cool to room temperature. Pour the brine over the breasts and stir in the lemon slices, onion, and garlic. Cover the dish with plastic wrap and let stand in the refrigerator for 2 hours, turning the breasts once or twice.

3. Set up the grill for direct grilling (see page 10 for charcoal or page 16 for gas) and preheat to high. When ready to cook, brush and oil the grill grate. Arrange the chicken breasts on the hot grate, all facing the same direction, at a 45 degree angle to the bars of the grate. Grill the breasts until cooked, 4 to 6 minutes per side, rotating the breasts 90 degrees after 2 minutes on each side to create an attractive crosshatch of grill marks. To test for doneness, poke a breast in the thickest part with your finger. It should feel firm to the touch.

4. Transfer the breasts to plates or a platter, then serve.

ALSO GOOD FOR:
This brine is well suited to all types of poultry, from quail and game hens to turkeys. Quail need only 1 hour brining; turkeys take overnight.

HOW TO GRILL STUFFED CHICKEN BREASTS

METHOD:
Direct grilling

COOKING TIME:
8 to 12 minutes

ADVANCE PREPARATION:
1 hour for soaking the sun-dried tomatoes

The breast is the part of the chicken barbecue fanatics love to hate. They hate it because it's bland and tends to dry out on the grill (the result of its leanness). That said, yearly we consume tons of boneless, skinless chicken breasts—and many of them cooked on the grill. Why? Well, they're quick and easy to prepare (you can grill them in less than 10 minutes). Their mild flavor makes them a blank canvas awaiting the grill master's culinary colors. One way to put flavor and moistness into chicken breasts is to stuff them, as I do in the recipe accompanying this technique.

Grilled Stuffed Chicken Breasts with mesclun

SETTING UP THE GRILL

1 To set up a charcoal grill for direct grilling, first light the charcoal in a chimney starter (see page 9).

2 Using a garden hoe or other long-handled implement, rake the burning coals into an even layer.

3 To see if the grill is preheated to high, use the test on page 10.

PREPARING THE CHICKEN

1 Using a piece of unflavored dental floss will enable you to cut clean, thin, even slices of soft goat cheese. Hold the floss taut between your hands and slice downward.

2 Remove the chicken tender (tenderloin) from the boneless, skinless breast. Lift it by the loose end and gently pull it up, using a knife to cut it off at the base.

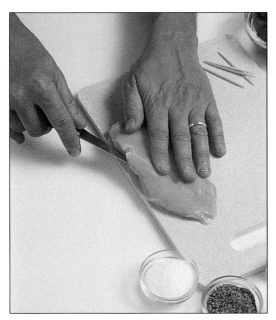

3 To cut a pocket in a chicken breast, place it at the edge of the cutting board with the thicker side facing out. Holding it flat with the palm of your free hand and holding the knife parallel to the cutting board, cut a deep pocket in the breast. (Do not cut all the way through.)

4 It's OK to make several successive cuts to create the pocket. The important thing is to try not to pierce the top or bottom of the breast (but it isn't the end of the world if you do). Once you've made the pocket, the breast is ready for stuffing.

5 Place two soaked sun-dried tomatoes in the pocket of each chicken breast.

6 Place two basil leaves and two slices of goat cheese in each pocket.

TIP

■ Each half chicken breast comes with a tenderloin or finger— a long slender muscle loosely attached to the underside of the breast, familiarly referred to as the tender. I like to save the tenders for satés (see page 254). They freeze well: Keep storing them in the freezer until you have enough for a whole saté recipe.

7 Pin the chicken breasts shut with oiled toothpicks.

8 Place the chicken breasts in a baking dish and sprinkle them with salt and pepper. Pour in olive oil and lemon juice and let the breasts marinate.

ON THE GRILL

1 Arrange the chicken breasts on the grill at a 45 degree angle to the bars of the grate. After 2 minutes, rotate each breast 90 degrees to create an attractive crosshatch of grill marks. The breasts you see here were turned over after grilling for about 6 minutes.

2 Use the finger poke test to check for doneness. The breasts should feel firm to the touch.

THE RECIPE

GRILLED STUFFED CHICKEN BREASTS

2 large, whole, boneless, skinless
   chicken breasts (each 12 to 16
   ounces) or 4 half breasts
   (each half 6 to 8 ounces)
8 sun-dried tomatoes, soaked
   in hot water for 1 hour,
   then drained

8 large fresh basil leaves
4 ounces creamy goat cheese
Coarse salt and black pepper
3 tablespoons extra-virgin
   olive oil
2 tablespoons lemon juice

SERVES 4

YOU'LL NEED:
Unflavored dental
floss for cutting
the goat cheese;
wooden
toothpicks,
soaked in oil

1. Cut the goat cheese into 8 slices as shown in Preparing the Chicken, Step 1 on page 240.

2. Cut each whole breast in half. Remove the tenders as shown in Step 2, and set them aside for later use (such as in the satés on page 254). Trim any sinews or excess fat off the breasts and discard. Rinse the breasts under cold running water, then drain and blot dry with paper towels. Cut pockets in the chicken breasts, as shown in Steps 3 and 4.

3. Stuff the chicken breasts with the sun-dried tomatoes, basil leaves, and goat cheese slices, and pin the breasts shut with toothpicks as shown in Steps 5 through 7. Place the chicken breasts in a nonreactive baking dish and season generously with salt and pepper. Pour the oil and lemon juice over the breasts and let

marinate, turning once or twice, while you preheat the grill.

4. Set up the grill for direct grilling (see page 10 for charcoal or page 16 for gas) and preheat to high. When ready to cook, brush and oil the grill grate. Arrange the breasts on the hot grate, all facing the same direction, at a 45 degree angle to the bars of the grate. Grill for 4 to 6 minutes per side, rotating the breasts 90 degrees after 2 minutes on each side to create an attractive crosshatch of grill marks. To test for doneness, poke a breast in the thickest part with your finger. It should feel firm to the touch.

5. Transfer the breasts to plates or a platter. Remove the toothpicks before serving. For a prettier presentation, cut the breasts crosswise into thin slices, using an electric knife or sharp carving knife.

VARIATIONS:
Chicken breasts can be filled with myriad stuffings: prosciutto, mozzarella, and sage leaves, for example, or smoked cheese, sliced kielbasa, and sauerkraut. The possibilities are limited only by your imagination.

METHOD:
Direct grilling

COOKING TIME:
8 to 12 minutes

ADVANCE PREPARATION:
30 minutes to
1 hour for
marinating
the chicken

HOW TO GRILL CHICKEN BREASTS UNDER BRICKS

Every grill jockey needs a couple of showstoppers—dishes so outrageously theatrical, you'll gain instant respect and admiration when you make them. American pit bosses have devised one such eyepopper: the beer-can chicken on page 216. Another also involves chicken and it comes from Italy: *pollo al mattone,* chicken grilled under a brick.

Two of Italy's most serious food cities claim parentage of this simple technique: Rome and Florence. And with good reason! It looks great. It tastes great. And the weight of the brick gives you killer 3-D grill marks—which makes this a perfect barbecue dish.

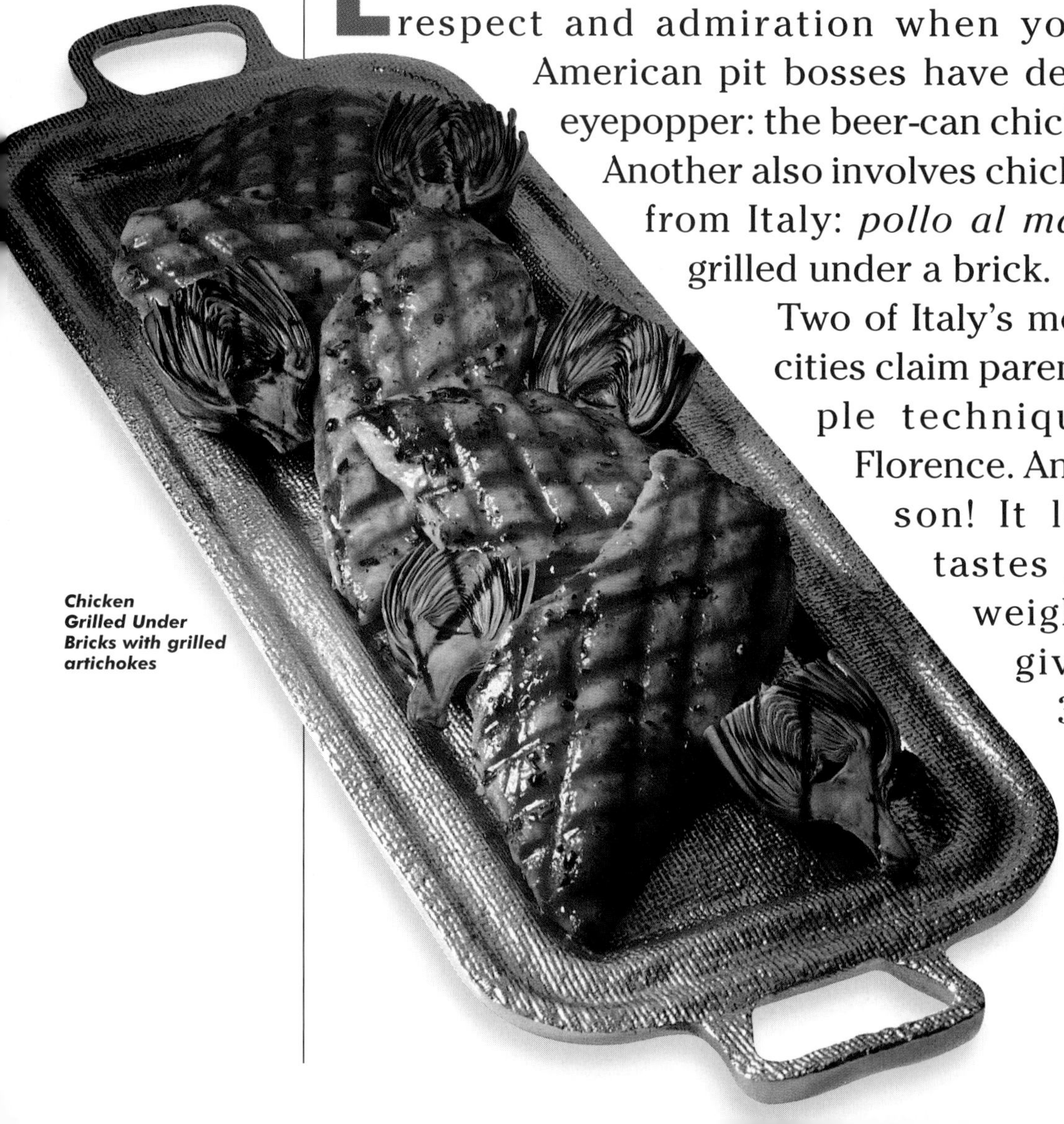

Chicken Grilled Under Bricks with grilled artichokes

SETTING UP THE GRILL

1 To set up a charcoal grill for direct grilling, first light the charcoal in a chimney starter (see page 9).

2 Using a garden hoe or other long-handled implement, rake the burning coals into an even layer.

3 To see if the grill is preheated to high, use the test on page 10.

PREPARING THE CHICKEN

Arrange the boneless, skinless chicken breasts in a baking dish and add olive oil, garlic, rosemary, hot red pepper flakes, salt, and cracked black peppercorns to marinate them. Squeeze the lemon juice through your fingers so you can catch any seeds. Cover and refrigerate the chicken.

ON THE GRILL

1 Wrap four bricks in aluminum foil. That way you don't have to scrub them clean.

2 Put a brick on top of each chicken breast. Rotate the breasts 45 degrees to create handsome grill marks after 2 minutes. Wear grill mitts when lifting the bricks.

TIPS

■ Tradition calls for *pollo al mattone* to be made with a spatchcocked whole chicken. You'll find instructions on how to spatchcock a chicken starting on page 221, and I urge you to try the recipe with a whole bird sometime. For the sake of speed and convenience, I call for boneless, skinless chicken breasts here.

■ I like to serve these chicken breasts with grilled artichokes that have been marinated in lemon juice and olive oil.

SERVES 4

YOU'LL NEED:
4 bricks, each
wrapped in
aluminum foil; oak
chunks for building
the fire, or 2 cups
wood chips
(preferably oak),
soaked for 1 hour
in cold water to
cover, then drained

T H E   R E C I P E

CHICKEN GRILLED UNDER BRICKS

2 large, whole, boneless, skinless
*   chicken breasts (12 to 16 ounces each)*
*   or 4 half breasts (each half 6 to 8 ounces)*
1 teaspoon coarse salt
1 teaspoon cracked black peppercorns

½ to 1 teaspoon hot red pepper flakes
1 tablespoon chopped garlic
1 tablespoon chopped fresh rosemary
Juice of 1 lemon
¼ cup extra-virgin olive oil

1. If using whole breasts, cut each in half. Trim any sinews or excess fat off the chicken breasts and discard. Rinse the breasts under cold running water, then drain and blot dry with paper towels. Sprinkle the breasts on both sides with the salt, cracked black pepper, and hot red pepper flakes. Sprinkle the breasts with the garlic and rosemary, patting them on with your fingers. Arrange the breasts in a nonreactive baking dish. Pour the lemon juice and oil over them and let marinate in the refrigerator, covered, for 30 minutes to 1 hour, turning several times.

2. Set up the grill for direct grilling (see page 10 for charcoal or page 16 for gas) and preheat to high. In the best of all worlds, you'd build your fire with oak chunks (see page 12). Alternatively, use gas or charcoal, plus soaked wood chips for smoke. If using a gas grill, place all the wood chips in the smoker box or in a smoker pouch (see page 17) and preheat until you see smoke.

3. When ready to cook, brush and oil the grill grate. If using a charcoal grill, toss the wood chips on the coals. Arrange the chicken breasts on the hot grate, all facing the same direction, at a 45 degree angle to the bars of the grate. Place a brick on top of each. Grill the breasts until cooked, 4 to 6 minutes per side, rotating the breasts 90 degrees after 2 minutes on each side to create an attractive crosshatch of grill marks. To test for doneness,

poke a breast in the thickest part with your finger. It should feel firm to the touch. Transfer the breasts to plates or a platter and serve at once.

Grilled Chicken Breasts

Grilling a plain chicken breast is easy—use the marinade in this recipe and grill the chicken without the bricks! The time will be about the same.

HOW TO GRILL CHICKEN WINGS

METHOD:
Direct grilling

COOKING TIME:
16 to 24 minutes

ADVANCE PREPARATION:
1 hour for marinating the wings

We are so used to enjoying chicken wings deep-fried (Buffalo style), we've forgotten how delectable they can be grilled. Wings are the perfect cut of chicken for grilling, possessing a high ratio of skin and bones to meat. The skin is the tastiest part of the chicken— especially when crisped by the fire—while the bones give the meat extra flavor.

A grill jockey I met in Malaysia taught me a nifty way to maximize the surface area of the wing exposed to the fire. He impaled the wings on long bamboo skewers to stretch them open to their fullest (more surface area means more crisp skin). The resulting kebabs look cool and make great finger food at a party.

East-West Buffalo Wings with Gorgonzola Sauce and celery sticks

SETTING UP THE GRILL

1 To set up a charcoal grill for direct grilling, first light the charcoal in a chimney starter (see page 9).

2 Using a garden hoe or other long-handled implement, rake the burning coals into an even layer.

3 To see if the grill is preheated to medium, use the test on page 10.

PREPARING THE CHICKEN

1 Skewer the chicken wings on bamboo skewers, starting at an inch or so above the wing tip. Extend each wing straight, so that it runs the length of the skewer.

2 Arrange the wings in a baking dish. Ladle the marinade over them. Cover and let marinate in the refrigerator for 1 hour.

ON THE GRILL: Grill the chicken wings for 8 to 12 minutes on each side. Note the use of aluminum foil to prevent the skewers from burning.

THE RECIPE

EAST-WEST BUFFALO WINGS

16 whole chicken wings (3½ pounds)

FOR THE MARINADE AND SAUCE:
1 cup (2 sticks) butter
4 cloves garlic, minced
4 scallions, trimmed, white parts minced,
green parts finely chopped,
for garnish
1 tablespoon peeled, minced
fresh ginger
1 cup Thai hot sauce (Sriracha) or
other hot sauce

3 tablespoons lime juice
1 teaspoon black pepper
Coarse salt

FOR SERVING (optional):
Gorgonzola Sauce (page 453)
4 ribs celery, cut in thirds lengthwise,
then cut crosswise into
3-inch sticks

1. Rinse the chicken wings under cold running water and blot dry with paper towels. Skewer the wings as shown in Preparing the Chicken, Step 1 on the facing page, and arrange them in a nonreactive baking dish.

2. Prepare the marinade: Melt 3 tablespoons butter in a nonreactive saucepan over medium heat. Add the garlic, scallion whites, and ginger and cook until fragrant but not brown, about 3 minutes. Add the remaining butter, the hot sauce, lime juice, and pepper, and season with salt to taste. Bring to a boil. Then remove from the heat and let cool to room temperature. Pour the mixture over the wings, turning the wings to coat evenly. Let marinate in the refrigerator, covered, for 1 hour.

3. Set up the grill for direct grilling (see page 10 for charcoal or page 16 for gas) and preheat to medium. When ready to cook, drain the wings, reserving any marinade (scrape the excess marinade off the wings with a spatula). Transfer the remaining marinade to a nonreactive saucepan and boil for 3 minutes. Place the wings on the hot grate. Grill until crisp and golden brown on the outside and cooked through, 8 to 12 minutes per side.

4. Transfer the wings to a platter and pour the boiled marinade over them. Sprinkle with the scallion greens and serve at once, with the Gorgonzola Sauce and celery sticks on the side, if desired.

SERVES 4 TO 8 AS AN APPETIZER

YOU'LL NEED:
16 long (12-inch), slender bamboo skewers, soaked for 1 hour in cold water to cover, then drained

VARIATIONS:
You can substitute almost any marinade in this book for this one. To make Bombay wings, for example, marinate the wings in the tandoori marinade following Steps 1 and 3 on page 185. To make Sichuan wings, use the Chinese Five-Spice Rub on page 442.

TIPS

■ Sriracha is a mildly hot chili sauce from Thailand (I like to think of it as Thai ketchup). Look for it at Asian markets, natural foods stores, and many supermarkets, or substitute your favorite hot sauce.

■ As with all marinades, you must rapidly boil this one for a good 3 minutes to sterilize it before using it as a sauce.

METHOD:
Direct grilling

COOKING TIME:
6 to 8 minutes

HOW TO GRILL YAKITORI

Chicken on a stick is Japan's national snack, enjoyed at crowded lunch counters and smoky yakitori parlors day and night. The basic recipe features tiny pieces of chicken grilled on slender bamboo skewers with a sweet-salty glaze made from sugar, soy sauce, and mirin (sweet rice wine). The variations are endless: white meat, dark meat, chicken skin, gizzards, and livers with an interspersing of scallions, leeks, shiitake mushrooms, or any other ingredient an imaginative griller might fancy. The essence of yakitori is its delicacy and its diminutive size. Note the double skewering technique here. Inserting two skewers through the meat side by side keeps the pieces of chicken from slipping.

Yakitori

SETTING UP THE GRILL

1 To set up a charcoal grill for direct grilling, first light the charcoal in a chimney starter (see page 9).

2 Using a garden hoe or other long-handled implement, rake the burning coals into an even layer.

3 To see if the grill is preheated to high, use the test on page 10.

PREPARING THE CHICKEN

1 When making yakitori, you want all the pieces to be the same length. Use one piece of scallion as a template to cut the rest into 1½-inch pieces.

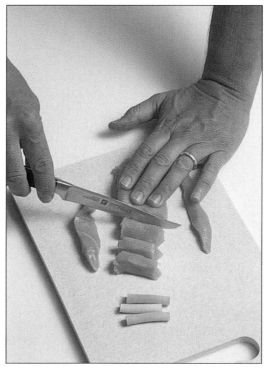

2 Cut the boneless, skinless chicken breasts across the grain into pieces the same size as the scallions.

TIPS

■ Like most of the world's barbecue buffs, the Japanese prefer the richness of the chicken's dark meat (the legs) for grilling. Since the breast is easier to prepare, I've suggested it in the recipe, but I encourage you to try yakitori sometime with thigh meat.

■ To simplify the recipe, you could cut ¾-inch squares of chicken and ¾-inch-long pieces of scallion and skewer them on individual skewers (use slightly thicker skewers).

■ Mirin is a Japanese sweet rice wine. Look for it in Japanese markets, natural foods stores, and most supermarkets. If it is unavailable, use sake or another dry rice wine (or even a dry white grape wine) and add a little more sugar.

TIP

■ A vegetable peeler
is the best tool for
removing thin strips of
lemon zest. You want
the zest (the oil-rich
outer rind), not the
bitter pith beneath it.

3 Lay the pieces of chicken and scallions out on the cutting board, alternating them. Allow three pieces of chicken and two of scallion per skewer. To double skewer them, hold the ingredients steady with one hand and slide in one skewer at a time. Double skewering keeps the pieces of chicken flat while grilling.

ON THE GRILL: Position the yakitori at the edge of the grate to protect the skewers from the fire. Start brushing the yakitori with the sauce after grilling for about 2 minutes on each side. The yakitori will be ready after grilling 3 to 4 minutes per side.

**SERVES 6 TO 8
AS AN APPETIZER,
4 AS A MAIN
COURSE**

YOU'LL NEED:
32 small (6-inch),
slender bamboo
skewers, soaked
for 1 hour in cold
water to cover,
then drained, or
more as needed

THE RECIPE

YAKITORI

FOR THE YAKITORI:
2 bunches scallions, trimmed
1½ pounds boneless, skinless
    chicken breasts

FOR THE YAKITORI SAUCE:
1 cup soy sauce
¾ cup sugar
½ cup mirin (sweet rice wine)
1 scallion, trimmed, white part gently
    crushed, green part cut into rings

1 clove garlic, gently crushed
    with the side of a cleaver
1 slice peeled fresh ginger
    (¼ inch thick), gently crushed
    with the side of a cleaver
1 strip lemon zest (½ by 2 inches)
Toasted sesame seeds (page 30),
    for garnish

1. Trim any sinews or excess fat off the chicken breasts and discard. Rinse the chicken breasts under cold running water, then drain and blot dry with paper towels. Cut the scallions and chicken breasts into uniform 1½-inch pieces and double skewer them as shown in Preparing the Chicken, Steps 1 through 3 on pages 251 and 252. Refrigerate, covered, until ready to grill.

2. Prepare the yakitori sauce: Place the soy sauce, sugar, mirin, scallion white, garlic, ginger, and lemon zest in a nonreactive saucepan and bring to a boil over medium heat. Let the sauce simmer until thick and syrupy, 5 to 10 minutes, stirring often to prevent scorching. Strain the sauce into a nonreactive bowl and let cool to room temperature. Set some aside to serve as a dipping sauce, if desired.

3. Set up the grill or hibachi for direct grilling (see page 10 for charcoal or page 16 for gas) and preheat to high. When ready to grill, brush and oil the grill grate. Place the yakitori at the edge of the hot grate so that the skewers are away from the heat. Grill the yakitori, turning after 2 minutes, to cook the outside of the meat. Begin basting with the sauce, and continue basting and turning until the chicken is cooked, 3 to 4 minutes per side. Alternatively, put the sauce in a shallow dish. When partially cooked, dip the yakitori in the sauce and continue grilling. The sauce should cook to a shiny glaze and the meat should feel firm to the touch when done.

4. Transfer the yakitori to plates or a platter and sprinkle with the scallion rings and sesame seeds. Although it's not strictly traditional, I like to serve a little reserved glaze in a tiny bowl as a dipping sauce.

ALSO GOOD FOR:
You can make the yakitori with any ingredients you fancy: pieces of chicken skin or liver, sections of asparagus or shiitake mushroom, folded shiso (perilla leaf), and so on. For that matter, the glaze is great with tiny kebabs of grilled shrimp, scallops, salmon, and other seafood.

METHOD:
Direct grilling

COOKING TIME:
2 to 4 minutes

HOW TO GRILL CHICKEN SATES

Chicken Satés with Asian Peanut Sauce

The saté burst on the dining scene in the United States in the 1980s with the opening of the first American Thai restaurants. It was love at first bite. We loved the explosive flavors of these tiny kebabs so much, we recrafted them in the American fashion. In this land of blast-furnace-size barbecue grills, the saté has grown to the size of a small shish kebab. But bigger doesn't always mean better, and I, for one, prefer the delicacy of the traditional Lilliputian saté from the Far East. Here is an authentic Thai chicken saté—rich with coconut milk and explosively seasoned with spices and chile. Sometimes, in order to win big you've got to think small.

SETTING UP THE GRILL

1 To set up a charcoal grill for direct grilling, first light the charcoal in a chimney starter (see page 9).

2 Using a garden hoe or other long-handled implement, rake the burning coals into an even layer.

3 To see if the grill is preheated to high, use the test on page 10.

PREPARING THE CHICKEN

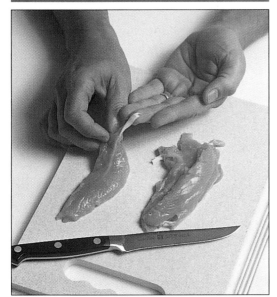

1 If you're using chicken tenderloins, you'll need to trim them. Find the tendon—the white sinewy part.

2 Place the tenderloin on the cutting board so the tendon is facing down. Holding the tendon with the fingers of one hand, slide a paring knife along the tendon, under the chicken meat, keeping the blade parallel to the cutting board. Cut the tender off the tendon. Discard the tendon.

TIPS

■ I like to make satés with chicken tenderloins (or tenders), the long, slender muscle found on the inside of a chicken breast. You can buy these at most supermarkets or save and freeze them when you prepare chicken breasts. You could also use thin slices of boneless breast or chicken thighs. The latter are used in Thailand.

■ The only trick to prepping chicken tenderloins is to remove the sinew found at one end. Follow the instructions at left. This isn't absolutely essential, but the tender will be a little tough if you don't.

3 Cut each tenderloin in half lengthwise.

4 Weave the chicken strips onto bamboo skewers.

5 Arrange the satés on a plate or baking dish and pour the marinade over them. Turn the satés several times during the 20 minute marinating time.

ON THE GRILL: When grilling the satés, place a folded sheet of aluminum foil under the skewers to keep them from burning. Turn the satés after 1 to 2 minutes, for a total of 2 to 4 minutes cooking time.

CHICKEN SATES

SERVES 4 TO 6
AS AN APPETIZER,
2 TO 3 AS A LIGHT
MAIN COURSE

YOU'LL NEED:
32 small (6-inch),
slender bamboo
skewers, soaked
for 1 hour in cold
water to cover,
then drained

*1 pound chicken tenderloins or
    boneless, skinless breasts*
2 tablespoons sugar
2 cloves garlic, minced
*1 stalk lemongrass, trimmed and
    minced (page 79), or
    2 strips lemon zest
    (½ by 2 inches), minced*
*1 Thai chile or jalapeño pepper,
    seeded and thinly sliced*
1½ teaspoons ground coriander
½ teaspoon ground turmeric

½ teaspoon black pepper
*¾ cup unsweetened coconut milk or
    heavy cream*
*3 tablespoons Asian fish sauce or
    soy sauce*
2 tablespoons lime juice
*3 tablespoons chopped fresh cilantro,
    for garnish*
*Asian Peanut Sauce (page 456),
    for serving*
*Cucumber Relish (optional; page 460),
    for serving*

1. Rinse the chicken tenderloins under cold running water and blot dry with paper towels. Prepare and skewer the satés as shown in Preparing the Chicken, Steps 1 through 4 on pages 255 and 256. Arrange the satés on a plate or in a baking dish so that the empty part of the skewers rest higher than the chicken.

2. Place the sugar, garlic, lemongrass, chile, coriander, turmeric, and pepper in a mortar and, using the pestle, pound to a fragrant paste, or place in a nonreactive mixing bowl and mash with the back of a wooden spoon. Stir in the coconut milk, fish sauce, and lime juice. Pour the marinade over the chicken satés (over the meat, not the skewers) and let marinate in the refrigerator, covered, for 20 minutes. Turn the satés once or twice so they marinate evenly.

3. Meanwhile, set up the grill or hibachi for direct grilling (see page 10 for charcoal or page 16 for gas) and preheat to high. When ready to cook, brush and oil the grill grate. Place the satés on the hot grate and grill until cooked, 1 to 2 minutes per side. If the skewers start to burn, slip a piece of aluminum foil under them to protect them. When done, the chicken will turn white and be firm.

4. Transfer the satés to plates or a platter, sprinkle with the cilantro, and serve with tiny bowls of Asian Peanut Sauce and Cucumber Relish, if desired.

ALSO GOOD FOR:
*Satés can be made
with any type of meat
or seafood—beef,
lamb, pork, rabbit,
fish, or shrimp—or
even with tofu. The
important thing is to
keep the satés small.*

HOW TO SMOKE A TURKEY

Every Thanksgiving I embark on a challenging mission—my quest to cook the perfect turkey. A whole turkey possesses white meat requiring a gentle heat to cook it without leaving it dry and stringy; dark meat that needs prolonged cooking to soften the tendons in the drumsticks; and skin, which should be as salty as a potato chip and as crackling crisp as cellophane. And therein lies the challenge. The solution lies in indirect grilling. The smoky sealed cooking environment produces a bird that's moist, tender, and perfumed with wood smoke. Moreover, cooking the bird outdoors leaves your oven free for the side dishes.

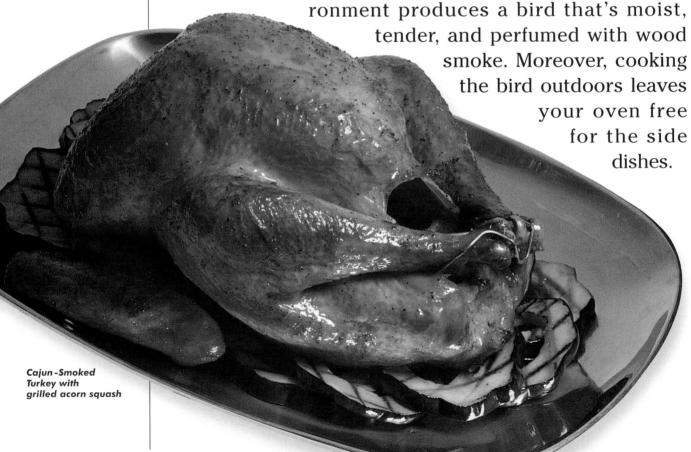

Cajun-Smoked Turkey with grilled acorn squash

SETTING UP THE GRILL

1 To set up a charcoal grill for smoking, first light the charcoal in a chimney starter (see page 9).

2 Place a drip pan in the center of the grill and divide the coals evenly on either side of it.

3 Place ½ cup of drained wood chips on each mound of coals.

PREPARING THE TURKEY

1 First draw the Injector Sauce into the kitchen syringe.

2 Inject a syringe full of sauce into each of the drumsticks. Note that I don't remove the metal clasp that the butcher provides to keep the turkey legs compact. There's enough room to remove the giblet packet and rinse out the interior when preparing the turkey, and it works as a truss during grilling.

TIP

■ One way to make a turkey moist is to use a kitchen syringe, sometimes called a Cajun injector (for a mail-order source, see page 481). My basic injector liquid is chicken broth, melted butter, lemon juice, and spices, and I use the syringe to squirt it deep into the leg and breast meat. You can buy commercial injector sauces, but many have a chemical taste, so I prefer to make my own. Just be sure to use finely ground spices so they won't clog the needle.

TIPS

■ When I smoke a turkey, I try to find an organic bird that's never seen the inside of a freezer. But such are the transformational powers of wood smoke that even a frozen supermarket bird will taste superior when it comes off the grill. Thaw a frozen bird in a roasting pan (or in a plastic garbage bag) in the refrigerator. It may take two or three days to thaw a large turkey.

■ Remove the packet of giblets from the neck and/or body cavity of the turkey before grilling it. This should sound like common sense, but every year people forget to do it.

■ Use a fairly light wood with turkey—apple and cherry are my favorites. You can get away with hickory, but mesquite will be too overwhelming.

3 Inject a syringe full of sauce into each of the thighs.

4 Inject a syringe full of sauce into the plumpest part of each side of the breast.

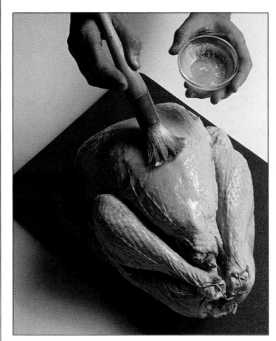

5 Brush the turkey skin all over with melted butter. This helps crisp the skin.

ON THE GRILL: If using a charcoal grill, add wood chips every hour to create plenty of smoke. A 12- to 14-pound turkey will be cooked through in 3 to 4 hours.

THE RECIPE

CAJUN-SMOKED TURKEY

1 turkey (12 to 14 pounds), completely thawed, if frozen
¾ cup Injector Sauce (recipe follows)

2 to 3 tablespoons melted butter or vegetable oil
Coarse salt and black pepper

1. Remove the packet of giblets from the neck and/or body cavity of the turkey and set aside for another use. If your turkey has a metal trussing clamp, leave it in place if possible. Remove and discard the fat just inside the body cavities of the turkey. Rinse the turkey, inside and out, under cold running water and then drain and blot dry. If your turkey does not have a metal clamp, truss it with butcher's string, as shown in Steps 1 through 8 on page 204.

2. Using a kitchen syringe, inject the Injector Sauce into the turkey as shown in Preparing the Turkey, Steps 1 through 4 on pages 259 and 260. Brush the outside of the turkey all over with the melted butter. Season all over with salt and pepper.

3. Set up the grill for indirect grilling (see page 12 for charcoal or page 16 for gas) and preheat to medium-low. If using a charcoal grill, place a large drip pan in the center. If using a gas grill, place all the wood chips in the smoker box or in a smoker pouch (see page 17) and preheat on high until you see smoke, then reduce the heat to medium-low.

4. When ready to cook, brush and oil the grill grate. If using a charcoal grill, toss 1 cup of wood chips on the coals. Place the turkey in the center of the hot grate, away from the heat, and cover the grill. Grill the turkey until cooked through, 3 to 4 hours. To test for doneness, insert an instant-read meat thermometer into the thickest part of a thigh, but do not touch the bone. The internal temperature should be between 170° and 180°F. Or wiggle a drumstick; it should move freely in the joint. If using charcoal, you'll need to add 12 fresh coals and ½ cup wood chips per side every hour. If the turkey starts to brown too much, cover it with aluminum foil.

5. Transfer the turkey to a platter, cover loosely with aluminum foil, and let rest for 10 minutes, then untruss. Carve and serve.

Injector Sauce

MAKES ¾ CUP

½ cup chicken broth (preferably homemade)
3 tablespoons butter
2 teaspoons lemon juice
1 teaspoon Cajun Rub (page 441)
Coarse salt, if needed

Combine the chicken broth, butter, lemon juice, and rub in a nonreactive saucepan over medium heat and cook just until the butter melts. Taste for seasoning, adding salt if necessary. Let the mixture cool to room temperature (or slightly warmer than room temperature—the butter should remain liquid), then put it in the kitchen syringe.

SERVES 12 TO 14

YOU'LL NEED: Kitchen syringe; 3 to 4 cups wood chips (preferably apple or cherry), soaked for 1 hour in cold water to cover, then drained; butcher's string (optional)

THE SMOKER METHOD: *Rinse and inject the turkey as described in the recipe. Preheat the smoker to 225° to 250°F following the manufacturer's instructions and the directions on page 24. Place the turkey in the smoker. If using a water smoker, place 1 quart dry white wine, cider, or water in the water pan before adding the turkey. For extra flavor, you may wish to add ¾ cup additional Injector Sauce to the water (you'll need to double the recipe). Smoke the turkey until cooked through, 6 to 7 hours, testing for doneness as directed in Step 4 of the recipe. Remember to add 24 fresh coals and 1 cup fresh wood chips every hour.*

METHOD:
Indirect grilling

COOKING TIME:
1½ to 2 hours

ADVANCE PREPARATION:
24 hours for curing the turkey breast

HOW TO GRILL TURKEY PASTRAMI

As a nice Jewish boy from Baltimore, I've been eating pastrami all my life, but it had never occurred to me that you could actually make it from scratch at home. Then I dined at the Park Avenue Cafe in New York City, where chef David Burke makes pastrami from just about everything—even salmon. The fact is pastrami is a curing and smoking process, not just a dish. Now I've become a pastrami fanatic, and one of my favorite iterations is turkey. It is slightly sweet, slightly salty, highly aromatic, delectably smoky, and surprisingly easy to make.

Turkey Pastrami

SETTING UP THE GRILL

1 To set up a charcoal grill for smoking, first light the charcoal in a chimney starter (see page 9).

2 Place a drip pan in the center of the grill and divide the coals evenly on either side of it.

3 Place ½ cup of drained wood chips on each mound of coals.

PREPARING THE TURKEY

1 If your turkey breast is bone-in, invert it, and using poultry shears, cut off the ribs.

2 Sprinkle one third of the rub on the underside of the breast.

TIP

■ Traditionally, the coriander seeds in the rub are cracked or coarsely crushed, not ground. There are several ways to do this—unfortunately, none of them effortless. You can crush the seeds in a large, deep mortar with a pestle (the seeds have a tendency to go flying, so the depth of the mortar is important). Or briefly grind them in a spice mill or well-cleaned coffee grinder, running the blade in brief bursts. Or wrap the seeds in a dish towel and crush them with the edge of a heavy skillet.

3 Sprinkle the remaining rub onto the skin of the turkey breast, being sure to lift the skin at the neck end and to put some of the rub into the neck cavity.

4 After the turkey cures for 24 hours in the refrigerator (covered with plastic wrap), the salt in the rub will have drawn out some of the water from it; you can see the liquid here at the bottom of the baking dish.

ON THE GRILL

1 Place the turkey on the grill grate, away from the heat. Add wood chips to the fire and replenish the coals after 1 hour, if using a charcoal grill.

2 Use an instant-read meat thermometer to test for doneness. The temperature in the thickest part of the breast should be at least 170°F. This will take 1½ to 2 hours.

THE RECIPE

TURKEY PASTRAMI

FOR THE RUB AND TURKEY:
3 tablespoons coriander seeds
3 tablespoons cracked black peppercorns
6 cloves garlic, minced
1 ½ teaspoons yellow mustard seeds
¼ cup coarse salt
¼ cup firmly packed brown sugar
¼ cup sweet paprika

1 tablespoon ground ginger
1 teaspoon ground mace (optional)
1 bone-in or boneless turkey breast
(4 to 5 pounds)

FOR SERVING:
Rye bread
Deli-style mustard

1. Make the rub: Coarsely crush the coriander seeds in a mortar with a pestle, in a spice mill or coffee grinder, or by wrapping them in a dish towel and crushing them with the edge of a heavy skillet. Combine the crushed seeds and the remaining rub ingredients in a mixing bowl and mix well with your fingers.

2. Rinse the turkey breast under cold running water, then drain and blot dry with paper towels. Using poultry shears, cut off the ribs, if necessary, as shown in Preparing the Turkey, Step 1 on page 263, and discard or save them for stock. Sprinkle and pat the rub on the turkey as shown in Steps 2 and 3. Cover the breast with plastic wrap or place in a large resealable plastic bag (you will need to turn the bag 2 or 3 times during the curing process) and let cure in the refrigerator for 24 hours.

3. Set up the grill for indirect grilling (see page 12 for charcoal or page 16 for gas) and preheat to medium-low. If using a charcoal grill, place a large drip pan in the center. If using a gas grill, place all the wood

chips in the smoker box or in a smoker pouch (see page 17) and preheat on high until you see smoke, then reduce the heat to medium-low.

4. When ready to cook, brush and oil the grill grate. If using charcoal, toss 1 cup of wood chips on the coals. Brush the excess rub off the turkey with a paper towel. Place the breast in the center of the hot grate over the drip pan, away from the heat; cover the grill. Grill the breast until tender, 1½ to 2 hours (the cooking time will depend on the size of the breast and the heat of the grill). To test for doneness, use an instant-read meat thermometer. The internal temperature should be at least 170°F. If using a charcoal grill, you'll need to add 12 fresh coals and ½ cup wood chips per side after 1 hour.

5. Transfer the turkey pastrami to a platter and let cool to room temperature, then refrigerate until cold. To serve, cut the pastrami into thin slices across the grain. Serve on rye bread slathered with mustard.

SERVES 8 TO 12

YOU'LL NEED:
**2 cups wood chips,
soaked for 1 hour
in cold water
to cover, then
drained; poultry
shears (optional)**

**THE SMOKER
METHOD:** *Prepare
the turkey breast as
described in the
recipe. Preheat the
smoker to 225° to
250°F, following
the manufacturer's
instructions and the
directions on page 24.
Place the cured turkey
breast in the smoker
and smoke until ten-
der, 3 to 4 hours. Add
24 fresh coals and 1
cup of wood chips
every hour. Test for
doneness as shown in
Step 2 on the facing
page.*

ALSO GOOD FOR:
*Beef brisket is the tra-
ditional meat for pas-
trami. Figure on ¼
cup rub per pound of
meat. An average
brisket (5 to 6 pounds)
will need to cure for
24 hours and cook
over medium-low
heat for 4 to 6 hours if
indirect grilled and
for 6 to 8 hours if
smoked at a low tem-
perature.*

METHOD:
Rotisserie grilling

COOKING TIME:
1½ to 2 hours

**ADVANCE
PREPARATION:**
6 to 24 hours
for marinating
the duck

HOW TO ROTISSERIE GRILL DUCK

There's an easy, mess-free way to cook duck. Simply roast it on the rotisserie of your grill. The slow, gentle turning is perfect for crisping the skin and melting out the fat. You wind up with a textbook perfect bird that's crisp outside, tender inside.

The recipe accompanying this technique is based on a Chinese method of smoking over a mixture of rice, tea, tangerine peel, and spices. Because it adds an extra step, I've made the tea smoking optional.

*Spit-Roasted Duck
with Chinese
Flavorings*

SETTING UP THE GRILL

1 To set up a rotisserie on a charcoal grill, first light the charcoal in a chimney starter (see page 9).

2 Position the rotisserie ring on the grill.

3 Mound the coals on one side of the grill, parallel to where the spit will be, and place drip pans in front of them.

PREPARING THE DUCK

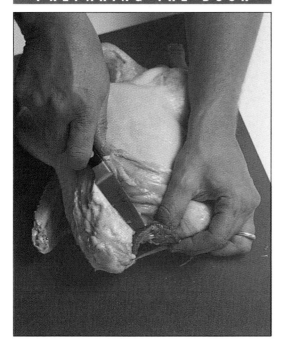

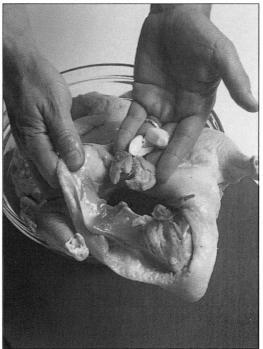

1 Lift the flap of neck skin, and using a paring knife, cut out the wishbone (this makes it easier to carve the cooked duck).

2 Place the crushed ginger, garlic, and scallion in the main cavity. Add a tablespoon of marinade to both cavities.

TIP

■ The Chinese like to loosen the skin from the duck body before roasting. This allows them to put a flavoring (a fragrant mixture of honey and five-spice powder in this case) under the skin, where it will perfume the meat. And loosening the skin helps the fat drain out, making for crisper duck. Loosening the skin is easier to do on fresh ducks than frozen (on some of the latter the skin is simply too fragile). You can always give it a try, following the procedure outlined on pages 208 and 209. Or skip this step and place half the marinade in the cavity and the other half on the outside of the duck.

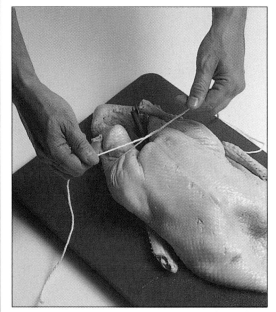

3 Use a 30-inch piece of butcher's string to truss the duck, starting with the legs. For complete instructions, follow Trussing Poultry, Steps 1 through 7 on page 204.

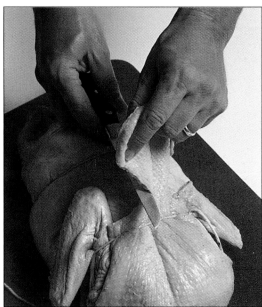

4 When the duck is trussed, cut off the excess neck skin.

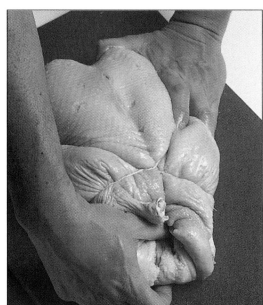

5 Turn the duck breast-side up and tuck the "pope's nose" (the tail) into the body cavity.

6 Place the duck in a baking dish, pour the remaining marinade over it, and carefully prick the duck skin all over with the tip of a carving fork. Marinate the duck, covered, in the refrigerator for at least 6 hours or as long as 24, turning it several times.

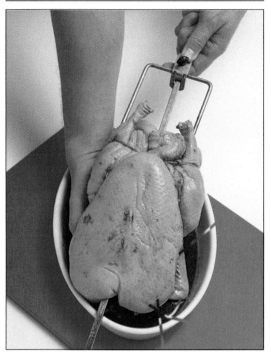

1 Push the spit through the duck, starting at the rear cavity.

2 Push the second set of prongs on the spit to hold the duck in place.

3 Insert the end of the spit in the rotisserie motor socket.

4 If your spit has a counter-weight, position it so that it counter-balances the duck.

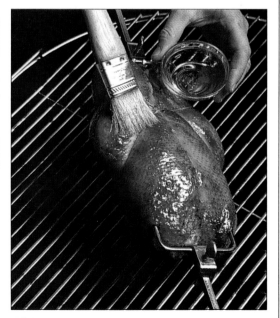

5 As the duck roasts on the rotisserie, brush it with sesame oil. After 1½ to 2 hours, it will be cooked to perfection.

TIP

■ A single duck will put out up to a cup of fat, so it's important to use a drip pan. This keeps your grill both clean and safe by eliminating the risk of flare-ups.

SERVES 2 TO 4

YOU'LL NEED:
1 cup wood chips
(optional), soaked
for 1 hour in cold
water to cover,
then drained;
rotisserie;
butcher's string

THE RECIPE

SPIT-ROASTED DUCK WITH CHINESE FLAVORINGS

1 duck (5 to 6 pounds)
¼ cup soy sauce
2 tablespoons honey
1 tablespoon Asian sesame oil, plus
   1 to 2 tablespoons for basting
1 teaspoon Chinese five-spice powder
   (page 442)

1 clove garlic, minced, plus 1 clove garlic,
   crushed
1 slice fresh ginger (¼ inch thick),
   lightly crushed
1 scallion, trimmed and lightly crushed
Tea-Smoking Mixture for Duck (optional;
   recipe follows)

1. Remove the packet of giblets from the duck's cavity and set aside for another use. Remove and discard the fat just inside the neck and body cavities. Rinse the duck, inside and out, under cold running water and then drain and blot dry, inside and out, with paper towels. Remove the wishbone as shown in Preparing the Duck, Step 1 on page 267.

2. Make the marinade: Combine the soy sauce, honey, 1 tablespoon oil, five-spice powder, and minced garlic in a bowl and stir.

3. Place the ginger, scallion, crushed garlic, and 1 tablespoon marinade in the body cavity of the duck and another tablespoon in the smaller neck cavity. Truss the duck as shown in Steps 1 through 7 on page 204 and Steps 3 through 5 on page 268. Place the duck in a baking dish and pour the remaining marinade over it. Gently prick the skin all over and let the duck marinate, covered, in the refrigerator for at least 6 hours, preferably 24, turning it several times.

4. Set up the grill for rotisserie grilling (see page 22) and preheat to high. If using a charcoal grill, place a large drip pan in the center. If using a gas grill with a smoker box, add all the wood chips and the Tea-Smoking Mixture, if desired (for the smoking mixture, line the smoker box with aluminum foil first), and preheat until you see smoke. If using a regular gas grill, place the wood chips and smoking mixture (again, if

VARIATION:
If you don't have a rotisserie, grill the duck using the indirect method instead, following the procedure on page 202 for grilling a chicken. Just be sure to have a large drip pan under the duck. It will take 2 to 2½ hours.

desired) in a smoker pouch (see page 17), and preheat until you see smoke.

5. Skewer the duck on the spit, as shown in Steps 1 and 2 on page 269. When ready to cook, if using a charcoal grill, place all the wood chips and the Tea-Smoking Mixture, if desired, on the coals. Attach the spit to the rotisserie mechanism as shown in Steps 3 and 4, and turn on the motor. Grill until the skin is dark golden brown and the meat is tender, 1½ to 2 hours. Baste with oil after 1 hour and every 15 minutes thereafter. If using a charcoal grill, you'll need to add 18 fresh coals after 1 hour. To test for doneness, insert an instant-read meat thermometer into the thickest part of a thigh, but not touching the bone. The internal temperature should be about 180°F.

Tea-Smoking Mixture for Duck

MAKES ENOUGH TO SMOKE 1 TO 2 DUCKS

⅓ cup white rice
⅓ cup black tea
⅓ cup firmly packed brown sugar
3 cinnamon sticks (each 3 inches long)
3 whole star anise
3 strips tangerine zest (each ½ by 2 inches)

Place all the ingredients in a small bowl and stir to mix.

HOW TO ROTISSERIE GRILL GAME HENS

METHOD:
Rotisserie grilling

COOKING TIME:
40 minutes to
1 hour

ADVANCE
PREPARATION:
30 minutes to
2 hours for
marinating the
game hens

The game hen is about the most perfect bird ever to grace a barbecue. It's leaner than a full-grown chicken but still fatty enough to give you gorgeous, crackling crisp skin, and it cooks fast—in maybe 40 minutes. You can grill a game hen using any of the methods included in this book for chicken, but my favorite way is on the rotisserie. The slow, gentle rotation crisps the skin and internally bastes the meat. The game hens come off the grill tender enough to pull apart with your fingers.

*Game Hens
Flavored with Herbs
and Mustard*

SETTING UP THE GRILL

1 To set up a rotisserie on a charcoal grill, first light the charcoal in a chimney starter (see page 9).

2 Position the rotisserie ring on the grill.

3 Mound the coals on one side of the grill, parallel to where the spit will be, and place drip pans in front of them.

PREPARING THE GAME HENS

1 Tunnel your fingers under the skin, working gently so as not to tear it. Loosen the skin from the breast meat, then the thighs and even the drumsticks.

2 Stand the game hen upright and spoon the herb paste between the skin and meat. Massage the bird with your fingers to spread the seasoning under the skin.

3 Insert whole sage leaves under the skin of the game hens. Try to center them on each side of the breasts.

4 Spoon the remaining herb paste over the game hens.

TIP

■ If a smoke flavor is desired, use 2 cups of wood chips. I would go for a mild wood, like cherry or oak, and I wouldn't bother to soak the chips.

ON THE GRILL

1 Thread the game hens onto the rotisserie spit, positioning the pronged clamps so that they go over the birds rather than into the meat. You'll need two pairs of prongs for four birds.

2 Insert the end of the spit into the rotisserie motor socket.

3 If your rotisserie spit has a counterweight, position it so that it counterbalances the game hens.

4 When the game hens are cooked (after 40 minutes to 1 hour), they'll be a rich golden brown. Note the two drip pans under the spit. Wear grill gloves to protect your hands when removing the spit from the motor and unspitting the hens.

SERVES 4

**YOU'LL NEED:
Rotisserie;
butcher's string**

THE RECIPE

GAME HENS
FLAVORED WITH HERBS AND MUSTARD

4 game hens (1 to 1¼ pounds each)
1½ cups loosely packed, stemmed
    mixed fresh herbs, such as
    basil, rosemary, oregano,
    thyme, marjoram, chives,
    and/or flat-leaf parsley
3 cloves garlic, roughly chopped

1 teaspoon coarse salt
½ teaspoon black pepper
¼ cup Dijon-style mustard
¼ cup lemon juice
½ cup extra-virgin olive oil, plus
    1 to 2 tablespoons oil for basting
8 whole fresh sage leaves

1. Remove the packet of giblets (if any) from the body cavities of the hens and set aside for another use. Remove and discard the fat just inside the neck and body cavities. Rinse the game hens, inside and out, under cold running water and then drain and blot dry, inside and out, with paper towels. Loosen the skin from the meat of the game hens as shown in Preparing the Game Hens, Step 1 on page 272.

2. Make the herb paste: Place the herbs, garlic, salt, and pepper in a food processor and process to finely chop. Add the mustard followed by the lemon juice and ½ cup of the oil to make a thick paste.

3. Holding the hens upright (place in a bowl or pot if necessary), spoon about one eighth of the herb paste into the space between the skin and the body of each hen, massaging the skin to spread the paste evenly over the hen. Insert 2 sage leaves under the skin of each hen, trying to position a leaf in the center of each side of the breast. Place 1 teaspoon herb paste into the cavity of each hen.

4. Truss the game hens, as shown in Steps 1 through 8 on page 204. Arrange the hens in a nonreactive roasting pan or baking dish and spoon the remaining herb paste over them. Let the hens marinate in the refrigerator, covered, for as little as 30 minutes (while you preheat the grill) or as long as 2 hours. The longer the hens marinate, the more intense the herb flavor will be.

5. Set up the grill for rotisserie grilling (see page 22) and preheat to high. When ready to cook, skewer the game hens on the spit, as shown in Step 1 on page 273. Attach the spit to the rotisserie mechanism, as shown in Steps 2 and 3, and turn on the motor. Grill the hens until golden brown on the outside and cooked through on the inside, 40 minutes to 1 hour. Brush the hens with the reserved oil as they roast. To test for doneness, insert an instant-read meat thermometer into the thickest part of a thigh but not so that it touches the bone. The internal temperature should be at least 170°F.

6. Transfer the hens to plates or a platter and let rest for 5 minutes. Remove the trussing strings and serve at once.

ALSO GOOD FOR:
Chicken or quail could be prepared the same way as these game hens. You'll have enough herb paste for two chickens or eight quail.

METHOD:
Direct grilling

COOKING TIME:
8 to 12 minutes

**ADVANCE
PREPARATION:**
30 minutes for
marinating
the quail

HOW TO GRILL QUAIL

Grilled quail began turning up on restaurant menus in the 1990s and has become something of a new American classic. Despite its diminutive size, quail is more flavorful than chicken, but not as gamy as squab or partridge. You can probably find it at your local supermarket (most likely frozen) or, at the very least, a good butcher shop.

In the old days, chefs would butterfly these little birds, but nowadays much of the quail sold in the United States comes with the breastbone, backbone, and rib cage removed and a wire frame inserted in the cavity to keep the bird spread flat. You can grill a quail with its frame, but I prefer removing it and using the three-skewer method instead.

*Grilled Quail with
Pear and Pine
Nut Salad*

SETTING UP THE GRILL

1 To set up a charcoal grill for direct grilling, first light the charcoal in a chimney starter (see page 9).

2 Using a garden hoe or other long-handled implement, rake the burning coals into an even layer.

3 To see if the grill is preheated to high, use the test on page 10.

PREPARING THE QUAIL

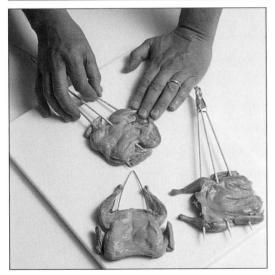

1 Lay the quail flat on the cutting board. Insert one bamboo skewer through the top portion of the quail, starting midwing on one side and coming out midwing on the other side. Insert a second skewer straight through the middle of the quail, and a third straight through from thigh to thigh. Note that these quail were bought whole, with breast- and backbones removed. The quail at the bottom still has a wire frame in its cavity.

2 Wrap the ends of the skewers with aluminum foil to hold them together. Sprinkle the quail on both sides with the spice rub.

TIPS

■ Most of the quail sold in the United States come frozen. This is not the end of the world, because the small, lean bird freezes well.

■ It's likely your quail will be partially boned and on a wire frame. If this is not the case, spatchcock the quail, as shown in Steps 1 through 4 on pages 221 and 222. The quail need to lie flat so you can grill them using the direct method.

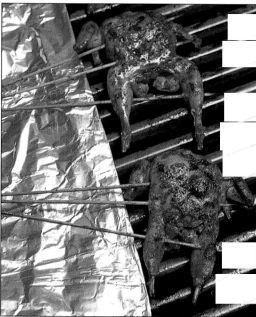

3 Pour the buttermilk over the quail.

ON THE GRILL: Grill the quail until nicely browned on both sides, 4 to 6 minutes per side. Place a sheet of aluminum foil under the skewers to keep them from burning.

SERVES 4

YOU'LL NEED:
12 long (10- to 12-inch), slender bamboo skewers, soaked for 1 hour in cold water to cover, then drained

THE RECIPE

GRILLED QUAIL WITH PEAR AND PINE NUT SALAD

4 quail (about 1 pound total)
1½ teaspoons coarse salt
1 teaspoon brown sugar
1 teaspoon sweet paprika
½ teaspoon ground coriander
½ teaspoon garlic powder
½ teaspoon ground cumin
¼ teaspoon ground cinnamon
1 teaspoon black pepper
1 cup buttermilk
1 tablespoon balsamic vinegar
1 tablespoon lemon juice
1 tablespoon honey

5 tablespoons hazelnut oil, walnut oil, or
    extra-virgin olive oil
3 tablespoons pine nuts, toasted
    (page 29)
3 tablespoons currants or dried cranberries
    (optional)
6 cups mesclun (mixed baby salad greens),
    washed and spun dry
6 ounces Roquefort cheese,
    crumbled
4 small ripe pears (preferably Bosc),
    halved lengthwise, cored,
    and rubbed with lemon

1. Remove the wire frames from the quail, if necessary. Or spatchcock the quail, as shown in Preparing the Chicken, Steps 1 through 4 on pages 221 and 222. Rinse the quail under cold running water and blot dry with paper towels. Insert 3 bamboo skewers in each quail, as shown in Preparing the Quail, Step 1 on page 277.

2. Combine 1 teaspoon salt with the brown sugar, paprika, coriander, garlic powder, cumin, cinnamon, and ½ teaspoon pepper in a bowl and stir to mix. Sprinkle the mixture over the quail on both sides, patting it onto the birds with your fingers. Sprinkle a little rub inside the quail, too. Pour the buttermilk over the quail and let marinate in the refrigerator, covered, for 30 minutes, turning once or twice.

3. Set up the grill for direct grilling (see page 10 for charcoal or page 16 for gas) and preheat to high.

4. Meanwhile, start the salad: Place the vinegar, lemon juice, honey, and ½ teaspoon each salt and pepper in a nonreactive mixing bowl and whisk to mix. Whisk in 3 tablespoons oil and the pine nuts and currants, if using. Place the greens and crumbled Roquefort on top of the dressing, but don't mix.

5. When ready to cook, remove the quail from the marinade and drain well. Brush and oil the grill grate. Place the quail on the hot grate and grill until cooked, 4 to 6 minutes per side, basting with 1 tablespoon of oil. Rotate the quail 90 degrees after 1½ minutes on each side to create attractive grill marks. The quail will be nicely browned on the outside and firm when cooked through.

6. Place the pear halves on the hot grate and grill 2 to 4 minutes per side, basting with the remaining 1 tablespoon of oil. The pear halves will be browned and tender when ready.

7. Toss the salad. Mound on plates and arrange 1 quail and 2 pear halves on each salad. Serve at once.

Note: Hazelnut oil is available at gourmet shops and many supermarkets and it has a wonderful nutty flavor that goes great in this autumnal salad. It's fairly perishable, however, so store the opened bottle of oil in the refrigerator.

VARIATIONS:
The recipe can be customized in any way you fancy. If you don't like Roquefort, for example, substitute goat cheese or Cheddar. Or you can use dried cranberries or cherries in place of the currants.

ALSO GOOD FOR:
The rub, buttermilk marinade, and salad in this recipe would work well with a variety of poultry and meats, from chicken and squab to pork chops, lamb loin chops, and venison.

FISH

METHOD:
Indirect grilling

COOKING TIME:
**45 minutes to
1 hour**

HOW TO GRILL A LARGE WHOLE FISH

When I was learning to cook, few Americans knew from grilled fish. Today, I don't have to convince you of its virtues. You are probably comfortable grilling tuna steaks or salmon fillets. But there comes a time when a griller wants to perform feats of fiery derring-do to impress a crowd. That's why every serious barbecue buff should know how to barbecue a whole salmon. Just don't let on that this is one of the easiest fish dishes in the world to cook.

*Whole Salmon with
Lemon and Dill and
Mustard-Dill Sauce*

SETTING UP THE GRILL

1 To set up a charcoal grill for indirect grilling, first light the charcoal in a chimney starter (see page 9).

2 Form two heat zones by raking the coals into two piles at opposite sides of the grill, using a long-handled implement, like a garden hoe.

3 If your grill has side baskets, divide the coals evenly between them. Note the drip pan in the center of the grill.

PREPARING THE FISH

1 Using kitchen shears, cut the fins and gills off the salmon. You can trim the ragged edges off the tail by making a V-shape cut, but this is strictly cosmetic.

2 Make a series of deep parallel slashes to the bone in each side of the fish. Place a slice of lemon and a sprig of dill in each to flavor the meat from the inside.

TIPS

■ If you live on the East Coast, you'll probably buy Atlantic salmon. This is a good thing, because Atlantics are rich, fat fish that aren't too big to fit on most grills. West Coasters have a choice between the smallish coho salmon, the mild medium-size sockeye, the pinkish-gray chum, and the luscious, formidable king salmon (also known as the Chinook). This last is what I used to demonstrate this technique and I've removed the head so the fish will fit on my grill.

■ A 23-inch kettle grill will accommodate a 7- to 10-pound salmon, and if the fish is still too large, you can gain another 4 inches by removing the head. A gas grill is trickier, as you'll be using the indirect method. Measure the diagonal length of that portion of the grill that won't be directly over the fire and purchase your fish accordingly.

MOVING THE FISH

To help get the fish on and off the grill, make a cardboard template slightly smaller than the fish. Wrap it in aluminum foil, shiny-side out, to keep the fish from sticking. Slide the cardboard support under the salmon to transfer it to the grill. Note how the cavity of the fish has been stuffed with lemon and dill.

ON THE GRILL: Baste the fish with the herb butter right after you put it on the grill and several more times throughout the grilling process. The salmon will take 45 to 60 minutes to be fully cooked.

SERVES 10 TO 12

YOU'LL NEED:
1 large piece of stiff cardboard;
2 cups wood chips or chunks (optional; preferably oak), soaked for 1 hour in cold water to cover, then drained

THE RECIPE

WHOLE SALMON WITH LEMON AND DILL

1 whole salmon (7 to 9 pounds with
  the head removed, somewhat
  heavier with the head on)
Coarse salt and black pepper
1 bunch fresh dill, 2 tablespoons
  chopped, the rest left in sprigs
2 lemons, thinly sliced and seeded

1 clove garlic, finely minced
6 tablespoons (¾ stick) butter,
  melted
Mustard-Dill Sauce (page 454),
  for serving
Dill sprigs, for serving (optional)

1. Set up the grill for indirect grilling (see page 12 for charcoal or page 16 for gas) and preheat to medium. If using a charcoal grill, place a drip pan in the center. If using a gas grill, place the wood chips, if desired, in the smoker box or in a smoker pouch (see page 17) and preheat to high until you see smoke, then reduce the heat to medium.

2. Cut a large piece of cardboard into a long rectangle that's almost as long as the fish and almost as wide (almost, but not quite—you don't want to see it under the fish). Wrap the cardboard in several layers of heavy-duty aluminum foil, shiny-side out, and set aside.

3. Trim the fish as shown in Preparing the Fish, Step 1 on page 283. Remove the gills or any fins, cutting off the latter with kitchen shears. Trim the tail. Rinse the fish, inside and out, under cold running water and then drain and blot dry, inside and out, with paper towels. Make 4 or 5 diagonal slashes to the bone in each side of the fish.

4. Season the cavity of the fish with salt and pepper and stuff it with half the dill sprigs and lemon slices. Tuck the remaining dill sprigs and lemon slices into the slashes in the sides of the fish.

5. Stir the chopped dill and the garlic into the melted butter. Brush the fish on both sides with some of this mixture. Season the fish generously on both sides with salt and pepper. Place the fish on the aluminum foil-wrapped cardboard.

6. When ready to cook, if using a charcoal grill, toss the wood chips on the coals, if desired. Place the salmon on its cardboard in the center of the hot grate away from the heat, and cover the grill. If you're working on a three-burner gas grill with a front-middle-rear burner configuration, place the fish over the middle burner. On a gas grill with a left-center-right configuration place the fish in the center on the diagonal, so the head and tail are near but not over the outside burners. Grill the salmon until cooked through, 45 minutes to 1 hour. Baste the salmon with the garlic-dill butter when you put it on the grill and then at 15-minute intervals, 4 bastings in all. To test for doneness, press the fish with your finger: It will break into clean flakes when fully cooked. Another test is to insert a metal skewer into the thickest part of the fish. When it is done, the skewer will come out very hot to the touch after 20 seconds. Alternatively, make a cut in the back of the fish and see if the meat next to the backbone looks cooked; if it is, it will be opaque, not translucent.

7. Transfer the fish to a large platter. Reseason the salmon with salt and pepper. To serve, run a knife along the backbone to separate the top fillet. Lift it off the bones in sections. Remove the bones and cut the fish crosswise into serving portions. Serve with the Mustard-Dill Sauce. Garnish with dill sprigs, if desired.

VARIATIONS:
There's no limit to the possible flavorings for whole fish. This recipe reflects a Scandinavian influence (dill and lemon). You could certainly vary the herbs to give the fish a different ethnic character. Whichever version you use, include the garlic.

For Mediterranean salmon, substitute basil and rosemary for the dill, and olive oil for the butter.

For Mexican salmon, substitute cilantro, sliced chiles, and limes for the dill and lemon slices; use olive oil in place of the butter.

For Pac-Rim salmon, substitute lemongrass, scallions, and basil for the dill, and fresh ginger slices for the lemon; use Asian (dark) sesame oil in place of the butter.

ALSO GOOD FOR:
Whole striped bass or snapper would be good grilled this way. Each will take 45 minutes to 1 hour.

METHOD:
Direct grilling

COOKING TIME:
12 to 20 minutes

ADVANCE PREPARATION:
30 minutes to
1 hour for
marinating the fish

HOW TO GRILL SMALL WHOLE FISH

When the first Europeans landed in the Caribbean, they found Arawak Indians grilling on a high wooden grate over a smoky fire. As distinctive as the cooking method were the indigenous seasonings: fragrant sprigs of thyme, fiery Scotch bonnet chiles, and sweet-scented allspice. A lot has changed since the days of Arawak cookouts, but Caribbean people still flavor their fish and meat with fresh herbs, tongue-blistering chiles, and allspice and still grill them. Here's a way to emulate their technique for grilling small fish.

French West Indian Snapper

SETTING UP THE GRILL

1 To set up a charcoal grill for direct grilling, first light the charcoal in a chimney starter (see page 9).

2 Using a garden hoe or other long-handled implement, rake the burning coals into an even layer.

3 To see if the grill is preheated to high, use the test on page 10.

PREPARING THE FISH

1 Using kitchen shears, trim the fins off the fish—here yellowtail snappers.

2 Trim the tails to give them a handsome V-shape. This is clearly for cosmetic reasons only.

TIPS

■ When selecting whole fish for grilling, choose a fish with a simple bone structure, weighing 1¼ to 1½ pounds (the weight won't change much after cleaning). Snapper would be the fish of choice in my neck of the woods (Miami). Other good candidates include pompano, porgy, redfish, black sea bass, and trout.

■ Fish has a tendency to stick to the grill. Enter the fish basket, a handy device that holds the fish between its hinged wire panels. The beauty of the fish basket is that you turn the basket, not the fish, so you never have a problem with delicate fish breaking or sticking. Be sure to spray the basket with oil before adding the fish.

3 Make a series of 3 or 4 deep parallel slashes to the bone in each side of each fish. This both helps the fish cook more quickly and evenly and enhances the absorption of the marinade.

4 Arrange the fish in a baking dish and stuff some of the marinade into the cavity of each. Spoon the remaining marinade on top and into the slashes in the fish.

PREPARING THE FISH BASKET

1 Spray the fish basket with oil. If you don't have spray oil, use a paper towel dipped in oil.

2 Place the fish in the oiled basket.

3 Close the basket and fasten it shut by sliding the ring on the handle.

ON THE GRILL: When you are ready to cook, put the fish basket with the fish inside on the grill. Turn the basket to cook the other side after 6 to 10 minutes and grill the fish for 6 to 10 minutes more.

FOR SERVING: To make Caribbean-style lime wedges, cut the sides off to obtain an oval section. When you squeeze the ends, the juice will flow easily—much more easily than from a conventionally cut lime wedge.

THE RECIPE

FRENCH WEST INDIAN SNAPPER

SERVES 4

YOU'LL NEED:
Fish basket or
fish grate
(optional)

4 small snappers or other small whole fish, cleaned and trimmed (1¼ to 1½ pounds each)

4 cloves garlic, minced

½ to 1 Scotch bonnet chile or other hot pepper, seeded and finely chopped (see Note)

1 teaspoon coarse salt

1 teaspoon black pepper

¾ cup lime juice

1 bunch chives or 4 scallions, finely chopped

2 shallots, thinly sliced

1 small onion, thinly sliced

3 tablespoons finely chopped flat-leaf parsley

2 tablespoons olive oil

4 sprigs fresh thyme or 1 teaspoon dried thyme leaves

4 dried bay leaves

4 allspice berries

Lime wedges, for serving

VARIATIONS:
Any small whole fish can be cooked in this manner using one of the many marinades in this book. The coconut shrimp marinade in Step 2 on page 320, for example, or Cuban mojo marinade in Step 1 on page 126 would be fantastic with snapper.

1. Rinse the fish, inside and out, under cold running water and then blot dry, inside and out, with paper towels. Trim the fish and make diagonal slashes in both sides, as shown in Preparing the Fish, Steps 1 through 3 on pages 287 and 288. Arrange the fish in a nonreactive baking dish just large enough to hold them.

2. Prepare the marinade: Place the garlic, Scotch bonnet, salt, and pepper in the bottom of a nonreactive mixing bowl and mash to a paste with the back of a wooden spoon. Add the lime juice and stir until the salt is dissolved. Stir in the chives, shallots, onion, parsley, and oil. Stuff some of this mixture into each of the fish cavities and some into the slits in the sides of the fish. Place a sprig or pinch of thyme, a bay leaf, and a whole allspice berry in each cavity. Pour the remaining marinade over the fish and let marinate in the refrigerator, covered, for 1 hour, turning once or twice.

3. Set up the grill for direct grilling (see page 10 for charcoal or page 16 for gas) and preheat the grill and the fish grate, if using, to high. When ready to cook, brush and generously oil the grill or fish grate or generously oil the fish basket, if using. Place the fish in the fish basket, as shown in Preparing the Fish Basket, Steps 1 through 3 on page 288. Place the fish or the fish basket on the hot grate and grill until the fish are cooked, 6 to 10 minutes per side (depending on the size of the fish), turning gently with a spatula or inverting the fish basket. To test for doneness, press the fish with your finger: It will break into clean flakes when fully cooked. The flesh will come cleanly away from the bones when pried loose with the tip of a paring knife, and a metal skewer inserted into the thickest part of the fish will come out very hot to the touch after 20 seconds. Transfer the fish to plates or a platter and serve at once with lime wedges.

Note: You can certainly use a milder chile than the Scotch bonnet.

HOW TO GRILL FISH ON THE SKIN

METHOD:
Direct grilling

COOKING TIME:
12 to 15 minutes

This is one of the easiest ways I know to cook fish and it never fails to make you look like a master. (It's so easy, I'm embarrassed to tell you how I do it—almost.) You grill a piece of fish fillet or whole side of fish on one side only—the skin side. You work over a moderate heat and cover the grill, combining the advantages of direct and indirect grilling.

This singular method has at least three benefits: The direct grilling makes the fish skin as crisp and tasty as a potato chip. Covering the grill enables the fish to cook from the top and the bottom simultaneously, eliminating the need to turn it (which is always a challenging business with fish fillets). Fish that's been cooked on the skin looks terrific—especially when you consider how little work it takes — you're looking at only 10 minutes preparation time.

Salmon with Mustard Glaze with bell-pepper-studded rice and grilled beets

SETTING UP THE GRILL

1 To set up a charcoal grill for direct grilling, first light the charcoal in a chimney starter (see page 9).

2 Using a garden hoe or other long-handled implement, rake the burning coals into an even layer.

3 To see if the grill is preheated to medium, use the test on page 10.

see page 9 ... page 10

PREPARING THE FISH

Brush the skin side of the salmon with oil or melted butter.

ON THE GRILL

1 Carefully spoon the glaze over the top of the fish.

TIP

■ The recipe with this technique calls for sections of salmon fillet with the skin on. Ask your fishmonger to cut them for you from a whole fillet. If you're careful, you could cook a whole side of salmon this way; use two spatulas to remove it from the grate.

2 Check the fish periodically to be sure the skin is crisp but not burnt. To do so, lift a corner of the fish with a spatula.

3 If the skin starts to burn before the fish and glaze are cooked through, slide a piece of folded aluminum foil under the salmon (you may want to use a grill glove— not your bare hands). This will keep the skin from burning. The fish will be done in 12 to 15 minutes.

THE RECIPE

SALMON WITH MUSTARD GLAZE

SERVES 6

FOR THE SALMON:
6 pieces of salmon fillets with skin on
(6 to 8 ounces each; ask your
fishmonger to cut them for you)
1 tablespoon olive oil or
melted butter
Coarse salt and black pepper

FOR THE GLAZE:
4 teaspoons toasted yellow mustard seeds
(page 29)
¾ cup mayonnaise
⅓ cup grainy mustard
1 tablespoon chopped fresh dill
1 teaspoon brown sugar (optional)
Coarse salt and black pepper

1. Run your fingers over the meat side of the salmon pieces, feeling for bones. Pull out any you find with needle-nose pliers or tweezers. Rinse the salmon under cold running water and then blot dry with paper towels. Brush the skin side of the fish with the oil and season both sides with salt and pepper.

2. Prepare the glaze: In a nonreactive mixing bowl whisk together 2 teaspoons

TIP

■ Because there are so few ingredients in this recipe, you need to use good ones: real mayonnaise, like Hellmann's, and a sharp, grainy mustard, like a Meaux-style one from France. To punch up the flavor and texture, I like to add toasted whole mustard seeds and fresh dill.

ALSO GOOD FOR:
Any fish with edible skin can be cooked this way, including striped bass, redfish, and snapper. Avoid fish with tough skin or tiny scales, like monkfish, sole, or flounder.

mustard seeds and the mayonnaise, mustard, dill, and brown sugar, if using. Add salt and pepper to taste.

3. Set up the grill for direct grilling (see page 10 for charcoal or page 16 for gas) and preheat to medium. When ready to cook, brush and oil the grill grate. Gently place the salmon pieces skin-side down on the hot grate. Spoon the glaze evenly over the tops of the fish pieces and sprinkle with the remaining mustard seeds. Cover the grill. Grill the salmon pieces until cooked through, 12 to 15 minutes. The skin will become dark and crisp. If it starts to burn, slide

folded rectangles of aluminum foil beneath each piece of fish to protect the skin as shown in Step 3 on page 293. To test for doneness, insert a metal skewer through the side. It should come out very hot to the touch after 20 seconds. The top of the fish should be lightly browned. Transfer the salmon to plates or a platter and serve at once.

HOW TO GRILL FISH FILLETS

METHOD:
Direct grilling

COOKING TIME:
8 to 12 minutes

ADVANCE PREPARATION:
30 minutes to 1 hour for marinating the fish

It's a cruel irony. The boneless fillet is America's favorite form of fish to eat, but it's also the most difficult to grill. The reason is simple: The skin and bones are what give fish its structure, so without them the fillet tends to fall apart or stick to the grill—or both. The secret is to use either a fish basket or fish grate. The former is a hinged wire basket in which you sandwich the fillets, the latter is a wire grid or flat metal plate with holes in it. The rigidity of the plate keeps the fish fillet from break-ing, while the holes allow smoke and fire flavors to reach the fish.

Garlic Halibut and red rice

SETTING UP THE GRILL

1 To set up a charcoal grill for direct grilling, first light the charcoal in a chimney starter (see page 9).

2 Using a garden hoe or other long-handled implement, rake the burning coals into an even layer.

3 To see if the grill is preheated to high, use the test on page 10.

(see page 9). ... the test on page 10.

TIPS

■ There are a few exotic ingredients in the recipe that accompanies this technique. Fish sauce is a malodorous, soy-sauce-like, Southeast Asian condiment made from pickled anchovies. Asian sesame oil is a lovely, nutty oil used in Japan and Korea. Cilantro root is used as a flavoring in Southeast Asia—it tastes like a cross between cilantro and parsley root. Additional cilantro leaves will work fine, too.

■ You can mix the marinade in your food processor, but you'll get an even richer flavor if you pound the garlic, sugar, ginger, and cilantro in a mortar with a pestle and then work in the remaining ingredients.

MARINATING THE FISH

1 To make the marinade, first reduce the garlic to an aromatic paste. This is most easily done in a mortar with a pestle.

2 Spoon the marinade over the fish. Turn the fillets a few times to coat them with the marinade.

PREPARING THE FISH BASKET

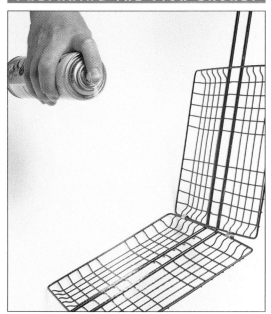

1 Spray the fish basket with oil. If you
don't have spray oil, use a paper towel
dipped in oil to oil the basket well.

2 Place the fish fillets in the oiled basket
and then fasten it shut.

ON THE GRILL

USING A FISH BASKET: Place the basket on
the grill. Wear grill gloves when turning the
basket: The metal gets very hot.

USING A FISH GRATE: Preheat the grate on
the grill. Oil it before putting on the fish.

TIPS

■ Be sure to oil the
fish basket or fish
grate before placing
the fish fillets in or on
it. No sense keeping
the fish off the
grill grate only to
have it stick to the
fish basket or grate.

■ Don't despair of
making the recipe if
you don't have a fish
basket or fish grate.
You can grill the fillets
directly on your grill
grate; just be sure to
brush and oil it
extremely thoroughly
before you put on the
fish. To further reduce
the chance of sticking,
brush the fillets with
vegetable or sesame
oil before placing
them on the grate.

DIRECTLY ON THE GRATE: Oil the preheated grate well, using a folded paper towel dipped in oil.

FINISHING THE FILLETS: A final brushing of sesame oil gives the fish grilled directly on the grate a handsome sheen.

SERVES 4

YOU'LL NEED:
Fish basket or fish grate (optional); spray oil (optional)

THE RECIPE

GARLIC HALIBUT

4 halibut fillets (6 to 8 ounces each)

FOR THE MARINADE:
6 cloves garlic, coarsely chopped
1 tablespoon peeled, grated ginger
1 tablespoon minced fresh cilantro leaves
1 teaspoon washed, chopped cilantro root
*   or 1 additional tablespoon cilantro leaves*
3 tablespoons sugar

¼ cup Asian fish sauce or soy sauce,
*   plus more for brushing*
3 tablespoons sake, Chinese rice wine,
*   or dry sherry*
3 tablespoons Asian (dark) sesame
*   oil, plus more for brushing*
*   (optional)*
1 teaspoon coarse salt
1 teaspoon black pepper

1. Rinse the fish fillets under cold running water and blot dry with paper towels. Arrange the fillets in a nonreactive baking dish just large enough to hold them.

2. Prepare the marinade: Pound the garlic, ginger, cilantro leaves and root, if using, and sugar to a paste in a mortar with a pestle as shown in Marinating the Fish, Step 1 on page 296 (start by pounding the garlic). Or purée in a minichopper or food processor. Work in the fish sauce, sake, sesame oil, salt, and pepper. Spoon the marinade on both sides of the fillets. Cover the fish with plastic wrap and let marinate in the refrigerator for 30 minutes to 1 hour, turning the fillets once or twice.

3. Set up the grill for direct grilling (see page 10 for charcoal or page 16 for gas) and preheat to high. When ready to cook, oil the fish basket, if using, or brush and oil the grill grate (see Note). Place the fillets in the basket as shown in Step 2 on page 297. If grilling directly on the grill grate, brush or spray the fillets themselves with oil.

4. Place the fish or the fish basket on the hot grate. Grill until each side of the fillets is browned and cooked through, 4 to 6 minutes per side. Because fish fillets tend to be fragile, I don't generally bother with rotating them to apply a crosshatch of grill marks. If grilling directly on the grate, brush the tops of the fillets with oil before gently turning them with a spatula. To test for doneness, press a fillet with your finger: It should break into clean flakes when fully cooked. Another test is to insert a metal skewer in the side of a fillet. When it is done the skewer will come out very hot to the touch after 20 seconds.

Note: To grill a fish fillet on a fish grate, place the grate on top of the regular grate and preheat to high. Oil the fish grate with a folded paper towel dipped in oil or lift it with tongs and spray with oil. As an added precaution against sticking, brush or spray the fillets themselves with oil. Arrange them on the hot fish grate. Grill the fillets as described in Step 4, turning them with a spatula onto a spot on the fish grate not previously occupied by a fillet. Continue grilling until done.

ALSO GOOD FOR:
If you live on the West Coast, halibut will be easy to find. This may be more challenging in the East. You could also make this recipe with fillets of salmon, bluefish, or sea bass—not to mention a good steak fish, like marlin or tuna.

METHOD:
Direct grilling

COOKING TIME:
4 to 12 minutes

**ADVANCE
PREPARATION:**
30 minutes to
2 hours for
marinating the fish

HOW TO GRILL FISH STEAKS

The steak is the easiest cut of fish to grill. Thick and compact, it won't fall apart the way fragile fish fillets do. Many fish steaks, like salmon and cod, have the added support of a section of backbone, which not only holds the fish together but adds flavor. The shape of a fish steak makes it easy to brand with grill marks, increasing its resemblance to beef even more. You can serve tuna charred on the outside and rare and juicy inside, just like your favorite cut of beef. You might even get that die-hard carnivore in your family—you know, the one whose physician has been urging him to eat less meat and more fish—to put a healthier steak on his plate!

*Basil-Grilled
Tuna with
Arugula and Yellow
Tomato Salad*

SETTING UP THE GRILL

1 To set up a charcoal grill for direct grilling, first light the charcoal in a chimney starter (see page 9).

2 Using a garden hoe or other long-handled implement, rake the burning coals into an even layer.

3 To see if the grill is preheated to high, use the test on page 10.

PREPARING THE FISH

1 Trim any dark, bloody sections off the tuna steaks.

2 Marinate the fish in the herb mixture. You need lots of oil to keep fish steaks from drying out when grilling.

TIPS

■ The most popular steak fish for grilling are tuna, swordfish, and salmon. Tuna and swordfish are quite lean, so they taste best when soaked in an oil-based marinade before grilling or when generously basted with oil as they cook. Salmon is well marbled, so it's less likely to dry out during grilling. But even it can benefit from a marinade—especially a sweet-salty mixture of sugar and soy sauce, as in the teriyaki marinade in Step 2, on page 417.

■ Tuna is the beefi-est of all seafoods, red in color and meaty to the tooth. Many people like to serve it rare in the center, just like beef. If you want to do this, buy sushi-quality tuna—the sort you'd get from a first-rate fishmonger.

TIPS

- Depending on where it's cut from, tuna may have dark or bloody spots. These are perfectly safe to eat, but they can taste a little fishy. I usually cut them off.

- If you like your tuna cooked through, try grilling steaks that are ½ inch thick. Thicker steaks have a tendency to dry out in the time it takes to cook them completely.

- I like a light smoke flavor here, so I don't bother soaking the wood chips.

ON THE GRILL

1 Slide a spatula under the fish steaks when rotating and turning them over. Don't use a barbecue fork, which will puncture the fish.

2 Rotate the fish 45 degrees to make an attractive crosshatch of grill marks. Grilled to rare the fish steaks will be done after 2 to 3 minutes per side; medium takes 4 to 6 minutes.

SERVES 4

YOU'LL NEED:
1 cup wood chips (optional; preferably oak), unsoaked

THE RECIPE

BASIL-GRILLED TUNA WITH ARUGULA SALAD

4 tuna steaks (¾ to 1 inch thick; 6 to 8 ounces each)
1 bunch fresh basil, washed and stemmed
4 cloves garlic, cut in half
3 strips lemon zest
Juice of 1 lemon (3 to 4 tablespoons)

1 tablespoon white wine vinegar
1 cup extra-virgin olive oil
1 teaspoon coarse salt
1 teaspoon black pepper
Arugula and Yellow Tomato Salad (recipe follows)

1. Trim any skin or dark or bloody spots off the tuna. Rinse the tuna under cold running water and blot dry with paper towels. Arrange the steaks in a nonreactive baking dish.

2. Combine the basil, garlic, lemon zest, lemon juice, vinegar, oil, salt, and pepper in a food processor or blender and purée until smooth. Pour this mixture over the tuna and let marinate in the refrigerator, covered, for 30 minutes to 2 hours, turning the tuna steaks several times.

3. Set up the grill for direct grilling (see page 10 for charcoal or page 16 for gas) and preheat to high. If using a gas grill, place the wood chips, if desired, in the smoker box or in a smoker pouch (see page 17) and preheat until you see smoke. When ready to cook, brush and oil the grill grate. If using a charcoal grill, toss the wood chips, if desired, on the coals. Drain the tuna steaks and arrange on the grill. Grill until cooked to taste, 2 to 3 minutes per side for rare, 4 to 6 minutes per side for medium, rotating the steaks 45 degrees after 2 minutes to create an attractive crosshatch of grill marks. The steaks should be nicely browned on the outside. Test for doneness using the poke method (see page 55): A rare steak will be quite

soft, with just a little resistance at the surface; a medium-rare steak will be gently yielding; and a medium steak will be quite firm. Transfer the steaks to plates or a platter and let rest for 3 minutes, then serve with the arugula salad.

Arugula and Yellow Tomato Salad

SERVES 4

1 bunch arugula, washed and spun dry
1 pint yellow cherry tomatoes (see Note), cut in half
3 tablespoons finely chopped red onion
2 tablespoons lemon juice
3 to 4 tablespoons extra-virgin olive oil
Coarse salt and black pepper

Combine the arugula, tomatoes, onion, lemon juice, and oil in a nonreactive bowl and gently toss to mix. Add salt and pepper to taste.

Note: Yellow cherry tomatoes are available at gourmet shops; if you can't find them, use red.

ALSO GOOD FOR:
You can use any fish steak for this recipe; for that matter, you can use the basil marinade for fillets or small whole fish.

VARIATIONS:
Many of the other marinades in this book work well with tuna steaks. For Indian-style tuna, for example, use the tandoori marinade in Tandoori Lamb Chops, Steps 1 and 3 on page 185. You can also season the tuna steaks with a dry rub like that in Step 1 of the Sichuan-spiced lamb chops on page 180.

METHOD:
Direct grilling

COOKING TIME:
About 12 minutes
for grilling the
onion and garlic,
plus 8 to 12
minutes for
grilling the fish

**ADVANCE
PREPARATION:**
1 hour for
marinating the fish

HOW TO GRILL FISH IN LEAVES

Long before grills and gridirons were invented, people cooked with live fire. Sometimes, they wrapped the food in edible leaves and cooked it right on or in the coals. This practice survives; you find it in countries as diverse as Mexico, Turkey, and Thailand. And while any type of meat or poultry can be grilled in leaves, the most popular food to cook that way is fish.

Why grill fish in leaves? First, fish is delicate and prone to drying out. A leafy wrapping seals in flavor and moistness, keeping the fish from sticking to the grate or falling apart. Moreover, the leaf imparts a distinctive flavor all its own, as you'll see in this dish from the Yucatán.

Bluefish in Banana Leaves with grilled chayote

SETTING UP THE GRILL

1 To set up a charcoal grill for direct grilling, first light the charcoal in a chimney starter (see page 9).

2 Using a garden hoe or other long-handled implement, rake the burning coals into an even layer.

3 To see if the grill is preheated to high, use the test on page 10.

PREPARING THE MARINADE

1 Grind the annatto seeds, cinnamon stick, bay leaf, and other dry seasonings for the spice paste in a spice mill. If you don't have a spice mill, use a coffee grinder.

2 Place the ground spices in a blender with the onion and garlic and the sour orange juice. The onion and garlic were grilled in advance.

TIPS

■ This technique features bluefish, a fat, rich, tender, highly flavorful fish that is loved by most people and loathed by some. That's because fresh bluefish is as sweet as butter; but when it's old, it's as fishy as musty hip waders. The best place to buy bluefish is from a fishmonger where the stock turns over frequently. Good substitutes for bluefish include salmon, halibut, and mahimahi (dolphinfish).

■ If you can't find banana leaves, you can use bottled grape leaves. Soak them in several changes of cold water to remove the excess salt. You'll need to use several leaves to wrap each piece of fish. You can also use aluminum foil to wrap the fish.

305...

1 Pour the marinade over the fish—in this case bluefish.

2 Quickly grill the banana leaf on both sides to make it soft and pliable.

3 Place the fish and flavorings in the center of a piece of leaf and fold over the sides.

4 Fold over the top and bottom of the banana leaf to completely enclose the fish.

5 Secure the flaps of the banana leaf packet with a toothpick.

ON THE GRILL: Grill the packets until the leaves are nicely browned. The fish is cooked after grilling 4 to 6 minutes per side.

THE RECIPE

BLUEFISH IN BANANA LEAVES

¼ medium onion
2 cloves garlic, peeled and skewered
    on a toothpick
½ teaspoon annatto seeds or paste or
    ½ teaspoon saffron threads
½ teaspoon black peppercorns
2 allspice berries
2 cloves
1 piece cinnamon stick (1 inch)
½ teaspoon dried oregano
1 dried bay leaf

6 tablespoons sour orange juice or
    lime juice
1 teaspoon coarse salt
2 pounds bluefish, skin removed,
    flesh cut into 8 uniform
    4-ounce portions
1 or 2 whole banana leaves
    (enough to make 8 pieces
    each 8 by 10 inches)
2 onion slices, cut crosswise into rings
8 sprigs fresh epazote, cilantro, or mint

1. Prepare the spice paste: Set up the grill for direct grilling (see page 10 for charcoal or page 16 for gas) and preheat to medium-high. When ready to cook, place the onion quarter and the garlic on the hot

grate and grill until lightly browned, 3 to 4 minutes per side for the garlic and 5 to 6 minutes per side for the onion (the onion and garlic can be grilled in advance). Alternatively, brown them for the same length of

SERVES 4

YOU'LL NEED:
Banana leaves
(optional);
wooden toothpicks
soaked for 1 hour
in cold water
to cover,
then drained

VARIATION:
You could vary or simplify the spice paste for seasoning the fish, using any of the marinade recipes in this book in place of this one.

time in a dry skillet over high heat or on a baking sheet under the broiler.

2. Place the annatto seeds, peppercorns, allspice, cloves, cinnamon, oregano, and bay leaf in a spice mill or coffee grinder and grind to a fine powder. Transfer the mixture to a blender or a food processor and add the sour orange juice, browned onion and garlic, the salt, and ¼ cup water. Purée until smooth.

3. Rinse the fish under cold running water and blot dry with paper towels. Arrange the fish in a nonreactive baking dish and pour the marinade over it, turning the pieces to coat evenly. Let marinate in the refrigerator, covered, for 1 hour.

4. Set up the grill for direct grilling (see page 10 for charcoal or page 16 for gas) and preheat to high. When ready to cook, if using fresh banana leaves, place them on the hot grate and grill until pliable, 10 to 20 seconds per side. Cut the banana leaves into 8 pieces 8 by 10 inches. Place a piece of banana leaf, dark-side down, on your work surface. Place a piece of fish in the center. Place an onion ring or two and a sprig of epazote on top of

the fish. Wrap up the fish in the banana leaf, as shown in Preparing the Fish, Steps 3 through 5 on pages 306 and 307.

5. Place the fish packets on the hot grate and grill until the banana leaves are nicely browned and the fish is cooked through, 4 to 6 minutes per side. To test for doneness, insert a metal skewer into a bundle. When the fish is fully cooked the skewer will come out very hot to the touch after 20 seconds. Or unwrap one bundle: The fish will break into clean flakes when pressed with your finger. Serve the fish in the banana leaves.

HOW TO SMOKE FISH

This is a technique near and dear to my heart, for I do it almost every Saturday. My wife likes her Sunday morning bagels with home-smoked salmon, you see, so smoking fish is a frequent ritual. Given its steep price and gastronomic cachet, smoked salmon may seem difficult to make at home. Although you *do* need to budget your time so that you have 4 hours for the fish to cure, you may be surprised to learn that the actual preparation time is measured in minutes, not hours. And you can do it on your backyard charcoal grill. The method in question here is hot smoking, which cooks the fish as well as smoking it. (Cold smoking is a more complicated process wherein the fish is smoked but remains essentially raw.) I've tried smoking salmon on a gas grill, but the results were unpredictable; it's hard to get enough smoke going. But smoking on a charcoal grill results in a terrific kipper-style salmon, and I can't think of a better topping for a toast point or bagel.

METHOD:
Indirect grilling

COOKING TIME:
15 to 20 minutes

ADVANCE PREPARATION:
4¼ hours for curing the fish

Rum-Smoked Salmon with bagels, cream cheese, and sliced tomato and onion.

SETTING UP THE GRILL

1 To set up a charcoal grill for smoking, first light the charcoal in a chimney starter (see page 9).

2 Place a drip pan in the center of the grill and divide the coals evenly on either side of it.

3 Place 1 cup of drained wood chips on each mound of coals.

(see page 9)

TIP

■ The world of fish smokers is divided between partisans of the dry cure and of the brine cure. The former is a sort of rub composed mainly of salt and sugar (2 parts of the latter to 1 part of the former). You thickly crust the fish with this mixture and it cures from the outside in. A brine is made by dissolving these seasonings in water—you soak the fish in the brine. I find you get a richer flavor with a dry cure than brine. But if you overcure the fish, it will become unpalatably salty, so you need to keep an eye on the clock.

PREPARING THE FISH

1 Cut the skin off the salmon. Starting at one corner, using a long, thin carving knife and holding the blade parallel to the cutting board, slide the knife between the flesh and the skin, pressing the skin against the board.

2 Holding the fish skin by one corner, continue cutting in a gentle sawing motion until you've removed the skin. Save the salmon skin for grilling—see page 313.

see page 313

3 Run your fingers over the top of the salmon fillet, feeling for bones. Pull out any you may find with needle-nose pliers or tweezers.

4 Pour the rum over the salmon and let it marinate for 15 minutes.

5 Drain and blot dry the salmon, then mix together the ingredients for the cure.

6 Bury the salmon in the fish cure.

T I P

■ The traditional
wood for smoking
salmon in the United
States—at least in the
Northwest—is alder.
Apple and cherry
are also good for
smoking. Hickory
and mesquite are
too strong.

7 Let the fish stand, covered, in the refrigerator for 4 hours. The salt in the cure
will draw liquid out of the salmon; you can
see it in the bottom of the baking dish here.

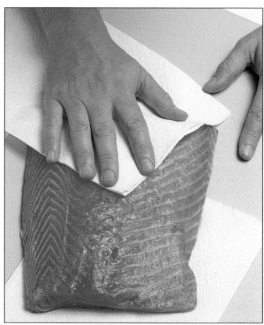

8 When ready to smoke, rinse the cure off
the salmon with cold running water and
blot the fish dry with paper towels.

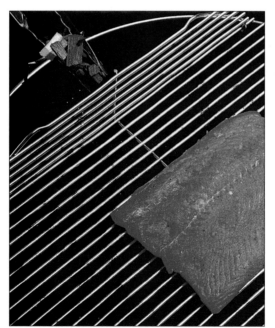

ON THE GRILL: Adding 2 cups more of wood
chips to the coals when you place the fish
on the grill generates the amount of smoke
needed.

TESTING FOR DONENESS: Press the fish—it
should feel firm and break into clean flakes
after 20 minutes. Use a spatula to transfer it
to a rack to cool.

RUM-SMOKED SALMON

1 salmon fillet (about 2 pounds)
1 cup dark rum
1 cup firmly packed brown sugar

½ cup coarse salt
1 tablespoon black pepper

1. Skin the salmon fillet and remove any bones as shown in Preparing the Fish, Steps 1 through 3 on pages 310 and 311. Rinse the salmon under cold running water and blot dry with paper towels. Lay the salmon in a baking dish just large enough to hold it and pour the rum over it. Let marinate for 15 minutes, then drain the salmon and blot dry with paper towels. Wipe out the baking dish.

2. Make the cure: Combine the brown sugar, salt, and pepper in a mixing bowl and mix well with your fingers. Spread one third of the cure over the bottom of the baking dish. Lay the salmon on top, skinned-side down, and sprinkle the remaining cure on top, patting it onto the fish with your fingertips. Cover the salmon with plastic wrap and let cure in the refrigerator for 4 hours.

3. Set up a charcoal grill for indirect grilling (see page 12), place a drip pan in the center, and preheat to medium-high. Rinse the cure off the salmon with cold running water and blot dry with paper towels. When ready to cook, toss 2 cups wood chips on the coals.

Brush and oil the grill grate. Place the salmon in the center of the hot grate over the drip pan away from the heat, toss the remaining wood chips on the coals, and cover the grill. Smoke the fish until cooked through, about 20 minutes. To test for doneness, press the top of the salmon with your finger. It should feel firm and break into clean flakes.

4. Transfer the salmon to a rack to cool. When cool, wrap it well in aluminum foil and refrigerate until cold. Serve cold or at room temperature. Smoked salmon will keep in the refrigerator, covered, for 3 to 5 days.

Salmon Chips

Salmon skin is so tasty, sushi masters have made it a delicacy in its own right. I think it's even better when grilled. Brush on both sides with Asian (dark) sesame oil. Season well with salt and pepper. Grill the skin directly over medium heat until crackling crisp, 10 minutes per side. Serve at once.

SERVES 6

YOU'LL NEED:
4 cups wood chips (preferably alder), soaked for 1 hour in cold water to cover, then drained; needle-nose pliers or tweezers

VARIATIONS:
If you have a smoker (see page 24), your job will be a lot easier. Follow the manufacturer's instructions for setting up the smoker and smoke the fish at 225°F for 1½ to 2 hours.

You can vary the flavor of the fish by replacing the sugar with a cup of another sweetener, like honey, molasses, or maple syrup (or even a mixture of sweeteners).

ALSO GOOD FOR:
Use this method to smoke any type of fatty fish, like bluefish.

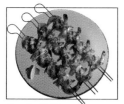

SHELLFISH

METHOD:
Direct grilling

COOKING TIME:
4 to 6 minutes

ADVANCE
PREPARATION:
1 to 2 hours
for marinating
the shrimp

HOW TO GRILL SHRIMP

Everybody loves grilled shrimp. Shrimp cooks quickly and evenly and the searing heat of live fire seems to bring out its natural sweetness. Its handsome size and shape are ideal for making kebabs, and shrimp readily absorbs the flavors of rubs and marinades.

The recipe accompanying this technique comes from Brazil, where shrimp is bathed in a tangy *tempeiro*—a marinade flavored with garlic, onion, peppers, cilantro, and coconut milk. The last counteracts shrimp's one potential shortcoming, a tendency to dry out during grilling. That's why shrimp is usually prepared with some sort of fat—marinated in yogurt or coconut milk, basted with oil or melted butter, or even wrapped in bacon.

*Brazilian Coconut
Shrimp Kebabs*

SETTING UP THE GRILL

1 To set up a charcoal grill for direct grilling, first light the charcoal in a chimney starter (see page 9).

2 Using a garden hoe or other long-handled implement, rake the burning coals into an even layer.

3 To see if the grill is preheated to high, use the test on page 10.

see page 9; page 10

TIP

■ Most of the shrimp sold in the United States has been frozen. As a result, it may taste a little dry or tough. To reinvigorate previously frozen shrimp, soak it for 30 minutes in salted water in the refrigerator. Use 2 tablespoons salt for 1 quart of cold water.

PEELING THE SHRIMP

1 To peel shrimp by hand, starting with the legs, remove the shell from the shrimp as though you were peeling a tangerine.

2 Pinch the bottom of the shell, just above the tail. The shrimp will pop out of the shell. Sometimes I leave the tails on.

DEVEINING THE SHRIMP

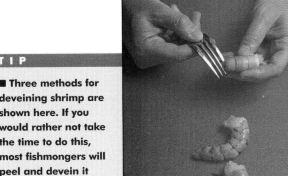

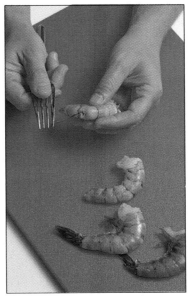

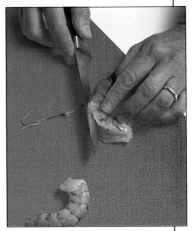

LAZY MAN'S WAY: Insert the tine of a fork roughly midway down the back of the shrimp and about ¼ inch deep. Gently pull the fork away from the shrimp; you'll pull out the vein with it. Note: This works often but not always. If the vein keeps breaking you'll have to use the butterfly method.

BUTTERFLY METHOD: Make a diagonal cut (one half of a V) in the back of the shrimp, about ¼ inch deep, just above the vein and running the length of the shrimp. Invert the shrimp and make another diagonal cut (the second half of the V) to remove the vein and flesh around it.

USING A DEVEINER: Insert the slender pointed end of the shrimp deveiner into the large end of the unpeeled shrimp just beneath the shell where the vein begins. Push the deveiner into the shrimp, straightening the shellfish as you go. The deveiner's serrated edge will cut through the shell, removing the shell and the vein.

PREPARING THE KEBABS

1 Cut the onion in eighths: First, cut it from top to root into quarters; then cut each quarter in half crosswise. This makes it easy to separate the onion into individual layers. Cut the flesh of the bell peppers off the core. This eliminates having to core and seed them. Cut the bell peppers into 1-inch squares, then triangles.

2 Thread the shrimp on skewers, alternating them with pieces of onion and bell pepper.

3 Spoon the marinade over the kebabs. It's easier to skewer the shrimp and vegetables before they're slippery with marinade.

ON THE GRILL: The shrimp are cooked through after grilling 2 to 3 minutes per side. Baste with butter during their last 2 minutes on the grill.

TIPS

■ Shrimp tend to spin when you place them on a single skewer. Two-pronged skewers solve this problem. If you don't have two-pronged skewers, skewer the shrimp on two slender bamboo skewers running parallel to each other (run one skewer through the shrimp and vegetables first, then insert the other).

■ Coconut milk is widely available canned. Be sure to get unsweetened coconut milk, not sweet coconut cream. If you are watching your fat intake, one company, A Taste of Thai, makes a reduced-fat coconut milk.

SERVES 4

YOU'LL NEED:
8 two-pronged
skewers or 16
slender bamboo
skewers, soaked
for 1 hour in cold
water to cover,
then drained

ALSO GOOD FOR:
*This marinade is
great for any type
of kebab—especially
scallops, fish, even
chicken. You can also
marinate fish steaks
and chicken breasts
in the coconut milk
mixture.*

THE RECIPE

BRAZILIAN COCONUT SHRIMP KEBABS

*32 jumbo or extra-large shrimp
(about 1½ pounds)*
2 onions
*1 large green bell pepper, plus ½ green bell
pepper diced*
*1 large orange, yellow, or red bell pepper,
plus ½ red pepper diced*
6 cloves garlic, cut in half
*1 piece (1 inch) fresh ginger, peeled and
thinly sliced*
*1 to 2 jalapeño peppers, seeded and diced
(for hotter kebabs, leave the seeds in)*

1 can (14 ounces) unsweetened coconut milk
3 tablespoons lime juice
2 tablespoons olive oil
1 teaspoon coarse salt, or more to taste
1 teaspoon white pepper, or more to taste
*⅓ cup chopped fresh cilantro or
flat-leaf parsley*
*3 tablespoons melted butter or olive oil
for basting (optional)*
Lime wedges, for serving

1. Rinse the shrimp under cold running water, then drain and blot dry with paper towels. Peel and devein the shrimp as shown starting on page 317. Cut 1 onion into 8 pieces, as shown in Step 1 on page 319. Break each piece into individual layers. Cut the flesh of the whole bell peppers off the cores, and then cut it into 1-inch triangles. Thread the shrimp and the onion and bell pepper triangles onto the skewers as shown in Step 2. Arrange the kebabs in a nonreactive baking dish.

2. Prepare the marinade: Cut the remaining onion in quarters. Finely chop the garlic, ginger, onion quarters, diced bell peppers, and jalapeño in a food processor. Add the coconut milk, lime juice, oil, salt, and white pepper. Taste for seasoning, adding salt and pepper as necessary. Add the cilantro and pulse a few times just to mix. Don't process the marinade too much after the cilantro is added or it will turn green. Alternatively, purée the ingredients in a blender, again adding the cilantro at the end and blending just to mix. Pour the marinade over the kebabs and let marinate for 1 to 2 hours in the refrigerator, covered,

turning the kebabs several times to ensure even marinating.

3. Set up the grill for direct grilling (see page 10 for charcoal or page 16 for gas) and preheat to high. When ready to cook, brush and oil the grate.

4. Place the shrimp kebabs on the hot grate and grill until the shrimp is cooked (it will be firm and white), 2 to 3 minutes per side. Baste the shrimp with the butter, if using, during the last 2 minutes of grilling.

5. Serve the shrimp at once with lime wedges. Unskewer the kebabs before eating, to avoid you or your guests burning your lips on the hot skewers.

HOW TO GRILL SHRIMP IN THE SHELL

METHOD:
Direct grilling

COOKING TIME:
4 to 6 minutes

ADVANCE
PREPARATION:
30 minutes
for marinating
the shrimp

Shrimp is one of the world's favorite shellfish, but a challenge that bedevils grillers everywhere: the tendency of this lean shellfish to dry out. One solution used from Portugal to Penang is to grill the shrimp in their shells, which shield the delicate meat from the fire, sealing in juices. The recipe I use to illustrate this technique is based on one from New Orleans. The locals call it "barbecued shrimp," but the shrimp aren't grilled. They stew in spices, fiery hot sauce, and finger-licking rich butter. It's time to harness the flavors of this dish to the service of the grill. Here's a New Orleans-style shrimp that's actually worthy of the name barbecue.

New Orleans-Style
Barbecued Shrimp
with grilled bread

SETTING UP THE GRILL

1 To set up a charcoal grill for direct grilling, first light the charcoal in a chimney starter (see page 9).

2 Using a garden hoe or other long-handled implement, rake the burning coals into an even layer.

3 To see if the grill is preheated to high, use the test on page 10.

PREPARING THE SHRIMP

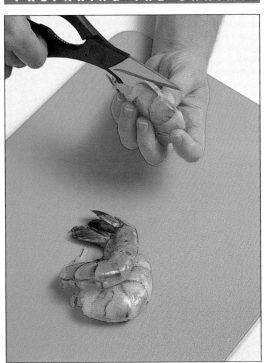 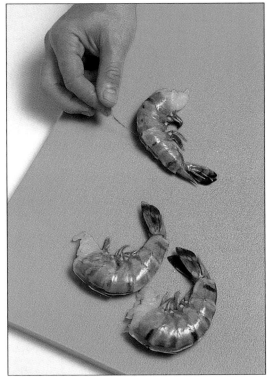

1 To devein the shrimp in their shells, use kitchen shears to make a lengthwise cut down the back of each shrimp.

2 Once the shell is cut, you can pull out the vein with your fingers or with the tine of a fork.

3 Skewer the shrimp. To ensure even grilling, position all the shrimp facing the same direction. Using two-pronged skewers, like the one here, keeps the shrimp from slipping or rotating during grilling. You can also use two single bamboo skewers.

ON THE GRILL: Cook the shrimp directly over a hot fire. They will be firm and white when fully cooked. This will take 2 to 3 minutes per side.

TIPS

■ You'll find a simple recipe for a Creole spice mix here, but if you're in a hurry, you could use your favorite commercial blend.

■ Louisianans would make this dish with whole shrimp (with the heads on). Indeed, the juices in the head are a special delicacy (you break off the heads and suck the juices). If you're feeling adventurous and you can find whole shrimp, by all means use them.

THE RECIPE

NEW ORLEANS-STYLE BARBECUED SHRIMP

2 pounds extra-large shrimp in their shells (about 48)
1 teaspoon cayenne pepper
1 teaspoon dried thyme
1 teaspoon dried oregano
1 teaspoon crumbled dried rosemary
1 teaspoon garlic powder
Coarse salt and black pepper
2 tablespoons olive oil
12 tablespoons (1½ sticks) butter
3 cloves garlic, minced
¾ cup bottled clam broth
¾ cup heavy cream

¾ cup beer
2 tablespoons Worcestershire sauce
2 tablespoons cane syrup, such as Steen's, or corn syrup, such as Karo, or more to taste
1 to 2 tablespoons hot sauce, such as Tabasco or Crystal, or more to taste
1 slice lemon (¼ inch thick), with rind but seeds removed
1½ tablespoons lemon juice, or more to taste
2 teaspoons sweet paprika
2 tablespoons chopped fresh flat-leaf parsley
Crusty bread (grilled; optional), for serving

SERVES 6 TO 8 AS AN APPETIZER, 4 AS A GENEROUS MAIN COURSE

YOU'LL NEED:
12 two-pronged skewers or 24 slender bamboo skewers, soaked for 1 hour in cold water to cover, then drained

1. Rinse the shrimp under cold running water and then drain and blot dry with paper towels. Cut the shrimp down the back and remove the veins as shown in Preparing the Shrimp, Steps 1 and 2 on page 322. Place the shrimp in a large mixing bowl.

2. Make the rub: Place the cayenne, thyme, oregano, rosemary, and garlic powder in a small bowl. Add 2 teaspoons salt and 1 teaspoon black pepper and stir to mix. Sprinkle all but 2 teaspoons of this mixture over the shrimp and toss to mix. Be sure to sprinkle a little rub into the cuts in the shells. Pour the oil over the shrimp and toss to mix. Let stand in the refrigerator, covered, for 40 minutes, while you make the sauce and build the fire.

3. Make the sauce: Melt the butter in a large nonreactive saucepan over medium heat. Add the garlic and cook until fragrant, but not brown, 2 minutes. Stir in the clam broth, cream, beer, Worcestershire sauce, cane syrup, hot sauce, lemon slice and juice, paprika, a little salt and pepper, and the reserved rub. Let the sauce simmer briskly, uncovered, until thick and flavorful, 10 to 15 minutes. Remove and discard the lemon slice. Taste for seasoning, adding

cane syrup, hot sauce, salt, and/or pepper as necessary; the sauce should be highly seasoned (see Notes).

4. Set up the grill for direct grilling (see page 10 for charcoal or page 16 for gas) and preheat to high. Thread the shrimp onto skewers as shown in Step 3 on page 323. When ready to cook, place the kebabs on the hot grate and grill until just cooked, 2 to 3 minutes per side, turning with tongs. When the shrimp are cooked, they'll be firm and white, with bright pink shells.

5. Unskewer the shrimp into individual soup bowls or one large bowl. Pour the sauce over the shrimp and toss to coat. Sprinkle with the parsley and serve with plenty of crusty bread (see Notes) for mopping up the sauce.

Notes: The sauce can be prepared up to 1 hour ahead. Reheat the sauce, whisking it, before serving.

If you wish to grill the bread, slice it and lightly butter both sides of each slice. Grill them for 1 minute on each side.

HOW TO GRILL SHRIMP ON A STICK TWO WAYS

METHOD:
Direct grilling

COOKING TIME FOR BOTH WAYS:
4 to 8 minutes

The shrimp kebab is a perfect party pass-around or hors d'oeuvre if there ever was one. It invites you to indulge in the primal pleasure of eating shrimp with your fingers, but the skewer keeps you tidier than when you devour the shrimp right out of the shells (for a deliciously messy version of the latter, see the barbecued shrimp on page 323). Here are two of my favorite ways to illustrate this technique—shrimp on a stick wrapped with smoky bacon and fragrant basil leaves and shrimp skewered on sugarcane with a dulcet rum glaze.

Shrimp on Sugarcane with Mount Gay Rum Glaze (top) and Bacon-Basil Shrimp on a Stick (bottom)

SETTING UP THE GRILL

1 To set up a charcoal grill for direct grilling, first light the charcoal in a chimney starter (see page 9).

2 Using a garden hoe or other long-handled implement, rake the burning coals into an even layer.

3 To see if the grill is preheated to high, use the test on page 10.

ON A SKEWER

PREPARING THE SHRIMP

TIP

■ Supermarket bacon will produce perfectly tasty kebabs, but for the height of perfection, use an artisanal smokehouse bacon, like one from Nueske Hillcrest Farm Meats (see Mail-Order Sources, page 481).

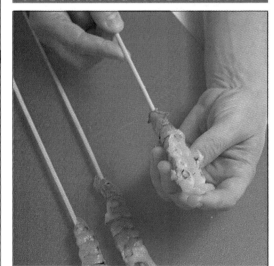

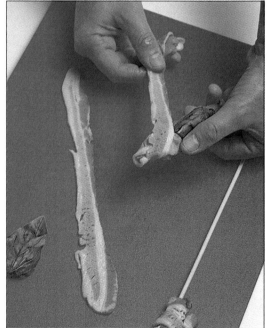

1 To skewer a peeled and deveined shrimp so that it is straight, hold it in a stretched-out position with one hand. Start at the tail end and insert a bamboo skewer into the shrimp so that it runs the full length. Keep unbending the shrimp with your fingers as you go.

2 After placing a whole basil leaf on the back of a shrimp, wrap it in a slice of bacon, starting at the top and turning the skewer to wind it on. Tuck under the top end of the bacon as you make the first wind.

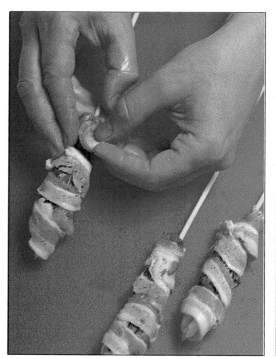

3 Tuck in the bottom end to secure the bacon on the shrimp.

ON THE GRILL: Cook the shrimp directly over high heat. Place a folded sheet of aluminum foil under the skewers to keep them from burning. The shrimp will be done and bacon will be well-browned and crisp after grilling 2 to 4 minutes per side.

VARIATIONS:
Substitute sage for the basil or prosciutto or pancetta for the bacon.

ALSO GOOD FOR:
Grill scallops, chicken tenders, or cubes of pork, veal, or beef on a stick: Wrap them with basil and bacon, skewer, and grill kebab style.

THE RECIPE

BACON-BASIL SHRIMP ON A STICK

24 jumbo or extra-large shrimp (about 1½ pounds), peeled and deveined (see pages 317 and 318)

24 fresh basil leaves
24 thin slices of bacon (each 6 to 7 inches long)

1. Rinse the shrimp under cold running water and then drain and blot dry with paper towels. Skewer the shrimp as shown on the facing page. Place a basil leaf on the back (the formerly rounded part) of each shrimp. Wrap each shrimp in a slice of bacon as shown at left and above.

2. Set up the grill for direct grilling (see page 10 for charcoal or page 16 for gas) and preheat to high.

3. When ready to cook, arrange the shrimp on the hot grate, placing a folded sheet of aluminum foil under the exposed portion of the skewers to keep them from burning. Grill the kebabs until the bacon is nicely browned and the shrimp are cooked through, 4 to 8 minutes in all, turning the kebabs to ensure even cooking. The shrimp will be firm and white when cooked through.

MAKES 24 PIECES; SERVES 6 TO 8 AS AN APPETIZER, 4 AS A LIGHT MAIN COURSE

YOU'LL NEED:
24 slender bamboo skewers (8 to 10 inches long), soaked for 1 hour in cold water to cover, then drained

ON SUGARCANE

PREPARING THE SUGARCANE

1 Trim off the ends of the sugarcane batons and cut each crosswise into 5-inch sections, using a sharp, heavy chef's knife.

2 Stand one of the cane sections on end. Working with a downward motion, cut the tough skin off the cane in thin lengthwise strips.

3 Again working with a downward motion, cut the cane into flat ¼-inch-thick strips. This is easier than it sounds because you'll be cutting along the grain of the cane.

4 Lay the cane strips flat on your cutting board. Cut each one lengthwise into ¼-inch-wide skewers.

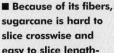

TIP

■ Because of its fibers, sugarcane is hard to slice crosswise and easy to slice lengthwise. A few taps with a pestle or hammer will help push the knife through when you are cutting against the grain.

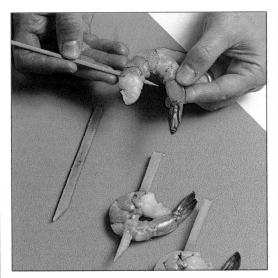

SKEWERING THE SHRIMP: Use a bamboo skewer to make two "leader" holes in the shrimp, one near the head end, one toward the tail. Insert the sugarcane skewers through these holes. Note that I have made a 90 degree cut off one end of each sugarcane skewer. This helps the skewer pierce the shrimp more easily.

ON THE GRILL: Arrange the shrimp cane kebabs on the grill grate. Brush them with glaze as they cook. The shrimp will be cooked through after 2 to 4 minutes per side.

SHRIMP ON SUGARCANE WITH MOUNT GAY RUM GLAZE

24 jumbo or extra-large shrimp (about 1½
    pounds), peeled and deveined
    (see pages 317 and 318)
½ cup firmly packed brown sugar
8 tablespoons (1 stick) butter,
    cut into 1-inch pieces
½ cup dark rum (preferably
    Mount Gay)

3 tablespoons Dijon-style mustard
1 tablespoon distilled white vinegar
¼ teaspoon ground cinnamon
¼ teaspoon ground cloves
¼ teaspoon black pepper, or more
    to taste
1 pinch coarse salt, or more
    to taste

1. Trim off the ends of the sugarcane and cut it into skewers as shown on the facing page. Rinse the shrimp under cold running water and then drain and blot dry with paper towels. Skewer the shrimp on the sugarcane as shown on the facing page.

2. Place the brown sugar, butter, rum, mustard, vinegar, cinnamon, cloves, pepper, and salt in a nonreactive saucepan and bring to a boil over high heat. Reduce the heat to medium and simmer until the mixture is thick and syrupy, 3 to 5 minutes. Taste for seasoning, adding salt and pepper as necessary. The recipe can be prepared up to 1 hour ahead to this stage; keep the shrimp in the refrigerator, covered. The glaze can be kept at room temperature.

3. Set up the grill for direct grilling (see page 10 for charcoal or page 16 for gas) and preheat to high. When ready to cook, brush

and oil the grill grate. Place the shrimp kebabs on the hot grate and grill until cooked, 2 to 4 minutes per side. Generously baste each with glaze once before turning and once before removing from the grill. The shrimp will be firm and white when cooked through. Serve any remaining glaze as a sauce on the side.

Note: Fresh sugarcane batons are sold nationwide at high-end food and produce markets and can be ordered from two companies: Melissa's and Frieda's (see Mail-Order Sources on page 481). To make your life really easy, Melissa's sells precut sugarcane swizzle sticks, which easily double as skewers. Cut them in half crosswise. Whole pieces of fresh sugarcane can often be found at Southeast Asian and Caribbean markets.

MAKES 24 PIECES; SERVES 6 TO 8 AS AN APPETIZER, 4 AS A LIGHT MAIN COURSE

YOU'LL NEED:
2 batons
(12-inch lengths)
of sugarcane
(enough to make
24 skewers,
each about
5 inches long and
¼ inch wide;
see Note)

VARIATION:
If you don't have sugarcane, make conventional kebabs using bamboo skewers and the rum glaze.

ALSO GOOD FOR:
Cubes of pork or chicken can be skewered on sugarcane and grilled like shish kebabs with the rum glaze.

METHOD:
Direct grilling

COOKING TIME:
THE FIRST WAY:
14 to 20 minutes;
THE SECOND WAY:
12 to 14 minutes

HOW TO GRILL A WHOLE LOBSTER TWO WAYS

There are at least three ways you can grill a lobster. You can cook it in a pile of seaweed directly on the coals in the style of a traditional clambake (the lobster cooks in the steam generated when the fire heats the damp seaweed). Or you can cut the lobster in half lengthwise and grill it over the coals—the second technique, which you'll find starting on page 333. The easiest way is simply to grill the whole lobster in its shell.

Grilled Lobster with Grilled Corn (page 361) and grilled new potatoes

SETTING UP THE GRILL

1 To set up a charcoal grill for direct grilling, first light the charcoal in a chimney starter (see page 9).

2 Using a garden hoe or other long-handled implement, rake the burning coals into an even layer.

3 To see if the grill is preheated to high, use the test on page 10.

TIP

■ When given the choice, I always prefer a female lobster to a male. The reason is simple: Females have more meat in the tail and sweeter flesh. And if it's summer, you might be lucky and land an egg-bearing lobster. Nothing is tastier than cooked lobster "caviar," the sweet, pleasantly waxy, delicately flavored roe. To tell the sex of a lobster, see below.

SELECTING A LOBSTER

1 A Maine lobster ready for grilling.

2 To identify the sex, turn the lobster over and look at the first set of swimmerets (tiny legs at the junction of the tail and the body). On a male (seen here), the swimmerets will be thick, hard, and rigid.

3 On a female lobster, the swimmerets will be thin, soft, and feathery.

GRILLED WHOLE

PREPARING THE LOBSTER

1 Position the tip of the knife in the center of the lobster's head.

2 Plunge the knife blade between the lobster's eyes. This kills the lobster instantly, although it may continue to twitch.

ON THE GRILL

1 Place the lobster on the grate on its back side.

2 Turn the lobster over and grill it belly-side down for the last 5 minutes. Stretch out the tail so the lobster lies flat.

3 To check the lobster for doneness, lift the carapace. When the lobster is fully cooked, the tomalley (the liver—the green stuff under the shell) will be set like custard.

GRILLED LOBSTER

SERVES 2

2 lobsters (1¼ to 1½ pounds each)
8 tablespoons (1 stick) butter, melted

2 tablespoons chopped fresh chives
(optional)

1. Set up the grill for direct grilling (see page 10 for charcoal or page 16 for gas) and preheat to high. Parboil the lobsters in 1 inch of water just until the shells turn red, about 2 minutes, or prepare them as shown on the facing page. When ready to cook, place the lobsters directly on the grate over the fire, back-side down. Close the grill lid. Grill the lobsters until the shells are a brighter red and the meat is cooked through and firm, but not tough, about 14 to 18 minutes for a 1¼-pound lobster; 16 to 20 minutes for a 1½-pound lobster. Turn the lobsters belly-side down for the last 5 minutes, stretching out the tails so the lobsters lie flat.

2. To test for doneness, lift the carapace (the shell over the back). Check the tomalley (the greenish liver); when it's set like custard, the lobsters are cooked.

3. Place the melted butter in 2 small bowls and add the chopped chives, if using. To eat, dip the lobster meat in the melted butter.

GRILLED SPLIT

SPLITTING A LOBSTER

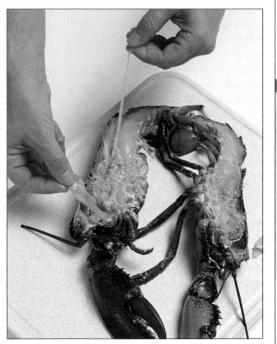

1 Kill the lobster as shown on the facing page. Then cut the lobster in half lengthwise, starting at the head and using a sharp knife. Work on a grooved cutting board to catch the juices; add these to the melted butter.

2 Remove the papery sac from the head of the lobster and discard it. Remove the vein running the length of the lobster's tail.

TIPS

■ You can also grill a lobster as is, without parboiling or cutting.

■ Many people like to cut lobsters in half before grilling. The advantage is that the flesh picks up more of the fire flavor and you can soak the meat with butter as it grills.

ON THE GRILL

1 Grill the lobster claws for 3 minutes before adding the body cut-side down and grilling for 3 minutes more.

2 Turn all the lobster pieces and grill for 6 to 8 minutes more. Baste the cut sides of the lobsters with melted butter during the last few minutes of grilling.

SERVES 2

THE RECIPE

GRILLED SPLIT LOBSTER

2 lobsters (1¼ to 1½ pounds each)
8 tablespoons (1 stick) butter, melted

2 tablespoons chopped fresh chives (optional)
Coarse salt and black pepper

1. Set up the grill for direct grilling (see page 10 for charcoal or page 16 for gas) and preheat to high.

2. Cut the lobsters in half as shown in Step 1 on page 333. Remove the papery sacs from the heads and the veins from the tails, as shown in Step 2. Remove the claws. Turn the lobsters over a bowl to collect the juices. Combine the butter and chives, if using.

3. When ready to cook, brush and oil the grill grate. Place the lobster claws on the hot grate and cover the grill. Grill for

3 minutes. Brush the cut side of each lobster half with some butter, sprinkle with salt and pepper, place cut-side down on the grill, and grill for 3 minutes. Turn, add the reserved juices, and grill cut-side up for 6 to 8 minutes more, until the flesh is firm, white, and just cooked, basting with some of the butter. Do not overcook. The claws will be cooked in 12 to 14 minutes in all; the body in 8 to 10 minutes.

4. Transfer the lobsters to plates or a platter and serve with the remaining melted butter.

HOW TO GRILL LOBSTER TAILS

METHOD:
Direct grilling

COOKING TIME:
8 to 12 minutes

ADVANCE PREPARATION:
30 minutes for marinating the lobster tails

Spiny lobsters (a.k.a. Florida lobsters, rock lobsters, or *langoustes*) look vaguely like Maine lobsters but have spotted, brown to tan bodies covered with formidable spines. They have no claws, and their tails are wider than those of Maine lobsters and are filled with firm, sweet, snowy white meat. The flavor lies somewhere between Maine lobster and shrimp, with a hint of scallop and monkfish. Usually only the tail portion is sold—a definite attraction for people who don't like handling whole live Maine lobsters. You simply split the tail and grill the lobster meat in the shell—it's one of the easiest shellfish to cook on the grill.

Spiny Lobster with Cilantro and Lime, Mango Salsa, and Boniato Mash

SETTING UP THE GRILL

1 To set up a charcoal grill for direct grilling, first light the charcoal in a chimney starter (see page 9).

2 Using a garden hoe or other long-handled implement, rake the burning coals into an even layer.

3 To see if the grill is preheated to high, use the test on page 10.

TIP

■ If you live in Florida or the Caribbean, you may be able to buy whole spiny lobsters. Cut them in half lengthwise (or have your fishmonger do it) and grill them as you would a split Maine lobster (see page 334). Depending upon the size, it will take 10 to 18 minutes.

PREPARING THE LOBSTER TAILS

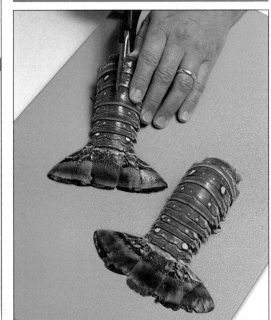

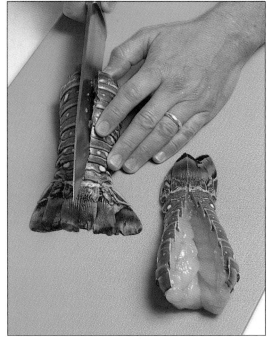

1 To butterfly the lobster tails before grilling, use kitchen shears to make a lengthwise cut through the hard top shell. You may want to wear clean gardening gloves to protect your hands.

2 Using a chef's knife, cut the tail meat in half lengthwise, slicing through the meat but not through the bottom shell. Note that once you've made this cut, you can open the lobster as I've done with the tail on the right.

ON THE GRILL

1 Place the lobster tails on the grate cut-side down to sear the meat.

2 After the tails have grilled for 3 minutes, turn them cut-side up so you can baste them with cilantro butter. Grill until done, 5 to 9 minutes more.

THE RECIPE

SERVES 4

SPINY LOBSTERS WITH CILANTRO AND LIME

FOR THE LOBSTERS:
4 spiny lobster tails (about
*   8 ounces each; see Note)*
2 cloves garlic, minced
Coarse salt and black pepper
2 limes, cut in half or in wedges
1 Scotch bonnet chile,
*   cut in half and seeded*

FOR THE CILANTRO-BUTTER BASTE:
6 tablespoons (¾ stick) butter
2 cloves garlic, minced
3 tablespoons chopped fresh cilantro

FOR SERVING (optional):
Lime wedges
Mango Salsa (page 460)
Boniato Mash (optional; recipe follows)

1. Butterfly the lobster tails as shown in Preparing the Lobster Tails, Steps 1 and 2 on page 336. Remove the vein running the length of the tails if you can find it (in some lobsters the vein is too small to locate). Place the lobster tails on a plate or in a non-reactive baking dish. Sprinkle the lobster meat with the garlic and season with salt and pepper. Squeeze the lime juice into the Scotch bonnet halves, then pour the juice over the lobster meat. Let marinate in the refrigerator, covered, for 30 minutes.

2. Prepare the cilantro butter: Melt the butter in a saucepan with the garlic and cilantro over medium heat. Cook until the garlic loses its rawness, but do not let it brown, about 2 minutes. Keep warm.

3. Set up the grill for direct grilling (see page 10 for charcoal or page 16 for gas) and preheat to high.

4. When ready to cook, brush and oil the grill grate. Brush the cut side of the lobster tails with some of the cilantro butter, place cut-side down on the hot grate, and grill for 3 minutes to sear the meat. Invert the tails and cook cut-side up until the flesh is white and firm but not dry, about 5 to 9 minutes. Brush the lobster tails twice more with the cilantro butter as they grill and again just before serving.

5. Place the grilled lobster tails on plates or a platter and serve with lime wedges, Mango Salsa, and, if desired, Boniato Mash.

Note: Spiny lobster season runs from the second week of August to the end of March in Florida—the time of year you're most likely to find them fresh. You can also buy it frozen. The popular rock lobster tails from South Africa are almost always sold frozen.

VARIATIONS:

For a Mediterranean twist, substitute lemon juice for the lime and basil for the cilantro. Omit the Scotch bonnet.

ALSO GOOD FOR:

This marinade is great for any type of seafood: Maine lobster, shrimp, scallops, fish steaks—for that matter, even chicken breasts.

Boniato Mash

SERVES 4

2 large boniatos (about 1½ pounds total; see Note), peeled and cut into ½-inch dice
Coarse salt
4 tablespoons (½ stick) butter
½ cup heavy cream
Black pepper
¼ teaspoon freshly grated nutmeg, or more to taste

1. Place the boniato in a large pot with cold salted water to cover and slowly bring to a boil over medium-high heat. Reduce the heat to medium and gently simmer the boniato until very tender, about 10 minutes.

2. Drain the boniato well and return to the pot. Mash with a potato masher. Or place the boniato in a mixer fitted with a paddle or dough hook and mash. You can also put it through a ricer. Do not use a food processor to mash the boniato or it will taste gummy. Add the butter and cream and continue mashing to form a creamy purée. Season with salt, pepper, and nutmeg to taste.

Note: Boniato is a Caribbean sweet potato with grayish-white flesh and the delicate flavor of roasted chestnuts. It is available at Hispanic and Caribbean markets as well as at many supermarkets.

HOW TO GRILL SOFT-SHELL CRABS

METHOD:
Direct grilling

COOKING TIME:
4 to 8 minutes

A soft-shell is a blue crab that has just shed its shell (crabs molt periodically so they can grow). It's particularly sweet and juicy in this stage, and you eat it shell and all. This may sound a little creepy, but it's like eating the sweetest imaginable crab between two really good potato chips. Traditionally, soft-shells are panfried, but grilling produces a crisp, succulent crab with a wonderful live-fire flavor. The only remotely tricky part is cleaning the crab, a process that can be traumatic for some people. I describe it in lurid detail on page 340, but you can always ask your fishmonger to clean the crabs for you, instead.

*Soft-Shell Crabs
with Tarragon
Tartar Sauce*

SETTING UP THE GRILL

1 To set up a charcoal grill for direct grilling, first light the charcoal in a chimney starter (see page 9).

2 Using a garden hoe or other long-handled implement, rake the burning coals into an even layer.

3 To see if the grill is preheated to high, use the test on page 10.

PREPARING THE CRABS

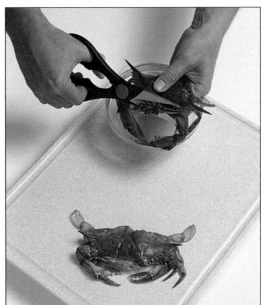

1 First use kitchen shears to cut the eyes and mouth off the front of the crab (this kills the crab instantly, although it may continue to wriggle). Work over a bowl to catch the juices, which you can pour over the crabs as they grill or save for fish soup.

2 Turn the crab on its back and lift and pull off the apron (the tab) on the belly.

3 Turn the crab over again (back-side up) and peel back the carapace on each side, starting with the point. Beneath it you'll find the gills (they look like elongated conical feathers).

4 Scrape or pull out the gills, using a paring knife or your fingers.

ON THE GRILL: Dip the crabs in melted garlic butter before arranging them on the grate. When fully cooked, the shells will turn deep red, 2 to 4 minutes per side.

TIPS

■ In order to crisp the shell, you need to baste the crabs fairly generously. I position a pan of melted butter by the side of the grill and dip the crabs in it right before grilling. If you follow suit, be careful about where you shake off the excess butter. You don't want to cause the coals to flare up.

■ Some people like to flour their crabs before buttering and grilling in the belief that you get a better crust. I've never found much of a difference, but you can certainly try this if you wish to.

SERVES 4 TO 8

THE RECIPE

SOFT-SHELL CRABS WITH TARRAGON TARTAR SAUCE

8 large soft-shell crabs
8 tablespoons (1 stick) butter
1 clove garlic, minced
1 cup mayonnaise
2 pickled jalapeño peppers, finely chopped
1 tablespoon drained capers
1 tablespoon chopped sour pickles (preferably French cornichons)
1 tablespoon lime juice

1 tablespoon finely chopped fresh chives or scallion greens
1 tablespoon finely chopped fresh tarragon leaves
2 teaspoons Dijon-style mustard
½ teaspoon black pepper
Ripe tomato slices, for serving
Lettuce leaves, for serving
Grilled and buttered white bread slices or buns, for serving

1. Clean the crabs as shown in Preparing the Crabs, Steps 1 through 4 on pages 340 and 341, or have your fishmonger do this for you. Melt the butter in a wide saucepan or frying pan with the garlic over medium heat and keep warm.

2. Combine the mayonnaise, jalapeños, capers, pickles, lime juice, chives, tarragon, mustard, and pepper in a nonreactive bowl and whisk to mix. Refrigerate the tartar sauce, covered, until ready to serve.

3. Set up the grill for direct grilling (see page 10 for charcoal or page 16 for gas) and preheat to high. When ready to cook, dip each crab in the garlic butter, shake off the excess, and place the crab on the grill. Grill until the crabs are cooked (the shells will become deep red), 2 to 4 minutes per side.

4. Transfer the crabs to plates or a platter and serve with the tomato slices, lettuce, tartar sauce, and buttered grilled bread or buns. Let everyone make his or her own sandwich.

VARIATIONS:
For Mediterranean soft-shells, dip the crabs in olive oil and baste them with lemon juice as they grill. Substitute 1 teaspoon each of chopped fresh basil and rosemary for the jalapeño peppers in the tartar sauce. For Cajun soft-shells, sprinkle the crabs with 1 teaspoon of Cajun seasoning and add ½ teaspoon of the seasoning to the tartar sauce.

HOW TO GRILL SCALLOPS ON ROSEMARY SKEWERS

METHOD:
Direct grilling

COOKING TIME:
4 to 6 minutes

When it comes to grilling shellfish, many folks overlook sea scallops. This is a shame, because nothing brings out a scallop's sweetness like the smoke flavor imparted by grilling. The following technique—grilling on a skewer fashioned from a fresh sprig of rosemary—can be used with all sorts of shell-fish. Besides the obvious dramatic impact (eyes pop at the novelty of nibbling a scallop off a rosemary sprig), the herb imparts an exquisite aroma.

Rosemary-Grilled Scallops

SETTING UP THE GRILL

1 To set up a charcoal grill for direct grilling, first light the charcoal in a chimney starter (see page 9).

2 Using a garden hoe or other long-handled implement, rake the burning coals into an even layer.

3 To see if the grill is preheated to high, use the test on page 10.

(see page 9) / see page 10

TIPS

■ Scallops are almost pure protein, so they tend to dry out when grilled. To keep them moist, marinate them in olive oil or wrap them in prosciutto or bacon. Or even do both, as you'll see here.

■ The most cost-effective way to buy rosemary for this recipe is to purchase a whole plant, not a bag of sprigs. Plants give you longer, sturdier sprigs, and they keep on producing rosemary for months.

PREPARING THE SCALLOPS

1 The crescent-shaped muscle on the side of the scallops is tough. If it hasn't already been removed from your scallops, pull it off with your fingers.

2 To make skewers for the scallops, strip the leaves off the bottom 1½ inches of the rosemary sprigs, using your thumb and forefinger.

3 Wrap each scallop in a strip of prosciutto. Pin the prosciutto in place by inserting a rosemary skewer through the side of the scallop. The base of the stem should extend just past the scallop.

ON THE GRILL: Turn the scallops 90 degrees after 1 minute on each side to create an attractive crosshatch of grill marks. Total cooking time is 2 to 3 minutes per side.

THE RECIPE

ROSEMARY-GRILLED SCALLOPS

1½ pounds sea scallops (28 to 32)
28 to 32 fresh rosemary sprigs
(each 3 to 4 inches long)
3 ounces prosciutto, sliced paper-thin

3 tablespoons extra-virgin olive oil
or basil oil
1 lemon, cut in wedges
Coarse salt and black pepper

1. Pull off and discard the small, crescent-shaped muscle from the side of any scallop that has one. Rinse the scallops under cold running water and then drain and blot dry with paper towels. Strip the bottom leaves off the rosemary sprigs, as shown in Preparing the Scallops, Step 2 on the facing page. Cut the prosciutto into strips just large enough to wrap around the scallops (about ¾ by 3½ inches).

2. Lay a scallop flat on your work surface. Wrap a piece of prosciutto around it and skewer it with a rosemary sprig. Repeat with the remaining scallops. Arrange the scallops on a plate or in a nonreactive baking dish. Drizzle the oil over both sides of the scallops, squeeze lemon juice over them (hold one hand under the lemon, fingers

together, to catch any seeds), and season with salt and pepper (go easy on the salt, as the prosciutto is fairly salty). Let marinate for 15 minutes while you light the grill.

3. Set up the grill for direct grilling (see page 10 for charcoal or page 16 for gas) and preheat to high. If you have a fish or vegetable grate (see page 477), place it on top and preheat it as well. You can also cook the scallops directly on the grill grate.

4. When ready to cook, brush and oil the grill grate. Place the skewered scallops on the hot grate and grill until just cooked, 2 to 3 minutes per side. The scallops are done when they turn white and feel firm (but just barely; they shouldn't feel hard). Serve at once.

MAKES 28 TO 32 SCALLOPS; SERVES 6 AS AN APPETIZER, 4 AS A MAIN COURSE

VARIATIONS:
You can certainly use other fresh herbs as skewers, especially stalks of lemongrass or thyme branches. You could also use strips of sugarcane.

ALSO GOOD FOR:
Shrimp grills beautifully on rosemary skewers (with or without the prosciutto), as do cubes of steak, fish, chicken, or even veal. You'll need to allow 2 to 3 minutes per side for 1-inch cubes of any of these.

METHOD:
Direct grilling

COOKING TIME:
5 to 8 minutes

HOW TO GRILL OYSTERS

Long before I lit my first charcoal, grill jockeys on Tomales Bay in central California were grilling oysters with barbecue sauce. And long before that, oystermen on the East Coast were staging oyster roasts on the barrier islands of the Carolinas. The fact is that something mystical takes place when you cook shellfish directly over a live fire—the searing heat makes oysters taste even more briny and more succulent than when cooked by other methods. And the shells burn ever so slightly, imparting a haunting smoke flavor.

Oysters with Wasabi Whipped Cream

1 To set up a charcoal grill for direct grilling, first light the charcoal in a chimney starter (see page 9).

2 Using a garden hoe or other long-handled implement, rake the burning coals into an even layer.

3 To see if the grill is preheated to high, use the test on page 10.

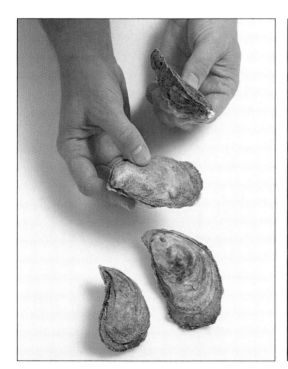

CHECKING FOR FRESHNESS: Gently tap the oysters on your work surface to make sure they close their shells. Discard any oysters that don't.

ON THE GRILL: Place the oysters on the grate with the deeper shell down to hold in the juices. The oysters are ready to eat the moment the shells pop apart, after 5 to 8 minutes. Serve them right away.

TIP

■ When buying oysters, make sure the shells are tightly closed or close when you tap the oyster a few times. The oysters should smell briny, not fishy. These are the tests for freshness, and you want to grill superfresh oysters only.

ALSO GOOD FOR:
Clams and mussels can be prepared the same way as the oysters. Clams will take 5 to 8 minutes, mussels 2 to 6 minutes.

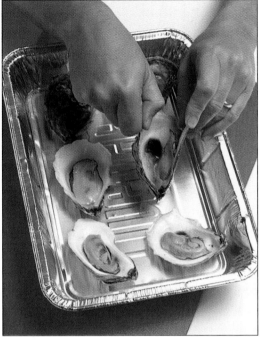 

BEFORE SERVING: Gently pry off the top shell with the oyster attached, and place the bottom shell in a pan, trying not to spill the juices. Pull the oyster off the top shell and place it in the bottom with the juices. The oysters in the pan are ready for a dab of Wasabi Whipped Cream—or just lemon, if you prefer.

MAKES 2 DOZEN OYSTERS; SERVES 4 TO 6 AS AN APPETIZER, 2 TO 3 AS A MAIN COURSE

THE RECIPE

OYSTERS WITH WASABI WHIPPED CREAM

VARIATIONS:
There's virtually no limit to the possible toppings for grilled oysters. Substitute white horseradish for the wasabi to make an English-style horseradish sauce. Or use curry powder to make a curry whipped cream. For a Mexican twist, top the oysters with salsa.

2 dozen large oysters
Wasabi Whipped Cream (page 455)

4 chives, cut into ¼-inch-long pieces

1. Set up the grill for direct grilling (see page 10 for charcoal or page 16 for gas) and preheat to high.

2. Scrub the oyster shells with a stiff brush to remove any grit or mud. Discard any oysters that fail to close when tapped.

3. When ready to cook, place the oysters on the grill with the more concave side down. Grill until the shells pop open, 5 to 8 minutes, or as needed.

4. Transfer the oysters to a pan or platter, discarding any that did not open. Pull off the top shells, cutting the adductor muscles with a paring knife if necessary. Pull the cooked oyster off the top shell and place it on the bottom shell with the oyster juices. Discard the top shells. Place a spoonful of Wasabi Whipped Cream on each oyster, sprinkle with chives, and serve at once.

HOW TO GRILL CLAMS AND MUSSELS

METHOD:
Direct grilling

COOKING TIME:
2 to 6 minutes

When it comes to cooking clams and mussels, the last place you probably think of is your grill. Not so barbecue buffs in Bordeaux, who have devised one of the world's most ingenious methods for cooking shellfish. They arrange mussels in a metal pan, pile dried pine needles on top, and set the whole thing on fire. Even if you don't have pine needles, you can cook both mussels and clams on the grill with delicious results. You'll never think of bivalves quite the same way again.

Shellfish with Sesame-Cilantro Butter

SETTING UP THE GRILL

1 To set up a charcoal grill for direct grilling, first light the charcoal in a chimney starter (see page 9).

2 Using a garden hoe or other long-handled implement, rake the burning coals into an even layer.

3 To see if the grill is preheated to high, use the test on page 10.

TIPS

■ When it comes to grilling clams, size matters. The smaller the better. Grilling tends to accentuate the toughness of a clam, so cherrystones or littlenecks are the best choices.

■ Mussels have a cluster of threads at the hinge (the place where the shells attach). This is sometimes called the beard. To remove these threads, pinch them between your thumb and forefinger and pull hard. Alternatively, use needle-nose pliers.

■ Use a stiff-bristled brush to scrub the mussel and clam shells. You want to remove every last bit of grit.

PREPARING THE SHELLFISH

1 Discard any shellfish with cracked shells or with open shells that fail to close tightly when tapped.

2 To beard a mussel, pull out and discard any threads at the hinge.

ON THE GRILL: Cook the mussels and clams just until the shells pop open, 2 to 6 minutes.

BEFORE SERVING: Toss the shellfish with the flavored butter.

THE RECIPE

SHELLFISH WITH SESAME-CILANTRO BUTTER

SERVES 4

2 pounds small clams
2 pounds mussels
8 tablespoons (1 stick) butter
3 tablespoons chopped fresh cilantro or
    flat-leaf parsley

2 cloves garlic, minced
2 tablespoons sesame seeds
Crusty bread, for serving

1. Set up the grill for direct grilling (see page 10 for charcoal or page 16 for gas) and preheat to high. Scrub the clams and mussels under cold running water, discarding any with cracked shells or shells that fail to close when tapped. Remove the threads at the hinges of the mussels.

2. Melt the butter in a saucepan over medium heat. Add the cilantro, garlic, and sesame seeds and cook until fragrant but not brown, about 2 minutes. Keep warm.

3. When ready to cook, arrange the clams and mussels on the hot grate, deep-shell-side down to hold the juices. Position the shells so that the bars of the grate hold them level. Grill over high heat just until

the shells pop open, 2 to 6 minutes. The cooking time depends on the size and freshness of the shellfish; clams have thicker shells than mussels and may take a little longer to open, so you may want to place the clams on the grill first.

4. Using tongs, transfer the shellfish to one large or four individual bowls, trying to keep the bottom shells level to hold in the juices. Discard any shellfish that did not open. Pour the sesame-cilantro butter over all and toss to mix. Serve with crusty bread for dunking in the sauce and eat the mussels and clams with your fingers.

VARIATIONS:
You can certainly vary the flavorings in the butter. A little curry powder would be a nice touch. For a low-fat version of the recipe, you could toss the bivalves with salsa instead of butter.

ALSO GOOD FOR:
If mussels and clams seem too exotic to grill, know that the sesame butter sauce is delicious with shrimp or scallops.

VEGETABLES
PLUS

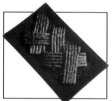

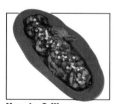

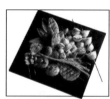

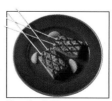

METHOD:
Direct grilling

COOKING TIME:
4 to 8 minutes

HOW TO GRILL ASPARAGUS
(and Other Long, Slender Vegetables)

Sesame-Grilled Asparagus

Grilling, more than any other cooking method, makes asparagus taste sweet and springlike. But, the slender stalks present a problem, for they tend to fall through the gaps in the grate. The Japanese have come up with an ingenious solution: They skewer the stalks crosswise with a toothpick or bamboo skewer, making them easy to turn with tongs, and you don't lose a single stalk to the fire.

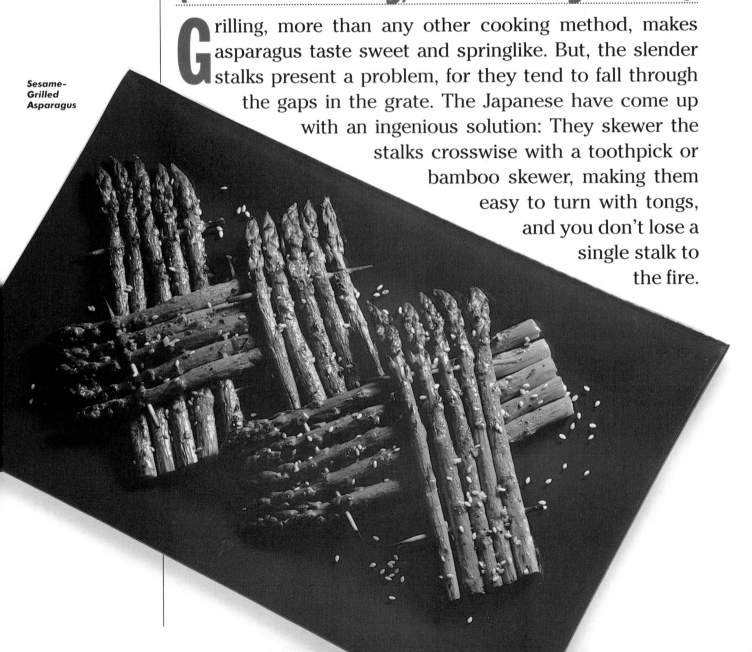

SETTING UP THE GRILL

1 To set up a charcoal grill for direct grilling, first light the charcoal in a chimney starter (see page 9).

2 Using a garden hoe or other long-handled implement, rake the burning coals into an even layer.

3 To see if the grill is preheated to high, use the test on page 10.

PREPARING THE ASPARAGUS

1 With one hand, hold an asparagus stalk at its base. Bend the stalk over with your other hand—the asparagus will break where the woody part ends and the tender part begins. Discard the base of the asparagus stalk.

2 Place 4 or 5 asparagus stalks next to one another. Skewer them crosswise in two places—just below the tips and 1½ inches from the bottom—with toothpicks or slender bamboo skewers. You will end up with something that looks like a raft.

ON THE GRILL: Grill the asparagus directly over the fire for 2 to 4 minutes per side. The asparagus rafts are easy to turn with tongs.

TIPS

■ When buying sesame oil be sure to choose a dark, roasted Asian variety. The nonroasted oils sold at natural foods stores lack the nutty flavor of the Asian product.

■ Leave a tiny bit of space between asparagus stalks when you make the rafts. This allows the asparagus to cook on all sides.

■ You can use untoasted sesame seeds here; the heat of the fire will toast them.

SERVES 4

YOU'LL NEED:
Wooden toothpicks
or slender bamboo
skewers, soaked
for 1 hour in cold
water to cover,
then drained

VARIATIONS:

*To make Italian
grilled asparagus,
substitute olive oil for
the sesame oil and
fresh lemon juice for
the soy sauce.
Sprinkle the hot
grilled asparagus
with chopped herbs
or freshly grated
Parmigiano-Reggiano
cheese. Or you can
baste the asparagus
with walnut or hazel-
nut oil and sprinkle it
with chopped nuts.*

*If you want to grill
asparagus without
skewering the stalks,
lay them on a veg-
etable grate (see
page 477).*

ALSO GOOD FOR:
*Asparagus isn't the
only vegetable you
can cook in a raft.
Any long, slender
vegetable, from okra
to sugar snap peas
to green beans or
scallions, can be
skewered in this
manner and grilled.*

THE RECIPE

SESAME-GRILLED ASPARAGUS

*1 pound asparagus (the stalks shouldn't
     be too thin)
2 tablespoons Asian (dark)
     sesame oil*

*1 tablespoon soy sauce
1 clove garlic, minced
Coarse salt and black pepper
2 tablespoons sesame seeds*

1. Set up the grill for direct grilling (see page 10 for charcoal or page 16 for gas) and preheat to high.

2. Snap off the woody bases of the asparagus and discard. Skewer 4 or 5 asparagus spears together, using tooth-picks or bamboo skewers, as shown in Preparing the Asparagus, Step 2 on page 355.

3. In a small bowl, combine the sesame oil, soy sauce, and garlic and stir with a fork to mix. Brush this mixture on the asparagus rafts on both sides. Season the asparagus with a little salt and lots of pepper.

4. When ready to cook, place the asparagus rafts on the hot grate and grill until nicely browned on both sides, 2 to 4 minutes per side. Sprinkle the asparagus rafts with the sesame seeds as they grill. You can serve the asparagus as rafts or unskewered.

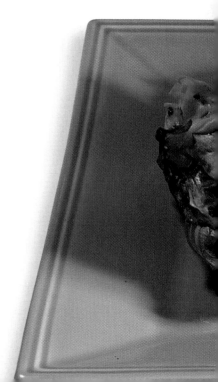

HOW TO BARBECUE CABBAGE

METHOD:
Indirect grilling

COOKING TIME:
1 to 1½ hours

This eye-popping technique is a favorite on the American barbecue circuit. The sight of a whole barbecued cabbage never fails to grab attention and it tastes as great as it looks. The cabbage here is stuffed with bacon and onions, anointed with butter and barbecue sauce, and grilled using the indirect method until it's tender enough to cut with a fork. Best of all, the preparation time is short, although you need to allow an hour or so for the cabbage on the grill. Thus, barbecued cabbage meets my three requirements for a truly great dish: It looks terrific, it tastes terrific, and it takes just a few minutes to prepare.

Barbecued Cabbage

1 To set up a charcoal grill for indirect grilling, first light the charcoal in a chimney starter (see page 9).

2 Form two heat zones by raking the coals into two piles at opposite sides of the grill, using a long-handled implement, like a garden hoe.

3 If your grill has side baskets, divide the coals evenly between them. Note the drip pan in the center of the grill.

PREPARING THE CABBAGE

TIP

■ The traditional cabbage for barbecuing is green cabbage. I also like the milder, sweeter flavor of a savoy cabbage. I suppose you could barbecue a red cabbage, although I haven't actually tried it (if you do, log onto my Web site, barbecuebible.com, and let me know how it goes).

1 Set the cabbage on a cutting board on its crown. Cut out the core by angling your knife about 3 inches down toward the center of the cabbage and cutting in a circle that is about 3 inches in diameter. The piece removed should look like a cone.

2 Pull out the core and discard it.

3 A 3-inch ring of crumpled aluminum foil will hold the cabbage upright while you work and as the cabbage cooks on the grill.

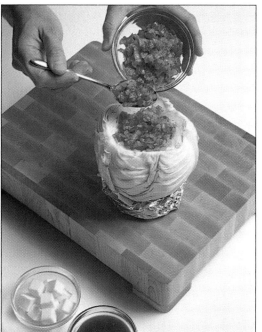

4 Spoon the bacon and onion mixture into the cavity of the cabbage.

5 Add the barbecue sauce and diced butter.

ON THE GRILL: Cook the cabbage for 1 to 1½ hours, using the indirect method. Add soaked wood chips to generate smoke.

TIPS

■ Some people like to wrap the cabbage in aluminum foil before grilling. This gives you softer, juicier cabbage, but it won't have a pronounced smoke flavor. One compromise would be to cook it for 30 minutes, unwrap it, add the wood chips to the fire, and finish grilling the cabbage unwrapped.

■ Be sure to present the whole barbecued cabbage to your guests—when the "wows" die down you can cut it up to serve.

SERVES 6 TO 8

YOU'LL NEED:
2 cups wood chips,
soaked for 1 hour
in cold water to
cover, then drained

VARIATIONS:
*For an eastern
European flavor,
substitute diced
kielbasa for the
bacon; for a Spanish
flavor, diced chorizo.
Either way, cook the
sausage with the
onions and don't
forget the barbecue
sauce.*

*You can barbecue the
cabbage by cooking it
in a smoker at 225°F
for 2½ to 3 hours.*

THE RECIPE

BARBECUED CABBAGE

4 tablespoons (½ stick) butter
4 slices bacon (¼ pound; preferably
    artisanal), cut crosswise into
    ¼-inch slivers
1 small onion, finely chopped

1 medium-size green cabbage (about 2 pounds)
¼ cup Basic Barbecue Sauce (page 447)
    or your favorite commercial brand
Coarse salt and black pepper

1. Melt 1 tablespoon of the butter in a skillet over medium heat. Add the bacon and onion and cook until just beginning to brown, 3 to 5 minutes. Drain the bacon and onion in a strainer over a bowl and reserve the drippings. Crumple a piece of aluminum foil and shape it into a ring about 3 inches in diameter.

2. Cut the core out of the cabbage as shown in Preparing the Cabbage, Steps 1 and 2 on page 358, and discard. Cut the remaining butter into dice. Stir the barbecue sauce into the bacon and onion mixture. Prop the cabbage upright on the aluminum foil ring, cavity facing up. Place the bacon and onion mixture in the cavity and top with as many pieces of butter as will fit. Using a basting brush, paint the outside of the cabbage with bacon drippings (save any remaining bacon fat for basting pork chops or making baked beans). Season the cabbage lightly with salt and generously with pepper.

3. Set up the grill for indirect grilling (see page 12 for charcoal or page 16 for gas) and preheat to medium. If using a gas grill, place all the wood chips in the smoker box or in a smoker pouch (see page 17) and preheat on high until you see smoke, then reduce the heat to medium.

4. When ready to cook, place the cabbage on its aluminum foil ring in the center of the hot grate away from the heat. If using a charcoal grill, toss all the wood chips on the coals. Cover the grill.

5. Grill the cabbage until very tender (when done it will be easy to pierce with a skewer), 1 to 1½ hours. If using a charcoal grill, you'll need to add 12 fresh coals per side after 1 hour if the cabbage is not done. To serve, peel off any dried-out or charred outside leaves and discard. Cut the cabbage into wedges and serve.

HOW TO GRILL CORN

METHOD:
Direct grilling

COOKING TIME:
8 to 12 minutes

A bitter controversy surrounds the best way to grill corn. At the heart of the debate is this: Does corn taste better grilled with the husk or without? Advocates of the former argue that the husk protects the delicate kernels from the harsh heat. Proponents of the huskless school (of which I'm a member) point out that corn steams rather than grills in the husk and that the husk blocks out that wonderful live-fire flavor. If you follow my huskless technique, which I use nightly in corn season, I'm ready to bet it will make you a convert—if you aren't already.

Grilled Corn

SETTING UP THE GRILL

1 To set up a charcoal grill for direct grilling, first light the charcoal in a chimney starter (see page 9).

2 Using a garden hoe or other long-handled implement, rake the burning coals into an even layer.

3 To see if the grill is preheated to high, use the test on page 10.

(see page 9), page 10

PREPARING THE CORN

1 Strip back the husk, starting at the top of the ear of corn; the motion is rather like that of peeling a banana. Leave the husk attached at the stem end.

2 Remove the corn silk and fold the husk back over the stalk. Tie the husk with string to form a handle.

TIPS

■ Buy corn in the husk. When you fold the husk back, it makes a handle for holding the corn while you eat it.

■ When buying corn, inspect it ear by ear (if allowed) by stripping back a portion of the husk. Look for ears with plump, juicy, fully formed kernels.

ON THE GRILL

1 Brush the corn with the garlic butter as it grills. The ears are cooked when golden brown, after 8 to 12 minutes. Note how the corn has been placed at the edge of the grill grate so the husks extend over the side away from the fire.

2 Another way to keep the husks from burning is to slide a sheet of aluminum foil under them.

THE RECIPE

GRILLED CORN

**MAKES 4 EARS;
SERVES 2 TO 4**

**YOU'LL NEED:
Butcher's string**

4 ears sweet corn in their husks
6 tablespoons (¾ stick) butter,
  at room temperature
2 tablespoons minced fresh flat-leaf parsley
1 clove garlic, minced
Coarse salt and black pepper

1. Set up the grill for direct grilling (see page 10 for charcoal or page 16 for gas) and preheat to high.

2. Fashion the husk of each ear of corn into a handle as shown in Preparing the Corn, Steps 1 and 2 on the facing page, and remove the corn silk.

3. Place the butter, parsley, and garlic in a mixing bowl and whisk or beat until smooth and creamy.

4. When ready to cook, lightly brush each ear of corn with a little of the garlic-parsley butter and arrange on the hot grate, positioning the ears in such a way that the husks are away from the fire. Grill the corn until the kernels are handsomely browned all over, 8 to 12 minutes in all, turning as needed, brushing with the remaining butter, and seasoning generously with salt and pepper. Remove the corn from the grill and serve at once.

VARIATIONS:
Dill, basil, or tarragon all make tasty alternatives to the parsley in the butter.

Grilled corn kernels make a delectable addition to salsas and salads. Lay the ears on their side and cut the kernels off the cob with broad lengthwise strokes of a knife.

HOW TO GRILL WHOLE EGGPLANTS

Grilled eggplant turns up in countries as varied as Japan, Iran, Israel, and Trinidad and Tobago. Most often the eggplant is charred in the skin to make some sort of dip—*baba ghanoush* in the Middle East, for example, or *choka* in the West Indies. Elsewhere, as in Turkey and Israel, it's diced and mixed with other grilled vegetables to make smoke-scented salads.

Cooking whole eggplant is one of the first things I teach in my grilling classes. The reason is simple: It's one of the few foods you can burn and still come out looking good. Indeed, not only can you burn the skin, you *should* burn the skin, for this is what gives you the smoke flavor.

Grilled Eggplant Dip with Grilled Pita Bread

SETTING UP THE GRILL

1 To set up a charcoal grill for direct grilling, first light the charcoal in a chimney starter (see page 9).

2 Using a garden hoe or other long-handled implement, rake the burning coals into an even layer.

3 To see if the grill is preheated to high, use the test on page 10.

PREPARING THE EGGPLANTS

1 To stud the eggplants with garlic, make slits in each, about ½ inch wide and deep, using the tip of a paring knife. Note how the garlic has been cut lengthwise into wedges.

2 Insert the garlic wedges in the slits in the eggplants.

TIPS

■ When buying eggplants for grilling, choose ones that are cylindrical rather than round or bulbous at one end. Cylindrical eggplants cook more evenly.

■ Female eggplants are marginally more tender than male. Females have a dimple at the end opposite the stem.

■ Don't feel obliged to stud the grilled eggplants with garlic as I do in the recipe illustrating this technique. The fact is millions of grill jockeys in the Middle and Near East grill their eggplants plain, adding raw garlic to the dip or salad. For a roasted-garlic flavor, stud the eggplants; for a fresh garlic flavor, don't.

TIPS

■ Tahini is a Middle Eastern sesame paste. Look for it in cans or jars at Middle Eastern markets and many supermarkets.

■ When puréeing the eggplant to make the dip, add the parsley at the last minute and process the dip in short pulses. Otherwise, the whirling processor blade will cause the parsley to color the dip green.

ON THE GRILL: Grill the eggplants until the skins are charred black all over, 20 to 30 minutes.

BEFORE MAKING THE DIP: Peel off the charred skin, exposing the smoky, garlic-scented eggplant flesh.

**MAKES ABOUT
2 CUPS;
SERVES 6 TO 8**

VARIATION:
To make a grilled eggplant salad, grill and peel the eggplants, as described at right, but chop them instead of puréeing them. Add some chopped grilled tomatoes, onions, and green bell peppers or horn peppers. Season the salad with lemon juice, olive oil, fresh garlic, plenty of chopped flat-leaf parsley, and some salt and pepper.

THE RECIPE

GRILLED EGGPLANT DIP

2 cylindrical eggplants (about 1 pound each)
*6 garlic cloves, each cut into 3 to 4
    lengthwise wedges*
3 tablespoons tahini
3 tablespoons extra-virgin olive oil
*2 tablespoons lemon juice, or more to taste,
    plus lemon wedges for serving*

½ teaspoon coarse salt, or more to taste
½ teaspoon black pepper
*3 tablespoons minced fresh flat-leaf
    parsley*
Lettuce leaves
Hot paprika
Grilled Pita Bread, for serving (page 189)

1. Set up the grill for direct grilling (see page 10 for charcoal or page 16 for gas) and preheat to high.

2. Make slits in each eggplant and insert the garlic as shown in Preparing the Eggplants, Steps 1 and 2 on page 365. When ready to cook, place the eggplants on the hot grate and grill until the skins are charred all over and the flesh is very soft, 20 to 30 minutes in all, turning with tongs. Transfer the eggplants to a plate to cool.

3. Peel the burnt skin off the eggplants. Don't worry about removing it all—a few

flecks add character. Coarsely purée the grilled eggplants with their garlic in a food processor. Add the tahini, 2 tablespoons of oil, the lemon juice, salt, and pepper. Taste for seasoning, adding salt or lemon juice as necessary; the mixture should be very flavorful. Add the parsley and process in short bursts, just to mix. Spoon the dip into a small bowl lined with lettuce leaves, drizzle with the remaining 1 tablespoon of oil, and sprinkle with paprika. Serve with lemon wedges and grilled pita bread.

HOW TO GRILL EGGPLANT SLICES

METHOD:
Direct grilling

COOKING TIME:
10 to 16 minutes

ADVANCE PREPARATION:
30 minutes for preparing the eggplants

Depending on how you cook it, eggplant can taste like one of several different vegetables. Grill it whole, and you bring out its soft, creamy, pâté-like qualities. Grill it sliced, and it acquires the soft, chewy consistency of a grilled mushroom or zucchini. Sliced grilled eggplant turns up across the world's barbecue trail because its texture soaks up the smoke and fire flavors like a sponge.

Inspired by the classic Italian *caprese* salad, the recipe that illustrates this technique features grilled eggplant slices topped with a sort of salsa made from diced tomatoes, fresh basil, and fresh mozzarella cheese. It's best to grill the eggplants ahead of time—even the day before you plan to serve them.

Eggplant Slices with Caprese "Salsa"

SETTING UP THE GRILL

1 To set up a charcoal grill for direct grilling, first light the charcoal in a chimney starter (see page 9).

2 Using a garden hoe or other long-handled implement, rake the burning coals into an even layer.

3 To see if the grill is preheated to high, use the test on page 10.

TIPS

■ Whenever I grill eggplant, I first use a French technique called disgorging. Sprinkling the slices with salt and letting them stand draws out the bitter juices, giving you a sweeter, milder-tasting grilled eggplant.

■ Disgorging also has a tenderizing effect on the eggplant. Is it absolutely essential? No, and many a time when I've been in a hurry, I've skipped this step. It does give you better-tasting eggplant, which is why I urge you to disgorge your eggplants before grilling.

■ As in the preceding technique, choose eggplants that are cylindrical, rather than bulbous: This gives you more uniform slices.

PREPARING THE EGGPLANTS

1 To disgorge the eggplants, arrange the slices in a single layer on a large rack placed over a baking dish or a rimmed baking sheet. Sprinkle both sides generously with coarse salt.

2 After 30 minutes, tiny beads of bitter juices will form on the surface of the eggplants. Rinse these off under cold water and blot the eggplants dry with paper towels.

ON THE GRILL: The eggplant slices will be done after grilling for 5 to 8 minutes on each side. To create an attractive crosshatch of grill marks, rotate them 90 degrees after 3 minutes of grilling.

EGGPLANT SLICES WITH CAPRESE "SALSA"

SERVES 6

FOR THE EGGPLANT:
2 cylindrical slender eggplants
  (about 1 pound each),
  cut crosswise into ½-inch slices
About 2 tablespoons coarse salt
3 tablespoons extra-virgin olive oil
2 teaspoons dried oregano
½ to 1 teaspoon black pepper
½ to 1 teaspoon hot red pepper flakes
  (optional)
3 cloves garlic, minced
3 tablespoons chopped fresh flat-leaf parsley

FOR THE CAPRESE "SALSA":
1 large, ripe tomato, seeded and cut into
  ¼-inch dice
1 piece fresh mozzarella cheese
  (about 5 ounces), drained, if necessary,
  and cut into ¼-inch dice
8 fresh basil leaves, slivered, plus a
  few whole sprigs for garnish
2 tablespoons extra-virgin olive oil
Coarse salt and black pepper
2 tablespoons lemon juice, plus lemon
  wedges for serving (optional)

1. Sprinkle the eggplant slices with the salt and let disgorge as shown in Preparing the Eggplants, Steps 1 and 2 on the facing page. Let the eggplants stand for 30 minutes.

2. Set up the grill for direct grilling (see page 10 for charcoal or page 16 for gas) and preheat to high.

3. Rinse the eggplant slices under cold water and blot dry with paper towels. Arrange on a baking sheet and drizzle 2 tablespoons of oil over them, rubbing the oil over the slices with your fingers or a pastry brush. Sprinkle the eggplant slices with half of the oregano, black pepper, hot pepper flakes, if using, garlic, and parsley. Turn the eggplant slices, drizzle with the remaining oil, and sprinkle with the remaining oregano, black pepper, hot pepper flakes, garlic, and parsley.

4. When ready to cook, arrange the eggplant slices on the hot grate and grill until nicely browned on both sides, 5 to 8 min-

utes per side. Rotate the slices 90 degrees after 3 minutes to create an attractive cross-hatch of grill marks. If the eggplant starts to burn before the slices are tender, lower the heat or move the slices to a cooler section of the grill. Transfer the eggplant slices to plates or a platter and let cool to room temperature. The grilled eggplants can be kept in the refrigerator, covered, for 24 hours. Arrange the eggplant slices in a shingle pattern, as pictured on page 367.

5. Make the *caprese* "salsa": Combine the tomato, mozzarella, basil, oil, and lemon juice in a nonreactive mixing bowl but don't mix them. The "salsa" can be prepared up to this stage several hours ahead and kept, covered, in the refrigerator.

6. When ready to serve, add salt and pepper to the "salsa" and gently toss to mix. Spoon the "salsa" over the eggplant and garnish with lemon wedges, if using, and basil sprigs.

VARIATIONS:
To make Argentine-style grilled egg-plants, cut the slices a little thicker (¾ to 1 inch). Grill for 6 to 10 minutes per side. Omit the caprese "salsa" and drizzle extra-virgin olive oil over the grilled egg-plants before serving.

The Japanese like to grill Asian eggplants that have been cut in half lengthwise. Using a sharp knife, score the skin to speed up the cooking. Brush the eggplants with Asian (dark) sesame oil before grilling. You'll need to grill the eggplant halves about 8 to 10 minutes per side.

HOW TO GRILL LETTUCE

At first glance, lettuce might seem like the *last* vegetable you'd attempt to cook on the grill. Given its propensity to wilt on a warm day, why would you ever expose it to fire? Yet Italians love grilled lettuce—they love the spotted, crinkled chiaroscuro of its looks and the way the leaves absorb the flavor of the fire. The secret lies in the choice of lettuce— the Italians grill firm, bitter lettuces, such as radicchio and endive, that can stand up to the searing heat.

Lettuces with Venetian Sweet-and-Sour Sauce

S E T T I N G   U P   T H E   G R I L L

1 To set up a charcoal grill for direct grilling, first light the charcoal in a chimney starter (see page 9).

2 Using a garden hoe or other long-handled implement, rake the burning coals into an even layer.

3 To see if the grill is preheated to high, use the test on page 10.

PREPARING THE RADICCHIO: Cut the radicchio into wedges and skewer them with slender bamboo skewers or toothpicks. (If your skewers are too long, you can cut them with kitchen shears.) Skewering keeps the radicchio wedges from falling apart.

ON THE GRILL: Baste the lettuces with oil as they grill. Grill each side of the radicchio and endives, 3 to 5 minutes per side.

TIPS

■ You can certainly serve grilled lettuce hot off the grill, but it's also tasty at room temperature. Thus, it's a good make-ahead dish to have on hand at a cookout, freeing up the grill for other items that require some last-minute attention.

■ I pair grilled lettuce with a thick, silky *agrodolce,* a sweet-sour sauce from Venice. The chocolate gives the sauce an earthy richness, a trick Mexicans have used for centuries in the preparation of *mole poblano.*

■ The wood chips are not soaked in the recipe that illustrates this technique. This gives you the flavor of wood grilling, not smoking.

■ Grill masters in Italy cook the lettuces dry. I like the extra flavor that comes from a light basting with olive oil.

THE RECIPE

LETTUCES WITH VENETIAN SWEET-AND-SOUR SAUCE

FOR THE SWEET-AND-SOUR SAUCE:
3 tablespoons extra-virgin olive oil
2 cloves garlic, peeled and gently crushed
 with the side of a knife
3 tablespoons pine nuts
3 tablespoons currants or raisins
⅓ cup balsamic vinegar,
⅓ cup honey
1 ounce semisweet chocolate,
 coarsely chopped
Coarse salt and black pepper
1 tablespoon butter

FOR THE LETTUCES:
2 small or 1 large head radicchio
2 medium Belgian endives, halved lengthwise
2 tablespoons extra-virgin olive oil

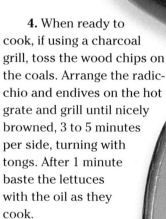

1. Make the sweet-and-sour sauce: Heat the oil in a saucepan over medium heat. Add the garlic and cook until lightly browned, about 3 minutes. Add the pine nuts and currants and cook, stirring, until the pine nuts are lightly browned, about 2 minutes. Stir in the vinegar, honey, and chocolate and bring to a boil. Simmer the sauce until thick and syrupy, 3 to 5 minutes, whisking to mix in the chocolate. Season the sauce with salt and pepper to taste. Remove the pan from the heat and whisk in the butter. (The sauce can be prepared up to 6 hours ahead and reheated.)

2. Set up the grill for direct grilling (see page 10 for charcoal or page 16 for gas) and preheat to high. If using a gas grill, place the wood chips in the smoker box or in a smoker pouch (see page 17) and preheat until you see smoke.

3. Cut the radicchio into wedges (each wedge should be about 1 inch thick at the outside edge). Run a slender bamboo skewer or toothpick crosswise through each wedge to hold the leaves together. You don't need to skewer the endives.

4. When ready to cook, if using a charcoal grill, toss the wood chips on the coals. Arrange the radicchio and endives on the hot grate and grill until nicely browned, 3 to 5 minutes per side, turning with tongs. After 1 minute baste the lettuces with the oil as they cook.

5. Transfer the grilled lettuces to plates or a platter and serve with the sauce in a bowl on the side or drizzle it over them. For a richer flavor, although a less handsome appearance, turn the lettuces a few times to soak up the sauce. Serve hot or warm.

HOW TO GRILL MUSHROOMS

METHOD:
Direct grilling

COOKING TIME:
6 to 10 minutes

Looking for a new way to cook mushrooms? Fire up your grill. Mushrooms readily absorb flavorful marinades, not to mention the scent of the fire and wood smoke. The only real challenge is cooking them evenly and keeping them from falling through the bars of the grate. This can be accomplished by skewering them (it's easier to turn one kebab than six individual mushrooms) or "stir-grilling" them in a grill wok or grill skillet. These look like a wok or frying pan made of perforated metal plate (see page 477). They allow you to toss the mushrooms, as you would in a wok, while the many holes let the smoke and fire flavors pass through. Stir-grilling must be done quickly over high heat to keep the loss of the mushroom juices to a minimum.

TIPS

■ Try to use a variety of mushrooms—the more, the better. Most gourmet shops carry at least a half-dozen different types of exotic mushrooms. Even your local supermarket probably has two or three varieties.

■ Grill shops sell a variety of skillet- and wok-type grilling devices. Look for one with a gracefully curved bottom and lots of holes.

Mexican Mushroom Mixed Grill

SETTING UP THE GRILL

1 To set up a charcoal grill for direct grilling, first light the charcoal in a chimney starter (see page 9).

2 Using a garden hoe or other long-handled implement, rake the burning coals into an even layer.

3 To see if the grill is preheated to high, use the test on page 10.

PREPARING THE MUSHROOMS

1 Trim the stems off the shiitakes, cutting them at the base of the caps. Pictured here (starting below my hand and running counterclockwise): oyster mushrooms, shiitakes, yellow oyster mushrooms, honshimeji, and crimini mushrooms.

2 If you don't have a grill wok, skewer the mushrooms by kind, taking care not to break the caps.

ON THE GRILL: Grill the mushroom kebabs, oiled-side down, on the grate for 3 to 5 minutes. Brush the second side with oil before turning and grilling for 3 to 5 minutes more. Better yet, toss all the mushrooms in oil and "stir-grill" in a grill wok (seen at the top of the photo) until tender and smoky, 6 to 10 minutes.

MEXICAN MUSHROOM MIXED GRILL

*1 pound mixed mushrooms (preferably
    exotic mushrooms, including
    shiitakes, morels, oyster
    mushrooms, hedgehog
    mushrooms, lobster mushrooms,
    and the like)*
3 tablespoons extra-virgin olive oil
2 cloves garlic, minced
Coarse salt and black pepper
*2 plum tomatoes, grilled (page 393),
    seeded, and diced*

*1 medium onion, quartered, grilled
    (page 380), and diced*
*2 jalapeño peppers or more to taste,
    grilled, sliced crosswise, and
    seeded (for a hotter mixed grill,
    leave the seeds in)*
*2 tablespoons chopped cilantro, plus small
    sprigs for garnish*
2 tablespoons lime juice
Thin lime slices, for garnish

1. Set up the grill for direct grilling (see page 10 for charcoal or page 16 for gas) and preheat to high. If using a gas grill, place the wood chips in the smoker box or in a smoker pouch (see page 17) and preheat until you see smoke.

2. Using a damp paper towel, wipe the mushrooms clean. Trim the mushrooms and cut any large ones in half or quarters, so that all are roughly the same size. When ready to cook, if using a charcoal grill, toss the wood chips on the coals.

3. "Stir-grill" method: Place the grill wok on the grill to preheat. When ready to cook, lightly spray the wok with oil, removing it from the grill when you do so. Toss the mushrooms with the oil and add them to the wok. Grill until the mushrooms are nicely browned, 6 to 10 minutes, shaking the wok

and stirring the mushrooms with tongs to ensure even grilling (use a grill mitt to handle the wok). Generously season the mushrooms with salt and pepper as they grill.

Skewer method: Skewer the mushrooms as shown in Preparing the Mushrooms, Step 2 on the facing page. When ready to cook, brush one side of the mushrooms with oil and season with salt and pepper. Grill the mushrooms 3 to 5 minutes per side, basting with oil before and after turning; when done the mushrooms will be browned and tender, 6 to 10 minutes in all.

4. Transfer the grilled mushrooms to a large bowl (unskewer if necessary). Stir in the tomatoes, onion, jalapeños, chopped cilantro, and lime juice. Add salt and pepper to taste. Garnish with the lime slices and cilantro sprigs and serve at once.

SERVES 4

YOU'LL NEED:
Grill wok or skillet
or 10 to 12
bamboo skewers,
soaked for 1 hour
in cold water to
cover, then
drained; 1 cup
wood chips
(preferably oak),
unsoaked; spray
oil (optional)

TIP

■ For extra flavor, I like to combine grilled mushrooms with grilled chiles, tomatoes, and onions. Grill them before you put on the mushrooms, as they take longer to cook and chop.

VARIATIONS:
For additional flavor add minced garlic and chopped cilantro or parsley to the olive oil before tossing it with or brushing it on the mushrooms. For a more European version of this dish, toss or baste the mushrooms with the Garlic-Herb Butter or Tarragon Butter on page 450. Substitute grilled bell peppers for the jalapeños and parsley or basil for the cilantro. You can also add crisped bits of bacon or pancetta.

METHOD:
Direct grilling

COOKING TIME:
7 to 9 minutes

**ADVANCE
PREPARATION:**
30 minutes to
3 hours for
marinating the
mushrooms

HOW TO GRILL PORTOBELLO MUSHROOMS

The portobello is the steak of the vegetable kingdom: It looks like a steak, it fills a plate (or a bun) like a steak, and there's even something meaty about its flavor, especially when the mushroom is grilled. If ever there was a mushroom for grilling, it's the portobello. Its broad cap rests securely on the grate and the gills readily absorb the smoke flavor. Portobellos contain less water than most mushrooms, so they can stand up to the heat of the grill. Their impressive size makes them easy to stud with garlic and other flavorings.

*Portobello
Mushrooms with
Garlic, Parmesan,
and Pine Nuts*

SETTING UP THE GRILL

1 To set up a charcoal grill for direct grilling, first light the charcoal in a chimney starter (see page 9).

2 Using a garden hoe or other long-handled implement, rake the burning coals into an even layer.

3 To see if the grill is preheated to high, use the test on page 10.

PREPARING THE PORTOBELLOS

1 Using a paring knife, cut the stems off the portobellos so they are flush with the caps.

2 Wipe the portobellos clean with a damp paper towel. Don't put the mushrooms under running water, or they'll become soggy.

3 Use a sharp object, such as the tip of a metal skewer or a tapered chopstick, to make a series of small holes in the gill side of the mushroom caps, ½ inch apart. Insert garlic and cheese slivers, rosemary leaves, and pine nuts in these holes.

4 Pour some marinade in the bottom of a baking dish. Arrange the portobellos in the dish, gill-side up, and pour the remaining marinade over them.

ON THE GRILL

1 Start grilling the portobellos gill-side down. Let them cook for 3 minutes.

2 Turn the portobellos and grill gill-side up. Ladle the reserved marinade into the mushroom caps. The portobellos will be done after 4 to 6 minutes.

PORTOBELLO MUSHROOMS WITH GARLIC, PARMESAN, AND PINE NUTS

4 large portobello mushrooms
  (8 to 10 ounces each)
2 large cloves garlic, cut into slivers
1 ounce Romano, Parmigiano-Reggiano, or
  other firm cheese, cut into slivers
1 sprig fresh rosemary, leaves stripped off the
  stem, or 2 teaspoons dried rosemary

2 tablespoons pine nuts
½ cup plus 2 tablespoons balsamic vinegar
½ teaspoon coarse salt
½ teaspoon black pepper
1 ⅓ cups extra-virgin olive oil,
  or more as needed
12 fresh basil leaves, thinly slivered

1. Trim the stems off the portobellos as shown in Preparing the Portobellos, Step 1 on page 377. Using a moist paper towel, wipe the caps clean. Using a sharp object, make a series of holes in the portobellos, as shown in Step 3 on the facing page. Insert garlic slivers in some of the holes, cheese slivers in others, rosemary leaves in others, and pine nuts in the remaining holes.

2. Combine ½ cup vinegar and the salt and pepper in a nonreactive mixing bowl and whisk until the salt is dissolved. Whisk in the oil and the basil. Pour some of the mixture in the bottom of a nonreactive baking dish and arrange the portobellos in it, gill-side up. Swish the mushrooms around to coat the bottoms with marinade. Spoon the remaining marinade over the portobellos. Let marinate in the refrigerator, covered, for as little as 30 minutes or as long as 3 hours.

3. Set up the grill for direct grilling (see page 10 for charcoal or page 16 for gas) and preheat to high.

4. When ready to cook, remove the mushroom caps from the marinade. Strain the marinade if the basil looks wilted. Whisk the remaining 2 tablespoons vinegar into the marinade. Arrange the portobellos on the hot grate, gill-side down. Grill for 3 minutes, then invert the portobellos and spoon on some of the reserved marinade. Continue grilling until the caps are browned and very tender, 4 to 6 minutes, rotating the caps 45 degrees after 2 minutes to create an attractive crosshatch of grill marks. If the caps brown too much, reduce the heat or move the mushrooms to a cooler part of the grill. Transfer to plates or a platter and serve at once.

VARIATIONS:
Many other flavorings can be used for studding the mushrooms: slivers of prosciutto, chorizo or other sausage, lemon zest, olives, almonds—the list has virtually no limits. The same goes for the marinade, which could be made with walnut or hazelnut oil. For a Pac-Rim portobello, stud the caps with slivers of ginger, garlic, and scallion, and marinate them in a mixture of Asian (dark) sesame oil, soy sauce, and mirin (sweet rice wine) or sherry.

Sometimes I make a portobello "brisket" for the vegetarians in the family. I brush the mushrooms with melted butter, season them with Basic Barbecue Rub (page 441), and slather them with Basic Barbecue Sauce (page 447), brushed on during the last few minutes of grilling. Cut the portobellos into thin, diagonal slices, just like you'd carve brisket.

METHOD:
Direct grilling

COOKING TIME:
8 to 16 minutes

HOW TO GRILL ONIONS AND GARLIC

I'd be hard pressed to name a culture that doesn't enjoy some sort of grilled onion—from Japanese *negi* (leeks) to Spanish *calçots* (giant green onions) to the grilled Bermuda onions so popular on steak sandwiches in the United States. There are good reasons for the grilled onion's popularity. Its high water content keeps the onion moist during grilling. The abundant plant sugars acquire a toffee flavor when caramelized by the high heat. The fire mellows the onion's breath-polluting pungency, while adding complexity to its overall flavor. Even the texture undergoes an interesting transformation, from wet and crisp to silky and soft.

Onion Mixed Grill

SETTING UP THE GRILL

1 To set up a charcoal grill for direct grilling, first light the charcoal in a chimney starter (see page 9).

2 Using a garden hoe or other long-handled implement, rake the burning coals into an even layer.

3 To see if the grill is preheated to high, use the test on page 10.

PREPARING THE ONION AND GARLIC

1 Thread onion quarters on slender bamboo skewers to keep them from falling apart during grilling. Onion slices should be cut thick (½ inch) and skewered through the rings with slender bamboo skewers or toothpicks. Skewer pearl onions whole.

2 Garlic is delicious grilled. Skewer peeled cloves on toothpicks. Or cut unpeeled whole garlic heads in half.

ON THE GRILL: From top to bottom: scallions, banana shallots, pearl onions, *cipollini,* garlic cloves (partially wrapped in foil), onion quarters, a half head of garlic, and a slice of Vidalia onion. Note the use of a vegetable grate.

TIPS

■ To maximize the flavor of a grilled onion, you need to cut it in quarters or slices.

■ Because garlic lacks the high water content of an onion, wrap it loosely in aluminum foil to prevent it from burning before it's cooked through.

■ A vegetable grate (see page 477) is a great help for grilling onion pieces. Preheat the vegetable grate when you light the grill, and spray or brush it with oil before grilling the onions.

ONION MIXED GRILL

SERVES 6

YOU'LL NEED:
12 slender bamboo
skewers or wooden
toothpicks, or
more as needed,
soaked for 1 hour
in cold water to
cover, then
drained; vegetable
grate (optional)

VARIATION:
*Onions are also deli-
cious roasted whole
in the embers—see
How to Roast Sweet
Potatoes in the
Embers, page 390.
Pick onions that are
between 2½ and 3½
inches across and
allow 20 to 30 min-
utes for them to roast.*

*2 to 3 pounds mixed onions, such as large
    sweet onions (Vidalias, Mauis, Walla Wallas,
    or Texas sweets), red onions, cipollini, pearl
    onions, banana or regular shallots, green
    onions, scallions, and/or garlic*
About ¼ cup extra-virgin olive oil

Coarse salt and black pepper
Honey-Balsamic Glaze (recipe follows)
*2 tablespoons minced fresh flat-leaf
    parsley*
*3 tablespoons toasted pine nuts
    (optional; page 29)*

1. If using large onions, peel and cut
each one lengthwise in quarters or crosswise into ½-inch slices. Skewer as shown in
Preparing the Onions, Step 1 on page 381.
If using *cipollini* or pearl onions, peel and
thread them on toothpicks or bamboo skewers. If using shallots, cut them in half. If
using green onions, cut large ones in half
lengthwise. If using scallions, leave them
whole. If using whole garlic heads, cut them
in half widthwise. If using garlic cloves, peel
and skewer them on toothpicks. Brush the
large onions, *cipollini,* pearl onions, and
shallots with oil. Green onions, scallions,
and garlic are generally grilled without oil.
Season everything with salt and pepper.

2. Set up the grill for direct grilling (see
page 10 for charcoal or page 16 for gas) and
preheat to high. If using a vegetable grate,
preheat it as well.

3. When ready to cook, spray or brush
the vegetable grate with oil or brush and oil
the grill grate. Arrange all the onions and
garlic on the hot grate. Grill until nicely
browned (even a little charred) on all sides,
4 to 8 minutes per side, or as needed. If any
of the onions start to burn, move them to a

cooler part of the grill. You may need to
loosely wrap the garlic cloves in aluminum
foil to keep them from burning.

4. Transfer the onions to a platter and
unskewer. Drizzle the Honey-Balsamic Glaze
over them and sprinkle with the parsley and
the pine nuts, if using. Serve hot or at room
temperature. You can grill the onions and
garlic several hours ahead of serving.

Honey-Balsamic Glaze

MAKES ABOUT ½ CUP

½ cup balsamic vinegar
3 tablespoons honey
2 tablespoons sugar
1½ tablespoons soy sauce

Place the vinegar, honey, sugar, and soy
sauce in a heavy, nonreactive saucepan and
bring to a boil over medium heat. Simmer
the mixture until thick, syrupy, and reduced
to about ½ cup, 6 to 8 minutes. The glaze
will thicken as it cools.

HOW TO GRILL PEPPERS

METHOD:
Direct grilling

COOKING TIME:
16 to 24 minutes

I t's hard to imagine a world without roasted peppers, those soft, smoky, flame-charred strips that turn up in antipasti, salads, sauces, soups, and sandwiches. Traditional recipes call for roasting the peppers on the stove or under the broiler, but the easiest way to roast a pepper is to grill it.

There are three dishes you can burn in this book and peppers is one of them. (The other two are found on pages 364 and 390.) By charring peppers, you actually make them sweeter. Roasted peppers are great to eat drizzled with olive oil or in salads. Purée them with olive oil, garlic, and cayenne to make rouille, a French sauce for fish.

*Grilled
Pepper
Salad*

SETTING UP THE GRILL

1 To set up a charcoal grill for direct grilling, first light the charcoal in a chimney starter (see page 9).

2 Using a garden hoe or other long-handled implement, rake the burning coals into an even layer.

3 To see if the grill is preheated to high, use the test on page 10.

ON THE GRILL

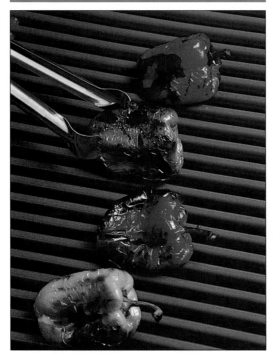

Arrange the peppers on the grate and grill until their skins are nicely charred, 4 to 6 minutes per side. Turn the peppers with tongs to ensure even charring.

SKINNING THE PEPPERS

1 Place the hot peppers in a baking dish and cover with plastic wrap. Let sit for 20 minutes as they cool down.

2 Pull or scrape the skin off the peppers, using your fingers or a paring knife. Don't worry about removing every last bit. A few burnt specks add character.

3 Cut out the stem end and discard.

4 Cut open the peppers and scrape out the veins and seeds with a knife.

THE RECIPE

SERVES 6 TO 8

GRILLED PEPPER SALAD

FOR THE PEPPERS:
2 red bell peppers
2 yellow bell peppers
2 green bell peppers

FOR THE DRESSING:
1 clove garlic, chopped
½ teaspoon coarse salt, or more to taste

1 tablespoon balsamic vinegar
1 tablespoon lemon juice
4 tablespoons extra-virgin olive oil
2 tablespoons chopped fresh flat-leaf parsley or slivered fresh basil
2 tablespoons toasted pine nuts (page 29)

1. Set up the grill for direct grilling (see page 10 for charcoal or page 16 for gas) and preheat to high.

2. When ready to cook, place all the peppers on the grate and grill until the skins are charred on all sides, 4 to 6 minutes per side (16 to 24 minutes in all), turning with tongs. Transfer the hot peppers to a baking dish and cover with plastic wrap. Alternatively, wrap each in a wet

VARIATIONS:

To make Argentinean-style grilled peppers, in place of the dressing, brush them with olive oil and sprinkle them with minced garlic and salt and pepper before grilling. Grill the peppers until the skins are a deep golden brown. Serve the peppers whole, instructing your guests to cut the flesh off the core.

To make Turkish-style grilled peppers, skewer several horn peppers (long, slender, twisted hot chiles) side by side on a flat metal skewer. Grill on both sides until darkly browned. Serve with grilled lamb or beef. Japanese grill jockeys prepare horn peppers this way also.

paper towel (the steam generated by the hot peppers and water helps you remove the skin). Let the peppers cool to room temperature, about 20 minutes.

3. Meanwhile, make the dressing. Place the garlic and salt in a nonreactive mixing bowl and mash to a paste with the back of a wooden spoon. Add the vinegar and lemon juice and whisk until the salt is dissolved. Whisk in the oil, parsley, and pine nuts.

4. Using the tip of a paring knife, scrape the burnt skin off the peppers and cut the flesh off the core, as shown in Steps 2 through 4 on page 385. Cut into quarters or strips and arrange the pepper pieces on a platter, alternating pieces of different colors. Stir the dressing and spoon it over the peppers. You can serve the salad right away, or let it sit for a few hours to allow the flavors to blend.

HOW TO SMOKE ROAST POTATOES

METHOD:
Indirect grilling

COOKING TIME:
1 to 1¼ hours

If you like baked potatoes (and who doesn't), you're going to *love* this technique. That's because smoke-roasted potatoes are one of the most addictive foods known to man. The high, dry heat of the grill produces a potato with a crackling crisp skin and a steamy, fluffy interior. The delicate flesh of the potato soaks up the smoke flavor, acquiring a style and distinction you never knew the friendly spud could possess. Top the potato with the traditional fixings—butter, sour cream, chopped fresh chives, and/or bacon bits made from scratch—and you won't even need a main course.

Smoked Potatoes with sour cream, bacon, and Grilled Scallions

SETTING UP THE GRILL

ALSO GOOD FOR:
Sweet potatoes and onions can be smoke roasted in their skins the same way. They'll take about 1 hour.

1 To set up a charcoal grill for smoking, first light the charcoal in a chimney starter (see page 9).

2 Place a drip pan in the center of the grill and divide the coals evenly on either side of it.

3 Place 1 cup of drained wood chips on each mound of coals.

PREPARING THE POTATOES

1 Prick each potato a half-dozen times with a fork, inserting the tines about ¼ inch into it. This will help the potatoes absorb the smoke and prevent them from exploding.

2 Brush the potatoes with melted butter or bacon drippings and season them generously with salt and pepper.

ON THE GRILL: Smoke roast the potatoes until they are very tender, 1 to 1¼ hours. The skins will be wrinkled. If you are using a charcoal grill, you may need to add more wood chips after an hour.

SMOKED POTATOES

FOR THE POTATOES:
4 large baking potatoes
  (preferably Idaho bakers)
2 to 3 tablespoons melted butter,
  bacon drippings, or melted lard
Coarse salt and black pepper

FOR SERVING:
Butter
Sour cream
2 to 4 slices of bacon, fried and diced
Whole grilled scallions
  (optional; page 380)

1. Set up the grill for indirect grilling (see page 12 for charcoal or page 16 for gas) and preheat to high. If using a gas grill, place all the wood chips in the smoker box or in a smoker pouch (see page 17) and preheat until you see smoke.

2. Prick each potato as shown in Preparing the Potatoes, Step 1 on the facing page. Brush or rub the potatoes all over with the melted butter. Season very generously with salt and pepper.

3. When ready to cook, if using a charcoal grill, toss 2 cups of the wood chips on the coals. Place the potatoes in the center of the hot grate, away from the heat, and cover the grill. Smoke roast the potatoes until cooked through; the skins will be crisp and the potatoes squeezably soft, 1 to 1¼ hours. You should be able to pierce the potatoes easily with a metal skewer. If using a charcoal grill, add 12 fresh coals and ½ cup fresh wood chips per side if the potatoes are still hard in the center after 1 hour.

4. Serve the potatoes with butter, sour cream, bacon bits, and grilled scallions, if desired.

⌒

SERVES 4

YOU'LL NEED:
2 to 3 cups wood chips (preferably hickory or oak), soaked for 1 hour in cold water to cover, then drained

VARIATION:
You can also barbecue potatoes. Cook them in a smoker at 225°F for 2½ to 3 hours.

TIPS

■ As logic would dictate, use a baking potato for smoking. The structure of its starch produces a lighter, fluffier smoked potato than that of a thin-skinned boiling potato. Yukon Golds are also good for smoking.

■ You can brush the potatoes with melted butter; however, you'll get an even richer flavor if you use bacon fat or melted lard.

■ Do not under any circumstances wrap these potatoes in aluminum foil. All you'll succeed in doing is locking out the smoke.

METHOD:
Roasting in the
embers

COOKING TIME:
40 minutes to
1 hour

HOW TO ROAST SWEET POTATOES
(and Other Root Vegetables)
IN THE EMBERS

**Ember-Roasted
Sweet Potatoes with
Maple-Cinnamon
Butter**

Long before there were grills, people cooked with live fire and they did so right in the embers. Roasting in the embers is a cooking technique especially well suited for root vegetables, such as potatoes, sweet potatoes, yams, onions, and beets. When you roast a vegetable in the coals, you sacrifice the exterior, but in the process of charring, you give the flesh inside an irresistible smoke flavor. Potatoes and yams emerge from the coals light and fluffy and beets and onions become incredibly sweet.

SETTING UP THE GRILL

1 To set up a charcoal grill for direct grilling, first light the charcoal in a chimney starter (see page 9).

2 Dump the lit coals from the chimney starter into the bottom of the grill.

3 Using a garden hoe or other long-handled implement, rake the burning coals into an even layer.

TIPS

■ You'll lose about 20 percent of the tuber to charring, so start with large ones. Choose vegetables of roughly the same shape and size, so they'll roast evenly.

■ To roast vegetables in the embers, obviously you need a charcoal grill. The embers can be charcoal or wood. If you have a gas grill, grill the vegetables in their skins over medium-high heat until the skins are black and charred. The flavor won't be quite as rich and smoky, but it will be close.

■ Unlike with the smoked potatoes on page 387, I find that ember roasting works best when you don't prick the tubers.

READY FOR ROASTING: Use tongs to place the sweet potatoes on the coals. Pictured here from top to bottom are Beauregard yams, ordinary sweet potatoes, and garnet yams.

ON THE COALS: Rest the potatoes directly on the coals, raking loose coals around them. When the bottoms become charred, turn the potatoes with tongs. The skins will be charred black when they are done, 40 minutes to 1 hour.

SERVES 4

YOU'LL NEED:
Large charcoal or
wood fire

ALSO GOOD FOR:
*Any round vegetable
with a sturdy skin
and/or a dense starch
structure is a candi-
date. Baking pota-
toes, onions, and
beets are delicious
roasted in the coals.
You can vary the fla-
vor of the butter to
suit the vegetable.
Potatoes do well with
Parmesan butter
(replace the maple
syrup and cinnamon
with freshly grated
Parmesan cheese and
black pepper), for
example. Balsamic
vinegar butter goes
well with roasted
onions; Roquefort
butter with roasted
beets.*

THE RECIPE

EMBER-ROASTED SWEET POTATOES WITH MAPLE-CINNAMON BUTTER

*6 tablespoons (¾ stick) butter,
    at room temperature*
1 tablespoon maple syrup

1 teaspoon ground cinnamon
*4 large sweet potatoes
    or yams*

1. Make the maple-cinnamon butter: Place the butter in a mixing bowl and whisk until light and fluffy. Whisk in the maple syrup and cinnamon. Alternatively, blend the ingredients in a mixer or food processor. Transfer the butter to a bowl or 4 ramekins and refrigerate until serving.

2. Build the fire as shown in Setting Up the Grill, page 391, and let it burn down to glowing coals. Rest the sweet potatoes on the embers. Using tongs or a hoe, rake any loose coals around the potatoes.

3. Roast the sweet potatoes until the skins are charred black and the centers are soft and steamy, 40 minutes to 1 hour. Turn the potatoes with tongs from time to time to ensure even roasting. Use a slender metal skewer to test for doneness; it should insert easily.

4. Remove the potatoes from the coals with tongs and brush away the ashes with a pastry brush. Let the sweet potatoes cool for a few minutes, then cut each in half lengthwise and place on plates or a platter for serving. Serve the sweet potatoes in their skins with the maple-cinnamon butter on the side. You'll eat only the center portion of the sweet potatoes.

HOW TO GRILL TOMATOES

METHOD:
Direct grilling

COOKING TIME:
6 to 10 minutes

Is there anything more delicious than biting into a luscious, red, squishily ripe tomato? Only one thing I can think of: biting into a luscious, red, squishily ripe tomato that's been grilled. The easiest way to grill a tomato is simply to place it on the grate over a hot fire. The skin will darken and blister, imparting a smoke flavor. Drizzle the best extra-virgin olive oil you can buy over the tomato and sprinkle it with coarse sea salt and freshly ground black pepper (and perhaps a little chopped garlic and fresh herbs). The recipe that I've chosen to illustrate this technique is a trifle more elaborate in that the tomato is seasoned with fried garlic and Parmesan cheese, which set off its smoke flavor.

TIPS

■ To recognize a truly ripe red tomato, use your eyes, nose, and fingers. A worthy specimen will be bright red; have a pleasing grassy, tomatoey aroma; and feel slightly yielding when squeezed gently.

■ Don't buy tomatoes that have been refrigerated, if you can help it, and never refrigerate a tomato yourself (the cold destroys the delicate texture and flavor).

*Garlic
Grilled
Tomatoes*

SETTING UP THE GRILL

1 To set up a charcoal grill for direct grilling, first light the charcoal in a chimney starter (see page 9).

2 Using a garden hoe or other long-handled implement, rake the burning coals into an even layer.

3 To see if the grill is preheated to high, use the test on page 10.

PREPARING THE GARLIC

1 To peel garlic, flatten the clove with the side of a large knife to loosen the skin.

2 Slip off the skin with your fingers. (By the way, note how beautifully ripe the halved tomatoes are.)

ON THE GRILL

1 First, grill the tomatoes cut-side down for 3 to 5 minutes. Rotate each 45 degrees after a couple minutes to create an attractive crosshatch of grill marks.

2 Turn the tomato halves cut-side up and carefully spoon the fried garlic over them. The tomatoes will be done after 3 to 5 minutes more grilling.

3 Cut the garlic clove crosswise into ¼-inch-thick slices. Lay these flat and pound them with the side of the knife, making sure the knife handle is off the edge of the cutting board. The garlic will pulverize instantly.

THE RECIPE

GARLIC GRILLED TOMATOES

6 ripe red tomatoes
Coarse salt and black pepper
6 cloves garlic
3 tablespoons extra-virgin olive oil

1 piece Parmigiano-Reggiano cheese (1 to 2 ounces)
1 to 2 tablespoons fresh thyme leaves

1. Cut the tomatoes in half crosswise. Season with salt and pepper.

2. Peel and pulverize the garlic as shown in Preparing the Garlic, Steps 1 through 3 on the facing page and above. Heat the oil in a small frying pan over medium heat. Add the pulverized garlic, and cook until just starting to turn golden brown, 1 to 2 minutes. Pour the garlic and oil into a heatproof bowl.

3. Set up the grill for direct grilling (see page 10 for charcoal or page 16 for gas) and preheat to high. If using a gas grill, place the wood chips, if desired, in the smoker box or in a smoker pouch (see page 17) and preheat until you see smoke.

4. When ready to grill, brush and oil the grill grate. If using a charcoal grill, toss the wood chips, if desired, on the coals. Place the tomatoes cut-side down on the

SERVES 6

YOU'LL NEED:
1 cup wood chips (optional; preferably oak), soaked for 1 hour in cold water to cover, then drained

VARIATION:

To make garlic-grilled plum or cherry tomatoes, place 12 whole plum tomatoes or 24 cherry tomatoes in a mixing bowl and toss with half of the olive oil and pulverized garlic, some salt and pepper, and half the thyme. Place the tomatoes on the hot grate (use a vegetable grate for the cherry tomatoes; see page 477). Grill until the skins are darkly browned and blistered, turning the tomatoes with tongs, 6 to 8 minutes in all. Transfer the tomatoes to a platter and sprinkle with the remaining oil, garlic, thyme, and the grated cheese. Serve at once.

hot grate and grill until nicely browned, 3 to 5 minutes, rotating them 45 degrees after 2 minutes to create an attractive crosshatch of grill marks. Turn the tomatoes with tongs, spoon the fried garlic over the tomatoes, and continue grilling

until the bottoms (the rounded parts) are nicely browned, 3 to 5 minutes.

5. Transfer the tomatoes to plates or a platter. Grate the Parmigiano-Reggiano over the tomatoes and sprinkle them with the thyme. Serve at once.

HOW TO GRILL ZUCCHINI AND YELLOW SQUASH

METHOD:
Direct grilling

COOKING TIME:
8 to 12 minutes

Zucchini is the quintessential vegetable of summer—and the quintessential vegetable for grilling. Its soft flesh readily takes on fire and smoke flavors, while its high water content keeps it moist during grilling. To maximize the fire flavor, I thinly slice the zucchini lengthwise. These broad slices present the greatest surface area to the fire, so they sear without getting soggy.

I like to grill zucchini and yellow squash together: The greens and yellows look great on a platter. They taste just as great at room temperature as they do hot off the grill, so you can prepare them in advance. But don't limit their preparation just to summer, for zucchini and yellow squash are plentiful and cheap year-round.

Zucchini and Yellow Squash with Greek Spices

SETTING UP THE GRILL

1 To set up a charcoal grill for direct grilling, first light the charcoal in a chimney starter (see page 9).

2 Using a garden hoe or other long-handled implement, rake the burning coals into an even layer.

3 To see if the grill is preheated to high, use the test on page 10.

(see page 9)
the test on page 10

TIPS

■ **Choose medium-size (5- to 8-inch-long) zucchini. The ratio of flesh to seed is greater than in the behemoths that invade gardens at the end of the summer. Likewise, choose small, tender yellow squash. Better yet, look for yellow zucchini. Scrub the vegetables with a nylon brush to remove any grit on the surface.**

■ **Grill the zucchini slices directly on the grate. If you have a lot of slices to grill, you may want to use a grill basket (see page 473).**

■ **Use wood chips if you'd like to impart a light wood flavor. I don't bother to soak the chips, which would produce a heavier smoke flavor.**

(see page 473)

PREPARING THE SQUASH

1 Cut the zucchini and yellow squash lengthwise into ¼-inch-thick slices.

2 Arrange the vegetable slices in a baking dish, sprinkle them with the herbs and seasonings, then drizzle with oil.

ON THE GRILL: Cook the squash until nicely browned, 4 to 6 minutes per side. Rotate the slices 90 degrees after 2 minutes on each side to create a handsome crosshatch of grill marks.

ZUCCHINI AND YELLOW SQUASH WITH GREEK SPICES

*2 to 3 medium zucchini
(about 1 pound in all)*
*2 to 3 medium yellow squash or
more zucchini (about 1 pound
in all)*
1 to 2 cloves garlic, minced
1 teaspoon dried oregano

1 teaspoon dried mint
½ teaspoon hot red pepper flakes
Coarse salt and black pepper
3 tablespoons extra-virgin olive oil
*Lemon wedges, for serving
(optional)*

1. Cut the zucchini and yellow squash lengthwise into ¼-inch slices. Arrange the slices on a platter or in a baking dish and sprinkle both sides with the garlic, oregano, mint, hot pepper flakes, and lots of salt and pepper. Drizzle 2 tablespoons oil over them, turning the slices several times to coat both sides. Let marinate for 15 minutes.

2. Set up the grill for direct grilling (see page 10 for charcoal or page 16 for gas) and preheat to high. If using a vegetable grate, preheat it as well. If using a gas grill, place the wood chips, if desired, in the smoker

box or in a smoker pouch (see page 17) and preheat until you see smoke.

3. When ready to cook, if using a charcoal grill, toss the wood chips, if desired, on the coals. Arrange the zucchini and yellow squash slices on the hot grate and grill until nicely browned on both sides, 4 to 6 minutes per side, rotating the slices 90 degrees after 2 minutes on each side to create an attractive crosshatch of grill marks.

4. Transfer to a platter. Drizzle the remaining 1 tablespoon of oil over the zucchini and yellow squash and garnish with lemon wedges, if using. Serve at once.

SERVES 4 TO 6

YOU'LL NEED:
**1 cup wood chips
(optional;
preferably oak),
unsoaked;
vegetable grate
(optional)**

VARIATIONS:
To give the zucchini a Moroccan flavor, add 1 teaspoon each ground cumin and coriander to the recipe.

Turn any leftover grilled zucchini or yellow squash into a salad (or grill extra). Cut them into 1-inch pieces. Season them with olive oil, lemon juice, minced garlic, and salt and pepper. You can also add grilled corn, tomatoes, and/or onions.

ALSO GOOD FOR:
The marinade used for squash is great when grilling any vegetable, from asparagus to sliced eggplants and onions.

METHOD:
Direct grilling

COOKING TIME:
8 to 10 minutes

HOW TO GRILL IN FOIL PACKETS

How do you grill small pieces of vegetables or seafood without a spit, skewer, or even a grill grate? If you ever belonged to the Boy Scouts or Girl Scouts, you probably remember the solution: grill them in an aluminum foil packet. The packets are a snap to assemble and the foil seals in the flavor and goodness.

The basic procedure is to wrap vegetables in aluminum foil along with herbs and spices and a little liquid. You throw the package on the coals (or on top of the grate). A short time later, you'll have a dramatically puffed foil vegetable pack that's bursting with enticing aromas.

Asian-Flavored Vegetables Grilled in Foil Packets

SETTING UP THE GRILL

1 To set up a charcoal grill for direct grilling, first light the charcoal in a chimney starter (see page 9).

2 Using a garden hoe or other long-handled implement, rake the burning coals into an even layer.

3 To see if the grill is preheated to high, use the test on page 10.

MAKING THE FOIL PACKETS

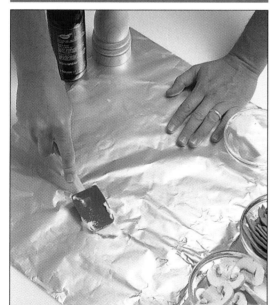

1 Spread a little butter in the center of what will become the bottom of the packet. Note that the dull side of the aluminum foil faces up now, so the shiny side will be on the outside when you close it up.

2 Arrange the sliced vegetables on top of the foil, starting with the harder, denser vegetables, like carrots. Light, watery vegetables, like mushrooms, go on top. Strew the flavorings (slivered ginger, garlic, scallions, and sesame seeds) on top. Sprinkle a few drops of soy sauce over the vegetables.

TIPS

■ Assemble the packets so that the shiny side of the aluminum foil faces out. This is purely cosmetic: It gives you a prettier package.

■ It's important to slice the vegetables thinly, so they cook quickly.

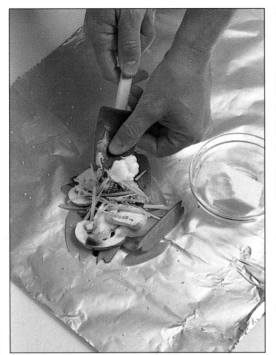

3 Place a piece of butter on top of the vegetables.

4 Fold half of the aluminum foil over the vegetables to make a rectangular packet.

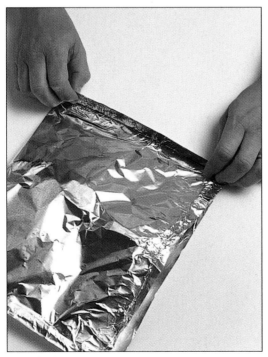

5 Fold the short sides over several times to make a tight seal.

6 Spoon in the rice wine.

7 Fold over and crimp the final edge to make a sealed packet.

ON THE GRILL: Place the packets on the grate over the fire. The packets will puff up after 8 to 10 minutes, signaling that they're done—like the one seen here on the bottom.

THE RECIPE

ASIAN-FLAVORED VEGETABLES GRILLED IN FOIL PACKETS

4 tablespoons (½ stick) unsalted
  butter
8 ounces carrots (3 to 4), sliced
  sharply on the diagonal in
  ⅛-inch-thick pieces
8 ounces snow peas, strings
  removed
8 ounces white (button) mushrooms,
  trimmed and sliced ⅛ inch thick
2 scallions, white part only,
  cut into matchstick slivers

1 piece (1 inch) fresh ginger, peeled,
  thinly sliced, and cut into
  matchstick slivers
2 cloves garlic, cut into matchstick
  slivers
4 teaspoons toasted sesame seeds
  (page 30)
1 tablespoon soy sauce
Coarse salt and black pepper
4 tablespoons Chinese rice wine,
  sake, or dry sherry

1. Place a sheet of aluminum foil, shiny-side down, one edge toward you, on the work surface. Smear a small piece of butter

in the center of the bottom half of the square. Arrange one quarter of the carrots, snow peas, and mushrooms in a mound on top of the butter. Arrange one quarter of the scallions, ginger, garlic, and sesame seeds on top. Sprinkle with a few drops of soy sauce and season with salt and pepper. Put another small piece of butter on top.

2. As shown in Steps 4 through 7 on pages 402 and 403, fold the top half of the aluminum foil rectangle over the vegetables and bring the edges together. Fold each side over several times to make a tight seal. Place 1 tablespoon of rice wine in the packet and seal the remaining edge. Repeat with the remaining ingredients to form three more packets. The packets can be prepared up to this stage 3 to 4 hours ahead. Keep them refrigerated, but let them return to room temperature before grilling.

3. Set up the grill for direct grilling (see page 10 for charcoal or page 16 for gas) and preheat to high.

4. When ready to cook, arrange the aluminum foil packets on the hot grate. Grill until the packets are dramatically puffed,

8 to 10 minutes. Serve at once.

5. Warn your guests to open the packets with a knife and fork and to avert their faces (just cut into the top of the packet). There will be a blast of steam when the packets are opened.

HOW TO GRILL QUESADILLAS

METHOD:
Direct grilling

COOKING TIME:
2 to 4 minutes

It wasn't so long ago that quesadillas—chewy-crisp flour tortillas filled with gooey melted cheese—burst upon our North American culinary landscape. It was love at first bite. In Mexico, quesadillas are traditionally cooked on a *comal* (a flat skillet). They can be baked in the oven, as is often the case in the United States. Now, I'm of the school that if something tastes great off the griddle or out of the oven, it probably tastes even better off the grill—even when that something is as flammable as a flour tortilla. The secret to grilling a quesadilla is to lower the heat and keep the cooking time brief in order to melt the cheese without burning the tortilla. It also helps to have a safety zone where you can move the quesadilla if it starts to burn (see the Tip on page 406). The effort is well worth it.

*Grilled Quesadillas
with Pico de Gallo
(page 458)*

TIP

■ Tortillas burn like paper. When grilling quesadillas, don't take your eyes off the grill for a second. It's a good idea to have a cool zone on your grill (see building a Three-Zone Fire, page 10, for charcoal or Direct Grilling, page 16, for gas). That way, if the tortillas start to burn, you can move them to safety.

1 To set up a charcoal grill for direct grilling, first light the charcoal in a chimney starter (see page 9).

2 Using a garden hoe or other long-handled implement, rake the burning coals into a three-zone fire (see page 10).

3 A three-zone fire gives you a coal-free safety zone.

ASSEMBLING THE QUESADILLAS

1 Arrange the cheese, tomatoes, chiles, scallions, and cilantro on half of each tortilla.

2 Fold up the tortillas over the filling.

ON THE GRILL: Grill the quesadillas until the tortillas are nicely browned and the cheese is melted, 1 to 2 minutes per side. Brush the quesadillas with melted butter as they grill.

GRILLED QUESADILLAS

8 flour tortillas (10 inches each)
6 ounces Jack or Cheddar cheese,
    thinly sliced
3 to 4 plum tomatoes, thinly sliced
3 to 4 fresh or pickled green and/or
    red jalapeño peppers, thinly sliced

4 scallions, trimmed and sliced
½ cup fresh cilantro leaves
3 tablespoons melted butter

1. Place the tortillas on a work surface. Arrange a few slices of cheese, tomato, and jalapeño on half of each tortilla. Top with some scallion and cilantro. Fold the tortillas in half. The quesadillas can be prepared up to this stage up to several hours ahead. Wrap the quesadillas tightly in plastic and refrigerate until ready to grill.

2. Set up the grill for three-zone direct grilling (see page 10 for charcoal or page 16 for gas) and preheat the hot zone to medium-high.

3. When ready to cook, place the quesadillas on the hot grate and grill until the tortillas are golden brown and the cheese is slightly melted, 1 to 2 minutes per side. Brush the outside of each quesadilla with the melted butter as it grills. Be prepared to move the quesadillas to a cooler part of the grill if they start to burn. Serve at once either whole or cut into wedges.

**MAKES 8;
SERVES 8 AS
AN APPETIZER,
4 AS A LIGHT
MAIN COURSE**

VARIATIONS:
You can stuff tortillas with just about anything—goat cheese and sun-dried tomatoes, Gouda cheese and roasted peppers, or sliced grilled chicken, duck, lobster, shrimp, or pork. You can also use corn tortillas instead of flour.

TIP

■ **To be strictly authentic, you'd use grated cheese and diced tomatoes. My method is quicker and gives you a more substantial quesadilla. If you prefer a milder quesadilla, seed the jalapeños.**

METHOD:
Direct grilling

COOKING TIME:
6 to 10 minutes
for grilling each
pizza

**ADVANCE
PREPARATION:**
1¼ to 2¾ hours
for making the
dough and
letting it rise

HOW TO GRILL PIZZA

Grilled pizza was popularized by George Germon and Johanne Killeen at their restaurant Al Forno in Providence, Rhode Island. The couple had the brainstorm to toss a sheet of raw pizza dough on the grate of their charcoal-burning grill. The crust browned and blistered, and soaked up the good grill flavors. It may have been a wacky idea, but it produced an irresistible pizza.

Because the crust tastes so great by itself, I tend to keep the toppings fairly simple. The grilled pizza that illustrates this technique comes with a colorful garnish of tomatoes, arugula, olives, onion, and mozzarella cheese. I deliberately leave portions of the crust bare because I enjoy the crunch of the grilled bread.

Grilled Pizza

SETTING UP THE GRILL

1 To set up a charcoal grill for direct grilling, first light the charcoal in a chimney starter (see page 9).

2 Using a garden hoe or other long-handled implement, rake the burning coals into a three-zone fire (see page 10).

3 A three-zone fire gives you a coal-free safety zone.

MAKING THE PIZZA DOUGH

1 Put the dry ingredients in the bowl of a food processor. Add the wet ingredients.

2 Process the dough in short bursts until it comes away from the side of the bowl.

TIPS

■ You can make the pizza dough by hand or in a mixer fitted with a dough hook, but I usually use a food processor. Ideally, the processor will have a plastic dough blade. If not, you can use the metal blade, but run the machine in short bursts.

■ The wetter your dough, the lighter and crisper the pizza. However, a really wet dough is hard to work with. But resist the temptation to add too much flour.

TIP

■ Unlike most pizzas, the dough here is stretched into a pizza shape on a baking sheet slathered with oil. Use plenty of oil: It helps the crust blister. George and Johanne make their pizzas in free-form rectangles—a practice I follow. Don't worry if it doesn't look perfect. Free form is the way to go. And don't be discouraged if your first effort feels awkward—stretching the dough becomes easier with practice.

3 Knead the dough by hand on a floured cutting board for a few minutes to give it a human touch.

4 Roll the dough into a ball and place it in an oiled bowl. Turn to coat it with oil all over.

5 Cover the dough with plastic wrap and let rise in a warm spot.

6 When the dough is ready it will be soft, spongy, and doubled in bulk. When you press it with your finger, an indentation will remain.

7 To shape the crust, place half the dough on an oiled baking sheet (the recipe makes enough for two crusts) and start stretching it out.

8 Gently stretch the dough to form a rough rectangle the size of the baking sheet (about 9 by 13 inches) and about ⅛ to ¼ inch thick.

ON THE GRILL

1 Once you are ready to cook, gently lift the dough by one end and flop it onto the hot part of the grill grate. Once it's firm enough to move, slide it to a cooler part of the fire.

2 When the bottom is browned and blistered after 3 to 5 minutes, turn the pizza crust over.

TIPS

■ Set up your grill for three-zone grilling (see building a Three-Zone Fire, page 10, for charcoal or Direct Grilling, page 16, for gas). Use the hot part for firming up the dough; the medium part for cooking it through and warming the toppings. The cool part of the grill is your safety zone.

■ For the best results, use fresh mozzarella, a ball of moist, sweet, pearl-white cheese frequently sold packed in water. Look for fresh mozzarella at Italian markets, cheese shops, and gourmet stores.

■ To simplify the work at the grill, I call for the onions, garlic, and tomatoes to be browned in a skillet. However, you can certainly cook the vegetables on the grill. (For instructions on grilling onions and garlic, see page 380; for tomatoes, page 393.)

1 After about a minute, when the second side begins to brown, move the crust to a cooler area of the grill and brush it with oil.

2 Add half of the toppings, starting with the mozzarella, then the tomato, onion, garlic, olives, and capers. The bottom of the crust will be done and the cheese melted after 2 to 4 minutes.

3 Slide the pizza onto a baking sheet and place half of the arugula on top.

MAKES 2 PIZZAS (9 BY 13 INCHES EACH); SERVES 4 AS AN APPETIZER, 2 AS A MAIN COURSE

THE RECIPE

GRILLED PIZZA

FOR THE DOUGH:
1 envelope active dry yeast
   (2½ teaspoons)
1 teaspoon sugar
1¼ cups warm water
3½ cups unbleached white flour,
   or more if necessary
1½ teaspoons coarse salt
About ¼ cup extra-virgin olive oil

FOR THE TOPPING:
1 bunch of arugula
2 to 3 tablespoons extra-virgin
   olive oil

3 cloves garlic, finely chopped
1 large onion, thinly sliced
Coarse salt and black pepper
2 medium-size red ripe tomatoes, cut
   crosswise into ¼-inch-thick slices
6 ounces fresh mozzarella cheese,
   thinly sliced
½ cup pitted black olives (preferably
   kalamata)
2 tablespoons capers, drained

Extra-virgin olive oil, for grilling
   the dough

1. Combine the yeast, sugar, and water in a small bowl and stir to mix. After 5 to 10 minutes, the mixture should look foamy. Place the flour and salt in the bowl of a food processor fitted with a plastic dough blade or a metal blade and pulse to mix. Add the yeast-water mixture and 2 tablespoons of oil and run the machine in short bursts to obtain a smooth, soft dough. It should be moist but not sticky. If necessary add more flour a spoonful at a time, running the machine between additions, until the dough is the proper texture. You can also make the dough in a mixer fitted with a dough hook: Place the yeast, sugar, and water in the mixer bowl. When foamy, add 2 tablespoons oil, and the salt and flour. Mix at low speed to form a smooth, soft dough.

2. Turn the dough out onto a work surface and knead it by hand for a few minutes. Lightly coat a large bowl with the remaining oil. Place the dough in the bowl, turning it to coat with oil. Cover the bowl with plastic wrap and let the dough rise in a warm spot until doubled in bulk, 1 to 1½ hours.

3. Punch down the dough and let rise until doubled in bulk again, 1 hour. This second rising isn't absolutely imperative, but your crust will be lighter if you have the time to do it.

4. Meanwhile, prepare the topping: Rinse the arugula and pat dry with paper towels. Heat 2 tablespoons of oil in a non-stick frying pan over medium heat. Fry the garlic until golden brown, 2 minutes. Transfer the garlic with a mesh skimmer to paper towels to drain. Add the onion to the pan. Cook over medium heat until caramelized to a dark golden brown, 6 to 10 minutes, adding salt and pepper to taste. You may need to lower the heat as the onion darkens. Transfer the onion to a platter. Heat the pan over high heat, adding the remaining 1 tablespoon oil if needed. Blot

the tomato slices dry on paper towels and season with salt and pepper. Quickly fry the tomato slices on both sides. Add the garlic and tomatoes to the platter with the onion.

5. Set up the grill for three-zone direct grilling (see page 10 for charcoal or page 16 for gas) and preheat the hot zone to high. When ready to cook, brush and oil the grill grate.

6. Generously oil two rimmed baking sheets. Place half the dough on one of the baking sheets and stretch it out to form a 9-by-13-inch rectangle that is ⅛ to ¼ inch thick. Repeat with the remaining dough and cover it with plastic wrap.

7. Starting from the far narrow side and using both hands, gently lift the first dough rectangle and drape it onto the grate over the hottest part of the fire. Within a minute or so, the underside of the dough will crisp and darken and the top will puff slightly. Using tongs and a spatula, slide the dough to a cooler part of the grill and cook until the bottom of the dough is browned and firm, 3 to 5 minutes. Brush the uncooked top with oil.

8. Using tongs and a spatula, invert the crust over a hotter part of the fire. Grill until this side, too, starts to crisp and darken, about 1 minute. Move the crust back to a cooler part of the grill and brush the top with oil. Arrange half of the cheese slices on the pizza, followed by half the fried tomato slices, caramelized onion, cooked garlic, olives, and capers. Cover the grill to melt the cheese. When the bottom crust is cooked, browned, and firm, 2 to 4 minutes more, slide the pizza onto a platter for serving. Top with half the arugula and season with salt and pepper. Cut into pieces and serve. While people are enjoying the first pizza, prepare the second one the same way (the pizza should be eaten as soon as it comes off the grill).

VARIATIONS:
There's no limit to the toppings for grilled pizza. You could certainly go the mozzarella, pepperoni, tomato sauce route (put the mozzarella on first, then the pepperoni, and finally the tomato sauce, so they cook in the proper order). Another of my favorites is crumbled Roquefort cheese, thinly sliced prosciutto, and grilled figs.

METHOD:
Direct grilling

COOKING TIME:
8 to 12 minutes

**ADVANCE
PREPARATION:**
2 to 3 hours for
pressing and
marinating
the tofu

HOW TO GRILL TOFU

For millions of Japanese, a barbecue just wouldn't be complete without grilled tofu. Wildly popular in Japan, it is served at rough-and-tumble yakitori parlors, tranquil Zen teahouses, and even at highfalutin restaurants. The traditional "barbecue sauce" for grilled tofu is a creamy, sweet-salty miso sauce, but you can also order it with *umeboshi* (pickled plum) sauce or a teriyaki sauce, like the one below. Taking on the grill flavors, as well as those in the marinade, grilled tofu makes a savory main dish that will please all guests, not just vegetarians.

*Tangerine
Teriyaki Tofu*

S E T T I N G   U P   T H E   G R I L L

1 To set up a charcoal grill for direct grilling, first light the charcoal in a chimney starter (see page 9).

2 Using a garden hoe or other long-handled implement, rake the burning coals into an even layer.

3 To see if the grill is preheated to high, use the test on page 10.

(see page 9) ... test on page 10

P R E P A R I N G   T H E   T O F U

1 To press the tofu, set it on a slanted cutting board in the sink and place a heavy skillet on top. The slant of the board lets the liquid drain off.

2 Cut the pressed tofu crosswise into ¾-inch-thick slices. Arrange these slices in a baking dish.

TIPS

■ You'll need extra-firm or firm tofu for this recipe (soft tofu won't stay on the skewers). To firm up tofu even further, press it under a weight to squeeze out some of the water.

■ Even when pressed, tofu is quite fragile, so I use two skewers to support it. The Japanese have a colorful name for this—*dengaku*—tofu on stilts.

TIPS

■ Star anise is a star-shaped spice with a smoky licorice flavor. Look for it in Asian markets and gourmet shops. If tangerines aren't in season, substitute oranges.

■ Tofu can have a tendency to stick to the grill grate, so the Japanese grill it suspended over the fire. You can do this by resting the ends of the skewers on bricks (see page 193). If you do this, you'll need to insert the skewers so that they extend well beyond the tofu on both ends. But if you brush and oil the grill grate well, you shouldn't have a problem grilling tofu directly on the grate.

3 Use a vegetable peeler to remove the zest (the oil-rich outer rind) of the tangerine.

4 Pour the marinade over the tofu and let it marinate in the refrigerator, covered, for 1 to 2 hours.

5 Push the skewers through the tofu, two skewers per slice. Only the tips of the skewers should extend through one end of the tofu.

ON THE GRILL: Grill the tofu directly on the grill grate (the grate should be well brushed and oiled). Brush the teriyaki sauce on the tofu as it grills. The tofu will be done after 4 to 6 minutes per side. For attractive cross-hatch grill marks, rotate the tofu 45 degrees after 2 to 3 minutes. Place aluminum foil under the skewers to protect them, if they start to burn.

T H E   R E C I P E

TANGERINE TERIYAKI TOFU

2 pounds extra-firm tofu
3 strips tangerine zest
½ cup soy sauce
½ cup sugar
½ cup tangerine juice
¼ cup Asian sesame oil
2 cloves garlic, peeled and crushed
  with the side of a knife
2 slices peeled fresh ginger (¼ inch thick),
  crushed with the side of a knife

2 whole star anise
½ teaspoon cornstarch dissolved
  in 2 teaspoons water
1 tablespoon lightly toasted
  sesame seeds (page 30),
  for garnish
2 scallions, green part only, finely
  chopped for garnish

1. Press the tofu for 1 hour as shown in Preparing the Tofu, Step 1 on page 415. Cut the tofu crosswise into ¾-inch-thick slices and arrange them in a nonreactive baking dish with the tangerine zest.

2. Combine the soy sauce, sugar, tangerine juice, sesame oil, garlic, ginger, and star anise in a nonreactive mixing bowl and whisk to mix. Pour the marinade over the tofu. Let marinate in the refrigerator, covered, for 1 to 2 hours, turning the tofu pieces several times to ensure even marinating.

3. Set up the grill for direct grilling (see page 10 for charcoal or page 16 for gas) and preheat to high. Strain the marinade into a saucepan. Skewer the tofu pieces as shown in Step 5 on the facing page. Bring the marinade to a boil over high heat.

Briskly simmer, uncovered, until syrupy, 5 to 10 minutes. Whisk in the dissolved cornstarch and boil until thickened, 30 seconds.

4. When ready to cook, brush and oil the grate well, then place the tofu on it. Grill the tofu until sizzling and well browned, 4 to 6 minutes per side. Protect the skewers with sheets of aluminum foil if they start to burn. The tofu is done when the surface is browned and sizzling. It will be hot throughout. Rotate the tofu 45 degrees after 2 to 3 minutes for crosshatch grill marks. Baste the tofu twice per side with the glaze as it cooks.

5. Transfer the tofu to plates or a platter. Spoon any remaining glaze over the tofu. Sprinkle it with the sesame seeds and scallion greens and serve at once.

MAKES 10 PIECES; SERVES 5 AS AN APPETIZER, 2 TO 3 AS A MAIN COURSE

YOU'LL NEED:
20 long, slender bamboo skewers, soaked for 1 hour in cold water to cover, then drained

VARIATIONS:
For Cuban-style tofu, use the marinade from Mojo-Marinated Pork Tenderloin, Step 1 on page 126; for Indian-style tofu, use the marinade from Tandoori Lamb Chops, Steps 1 and 3 on page 185.

ALSO GOOD FOR:
Use the tangerine teriyaki marinade on chicken breasts, flank steaks, pork chops, shrimp, and salmon or snapper fillets or steaks.

HOW TO GRILL GARLIC BREAD

The grill was the original toaster, and it's still the best way to toast bread. If you have any doubt, just go to Italy, where *bruschetta* (toasted bread rubbed with raw garlic and drizzled with olive oil) is still cooked over burning embers. From *bruschetta* to grilled garlic bread is just a small jump, and it's a jump that's well worth making. For if you like garlic bread (and who doesn't?), you're going to love this version, which is smokily charred on the grill.

*Grilled Garlic
Parsley Cheese
Bread*

SETTING UP THE GRILL

1 To set up a charcoal grill for direct grilling, first light the charcoal in a chimney starter (see page 9).

2 Using a garden hoe or other long-handled implement, rake the burning coals into a three-zone fire (see page 10).

3 A three-zone fire gives you a coal-free safety zone.

TIP

Bread is highly flammable and so is melted butter. Never leave your grill or divert your attention when grilling bread. A three-zone fire gives you a cool area to move the bread slices to if they start to burn (see building a Three-Zone Fire, page 10, for charcoal or Direct Grilling, page 16, for gas).

PREPARING THE BREAD

1 Slice the bread lengthwise sharply on the diagonal into ½-inch-thick slices. Use a serated knife to cut, starting on the top of the loaf.

2 Cream the butter, whisking it until it is light and fluffy, then add the garlic, parsley, pepper, and Parmesan.

3 Using a spatula or pastry brush, generously spread the garlic butter on both sides of the slices of bread.

4 Grill the bread until golden brown on both sides, 1 to 3 minutes per side. Keep a close watch on the grill as the bread can burn quickly.

MAKES 16 SLICES; SERVES 8

T H E   R E C I P E

GRILLED GARLIC PARSLEY CHEESE BREAD

1 loaf French bread (20 to 24 inches long)
12 tablespoons (1½ sticks) salted
*   butter, at room temperature*
3 cloves garlic, minced

¼ cup finely chopped fresh parsley
½ teaspoon black pepper
¼ cup freshly grated Parmigiano-
*   Reggiano cheese*

1. Set up the grill for three-zone direct grilling (see page 10 for charcoal or page 16 for gas) and preheat the hot zone to medium-high.

2. Cut the bread sharply on the diagonal into ½-inch-thick slices as shown in

Step 1 on page 419. Alternatively, cut the bread into fingers by first cutting it crossways into 6-inch pieces, then lengthwise into quarters. Arrange the bread slices on a tray or baking sheet to facilitate moving them from the kitchen to the grill.

3. Place the butter in a medium-size bowl and cream it using a whisk or wooden spoon. Add the garlic, parsley, pepper, and Parmigiano-Reggiano and beat until the butter is light and fluffy. Alternatively, you can do the beating in a mixer or food processor. Using a spatula or pastry brush, spread the garlic butter on both sides of the bread slices.

4. When ready to cook, place the buttered bread on the hot grate and grill until golden brown on both sides, 1 to 3 minutes per side. Don't take your eyes off of the grill for a second, as the bread will burn quickly. If it starts to burn, use tongs to move the slices to a cooler area of the grill. Remove from the grill and serve at once.

VARIATIONS:

You can vary the bread and substitute olive oil, walnut, or hazelnut oil for the butter, cilantro or basil for the parsley, and Gorgonzola or Roquefort for the Parmigiano-Reggiano. You could even add minced cooked bacon, pancetta, or prosciutto to the butter.

How to Grill Pineapples and Other Fruit **424**

How to Fire Roast Pears and Other Fruit **428**

How to Grill Crème Brûlée **432**

DESSERTS

Dessert on the grill? The very notion would have been unthinkable only a decade ago, but today, any self-respecting grill jockey needs a few dessert recipes in his or her repertory. Which brings us to the shortest chapter in the book, but also the sweetest: desserts you can cook on the grill. You'll learn how to grill fruit using both the direct and indirect methods, how to caramelize a crème brûlée the old-fashioned way (using a flame-heated poker), and even how to make an updated version of that childhood cookout favorite, the s'more. So fire up your grill and get ready for some just desserts.

How to Make S'mores **436**

METHOD:
Direct grilling

COOKING TIME:
8 to 12 minutes

HOW TO GRILL PINEAPPLES AND OTHER FRUIT

Grilled fruit is a great way to bring a barbecue to a festive close. In markets throughout Thailand or Indonesia you'll find grill jockeys dipping fruits like bananas in coconut milk and palm sugar and searing them over hibachis. From bananas it's a short leap to another tropical fruit that tastes great grilled this way: pineapple. Indeed, any juicy fruit is a candidate.

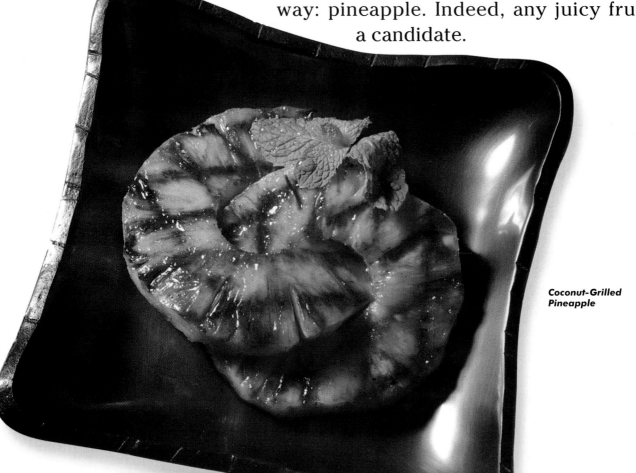

Coconut-Grilled Pineapple

SETTING UP THE GRILL

1 To set up a charcoal grill for direct grilling, first light the charcoal in a chimney starter (see page 9).

2 Using a garden hoe or other long-handled implement, rake the burning coals into an even layer.

3 To see if the grill is preheated to high, use the test on page 10.

PREPARING THE PINEAPPLE

1 Grab the pineapple firmly in one hand and its leaves in the other. Twist them in opposite directions to separate the leaves from the fruit.

2 Cut off the rind, first from the top and bottom of the pineapple, then from the sides. Cut it off in lengthwise strips, slicing deep enough to remove the eyes.

TIPS

■ The easiest way to get unsweetened coconut milk is to buy it canned—look for it in the ethnic foods section of your supermarket. Both Thai and Latin American brands are widely available. Two good Thai brands are Chaokoh and A Taste of Thai (the latter comes in a low-fat variation for health-conscious eaters).

■ When buying a pineapple, look for a golden or yellow rind; this indicates a ripe, sweet fruit. One good brand is Dole's Premium Select. You'll get between 8 and 12 slices from one pineapple.

TIP

■ If you like, save the pineapple rind to use as a fuel for smoking. Use it for Caribbean grilled dishes, like the grilled snapper on page 289 or even Jamaican jerk (see page 115).

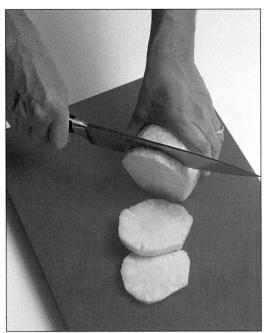

3 Cut the pineapple crosswise into ½-inch-thick slices.

4 Use a melon baller or fruit corer to remove the fibrous core from the center of each slice.

ON THE GRILL

1 Dip both sides of each pineapple slice first in coconut milk, then in cinnamon sugar, shaking off the excess. Place the pineapple slices on the oiled grill grate.

2 Grill the pineapple until browned on both sides, 4 to 6 minutes per side. Rotate the slices 60 degrees after 2 minutes to create an attractive crosshatch of grill marks.

SERVES 4 TO 6

COCONUT-GRILLED PINEAPPLE

1 ripe golden pineapple
1 can (14 ounces) unsweetened
*   coconut milk*
1½ cups turbinado sugar
*   or granulated sugar*

1 teaspoon ground cinnamon
Sprigs of fresh mint, for garnish
1 quart vanilla ice cream or
*   frozen yogurt, for serving*
*   (optional)*

1. Set up the grill for direct grilling (see page 10 for charcoal or page 16 for gas) and preheat to high.

2. Peel, slice, and core the pineapple as shown in Preparing the Pineapple, Steps 1 through 4 on pages 425 and 426. Shake the coconut milk well before opening the can. Pour it into a wide, shallow bowl. Place the sugar and cinnamon in another wide, shallow bowl and stir with a fork to mix.

3. When ready to cook, brush and oil the grill grate. Dip each pineapple slice first in coconut milk, then in the sugar mixture, shaking off the excess between each dipping. Arrange the slices on the hot grate and grill until nicely browned on both sides, 4 to 6 minutes per side. If a crosshatch of grill marks is desired, rotate each slice 60 degrees after 2 or 3 minutes on each side. Transfer the pineapple slices to plates or a platter for serving and garnish with mint sprigs. Or serve in bowls over ice cream, if desired. The pineapple can be served either hot or cold.

VARIATION:
A great variation on this recipe is to substitute melted unsalted butter for the coconut milk for dipping. Do not shake off the excess butter (or any oil) near the grill.

ALSO GOOD FOR:
This recipe also works well with bananas and stone fruit, such as peaches, plums, or nectarines. Use small bananas or cut large bananas in half crosswise sharply on the diagonal. When grilling stone fruit, cut them in half and remove the pits.

METHOD:
Indirect grilling

COOKING TIME:
**40 minutes
to 1 hour**

HOW TO FIRE ROAST PEARS AND OTHER FRUIT

Baked apples and pears are two of the most satisfying and comforting desserts. This led me to wonder how they would taste smoke roasted. The answer is terrific. The subtle smoke flavor counterpoints the earthy sweetness of the fruit. Then there's the theatrical value of lifting the lid to expose a gorgeous dessert on the grill. For a touch of drama, I usually roast pears instead of apples. I think you'll find the combination of pear, butter, brown sugar, and wood smoke to be irresistible. And I wouldn't say no to a side of vanilla ice cream, either!

*Smoke-Roasted
Pears*

SETTING UP THE GRILL

1 To set up a charcoal grill for indirect grilling, first light the charcoal in a chimney starter (see page 9).

2 Form two heat zones by raking the coals into two piles at opposite sides of the grill, using a long-handled implement, like a garden hoe.

3 If your grill has side baskets, divide the coals evenly between them.

PREPARING THE PEARS

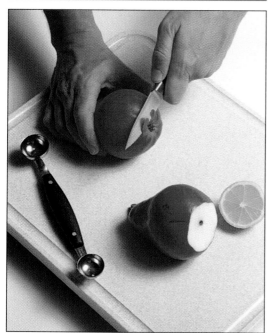

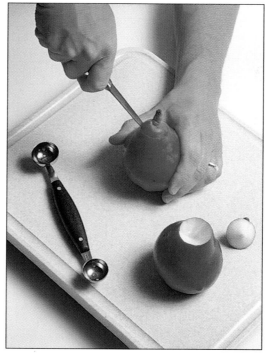

1 Using a paring knife, cut a thin slice off the bottom of each pear so it can stand upright without wobbling. Use lemon to rub the cut edge so it doesn't become discolored.

2 Using a paring knife, cut out the stem end (remove it in a neat inverted cone).

TIPS

■ My favorite pear for this dessert is the luscious, fleshy, red-skinned Comice. You can also use Bosc or Anjou pears. The fruit should be ripe but not soft.

■ To help the pears stand upright, I cut a thin slice off the bottom. This works for any fruit with a rounded bottom.

3 Using a melon baller, scoop out the core and seeds.

4 Stuff the filling into the cavity. Note: I like to dice the fruit that's around the core (leaving out the seeds, of course) and add it to the filling mixture. I've done that here.

ON THE GRILL: Place the stuffed pears in an aluminum foil pan and set it on the grill. Adding wood chips generates smoke. If you are using charcoal, put wood chips on the coals after the pears on the grill. For gas, you'll need to preheat the chips in the smoker box or in a smoker pouch. The pears are done when nicely browned and soft on the sides, after 40 minutes to 1 hour.

SERVES 6

YOU'LL NEED:
1 lightly oiled aluminum foil pan large enough to hold 6 pears;
1 cup wood chips (preferably apple, pear, cherry, or maple), soaked for 1 hour in cold water to cover, then drained

---

T H E   R E C I P E

SMOKE-ROASTED PEARS

6 large ripe pears
½ lemon
5 tablespoons butter, at room temperature
5 tablespoons brown sugar
5 tablespoons graham cracker crumbs or ground hazelnuts

½ teaspoon grated lemon zest
½ teaspoon ground cinnamon
¼ teaspoon grated nutmeg
½ teaspoon ground cloves
1 tablespoon rum
1 teaspoon vanilla extract

1. Cut a thin slice off the bottom and remove the top from each pear as shown in Preparing the Pears, Steps 1 and 2 on page 429. Discard the bottom slices and set the tops aside. Core the pears, using a melon baller. Rub the cut bottoms and tops with the cut side of the lemon to prevent browning. Squeeze a few drops of juice into the cavities.

2. Prepare the filling: Beat the butter and brown sugar in a mixing bowl with a wooden spoon. Beat in the graham cracker crumbs, lemon zest, cinnamon, nutmeg, cloves, rum, and vanilla. Spoon the butter mixture into the pears and loosely place the caps on top. Arrange the pears in the lightly greased aluminum foil pan. The recipe can be prepared up to this stage several hours ahead.

3. Set up the grill for indirect grilling (see page 12 for charcoal or page 16 for gas) and preheat to medium. If using a gas grill, place the wood chips in the smoker box or in a smoker pouch (see page 17) and preheat on high until you see smoke, then reduce the heat to medium.

4. When ready to cook, place the pan with the pears in the center of the hot grate, away from the heat. If using a charcoal grill, toss the wood chips on the coals. Cover the grill and smoke roast the pears until nicely browned and soft on the sides, 40 minutes to 1 hour. Serve at once.

VARIATION:
You can change the ingredients in the filling, adding ground nuts, candied ginger, or other flavorings.

ALSO GOOD FOR:
Apples and quinces taste delicious smoke roasted this way.

METHOD:
Indirect grilling

COOKING TIME:
35 to 45 minutes
for cooking the
crèmes brûlées,
plus at least
4 hours to
chill them

HOW TO GRILL CREME BRULEE

It may seem odd to include this exquisitely creamy dessert in a book on grilling. But the original crème brûlée was "burnt" (caramelized) with a flame-heated iron, and today chefs use the ultimate live-fire device—a blowtorch—for caramelizing the sugar. The whole notion of a live-fire dessert set me thinking how to make crème brûlée even more fiery. So, to spice up the recipe, I added chipotle chiles to the mix and smoked the custards on the grill, using the indirect method. The process may sound a little involved, if not weird, but the chiles and smoke actually make the custards taste richer and sweeter.

*Chipotle
Crèmes Brûlées*

SETTING UP THE GRILL

1 To set up a charcoal grill for indirect grilling, first light the charcoal in a chimney starter (see page 9).

2 Form two heat zones by raking the coals into two piles at opposite sides of the grill, using a long-handled implement, like a garden hoe.

3 If your grill has side baskets, divide the coals evenly between them.

PREPARING THE CUSTARD

1 Cut the vanilla bean in half to expose the tiny seeds. Also shown here are a whole vanilla bean, a cinnamon stick, and dried chipotle chiles.

2 Add the halved vanilla bean, cinnamon stick, and chipotles to the cream and gently simmer on the stove for 10 minutes.

3 After it has cooled to room temperature, whisk the cream into a mixture of egg yolk and sugar to make a custard.

4 Strain the custard into crème brûlée dishes. The dishes are in a roasting pan that will serve as a water bath.

TIPS

■ Chipotle chiles are smoked jalapeño peppers. You can buy them dried or canned. I normally prefer the robust flavor of canned chipotles, but for this recipe, mild dried chipotles are better for infusing the cream. The chipotles add a gentle smoky flavor and only a whisper of heat.

■ A crème brûlée dish is a small, shallow, round ceramic dish (often with fluted sides) that looks like a miniature gratin dish. Look for them in any cookware shop.

TIPS

■ The custards for the crèmes brûlées cook in a water bath—a roasting pan filled with about ½ inch of hot water. This provides a moist, gentle heat that keeps the custards soft and creamy. Add the water once the custards are on the grill so you don't have to worry about it sloshing around as you carry the pan.

■ The traditional way to caramelize a crème brûlée is with a flat, round iron called a salamander heated in the fire. You can heat it directly in the coals of a charcoal fire (just be sure to tap it against the side of the grill to knock off the ash). Or heat it on the grate of a gas grill. Touching the hot iron to the tops of the custards produces a dramatic hiss and puff of smoke—theatrics guaranteed to bring down the house at any cookout.

ON THE GRILL

1 Place the custards on the grill in the center, away from the heat. Add hot water to the roasting pan to make the water bath. The custards will be set after 25 to 35 minutes on the grill.

2 To reinforce the smoke flavor, add wood chips to the coals, if you're using charcoal. If you are using gas, put them in the smoker box or make a smoker pouch when you preheat the grill.

CARAMELIZING THE SUGAR

1 Once the custards are chilled (after about 4 hours in the refrigerator), sprinkle the tops with turbinado or granulated sugar.

2 Heat the iron in the coals, if you are using charcoal. If you have a gas grill, heat it on the grate or the side burner.

3 Tap the hot iron to knock off any ash and then press it lightly on top of each crème brûlée; the sugar will caramelize. You may need to reheat the iron as you work.

4 Or use a blowtorch to caramelize the sugar. Point the flame at the top of a crème brûlée. The nozzle should be 3 inches above the surface.

CHIPOTLE CREMES BRULEES

3 cups heavy cream
2 dried chipotle chiles, torn open and seeded
    (for a spicier dessert, leave the seeds in)
1 vanilla bean, cut in half lengthwise
1 cinnamon stick

8 egg yolks
1 whole egg
⅓ cup granulated sugar
3 to 4 tablespoons turbinado sugar
    or more granulated sugar

1. Combine the cream, chipotles, vanilla bean, and cinnamon stick in a heavy saucepan over medium-low heat and cook at the gentlest possible simmer for 10 minutes. Remove the pan from the heat and let the cream mixture cool to room temperature.

2. Combine the egg yolks, whole egg, and granulated sugar in a large bowl and whisk just to mix. Whisk the cooled cream mixture into the yolk mixture. Strain this mixture into crème brûlée dishes or ramekins. Place the filled dishes in a roasting pan. Bring 1 quart water to a boil.

3. Meanwhile, set up the grill for indirect grilling (see page 12 for charcoal or page 16 for gas) and preheat to medium. If using a gas grill, place the wood chips in the smoker box or in a smoker pouch (see page 17) and preheat on high until you see smoke, then reduce the heat to medium.

4. When ready to cook, place the roasting pan in the center of the hot grate away from the heat. Add ½ inch of boiling water to the pan, taking care not to splash any on the custards. If using a charcoal grill, toss the wood chips on the coals. Cover the grill

and grill the custards until just set, 25 to 35 minutes. To test for doneness, tap one of the dishes. The mixture should wiggle, not ripple, indicating the custard is set. Transfer the custards to a rack to cool to room temperature, then refrigerate until cold, about 4 hours. You can prepare the custards up to this stage the day before.

5. If using a crème brûlée iron, set up the grill for direct grilling (see page 10 for charcoal or page 16 for gas) and preheat to high. When ready to cook, sprinkle a thin layer of turbinado sugar (or granulated sugar) on top of each custard. If using an iron and charcoal to brûlée the custards, heat the iron in the coals as shown in Step 2 on the facing page. Tap the iron to knock off any ash. If using an iron and a gas grill, heat the iron on the grate. Press the iron lightly on the top of a custard to caramelize the sugar. Repeat with the remaining custards. Reheat the iron as needed to produce instant caramelization (this may be necessary after caramelizing 2 or 3 crèmes brûlées). Alternatively, caramelize the sugar using a blowtorch, as shown in Step 4. Serve at once.

SERVES 6

YOU'LL NEED:
6 crème brûlée dishes or ramekins 3½ to 4 inches in diameter; 1 cup wood chips (preferably cherry or apple), soaked for 1 hour in cold water to cover, then drained; a crème brûlée iron (salamander) or a blowtorch

---

TIP

■ Cookware shops sell kitchen blowtorches that are specially designed for caramelizing crème brûlée. But you can certainly use a hardware store blowtorch, as you see on the facing page.

VARIATIONS:
To make a traditional crème brûlée, omit the chipotles and the cinnamon stick. To make a coffee crème brûlée, infuse the cream with ½ cup dark-roasted coffee beans. To make lemon crème brûlée, infuse the cream with 6 strips of lemon zest (the oil-rich outer rind).

METHOD:
Direct grilling

COOKING TIME:
3 to 5 minutes

HOW TO MAKE S'MORES

Remember s'mores? That gooey sandwich of graham crackers, marshmallow, and chocolate you ate around the campfire when you were a kid? The burning marshmallow melted the chocolate bar, turning the s'more into an exquisite mess. It burned your fingers and dirtied your face, and nothing tasted quite so sinfully delicious. Here you'll find my take on the humble s'more—a princely sandwich made with shortbread cookies and designer chocolate. The childhood joy of burning the marshmallows and assembling and eating the s'mores remains the same.

Shortbread
S'mores

SETTING UP THE GRILL

1 To set up a charcoal grill for direct grilling, first light the charcoal in a chimney starter (see page 9).

2 Dump the lit coals from the chimney starter into the bottom of the grill.

3 Using a garden hoe or other long-handled implement, rake the burning coals into a layer.

ROASTING THE MARSHMALLOWS

1 If you are using charcoal, you can roast the skewered marshmallows directly over the coals; it will take 3 to 5 minutes.

2 With a gas grill you can roast the marshmallows over the side burner, if it has one. If not, hold them just above the grate to roast.

MAKING THE S'MORES: Sandwich a hot marshmallow between chocolate and two shortbread cookies. Squeeze until the chocolate is melted and gooey, then eat.

SERVES 6

YOU'LL NEED:
6 long metal or
bamboo skewers
or sticks,
bamboo skewers
soaked for
1 hour in cold
water to cover,
then drained

T H E   R E C I P E

SHORTBREAD S'MORES

12 shortbread cookies
6 squares (each 2 inches) superior dark
chocolate

6 large marshmallows

1. Arrange the cookies on a platter, topping half with squares of chocolate. Set up the grill for direct grilling (see page 10 for charcoal and page 16 for gas) and preheat to high. Or if using a gas grill that has one, light the side burner.

2. When ready to cook, if using a charcoal grill, rake the lit coals into a mound (don't place the top grate on the grill). Skewer the marshmallows on skewers or sticks and hold them over the fire. Roast until browned, or even black, rotating the marshmallows to ensure even cooking. This will take 3 to 5 minutes. You can even set the marshmallows on fire (again, rotate the skewers to ensure even burning). If you've lit your marshmallow, blow out the fire.

3. Immediately position each marshmallow on top of a piece of chocolate. Place another cookie on top and press down to squish the marshmallow into the chocolate. Pull out the skewer. Wait for a few seconds for the hot marshmallow to melt the chocolate, then eat the s'more like a sandwich.

Note: Never succumb to the temptation to eat a hot marshmallow directly off a metal skewer: You'll burn your lips (I speak from sad experience).

RUBS, SAUCES & CONDIMENTS

This chapter brings us to what separates the men from the boys, the pros from the amateurs, the true grill masters from the folks who merely play with fire. I'm talking about the rubs, mops, butters, barbecue sauces, and condiments that make good barbecue great and great barbecue unforgettable. These not-so-subtle flavor enhancers will light up your mouth like Fourth of July fireworks.

Rubs are mixes of spices (freshly ground, when possible), herbs, and seasonings that are massaged onto meats before the actual cooking—thus the term *rub*. A mop is a flavorful liquid, often vinegar based, that you brush or swab onto the meat while it cooks. The traditional way to apply it was to swab it on with a clean floor mop—and so the term *mop*. Like mops, flavored butters can be used for basting and slathering (they're particularly good on grilled bread), and I never met a grilled steak that wasn't improved by a golden dollop of flavored butter melting on top.

For many people, the sauce is the soul of barbecue. Barbecue sauces can be used for mopping or basting but are most commonly served over or on the side of the finished dish. They vary from dish to dish and region to region, and there are probably as many different types of barbecue sauces as there are individual grill jockeys. As for condiments, they include the salsas, chutneys, and relishes used by pit masters from Albuquerque to Bombay to give food hot off the grill a final bit of jazz.

HOW TO MAKE RUBS

Clockwise from large bowl at top (all recipes can be found in this section): Java Rub, Mucho Macho Pepper Rub, Chinese Five-Spice Rub, Basic Fish Cure, Mediterranean Herb Rub, and Basic Barbecue Rub. Cajun Rub, small bowl in center; Sesame Seasoning, large bowl in center.

Rubs are the basic seasonings of barbecue—simple mixes of salt, sugar, and spices or herbs that add complex layers of flavor to your food. There are two basic ways to use a rub. You can sprinkle it on food just before grilling, in which case the rub acts as a seasoning. Or you can apply it several hours or even a day in advance, in which case the rub both seasons and cures the meat. The second way gives you the deep layers of flavor that are characteristic of true barbecue. By the way, the proper way to apply a rub is to sprinkle it over the food, then gently rub it on with your fingertips.

THE RECIPE
BASIC BARBECUE RUB

MAKES ABOUT 1 CUP

OK, this is ground zero—the *ur* American barbecue rub. Use it on ribs, pork shoulders, chickens—anything you want to taste like American barbecue. Use 2 to 3 teaspoons per pound of meat. A 4-pound chicken will take 1½ to 2 tablespoons. You'll find hickory-smoked salt available in the spice rack of most supermarkets. To make a spicier rub, substitute hot paprika for some or all of the sweet paprika.

¼ cup firmly packed brown sugar
¼ cup sweet paprika
3 tablespoons black pepper
3 tablespoons coarse salt
*1 tablespoon hickory-smoked salt or
   more coarse salt*
2 teaspoons garlic powder
2 teaspoons onion powder
2 teaspoons celery seeds
1 teaspoon cayenne pepper

Combine all the ingredients in a mixing bowl and stir to mix. (Actually, your hands work better for mixing than a spoon or whisk does. Use your fingers to break up any lumps of brown sugar.) Store the rub in an airtight jar away from heat or light; it will keep for at least 6 months.

THE RECIPE
BASIC FISH CURE

MAKES ABOUT 1½ CUPS

If you love smoked fish as much as I do, you'll want to make your own cure. Here's a basic one that you can customize as you desire. For example, make it with white, turbinado, or maple sugar instead of brown. Or add any herb or spice you may fancy. Use ¾ cup per pound of fish meat.

1 cup firmly packed brown sugar
½ cup coarse salt
1 tablespoon black pepper
1 tablespoon dried dill (optional)
1 tablespoon mustard powder (optional)

Combine all the ingredients in a small mixing bowl and stir to mix. (Actually, your fingers work better for mixing than a spoon or whisk does.) Store the rub in an airtight jar away from heat and light; it will keep for at least 6 months.

THE RECIPE
CAJUN RUB

MAKES ABOUT ¾ CUP

Born in the bayous of Louisiana and immortalized by the pan-blackened redfish of Louisiana legend Paul Prudhomme, this rub will lend a Cajun accent to anything on which you sprinkle it, especially chicken, steak, and seafood. Use 2 to 3 teaspoons per pound of meat. A 4-pound chicken will take 1½ to 2 tablespoons.

¼ cup coarse salt
¼ cup sweet paprika
1 tablespoon garlic flakes
1 tablespoon onion flakes
1 tablespoon dried thyme leaves
1 tablespoon dried oregano
1 tablespoon black pepper
2 teaspoons white pepper
1 to 2 teaspoons cayenne pepper
1 teaspoon ground bay leaf

SPICING UP THE SPICES

■ One way to boost the flavor of any rub is to start with whole spices and grind them as you need them. Whole spices contain more aromatic oils than ground spices. It's sort of like grating your Parmesan fresh each meal rather than using a jar of pregrated cheese. Grind your spices in a spice mill or coffee grinder. I find that propeller-type grinders (the sort that look like miniature blenders) work best.

Combine all the ingredients in a mixing bowl and stir to mix. (Actually, your fingers work better for mixing than a spoon or whisk does.) Store the rub in an airtight jar away from heat or light; it will keep for at least 6 months.

THE RECIPE
CHINESE FIVE-SPICE RUB

MAKES ABOUT ¾ CUP

Rubs are primarily found in the West, but for centuries, the Chinese have used a fragrant mixture of star anise, fennel seeds, Sichuan and white peppercorns, cinnamon, and cloves to spice up their poultry and pork. Called five-spice powder, the mix varies from chef to chef and may include as few as four spices or as many as seven. To make a rub, I've added salt and brown sugar to a spice powder blend. Use 2 to 3 teaspoons per pound of meat. A 5-pound duck will take 1½ to 2 tablespoons.

FOR THE FIVE-SPICE POWDER:
3 whole star anise
2 tablespoons Sichuan peppercorns
1 tablespoon white peppercorns
1 tablespoon fennel seeds
½ teaspoon whole cloves
½ cinnamon stick

FOR THE RUB:
¼ cup coarse salt
¼ cup firmly packed brown sugar

1. Prepare the five-spice powder: Preheat a dry skillet over medium heat. Add the star anise, Sichuan and white peppercorns, fennel seeds, cloves, and cinnamon and toast until fragrant, 2 to 4 minutes. Don't overtoast, or the spices will be bitter. Transfer the spices to a bowl to cool. Grind the spices to a fine powder in a mortar with a pestle or in a spice mill.

2. Return the toasted spices to the bowl and mix in the salt and brown sugar (the best tool for mixing is your fingers). Store the rub in an airtight jar away from heat and light; it will keep for at least 6 months.

MAKING A RUB

1 Toast the spices in a skillet until they are fragrant. Here I'm making the Chinese Five-Spice Rub.

2 Pulverize the spices in a mortar with a pestle or grind them in a spice mill. If you haven't got a spice mill, you can use a coffee grinder. Once you've mixed in any additional ingredients, store the rub in an airtight jar away from heat or light.

THE RECIPE
JAVA RUB

MAKES ABOUT ¾ CUP

Coffee may seem like an odd ingredient for a rub, but competition 'que heads use it and win big with it. The bittersweet flavor of the coffee rub goes great on beef (especially brisket) and pork. Use 2 to 3 teaspoons per pound of meat. For extra flavor start with the same quantity of whole peppercorns and cumin and coriander seeds and toast them and grind them yourself.

6 tablespoons ground coffee
2 tablespoons coarse salt
2 tablespoons brown sugar
2 tablespoons sweet paprika
2 teaspoons black pepper
2 teaspoons garlic powder
2 teaspoons onion powder
1 teaspoon ground cumin
1 teaspoon ground coriander
1 teaspoon unsweetened cocoa powder

Combine all the ingredients in a mixing bowl and stir to mix. (Actually, your fingers work better for mixing than a spoon or whisk does.) Store the rub in an airtight jar away from heat and light; it will keep for at least 6 months.

THE RECIPE
MEDITERRANEAN HERB RUB

MAKES ABOUT 1 CUP

French *herbes de Provence* meet Kansas City barbecue rub in this fragrant seasoning, which tastes terrific on lamb, chicken, and seafood. Use 2 to 3 teaspoons per pound of meat. A 4-pound chicken will take 1½ to 2 tablespoons.

3 tablespoons dried tarragon
3 tablespoons dried oregano
3 tablespoons dried dill
3 tablespoons dried thyme
3 tablespoons dried rosemary
3 tablespoons coarse salt

2 tablespoons lemon pepper (see Note)
1 tablespoon garlic flakes

Combine all the ingredients in a mixing bowl and stir to mix. (Actually, your fingers work better for mixing than a spoon or whisk does.) Store the rub in an airtight jar away from heat and light; it will keep for at least 6 months.

Note: Lemon pepper is exactly that— ground black peppercorns flavored with lemon zest. You can buy it at most supermarkets, order it by mail, or make your own following the recipe in *Barbecue! Bible Sauces, Rubs, and Marinades.*

THE RECIPE
MUCHO MACHO PEPPER RUB

MAKES ABOUT ¾ CUP

The peppercorns and pepper flakes in this rub give it a good "ouch" quotient. This is exactly what you want when a steak or pork chop calls for a spice mix that bites back. This is a baby ouch, but you could certainly up the ante by adding more hot pepper flakes or black peppercorns. Use 2 to 3 teaspoons per pound of meat. A 4-pound chicken will take 1½ to 2 tablespoons.

3 tablespoons coarse salt
3 tablespoons cracked black peppercorns
3 tablespoons hot red pepper flakes
3 tablespoons onion flakes
3 tablespoons dried parsley

Combine all the ingredients in a mixing bowl and stir to mix. (Actually, your fingers

TOASTING YOUR WAY TO FLAVOR

■ Another way to increase the flavor of a rub is to toast the whole spices in a dry skillet over medium heat. Toasting brings out the aromatic oils and lightly caramelizes the spices (think of what roasting does for a coffee or cocoa bean). Spices toast best in a dry cast-iron or stainless steel skillet; don't use a nonstick pan. Remember that the spices will continue toasting even after the pan comes off the heat, so have a heatproof bowl ready to pour them into. Don't toast the spices too much, or they'll burn and become bitter.

Use your fingers to sprinkle the rub over the food, here a brisket, and then massage it on.

work better for mixing than a spoon or whisk does.) Store the rub in an airtight jar away from heat or light; it will keep for at least 6 months.

THE RECIPE
SESAME SEASONING

MAKES ABOUT ¾ CUP

For great barbecue, say "Open sesame." The tiny seeds add a great nutty flavor to rubs. This one gives you a triple blast of sesame flavor, with white sesame seeds, toasted sesame seeds, and black sesame seeds (the last are available at Japanese markets). It goes particularly well with grilled fish and vegetables, as well as with grilled pork and chicken. Use 2 to 3 teaspoons per pound. Unlike most rubs, Sesame Seasoning tastes best sprinkled on after the food comes off the grill.

½ cup white sesame seeds
¼ cup black sesame seeds
¼ cup coarse salt
1 tablespoon garlic flakes

1. Preheat a small dry cast-iron or stainless steel skillet over medium heat. Add half the white sesame seeds and toast until fragrant and golden brown, 2 to 4 minutes. Don't overtoast or the seeds will be bitter. Transfer the toasted sesame seeds to a small heatproof bowl and let cool. (The reason for toasting only half of the sesame seeds is aesthetic as well as gastronomic; it gives you three different color seeds with three distinct flavors.)

2. Add the remaining ingredients and stir to mix. Store the rub in an airtight jar away from heat and light; it will keep for at least 6 months.

THE RECIPE
TEXAS CHILI RUB

MAKES ABOUT 1 CUP

Texas is beef country, and this no-nonsense rub will add drama to any meat, from steak to brisket. Use 2 to 3 teaspoons per pound of meat. The chipotle chiles (smoked jalapeños) add an assertive smoke flavor. For a hotter rub, don't bother seeding the chipotles. Dried chipotles are available at gourmet shops and many supermarkets, or see the Mail-Order Sources on pages 481 and 482.

1 to 2 dried chipotle chiles, torn open
*   and seeded*
2 tablespoons black peppercorns
1 tablespoon cumin seeds
1 tablespoon coriander seeds
1 tablespoon yellow mustard seeds
¼ cup coarse salt
¼ cup mild chili powder or paprika
2 tablespoons brown sugar
1 tablespoon garlic flakes
1 tablespoon onion flakes
1 tablespoon dried oregano

1. Preheat a small dry cast-iron or stainless steel skillet over medium heat. Add the chipotles, peppercorns, and the cumin, coriander, and mustard seeds and toast until fragrant, 2 to 4 minutes. Put the chipotles in first, as it takes them longest to toast. Don't overtoast, or the spices will be bitter. Transfer the spices to a heatproof bowl to cool.

2. Grind the spices to a fine powder in a mortar with a pestle or in a spice mill. Return them to the bowl and mix in the remaining ingredients (use your fingers for mixing). Store the rub in an airtight jar away from heat and light; it will keep for at least 6 months.

HOW TO MAKE MOP SAUCES

Mop sauces are intensely flavorful liquids used to baste foods during grilling. Most mops are vinegar based, with salt, pepper, and hot pepper flakes or cayenne added for seasoning. Additional flavor often comes in the form of sliced onion, garlic, and chiles. Unlike barbecue sauces, mops contain no sugar, so you don't have to worry about them burning when exposed to heat for prolonged periods of time.

Mops are part of the barbecue tradition in the United States—especially in Tennessee and the Carolinas. They are usually destined for pork (especially whole hogs and pork shoulders) and chicken.

THE RECIPE

BASIC BARBECUE MOP SAUCE

MAKES ABOUT 2 CUPS

Here's a simple all-purpose vinegar mop that's great on pork or chicken—or just about anything else you care to put on the grill. The recipe makes enough for two chickens or 4 to 5 pounds of ribs or pork.

2 cups distilled white vinegar
1 tablespoon coarse salt
1 teaspoon black pepper, or more to taste
1 teaspoon hot red pepper flakes, or more to taste
1 small onion, thinly sliced
1 jalapeño pepper, thinly sliced

Place the vinegar, salt, black pepper, and hot pepper flakes in a nonreactive bowl and whisk until the salt dissolves. Stir in the onion and jalapeño. Taste for seasoning, adding black pepper or hot pepper flakes as necessary. Brush on grilled chicken or pork once the outside is cooked. The mop sauce can be made several hours in advance but use it the same day.

MOPPING UP

■ Mops are one of the great outlets for individualism in American barbecue. Feel free to customize the Basic Barbecue Mop recipe at left to your taste. Possible additions could include: beer, wine, whiskey, herbs, garlic, lemon juice, and/or olive oil. Use beer, wine, or lemon juice in place of some of the vinegar. Whiskey and olive oil can be added along with the vinegar.

■ For safety's sake, don't start mopping the meat until the outside is cooked. This in effect sterilizes the surface, eliminating the risk of any bacterial contamination.

The traditional tool for applying a mop sauce is a barbecue mop.

TAKING THE CHILL OFF

■ If you have made your barbecue sauce ahead, remember to take it out of the refrigerator to warm to room temperature before serving. It will have more flavor and won't make your hot food cold.

HOW TO MAKE BARBECUE SAUCES

Sauce is barbecue's lifeblood. This statement might be disputed by a few ornery Texans (who would argue that the essence of true barbecue is long, slow cooking and wood smoke). For the rest of the world it simply isn't barbecue without the sauce. But what sauce? Sauces vary from region to region, stirring strong emotions when local traditions are violated. In the United States alone there are more than 700 commercial barbecue sauces, and I've sampled hundreds more abroad. So, picking a few sauces to include here was a bit like naming the ten best rock songs of the century. Entertaining, but all but impossible.

All the barbecue sauces in this section can be used during grilling—for slathering on meats or chicken—as well as for serving with the finished barbecue. Sugar-based sauces should be applied toward the end of grilling to keep the sugar from burning. Starting on page 452, you'll find a wide variety of table sauces.

Clockwise from the red bowl at top (all recipes can be found in this section or in the section beginning on page 452): White Barbecue Sauce, North Carolina Vinegar Sauce, Mustard Barbecue Sauce, Basic Barbecue Sauce, Hoisin Barbecue Sauce, and Asian Peanut Sauce. Three-Herb Chimichurri, center.

THE RECIPE

BASIC BARBECUE SAUCE

MAKES ABOUT 2½ CUPS

This is the type of sauce that most people in the United States think of as barbecue sauce: Brown sugar and molasses make it sweet; liquid smoke makes it smoky—there isn't a Kansas City pit boss around who wouldn't recognize it as local. Slather it on ribs and chicken, spoon it over pork shoulder, and serve it with anything else you may fancy. You won't be disappointed.

2 cups ketchup
¼ cup cider vinegar
¼ cup Worcestershire sauce
¼ cup firmly packed brown sugar
2 tablespoons molasses
2 tablespoons prepared mustard
1 tablespoon Tabasco sauce
1 tablespoon of your favorite barbecue rub (or the Basic Barbecue Rub on page 441)
2 teaspoons liquid smoke
½ teaspoon black pepper

Combine all the ingredients in a nonreactive saucepan and bring slowly to a boil over medium-high heat. Reduce the heat to medium and gently simmer the sauce until dark, thick, and richly flavored, 10 to 15 minutes. Transfer the sauce to clean (or even sterile) jars and store in the refrigerator. It will keep for several months.

THE RECIPE

HOISIN BARBECUE SAUCE

MAKES ABOUT 2 CUPS

Chinese five-spice powder and hoisin sauce give this dark, thick barbecue sauce a sweet, smoky, anise-flavored finish, which makes it ideal for Asian-style barbecued ribs, spit-roasted duck (see page 270), or any other Asian grilling. Hoisin sauce is a thick, sweet table sauce made with soybeans, spices, and sugar. Look for it at Asian markets and most supermarkets.

½ cup hoisin sauce
½ cup ketchup
½ cup sake, Chinese rice wine, or dry sherry
2 to 4 tablespoons Thai hot sauce (Sriracha) or other hot sauce
1 tablespoon rice vinegar or distilled white vinegar
2 teaspoons peeled, minced fresh ginger
1 clove garlic, minced
1 teaspoon five-spice powder (page 442), see Note, or use a good commercial brand

Combine all the ingredients in a nonreactive saucepan and bring slowly to a boil over medium heat. Reduce the heat slightly and gently simmer the sauce until thick and richly flavored, about 5 minutes. Transfer the sauce to clean (or even sterile) jars and store in the refrigerator. It will keep for several months.

Note: Use only the ingredients for the five-spice powder blend from the recipe for Chinese Five-Spice Rub.

MAKING THE BASIC BARBECUE SAUCE: *Put the ingredients for the sauce in a pot, and stir to mix. After slowly bringing them to a boil, simmer until the sauce is thick and richly flavored. Notice how I place my thumb over the mouth of the liquid smoke bottle to control the flow of this powerful flavoring.*

IN THE SAUCE

■ A good barbecue sauce is a study in balance. Play the sweetness of brown sugar or molasses against the acidity of vinegar or lemon juice. Match the fruitiness of apple cider or marmalade with the earthy pungency of garlic and onion. And above all, don't forget: Where there's smoke, there's fire. Use liquid smoke to give you the former and a blast of hot sauce or cayenne pepper to turn up the heat.

THE RECIPE
MUSTARD BARBECUE SAUCE

MAKES ABOUT 1½ CUPS

Mustard goes great with grilled sausage, ham steak, pork chops, and other rich meats. Perhaps that's the rationale behind the mustard barbecue sauces that are popular in Georgia and South Carolina. Serve this version with any type of barbecued pork. It's not half bad with chicken, either. To be strictly authentic, you'd use yellow ballpark mustard. But I like the punch of a Dijon mustard or a grainy mustard from Meaux.

2 tablespoons yellow mustard seeds
1 tablespoon butter
1 slice bacon, thinly slivered
½ onion, finely diced
1 cup Dijon-style or grainy mustard
½ cup cider vinegar
½ cup firmly packed brown sugar
2 tablespoons molasses
Coarse salt and black pepper

1. Toast the mustard seeds in a dry nonreactive saucepan over medium heat until lightly browned, 2 to 3 minutes. Transfer the mustard seeds to a small heatproof bowl to cool.

2. Add the butter, bacon, and onion to the pan and cook over medium heat until the onion is lightly browned, 3 to 4 minutes. Stir in the mustard, vinegar, brown sugar, molasses, and half of the toasted mustard seeds and gradually bring to a boil. Reduce the heat and gently simmer the sauce until thick and richly flavored, 5 minutes. Add salt and pepper (plenty of the latter) to taste.

3. Transfer the sauce to clean (or even sterile) jars and store in the refrigerator. Store the remaining toasted mustard seeds in an airtight container and sprinkle them over the sauce just before serving. The sauce will keep for at least 5 days.

THE RECIPE
NORTH CAROLINA VINEGAR SAUCE

MAKES ABOUT 2¼ CUPS

While thin, clear, vinegary sauce sure doesn't look like your typical American barbecue sauce, North Carolina pulled pork (see page 109) would be sorry stuff without it. Mix the sauce with shredded or chopped meats after they are cooked (you don't really use it as a slather).

2 cups cider vinegar
3 tablespoons ketchup
2 tablespoons brown sugar
4 teaspoons coarse salt
1 tablespoon Tabasco or other
*   hot sauce*
1 to 2 teaspoons hot red pepper flakes,
*   or more to taste*
1 to 2 teaspoons black pepper

Combine all the ingredients in a nonreactive mixing bowl and whisk until the salt and brown sugar dissolve. Taste for seasoning, adding hot pepper flakes as necessary. Transfer the sauce to clean (or even sterile) jars and store in the refrigerator. It will keep for several months.

HOW TO MAKE FLAVORED BUTTERS

When asked the secret to great cuisine, the legendary French chef Fernand Point exclaimed, *"Du beurre, du beurre, et encore du beurre!"* ("Butter, butter, and yet again more butter!") His advice certainly holds for barbecue. Brushing steaks or chops with butter adds elegance. A disk of herb or garlic butter melting like snowflakes can turn an everyday grilled fish steak into a minor masterpiece. Flavored butters are simplicity itself to make—and as quick as creaming butter, which is really all you're doing. You'll find a few of my favorites here.

PREPARING FLAVORED BUTTER

1 After creaming the butter with herbs, garlic, and/or cheese, spread it on a sheet of plastic wrap, as seen here, or on parchment paper.

2 Roll up the flavored butter in the plastic wrap, making a compact cylinder.

3 Twist the ends of the plastic wrap to seal the butter. Refrigerate until firm. You can also freeze the flavored butter for up to 3 months.

THE RECIPE

TARRAGON BUTTER

MAKES ABOUT 1/2 CUP

Tarragon has a delicate flavor reminiscent of licorice, which makes it perfect for serving with grilled seafood, chicken, and steaks. (You must use fresh tarragon, as the herb loses most of its flavor when dried.) Think of this butter as béarnaise sauce without the elbow grease. This recipe will give you more butter than you need for the strip steaks on page 65, but it's easier to roll up a larger batch. Of course, you could substitute any fresh herb for the tarragon.

*3 tablespoons finely chopped fresh
    tarragon leaves or other fresh herb*
*1/2 teaspoon finely grated lemon zest,
    plus a few drops of fresh lemon juice*
1/2 teaspoon black pepper
*8 tablespoons (1 stick) salted butter,
    at room temperature*

1. Place the tarragon, lemon zest and juice, pepper, and butter in a small mixing bowl and beat with a wooden spoon until light and fluffy. Alternatively, you can do the beating in a mixer or food processor.

2. As shown in Steps 1 through 3 on page 449, lay a 12-inch-square piece of plastic wrap or parchment paper on your work surface and mound the flavored butter in the center. Roll it up into a cylinder, twisting the ends to compact the butter. Chill the butter in the refrigerator or freezer until firm. The flavored butter will keep for up to 5 days in the refrigerator or up to 3 months in the freezer. To use, unwrap the roll and cut crosswise into 1/2-inch slices.

THE RECIPE

GARLIC-HERB BUTTER

MAKES ABOUT 1/2 CUP

Garlic and grilling go together like smoke and fire. I like to tuck disks of this garlicky butter into hamburgers (see page 101); they'll ooze when you take a bite. It's also delicious brushed on grilled bread, shellfish, fish steaks of all sorts, lamb and beef kebabs—in short, just about anything.

*3 tablespoons finely chopped mixed
    fresh herbs, including parsley,
    chives, basil, oregano, and/or
    tarragon leaves*
1 clove garlic, minced
1/2 teaspoon black pepper
*8 tablespoons (1 stick) salted butter,
    at room temperature*

1. Place the herbs, garlic, pepper, and butter in a small mixing bowl and beat with a wooden spoon until light and fluffy. Alternatively, you can do the beating in a mixer or food processor.

2. As shown in Steps 1 through 3 on page 449, lay a 12-inch-square piece of plastic wrap or parchment paper on your work surface and mound the flavored butter in the center. Roll it up into a cylinder, twisting the ends to compact the butter. Chill the butter in the refrigerator or freezer until firm. The flavored butter will keep for up to 5 days in the refrigerator or up to 3 months in the freezer. To use, unwrap the roll and cut crosswise into 1/2-inch slices.

ZESTING LEMON

One quick way to zest a lemon is to remove the outer rind in strips with a vegetable peeler (be sure you take off only the yellow rind; the white pith is bitter). If the recipe calls for grated zest, use a grater or zester or grind strips of zest to a powder in a spice mill.

ROASTED GARLIC BUTTER

MAKES ABOUT ½ CUP

Think of this topping as garlic butter that's been to finishing school. The garlic is roasted, which mellows its nose-jarring pungency. Roasting also brings out garlic's sweetness—a sweetness that is echoed in the cheese (freshly grated Parmigiano-Reggiano). I originally developed this butter for stuffing under the skin of a chicken before grilling it (see page 207), but it's also amazing brushed on grilled bread (page 418). For that matter, a dollop of Roasted Garlic Butter would be most welcome on a grilled fish fillet, chicken breast, or veal chop.

1 head garlic
6 tablespoons (¾ stick) butter, at room
*   temperature*
2 tablespoons finely chopped mixed
*   fresh herbs, including flat-leaf*
*   parsley, chervil, basil, rosemary,*
*   oregano, and/or chives*
3 tablespoons freshly grated
*   Parmesan cheese*
Coarse salt and black pepper

1. Set up the grill for direct grilling (see page 10 for charcoal or page 16 for gas) and preheat to medium.

2. Loosely wrap the head of garlic in aluminum foil, leaving the top open so you can watch it as it grills. When ready to cook, place the garlic on the hot grate. Grill until very soft, 30 to 40 minutes, turning occasionally with tongs (turn the garlic, leaving the foil on the grill to protect the garlic). Don't let the garlic burn. Alternatively, you can roast the garlic in a preheated 350°F oven. The cooking time will remain the same. Transfer the head of garlic to a plate and let cool to room temperature.

3. Place the butter, herbs, and Parmesan in a small mixing bowl and beat with a wooden spoon until light and fluffy. Cut the garlic head in half through the cloves and squeeze the garlic from each half into the flavored butter. Season with salt and pepper and beat to mix.

4. As shown in Steps 1 through 3 on page 449, lay a 12-inch-square piece of plastic wrap or parchment paper on your work surface and mound the flavored butter in the center. Roll it up into a cylinder, twisting the ends to compact the butter. Chill the butter in the refrigerator or freezer until firm. The flavored butter will keep for up to 5 days in the refrigerator or up to 3 months in the freezer. To use, unwrap the roll and cut crosswise into ½-inch slices.

ROASTING GARLIC

1. Loosely wrap a head of garlic in aluminum foil to keep it from burning on the grill. Roast it until soft, 30 to 40 minutes.

2. Cut the grilled garlic head in half through the cloves.

3. Once the garlic has been roasted, it is easy to squeeze it out of its skin and mash with a spoon.

STAND-ALONE SAUCES

The secret to being well dressed is mastering the art of accessorizing. A single strand of pearls can turn that SBD (Simple Black Dress) into a sartorial masterpiece. So it is with barbecue. Following are some of the best sauces to accessorize yours—whether the food served is simply grilled or lengthily smoked. In contrast to the sauces starting on page 446, these are stand-alone: You don't use them for slathering or basting; you serve them alongside grilled vegetables, seafood, or meats.

THE RECIPE

BÉARNAISE MAYONNAISE

MAKES ABOUT 1½ CUPS; SERVES 6 TO 8

Beef tenderloin with béarnaise sauce is one of the glories of classical French cuisine. Given fresh tarragon's affinity for grilled beef, it's easy to see why. Like all egg-based sauces, béarnaise can be tricky to make, so I came up with a béarnaise-flavored mayonnaise that has all of the classic's vibrant flavor and none of its temperamental chemistry. It's the perfect accompaniment for the Herb-Crusted Grilled Beef Tenderloin on page 50.

1 to 2 shallots, minced (about ¼ cup)
½ teaspoon coarsely ground black
  peppercorns
½ cup dry white wine

3 tablespoons white wine vinegar or distilled
  white vinegar, or more to taste
Coarse salt
3 to 4 sprigs fresh tarragon, stemmed
  (enough to make 3 tablespoons chopped)
1¼ cups mayonnaise

1. Place the shallots, peppercorns, wine, and vinegar in a nonreactive saucepan and bring to a boil. Boil the mixture until only ¼ cup remains, about 8 minutes. Transfer the mixture to a small nonreactive mixing bowl and let cool.

2. Bring 1 cup salted water to a boil in a saucepan. Blanch the tarragon for 10 seconds, drain well in a strainer, rinse with cold water, and drain again. Blot the tarragon dry with a paper towel and finely chop. Add the blanched tarragon and mayonnaise to the wine mixture and whisk to mix. Taste for seasoning, adding salt or a few drops of vinegar as necessary; the Béarnaise Mayonnaise should be highly seasoned. It will keep in the refrigerator, covered, for at least 5 days.

Sauces are an integral part of barbecue, and, of course, the quickest and easiest sauce of all is fresh lemon juice. Seafood, chicken, and even lamb taste downright bland without it. Here's how to cut lemon wedges that are easy to squeeze and seed-free.

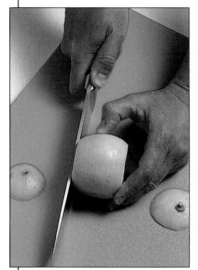

1 Cut the ends off the lemon as shown here.

2 Cut the lemon in half lengthwise. Stand each half on end and cut it into wedges. Note how each wedge has flat ends for easy squeezing.

3 Remove any seeds and cut off the white fibrous center; the lemon is now ready to use.

THE RECIPE

GORGONZOLA SAUCE

MAKES ABOUT 2½ CUPS, ENOUGH FOR 16 CHICKEN WINGS

Blue cheese sauce was popularized in Buffalo, New York, as an accompaniment for spicy chicken wings. My own contribution to the tradition is a sauce made with that powerful aristocrat of the European blue cheeses, Italian Gorgonzola. I like to serve this sauce with the East-West Buffalo Wings on page 249, but you could also use it as a dip for grilled shrimp or vegetables.

*4 ounces Gorgonzola cheese
　(rind trimmed off)*
1 cup mayonnaise
1 cup sour cream
¼ cup minced onion
½ teaspoon black pepper
Coarse salt, if neccessary

Push the cheese through a strainer or sieve into a mixing bowl. Stir in the mayonnaise, sour cream, onion, and pepper. It's unlikely you'll need salt (the cheese is quite salty already), but taste for seasoning and add a little if necessary. You can make the sauce up to 4 hours in advance.

WHITE BARBECUE SAUCE

MAKES ABOUT 1¾ CUPS; SERVES 6 TO 8

When you're looking for something different to serve with barbecued chicken, turkey, and even pork, this attention grabber is just what the doctor ordered. White barbecue sauce originated at the legendary Big Bob Gibson Barb-B-Q in Decatur, Alabama, but today you find it throughout the northern part of the state. Here's my version. You must use real mayonnaise.

1 teaspoon coarse salt, or more to taste
1 teaspoon black pepper
½ teaspoon sugar
2 tablespoons minced onion
1 clove garlic, minced
1 cup mayonnaise
½ cup distilled white vinegar, or more to taste

Combine the salt, pepper, sugar, onion, and garlic in a small nonreactive mixing bowl and mash to a paste with the back of a wooden spoon. Stir in the mayonnaise and vinegar. Taste for seasoning, adding salt or vinegar as necessary. Transfer the sauce to clean (or even sterile) jars and store in the refrigerator for 4 to 5 days.

MUSTARD SAUCE

MAKES ABOUT 1½ CUPS; SERVES 8

Here's a simple mustard sauce you can use not only with beef (like the Herb-Crusted Grilled Beef Tenderloin on page 50) but also with grilled pork, poultry, and even seafood. The whole mustard seeds add crunch. Yellow mustard seeds are the most common, but to add interest and color, you could use a blend of yellow, brown, and black—the last are available at Indian markets.

2 tablespoons mustard seeds
½ cup Dijon-style or grainy mustard
  (or a mixture of the two), or more to taste
½ cup mayonnaise
½ cup sour cream
2 teaspoons Worcestershire sauce, or more to taste

Toast the mustard seeds in a dry skillet over medium heat until fragrant and lightly browned, 2 to 3 minutes. Do not let burn. Transfer to a heatproof bowl. Whisk in the prepared mustard, mayonnaise, sour cream, and Worcestershire sauce. Taste for seasoning, adding mustard and Worcestershire sauce as necessary. The sauce will keep in the refrigerator, covered, for at least 5 days.

MUSTARD-DILL SAUCE

MAKES 3 CUPS; SERVES 12

Salmon has a natural affinity for mustard and dill—a combination appreciated by millions of Scandinavians, who add dill to their gravlax and serve mustard sauce with their smoked and cured salmon. Both cut the oily richness of the fish, as does lemon—my own addition to the tradition. Serve this sauce with the Whole Salmon with Lemon and Dill on page 284. It's also delicious with grilled chicken or Turkey Pastrami (see page 265).

1½ cups mayonnaise

¾ cup sour cream

½ cup Dijon-style or honey mustard (use honey mustard if you like a touch of sweetness)

⅓ cup chopped fresh dill, plus whole sprigs for garnish

2 tablespoons lemon juice, or more to taste

½ teaspoon finely grated lemon zest

½ teaspoon coarse salt, or more to taste

½ teaspoon black pepper, or more to taste

Place all the ingredients in a nonreactive mixing bowl and whisk to mix. Taste for seasoning, adding lemon juice, salt, and pepper as necessary. Serve the sauce in a bowl or in individual ramekins, garnished with dill sprigs.

THE RECIPE

WASABI WHIPPED CREAM

MAKES ABOUT 1½ CUPS; SERVES 6 TO 8

Who says whipped cream has to be sweet and served with dessert? Not the young Turks of contemporary American cuisine, who flavor whipped cream with fresh herbs, vodka, even horseradish. And certainly not this barbecue addict, who loves the way dollops of it melt on well-charred steaks or seafood. The singular condiment here pits the fiery bite of wasabi against the cooling richness of whipped cream. I like to serve it on grilled oysters (see page 348) and with beef tenderloin (see page 50), but you can also spoon it over any sort of grilled fish (especially salmon), beef, or shellfish.

1 tablespoon wasabi powder

1 cup heavy cream, chilled

½ teaspoon lemon juice, or more to taste

Coarse salt

Mix the wasabi with 1 tablespoon of water in a small bowl and stir to form a paste. Let stand for 5 minutes. Meanwhile, working in a chilled bowl, beat the cream with an electric mixer until soft peaks form. Fold in the wasabi mixture and lemon juice; season with salt. Taste for seasoning, adding lemon juice and salt as necessary; the cream should be highly seasoned. The whipped cream can be made several hours ahead and kept in the refrigerator, covered.

THE RECIPE

HERBED HORSERADISH SAUCE

MAKES ABOUT 2 CUPS; SERVES 8 TO 12

Roast beef and horseradish sauce are as English as Big Ben. Fresh herbs add a Mediterranean touch. But don't just serve this with the Hickory-Smoked Prime Rib on page 35. It would be a great addition to steaks and grilled fish.

1 piece (2 inches long and 1 to 1½ inches across; about 2 ounces) fresh horseradish root, peeled, or 2 to 3 tablespoons prepared white horseradish

½ cup sour cream

2 tablespoons chopped mixed fresh herbs, including oregano, rosemary, basil, and/or flat-leaf parsley

1 tablespoon lemon juice, or more to taste

½ teaspoon grated lemon zest

½ teaspoon coarse salt, or more to taste

½ teaspoon freshly ground black pepper, or more to taste

1 cup heavy cream, chilled

Grating fresh horseradish right before you use it will give you the strongest flavor.

WASABI

■ Wasabi is an intense green root often described as Japanese horseradish. It's usually sold in powdered form: You mix it with water to obtain a fiery green paste that looks like a dab of toothpaste. Look for wasabi in natural foods stores and Asian markets.

1. If using fresh horseradish, finely grate it or chop it in a food processor fitted with a metal blade. (If using the food processor, cut the horseradish into ¼-inch-thick slices before processing.) Whichever method you use, take care not to breathe the potent horseradish fumes.

2. Combine the grated horseradish, sour cream, herbs, lemon juice, lemon zest, salt, and pepper in a nonreactive bowl and whisk to mix.

3. Place the cream in a large chilled bowl and beat it with an electric mixer until soft peaks form. Gently fold the whipped cream into the sour cream mixture. Taste for seasoning, adding salt, pepper, and lemon juice as necessary. Refrigerate, covered, until serving. The horseradish sauce tastes best served within a couple of hours of making, but it will keep for a few days in the refrigerator.

THE RECIPE
ASIAN PEANUT SAUCE

MAKES ABOUT 2 CUPS; SERVES 8

This sweet, nutty peanut sauce (or any one of a hundred variations) is the traditional accompaniment to the satés (tiny kebabs) of Southeast Asia. As well as being good with any type of saté, the sauce goes well with the Garlic Halibut on page 298. Unsweetened coconut milk is available in cans from Asian markets, gourmet shops, and most supermarkets. If you can't find it, substitute equal parts of heavy cream and chicken broth.

2 tablespoons vegetable oil
3 cloves garlic, minced
1 to 3 Thai chiles or jalapeño peppers, seeded and minced (for a hotter sauce, leave the seeds in)
1 tablespoon peeled, minced fresh ginger
1 large or 2 medium shallots, minced
⅔ cup chunky peanut butter
1⅓ cups unsweetened coconut milk
3 tablespoons finely chopped fresh cilantro
3 tablespoons Asian fish sauce or soy sauce, or more to taste
1 tablespoon lime juice, or more to taste
1 tablespoon brown sugar, or more to taste
1 teaspoon ground coriander
½ teaspoon black pepper

1. Heat the oil in a wok or saucepan over medium heat. Add the garlic, chiles, ginger, and shallots and cook to a rich golden brown, 3 to 5 minutes. Reduce the heat to caramelize the garlic and shallots without burning them.

2. Stir in the peanut butter and cook for 1 minute. Add the remaining ingredients and simmer the sauce until thick and richly flavored, 3 to 5 minutes, whisking to blend the ingredients. If the sauce is too thick (it should be pourable), add a little water. Taste for seasoning, adding fish sauce, lime juice, and brown sugar as necessary. Transfer the sauce to clean (or even sterile) jars and store in the refrigerator for at least 5 days.

THE RECIPE
ASIAN PEAR DIPPING SAUCE

MAKES ABOUT 1½ CUPS; SERVES 6 TO 8

The delicate interplay of fruity and salty flavors makes this sauce the perfect accompaniment to almost any type of grilled meat, especially lamb, like the Sesame-Ginger Leg of Lamb on page 168, or seafood. The Asian pear adds a moist, sweet crunch.

⅔ cup soy sauce
⅔ cup sake, Chinese rice wine, or
    dry sherry
⅓ cup sugar
1 Asian pear, peeled, halved, cored,
    and finely chopped
3 scallions, trimmed and finely chopped
2 tablespoons toasted sesame seeds
    (page 30)
½ teaspoon black pepper, or more to taste

Place the soy sauce, sake, and sugar in a nonreactive mixing bowl and stir until the sugar dissolves. Stir in the pear, scallions, sesame seeds, and pepper. Divide the sauce among small bowls for dipping.

THE RECIPE
VIETNAMESE DIPPING SAUCE

MAKES ABOUT 1 CUP; SERVES 4

Wherever Vietnamese eat barbecue, this delicate dipping sauce turns up. The complex layering of flavors—sweet, sour, salty, and hot—goes well with the rich taste of grilled pork, like the Asian Flavor Baby Back Ribs on page 143. Fish sauce is a malodorous condiment made with pickled anchovies; if you can't find it, or don't care for it, substitute soy sauce.

1 thick piece carrot (3 inches long)
3 tablespoons sugar, or more to taste
2 cloves garlic, minced
½ cup warm water
¼ cup Asian fish sauce
¼ cup lime juice, or more to taste
1 tablespoon rice vinegar or more
    lime juice

1 to 2 serrano peppers or Thai chiles,
    cut crosswise into paper-thin slivers
¼ teaspoon black pepper

1. Using a vegetable peeler, slice the carrot lengthwise into paper-thin strips. Stack the strips 4 high and cut lengthwise into hair-thin slivers. Rinse these slivers in a strainer under cold water and blot dry with paper towels.

2. Place the sugar and garlic in a nonreactive mixing bowl and mash to a paste with the back of a wooden spoon. Add the water, fish sauce, lime juice, and rice vinegar and stir until the sugar dissolves. Stir in the serrano pepper and black pepper. Taste for seasoning, adding sugar or lime juice as necessary; the sauce should strike a delicate balance between sweet, sour, and salty. Pour the sauce into tiny bowls for dipping.

THE RECIPE
THREE-HERB CHIMICHURRI

MAKES ABOUT 3 CUPS; SERVES 4

Ten years ago, few North Americans had ever heard of *chimichurri*. Today this piquant parsley and garlic sauce, served with grilled beef in Argentina, has found a strong following in the United States. A traditional *chimichurri* would contain only parsley, and you can certainly make it this way, using 2½ cups of parsley leaves. I like to round out the flavor with fresh mint and cilantro, as you'll see here. *Chimichurri* is the obvious partner for *churrasco* (see page 51), but it's equally good with any kind of grilled beef or chicken. The minted version is particularly good with lamb.

MAKING CHIMICHURRI

1 Place the garlic and herbs in a food processor and finely chop them, then add the remaining spices.

2 With the machine running, add the olive oil in a thin stream, followed by the vinegar and water. Process until thick.

*1 packed cup washed, stemmed, fresh
   flat-leaf parsley leaves*
*1 packed cup washed, stemmed, fresh cilantro
   leaves*
½ packed cup washed, stemmed fresh mint leaves
6 cloves garlic, coarsely chopped
1 teaspoon coarse salt, or more to taste
½ teaspoon black pepper
½ teaspoon hot red pepper flakes
1 cup extra-virgin olive oil
⅓ cup distilled white vinegar, or more to taste
⅓ cup cold water

Combine the parsley, cilantro, mint, and garlic in a food processor and finely chop. Add the salt, black pepper, and hot pepper flakes and process to blend. Add the oil, vinegar, and water and continue processing to make a thick sauce. Taste for seasoning, adding salt or vinegar as necessary; the *chimichurri* should be highly seasoned. Serve within a few hours.

THE RECIPE
PICO DE GALLO

MAKES ABOUT 2 CUPS;
SERVES 6 TO 8

The basic Tex-Mex relish, *pico de gallo* is easy to make, but you must use juicy ripe red tomatoes and crisp white onions to get the full effect. Of course it goes with Beef Fajitas (see page 90), but you can serve it with any kind of grilled beef or even quesadillas.

1 clove garlic, minced
½ teaspoon coarse salt, or more to taste
2 ripe red tomatoes, seeded and finely diced
*2 to 6 serrano or jalapeño peppers, seeded and finely
   diced (for a hotter salsa, leave the seeds in)*
½ medium white onion, finely diced (about ½ cup)
¼ cup finely chopped fresh cilantro
3 tablespoons lime juice, or more to taste

Place the garlic and salt in a medium-size nonreactive mixing bowl and mash to a paste with the back of a wooden spoon. Add the remaining ingredients and gently toss to mix. Taste for seasoning, adding salt or lime juice as necessary. It will taste best served within a few hours of being made.

THE RECIPE
TOMATO-PEPPER SALSA

MAKES ABOUT 3 CUPS;
SERVES 6

Part salsa, part salad, this simple relish is 100 percent delicious. Argentineans call it *salsa criolla* (Creole sauce). If you are serving it with the Argentinean Rib Steaks (see page 93), you can make it while the meat is marinating. It will also go well with grilled beef, chicken, or seafood.

2 ripe tomatoes (about 1 pound total),
    seeded and cut into ¼-inch dice
1 medium (or ½ large) sweet onion,
    cut into ¼-inch dice (about 1 cup)
½ green bell pepper, cut into ¼-inch dice
½ yellow bell pepper, cut into ¼-inch dice
2 tablespoons extra-virgin olive oil
2 tablespoons red wine vinegar, or more to taste
3 tablespoons chopped fresh flat-leaf parsley
1 teaspoon dried oregano
Coarse salt and black pepper

Combine the tomatoes, onion, bell peppers, oil, vinegar, parsley, and oregano in a nonreactive mixing bowl and toss to mix. Season the salsa with salt and pepper. Taste for seasoning, adding vinegar or salt as necessary. The salsa should be highly seasoned. You can make the salsa up to 4 hours ahead; store it, covered, in the refrigerator. Let it return to room temperature before serving. You may need to reseason it before serving.

THE RECIPE
SALSA VERDE

MAKES 2½ TO 3 CUPS; SERVES 6

One of the cornerstones of Mexican cuisine, *salsa verde*, a cooked tomatillo salsa, is an indispensable part of Beef Fajitas (see page 90). It also goes well with anything Mexican, like the quesadillas on page 407 and the Bluefish in Banana Leaves on page 307. The traditional way to cook the vegetables is by roasting them on a *comal* (a flat skillet), but you could also char them on the grill. Tomatillos are round green fruits that look like husk-covered green

SEEDING A TOMATO

1 To seed a tomato, cut it in half crosswise and hold it cupped in your hand, cut-side out.

2 Gently squeeze the tomato to wring out the seeds. Use your fingertips or the handle of a spoon to scoop out any that are hard to get.

cherry tomatoes (actually, they're cousins of the gooseberry). Simply pull off the papery husk before using the tomatillos.

1 pound fresh tomatillos, husked
½ medium white onion, cut in half again
3 cloves garlic, peeled
3 to 5 serrano chiles or jalapeño peppers, seeded
    (for a hotter salsa, leave the seeds in)
¼ cup chopped fresh cilantro
½ teaspoon sugar, or more to taste
½ teaspoon coarse salt, or more to taste
½ teaspoon black pepper
½ to 1 cup chicken or vegetable stock or water

1. Heat a *comal* or a medium-size skillet over medium-high heat. Place the tomatillos in the skillet and cook until lightly browned on all sides, turning with tongs, 6 to 8 minutes. Add the onion, garlic, and chiles to the pan and roast until lightly browned, 8 to 10

CORING PEPPERS

The easiest way to seed and core a bell pepper is to cut off the sides, leaving the core behind, as shown here.

minutes for the onion, 4 to 6 minutes for the chiles and garlic. Alternatively, direct grill the vegetables over a hot fire. Transfer to a plate to cool.

2. Place the roasted vegetables in a food processor with the cilantro, sugar, salt, and pepper and process to a coarse purée. Add stock or water as needed to obtain a pourable sauce. Transfer this mixture to a nonreactive saucepan and simmer over medium-high heat until thick and richly flavored, 5 minutes. Taste for seasoning, adding salt or sugar as necessary.

RIPENING MANGOES

■ To ripen a mango, leave it at room temperature until very fragrant and gently yielding when squeezed. You can't go by color, as some mangoes remain green even when ripe. Warning: Some people are allergic to mango sap. If you have sensitive skin, wear rubber gloves.

THE RECIPE
MANGO SALSA

MAKES ABOUT 3 CUPS; SERVES 4

Mango salsas began turning up on America's tables in the 1990s. Their kaleidoscopic colors and explosively hot, fruity flavors make them a hit at summer cookouts. Here's a mango salsa you can serve with any sort of grilled poultry or with the Spiny Lobsters with Cilantro and Lime on page 337.

1 ripe mango, peeled, seeded, and diced
1 cucumber, scrubbed, seeded, and diced
½ medium red onion, diced
¼ cup chopped fresh cilantro
½ Scotch bonnet chile or other hot chile,
*   seeded and minced (for a hotter salsa,*
*   leave the seeds in)*
3 tablespoons lime juice, or more to taste
1 tablespoon brown sugar, or more to taste

Combine all the ingredients in a nonreactive mixing bowl and stir to mix. Taste for seasoning, adding lime juice or brown sugar as necessary. The salsa will taste best when served within a few hours of being made.

THE RECIPE
CILANTRO CHUTNEY

MAKES ABOUT 1 CUP; SERVES 4

Indians and Afghans share a love for this pungent green sauce, made with fresh cilantro and jalapeño peppers. It's great with Ground Lamb Kebabs (see page 193), Tandoori Lamb Chops (see page 185), and Saffron-Grilled Chicken (see page 234).

1 bunch fresh cilantro (about 1 cup packed)
2 cloves garlic, chopped
1 to 3 jalapeño peppers, seeded and chopped
*   (for a hotter chutney, leave the seeds in)*
3 tablespoons chopped walnuts
2 tablespoons chopped onion
¼ cup lemon juice, or more to taste
1 tablespoon vegetable oil
1 teaspoon coarse salt, or more to taste
½ teaspoon black pepper, or more to taste
½ teaspoon sugar

Combine all the ingredients in a blender and purée to a paste, scraping down the sides of the blender a few times and adding 4 to 5 tablespoons water, as needed to obtain a pourable sauce. Taste for seasoning, adding salt, pepper, or lemon juice as necessary. The chutney should be flavorful and piquant. It will keep for several days, in the refrigerator, covered, but tastes best served within a few hours of being made.

THE RECIPE
CUCUMBER RELISH

MAKES ABOUT 2 CUPS; SERVES 4 TO 6

This crisp, colorful relish exists in many incarnations throughout the world of barbecue. The cool, moist crunch of the cucumber and onion provides a welcome contrast to the flame-charred taste of grilled fare. Thai in inspiration, this one is perfect served with the Lemongrass Beef Satés on page 81 or the Chicken Satés on page 257.

1 cucumber
¼ cup sugar, or more to taste
1 clove garlic, minced
½ teaspoon coarse salt, or more to taste
½ teaspoon black pepper
¼ cup distilled white vinegar
⅓ cup diced red onion
3 tablespoons chopped fresh cilantro
2 tablespoons finely chopped dry-roasted
    peanuts (optional)

1. Peel the cucumber, removing the skin in lengthwise strips; leave a little skin between each strip. Cut the cucumber in half lengthwise, remove the seeds with a spoon or melon baller, and cut the cucumber flesh into ½-inch dice.

2. Place the sugar, garlic, salt, and pepper in a nonreactive mixing bowl. Mash with the back of a wooden spoon to a paste. Add the vinegar and ¼ cup water and stir until the sugar and salt dissolve. Stir in the diced cucumber and the onion and cilantro. Taste for seasoning, adding salt or sugar as necessary. Sprinkle with peanuts, if using, and serve at once.

THE RECIPE
SHALLOT MARMALADE

MAKES ABOUT 1 CUP; SERVES 6

While it may look like marmalade, this tangy relish sure doesn't taste like it! Not with the addition of shallots, wine, and balsamic vinegar. Serve it with Herb-Crusted Grilled Beef Tenderloin (see page 50), Juniper-Flavored Filets Mignons (see page 69), or any grilled steak.

1 pound shallots, thinly sliced
    (about 4 cups)
2 cups dry red wine
¼ cup balsamic vinegar, or
    more to taste
¼ cup honey, or more to taste
2 tablespoons sugar
1 pinch cayenne pepper
1 pinch ground cloves
About ½ teaspoon coarse salt
About ½ teaspoon black pepper

1. Place all the ingredients (use only a little salt and pepper to begin with) in a large nonreactive sauté pan with 2 cups water. The shallots should be completely covered. Bring the mixture to a boil, reduce the heat to medium, and gently simmer the shallots, uncovered, until the liquid is completely absorbed, 30 to 40 minutes. Stir from time to time, more frequently at the end. You may need to lower the heat to keep the shallots from burning.

2. Taste for seasoning, adding salt, pepper, vinegar, or honey to taste. The marmalade should be a little sweet, a little sour, and very highly seasoned. Transfer to clean (or even sterile) jars and store in the refrigerator for up to several weeks.

PEELING CUCUMBERS

■ When I peel a cucumber, I like to leave thin lengthwise strips of skin between the peelings. That way, when you slice the cucumber cross-wise, you get an attractive stippling of green.

MARMALADE VARIATIONS:

Marmalades can be made with other members of the allium family, especially red and/or white onions; use 2 pounds. You can also make a leek marmalade this way; you'll need 2 pounds of whole leeks (1 pound when trimmed). If you are using leeks, substitute white balsamic vinegar or white wine vinegar for regular balsamic vinegar and dry white wine for the red.

WEIGHT CONVERSIONS

U.S.	METRIC	U.S.	METRIC
½ oz	15 g	7 oz	200 g
1 oz	30 g	8 oz	250 g
1½ oz	45 g	9 oz	275 g
2 oz	60 g	10 oz	300 g
2½ oz	75 g	11 oz	325 g
3 oz	90 g	12 oz	350 g
3½ oz	100 g	13 oz	375 g
4 oz	125 g	14 oz	400 g
5 oz	150 g	15 oz	450 g
6 oz	175 g	1 lb	500 g

APPROXIMATE EQUIVALENTS

1 stick butter = 8 tbs = 4 oz = ½ cup

1 cup all-purpose presifted flour or
   dried bread crumbs = 5 oz

1 cup granulated sugar = 8 oz

1 cup (packed) brown sugar = 6 oz

1 cup confectioners' sugar = 4½ oz

1 cup honey or syrup = 12 oz

1 cup grated cheese = 4 oz

1 cup dried beans = 6 oz

2 large eggs = about 2 oz = about ¼ cup

1 egg yolk = about 1 tbs

1 egg white = about 2 tbs

Please note that all conversions are approximate but close enough to be useful when converting from one system to another.

LIQUID CONVERSIONS

U.S.	IMPERIAL	METRIC
2 tbs	1 fl oz	30 ml
3 tbs	1½ fl oz	45 ml
¼ cup	2 fl oz	60 ml
⅓ cup	2½ fl oz	75 ml
⅓ cup +1 tbs	3 fl oz	90 ml
⅓ cup +2 tbs	3½ fl oz	100 ml
½ cup	4 fl oz	125 ml
⅔ cup	5 fl oz	150 ml
¾ cup	6 fl oz	175 ml
¾ cup +2 tbs	7 fl oz	200 ml
1 cup	8 fl oz	250 ml
1 cup +2 tbs	9 fl oz	275 ml
1¼ cups	10 fl oz	300 ml
1⅓ cups	11 fl oz	325 ml
1½ cups	12 fl oz	350 ml
1⅔ cups	13 fl oz	375 ml
1¾ cups	14 fl oz	400 ml
1¾ cups +2 tbs	15 fl oz	450 ml
2 cups (1 pint)	16 fl oz	500 ml
2½ cups	20 fl oz (1 pint)	600 ml
3¾ cups	1½ pints	900 ml
4 cups	1¾ pints	1 liter

OVEN TEMPERATURES

FAHRENHEIT	CELSIUS GAS MARK		FAHRENHEIT	CELSIUS GAS MARK	
250	½	120	400	6	200
275	1	140	425	7	220
300	2	150	450	8	230
325	3	160	475	9	240
350	4	180	500	10	260
375	5	190			

Note: Reduce the temperature by 20°C (68°F) for fan-assisted ovens.

GRILLS AND GEAR

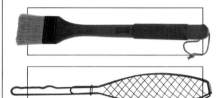

Any craftsman knows the importance of having the proper tools. Grilling is no different. Sure you can grill on a charcoal-filled brazier with a pair of primitive tongs. But the job will be easier and the results better if you start with the best tools. In the case of barbecue, this means the grills themselves, not to mention the accessories, which range from the ever-essential tongs and basting brushes to specialized rib racks, fish baskets, and kitchen syringes. You also need to get the fire started and have the right fuels and smoking materials, which include everything from lump charcoal to wood chunks to lava stones and ceramic briquettes for gas grills. In the following pages, you'll learn about the essential and not so essential (but fun) equipment you need to become a master griller. The sources for many of these are listed in the mail-order section on pages 481 and 482.

GRILLS

Before you can become a master griller, you have to have a grill. This has never been easier because a grill enthusiast has a huge variety of grills and smokers to choose from— from a $10 hibachi to a $10,000 super-grill. You don't need to spend a fortune to buy a great grilling machine. (Some of the best barbecue I've ever tasted was cooked on a car wheel rim filled with charcoal in Vietnam.) The fact is you can get a decent charcoal grill for less than $100 and a decent gas grill for less than $300. Of course, if you're so inclined, you can spend an enormous amount of money on a state-of-the-art supergrill. Here's a look at the major types of grills and what they're good for.

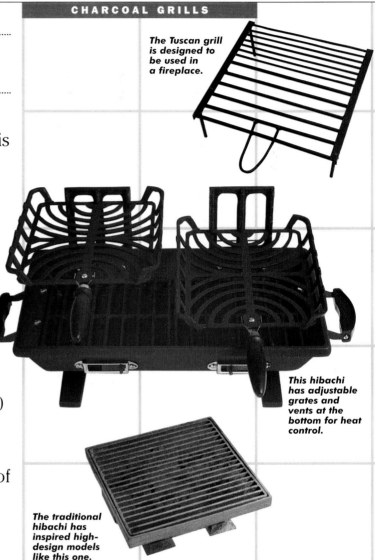

The Tuscan grill is designed to be used in a fireplace.

This hibachi has adjustable grates and vents at the bottom for heat control.

The traditional hibachi has inspired high-design models like this one.

CHARCOAL GRILLS

For many grill jockeys, charcoal represents the ultimate thrill in grilling. For others, it's the ultimate hassle. Charcoal burns hotter and drier than gas, so it's great for searing steaks and other meats. Charcoal grills have two other advantages over gas grills: They work better for smoking and you can also use wood as a fuel.

Charcoal grills are somewhat messy to use and require frequent prodding and attention. So naturally, diehard barbecue buffs adore them. If you like the process of building and tending a fire, a charcoal grill is for you.

TUSCAN GRILL: The Tuscan is the simplest of all grills, a sturdy metal grate with legs, so you can position it over a fire. Italians in general and Tuscans in particular use these grills in their fireplaces. You let the wood or charcoal burn down to embers and shovel them under the grate. The food goes on top. More elaborate versions feature a double grate attached at one end with a hinge. You place your steak or portobello mushrooms between the grates and turn the device over when one side is grilled.

■ **What to look for when buying a Tuscan grill:** Sturdy construction; legs that raise the grill at least 4 inches above the floor of your fireplace; and grates with variably spaced bars that can hold both large and small pieces of food.

HIBACHI: The hibachi is the traditional grill in Japan and variations are found throughout Asia. It consists of a small metal firebox with grates positioned over the coals. Hibachis are made of thick, heavy metal to hold in the heat. Their small size makes them highly portable and allows you to place one on a table outside, so you can grill in front of your guests (if you do so, be sure to have insulation underneath). You control the heat by means of vents at the bottom. Many hibachis come

Wire rails, left, and removable metal side baskets, top, will contain coals for indirect grilling on kettle grills that do not come with side baskets.

The Weber kettle grill has become an American icon.

The Smokey Joe is a portable kettle-type grill.

with grates you can position closer to or farther away from the coals for additional heat control. (A split or double grate enables you to cook some foods at a higher temperature, some at a lower one.) Hibachis are designed for the direct grilling of small cuts of meats—teriyaki, yakitori, satés, kebabs, chicken breasts, and small steaks. This makes sense, because Asians love tiny kebabs and pieces of meat they can pair with rice noodles or wrap in lettuce leaves.

■ **What to look for when buying a hibachi:** Sturdy construction; a thick heavy firebox with adjustable vents at the bottom; and split or double grates you can raise and lower.

KETTLE GRILL: The bowl-shaped kettle grill has been the workhorse of barbecue in the United States ever since an Illinois metalworker fashioned one from two halves of a nautical buoy in 1952. (His name was George Stephen and he went on to found the Weber-Stephen grill company.) The virtue of the kettle grill is its simplicity: You put the coals in the bottom and place the food on a grate above them. This makes direct grilling a snap, and the high sides protect the fire from wind. But the real genius of the kettle grill is its vent system and domed lid. These enable you to turn a kettle grill into a smoker by using a technique known as indirect grilling. The kettle-shaped grill is a trade-marked Weber product, but

kettle-type grills (with domed covers) come in many shapes and sizes. One popular model looks like a square pillow.

■ **What to look for when buying a kettle grill:** Sturdy legs and construction; a bottom grate for holding the coals above the bottom of the firebox; a top grate; and vents at the top and bottom of the grill, so you can control the heat. Optional features include an ash catcher; a hinged grate, which allows you to add charcoal and wood to the fire with-

FEATURES TO LOOK FOR

Every grill has its strengths and weaknesses. Here are some of the features I look for when buying one—some apply to charcoal, some to gas, and some to both.

ADJUSTABLE VENTS at the top, seen here, and bottom of a charcoal grill. Here they're partially opened, allowing for moderate heat. Closing the vents will lower the heat—and eventually put out the fire.

AN ASH CATCHER is handy to have on a charcoal grill. Slide the vent lever back and forth a few times to knock the ashes through the vent holes into the catcher. When the ash catcher is full, simply take it off and discard the ashes. *Never* put hot ashes with other trash or into a plastic trash can.

A grill that can hold disposable aluminum foil drip pans, like the Weber Genesis, at bottom, makes clean up easy.

A SIDE BURNER is useful for heating barbecue sauces and, yes, even roasting marshmallows.

The red markers on the **GAS GAUGE** of the grill seen above tell you when it's time to refill your gas tank.

A **DRIP PAN** or catch pan is essential for a gas grill. Char-Broil's grill has a simple cup like the one shown at top.

Weber gas grills employ **FLAVORIZER BARS**. The gas flames heat the bars to create a strong, even source of heat. Dripping fat and meat juices vaporize when they hit the bars, creating a delicious smoke flavor.

The DCS grill uses a **CERAMIC HEATING ELEMENT**. The gas flames heat the ceramic bars red hot, making for a strong, steady source of heat.

The Barbecook grill has a built-in chimney starter.

---

out removing the food; a rotisserie attachment; side tables; and a thermometer built into the lid.

If your kettle grill does not have side baskets, you can buy wire rails that corral the coals, keeping the piles on each side of the grill neat and concentrated for indirect grilling. Or you can buy metal side baskets (these are manufactured by Weber). Position them at opposite sides of the grill (under the grate that holds the food)

and fill them with blazing coals and wood chips for smoking.

BARBECOOK GRILL: The Barbecook grill, manufactured in Belgium, is a charcoal grill with a chimney starter built into the base. To control the heat you adjust the vents and raise and lower the grill grate.

This handsome grill is one of the best-selling charcoal grills in Europe. Its sales are increasing in North America—especially in high-end cook-

ware and barbecue shops. Accessories include a dome-shaped lid, which allows for indirect grilling.

CERAMIC COOKER: This curious grill arrived on the American barbecue scene in 1974. It is modeled on a Japanese *kamado,* a domed, charcoal-fired clay oven that's been used in the Far East for thousands of years. The heavy ceramic smoker grill consists of a firebox with a grate in the middle and a domed lid that's

tall enough to accommodate a large turkey. The thick clay walls maintain a steady, even temperature, so even a little charcoal will keep the cooker going for several hours (this also enables you to cook at a very low temperature). Vents at the top and bottom allow you to control the heat. The tight-fitting lid seals in moisture, which keeps food exceptionally moist and tender. Ceramic cookers work on a hybrid principle: The food is positioned directly over the

The coal holder of the Big Green Egg has perforations to allow air to fuel the fire.

This Big Green Egg, a ceramic cooker, will grill for several hours using only a small amount of charcoal.

A table grill should have grates that can be adjusted to varying distances from the heat; on this model it's done with gears.

coals, as in direct grilling, but because the grate sits so high above the coals, the cooking process is more like that of indirect grilling. A perforated ceramic coal holder allows air to enter from below the coals, which fuels the fire and facilitates air flow from top to bottom. The Big Green Egg is the best known ceramic cooker, but other companies make similar devices.

■ **What to look for when buying a ceramic cooker:** Thick walls of heat-resistant, kilned ceramic; a tight-fitting seal around the lid; a safety catch that prevents the lid from falling shut (it's heavy); air vents at the top and bottom; "shoes" (ceramic supports that keep the hot cooker an inch or so above your deck); side tables; housing in a rolling cart.

TABLE GRILL: As the name suggests, the table grill looks like a large table, the top of which is a shallow box that holds charcoal or can be fitted for gas. Most table grills have adjustable grates so you can raise and lower the cooking surface to control the heat. Some allow you to do this by means of a notched support that can hold the grate at a variety of heights. Some use gears. Table grills are designed chiefly for direct grilling, but many have fittings for rotisseries. These grills are popular for backyard grilling in Australia and are sporadically available in the United States. (They're used for institutional grilling: barbecue festivals, country club cookouts, church barbecues, and the like.) The best place to look for a table grill is at a party rental company.

■ **What to look for when buying or renting a table grill:** Sturdy construction with solid legs; a grill that can be raised and lowered; and a fitting for a rotisserie.

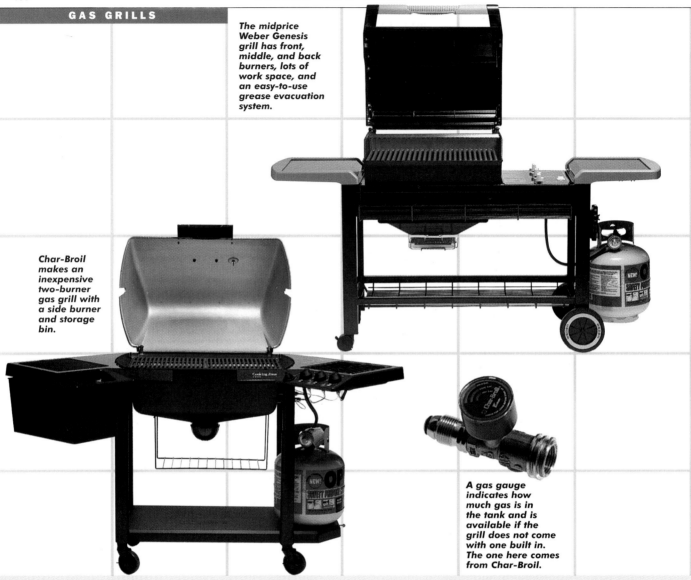

The midprice Weber Genesis grill has front, middle, and back burners, lots of work space, and an easy-to-use grease evacuation system.

Char-Broil makes an inexpensive two-burner gas grill with a side burner and storage bin.

A gas gauge indicates how much gas is in the tank and is available if the grill does not come with one built in. The one here comes from Char-Broil.

GAS GRILLS

Americans love gas grills. Since their introduction in the 1960s, gas grills have become more and more popular. Today, 60 percent of grill owners in the United States have a gas grill. The gas grill offers several advantages: It's clean, quick, and easy to use. It starts at the push of a button and maintains a consistent temperature for hours.

In the old days, there were several drawbacks to gas grills. They didn't get as hot as charcoal grills and their heat was more humid (water vapors are released when propane is burned). Also, traditionally, it was difficult to smoke on a gas grill. Newer generations of grills burn hotter and have smoker boxes with dedicated burners. So the problems that plagued gas grills are fast disappearing.

Most gas grills work on a similar principle: The fire burns from one or more gas burner tubes, heating some sort of cooking element positioned between the grate and the burners. The burner tubes come in many configurations—straight, U-shaped—arranged side by side or from the front to the back of the grill. A grill with rows of burners running side to side is great for rotisserie grilling. A grill with three or four burners running front to back gives you more room for indirect grilling.

The burners heat cooking or heating elements that vary from grill to grill, ranging from lava stones (see page 480) to metal plaques to ceramic rods or Flavorizer bars. These elements spread the heat of the fire evenly and keep the fat from dripping directly on the burners.

INEXPENSIVE GAS GRILL:
Char-Broil has a simple gas grill, above left, with two burners (front and rear), plus a burner at the side for heating barbecue sauces, among other things. There are two side tables, a

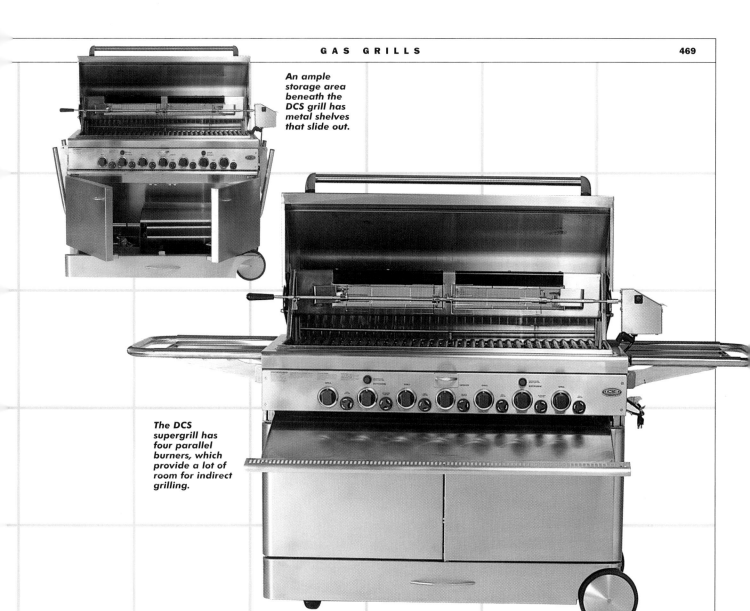

An ample storage area beneath the DCS grill has metal shelves that slide out.

The DCS supergrill has four parallel burners, which provide a lot of room for indirect grilling.

storage bin, and a thermometer that indicates the cooking temperature. The grill grate is made of heavy cast iron and the rounded drip pan on the bottom collects the fat. Cast iron and thick stainless steel are the best surfaces for grill grates.

MIDPRICE GAS GRILL:

Weber's popular Genesis gas grill, center, has three burners arranged in a front-middle-back configuration. The thermometer is built in and there are a gas gauge and a

convenient fat collection system, which funnels grease into a disposable aluminum foil catch pan. The cooking grate is porcelainized and there is a wire warming rack above the grate.

GAS SUPERGRILL: The stainless steel behemoth by DCS, right, has four parallel burners running front to back, a separate smoker box with a dedicated burner, and a rotisserie with a heavy-duty motor. The grate is porcelainized steel.

The fat collection system of this and many gas super-grills is a metal shelf under the burners. It may gather every drip, but it's awkward to empty.

■ **What to look for when buying a gas grill:** At least two and ideally three or four burners. A heavy metal grate with thick bars, preferably of cast iron or stainless steel. An easy-to-use fat collection system with a removable catch pan. Sturdy construction and a cart with wheels and a storage

compartment. A gas gauge and a thermometer are useful features. (If your gas grill lacks a gas gauge, you can buy one to install on the tank between the outflow nozzle and the gas hose.) Attractive optional features include a built-in rotisserie or rotisserie attachment with a heavy-duty motor, a side burner, and a slide-out smoker box with a dedicated burner, preferably located on one side of the grill, not in the center.

PSEUDOGRILLS

Char-Broil makes an electric grill with a lid that is insulated with corrugated aluminum.

The electric grill's thermostat: For the best flavor, set it on high.

A grill pan with high, clearly delineated raised ridges, like this one from Le Creuset, will make the best grill marks.

PSEUDOGRILLS

This catch-all category includes cooking devices that have grill-like properties but that don't necessarily use live fire as a heat source.

ELECTRIC GRILL: The best electric grills function like inverted broilers, giving you the searing and grill marks you'd get on a conventional grill. On some models you can even sneak in chunks of wood to generate a smoke flavor. The thermostat allows you to regulate the heat. The drawbacks are the lack of a real live-fire flavor and the fact that on most models you can't grill using the indirect method. Most of the recipes in this book that employ the direct grill method can be made using an electric grill.

■ **What to look for when buying an electric grill:** Sturdy construction and thermostatic control.

GRILL PAN: When it comes to putting a handsome cross-hatch of grill marks on a steak or chicken breast, a grill pan will do the job as effectively as an outdoor grill. Simply pre-heat over a hot gas or electric burner (be sure to have your exhaust fan running full bore to clear out the smoke). The downside to grill pans is that what you're really doing is pan-frying, not grilling.

■ **What to look for when buying a grill pan:** A thick, heavy pan made of cast iron, steel, or another sturdy metal.

SMOKERS

VERTICAL WATER SMOKER: No, it's not R2D2 from *Star Wars*. The simple, inexpensive barrel-shaped smoker, shown at left on the facing page, does a stellar job of transforming turkeys, pork shoulders, and spareribs into morsels of tender, smoky perfection. It has a removable domed top and a firebox. The genius of a water smoker lies in the deep drip pan you position in the center of the smoker. Filled with

SMOKERS

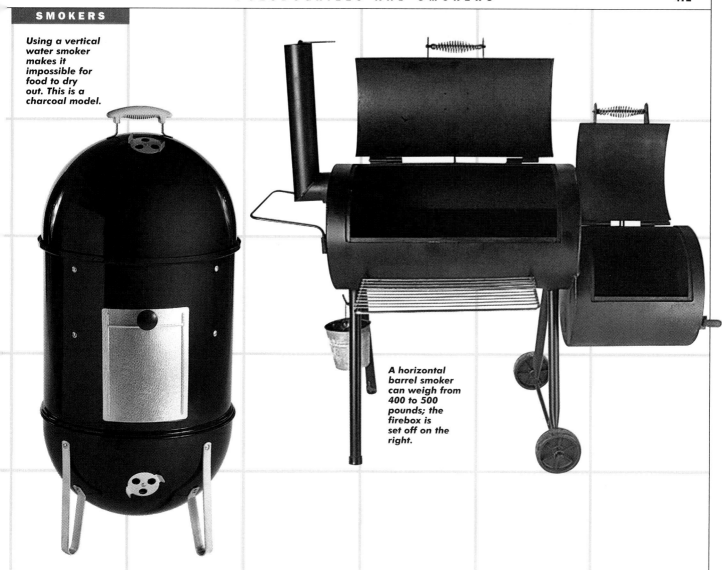

Using a vertical water smoker makes it impossible for food to dry out. This is a charcoal model.

A horizontal barrel smoker can weigh from 400 to 500 pounds; the firebox is set off on the right.

water, beer, wine, or another flavorful liquid, it creates a moist, steamy, smoking environment. You light the fire in the bottom of the smoker and place a pan of wood chips over it. Adjust the vents on the top and bottom to obtain the desired airflow and temperature and you're ready to smoke. The only drawback is that because of the low cooking temperature (225° to 250°F) and the moist smoking environment, your food never acquires a crisp crust.

Water smokers come in both charcoal-fired and electric models. The charcoal-fired ones require restoking every hour. You simply plug an electric water smoker in and forget about it. The ultimate difference in the taste is minimal.

■ **What to look for when buying a water smoker:** Sturdy construction; top and bottom vents to control the airflow and heat; a door in the front to allow you to add fresh charcoal and wood; a built-in thermometer.

HORIZONTAL BARREL SMOKER: If you want to make professional tasting, fork-tender briskets and dark, smoky ribs, the horizontal barrel smoker, shown at right, above, is the machine to do it. Barrel smokers have two parts: an offset firebox and a cylindrical smoking or cooking chamber. Most backyard barrel smokers burn charcoal or small logs. The heat is controlled by opening or closing the dampers on the firebox and at the top of the chimney. Horizontal barrel

smokers operate at a low temperature: 225° to 250°F. Low and slow is the essence of barrel smoking.

■ **What to look for when buying a barrel smoker:** Thick, heavy construction—at least ⅜-inch-gauge steel; adjustable vents on the firebox and chimney; prep racks on the front of the firebox; a drip spout with a bucket for collecting the fat; wheels to make moving it easier.

GRILLING GEAR

It used to be that a griller needed only tongs, a spatula, and a barbecue fork. My, how times have changed! Today's grill meisters have at their disposal literally hundreds of different grill accessories—some indispensable, others downright silly; all designed to enhance showmanship and make the act of live-fire cooking safer, more efficient, and more fun. Here are the essentials, as well as some clever, sometimes timesaving, gadgets that may actually work. (You'll find only things that are specifically for grilling here, not things like the knives and poultry shears that any well-equipped kitchen should have.)

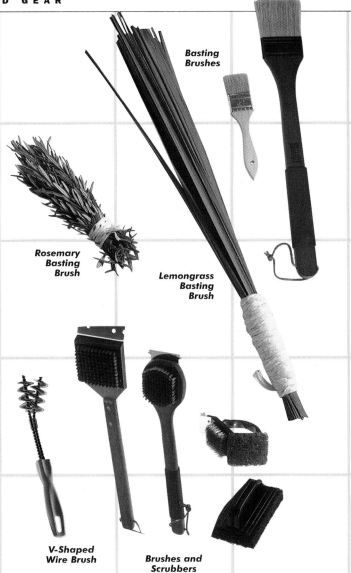

Basting Brushes

Rosemary Basting Brush

Lemongrass Basting Brush

V-Shaped Wire Brush

Brushes and Scrubbers

BASTING BRUSHES: Essential for brushing oils, bastes, glazes, and sauces on grilling food; the best barbecue basting brushes have long wooden handles and natural bristles. When working with messy sauces, I often use a cheap, natural-bristle paintbrush. Avoid nylon basting brushes, which will melt. For extra flavor, use bunches of herbs as basting brushes.

BRUSHES AND SCRUBBERS: A good grill grate brush will have a long, sturdy handle, a stiff, wide wire brush head, and a scraper at the end for dislodging burnt-on pieces of debris (a long handle is essential for working on a hot grill). A V-shaped wire brush is useful for scrubbing the individual bars of a particularly dirty grate. A grill scrubber should have a tough fiber pad for cleaning grates and fireboxes.

DRIP PANS: Aluminum foil drip pans are indispensable. Not only are they essential for positioning under the grate of the grill to catch fat, you can use them to soak wood chips and keep cooked foods warm on the side of the grill. You'll find heavy-duty aluminum foil drip pans at your local supermarket or barbecue shop. Buy a variety of sizes.

FIRE EXTINGUISHER: While grilling is fun, it should also be executed safely. Minor flare-ups can be controlled with a water pistol or a sprinkling of salt. In case of bigger flare-ups have a fire extinguisher armed and ready. You want a dry chemical type. An extinguisher remains charged and ready to use for several years—provided that it's not used. If you do use it, have it professionally recharged and inspected, or get another extinguisher. Another piece of safety equipment not pictured here is a bucket of sand (for extinguishing grease fires on the ground).

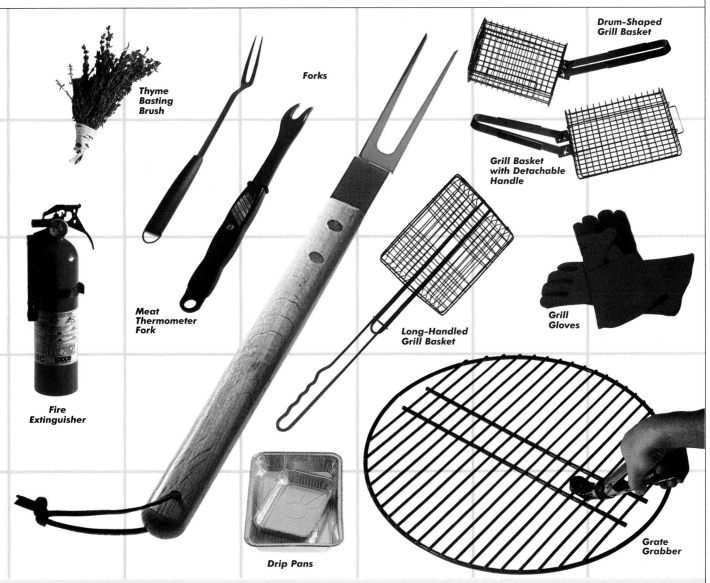

Thyme
Basting
Brush

Forks

Drum-Shaped
Grill Basket

Grill Basket
with Detachable
Handle

Meat
Thermometer
Fork

Fire
Extinguisher

Long-Handled
Grill Basket

Grill
Gloves

Drip Pans

Grate
Grabber

FORKS: Guys who don't know any better use forks to poke holes in steaks and burgers, thereby draining the juices onto the coals. The tines of a barbecue fork are good for sliding between the bars of the grate to lift up food when it's sticking to the grate, but don't stick them into the meat.

GLOVES: Indispensable for handling anything hot on or off the grill. Leather or suede gloves give you the best insulation. For maximum protection, choose a long-sleeve glove that comes most of the way up your arm. Grilla Gear's suede gloves, seen above, are thick, well-padded, and long.

GRATE GRABBER: A plierlike device that helps you to lift a hot grate off the grill when it's time to replenish the charcoal, if your grill is not hinged. The one above is available from the Big Green Egg Company.

GRILL BASKETS: If you've ever tried to grill a fragile fish steak, cheese sandwich, or vegetable burger, only to have it stick to the grate, you'll appreciate the value of the hinged grill basket. You insert the food between the hinged wire panels. When it's time to turn, you invert the basket, not the fragile food. The long-handled grill basket seen above has a metal ring that slides over the handle to fasten the panels together. The handle on Charcoal

Companion's large grill basket comes off so you can close the grill lid over the basket. The drum-shaped grill basket shown at top (also from Charcoal Companion) allows you to rotate a basketful of cubed vegetables. It has eight sides and a detachable handle.

FISH BASKETS: Whole fish and fish fillets are notorious for sticking to grates. The grill basket solves this problem. To prevent the fish from sticking or

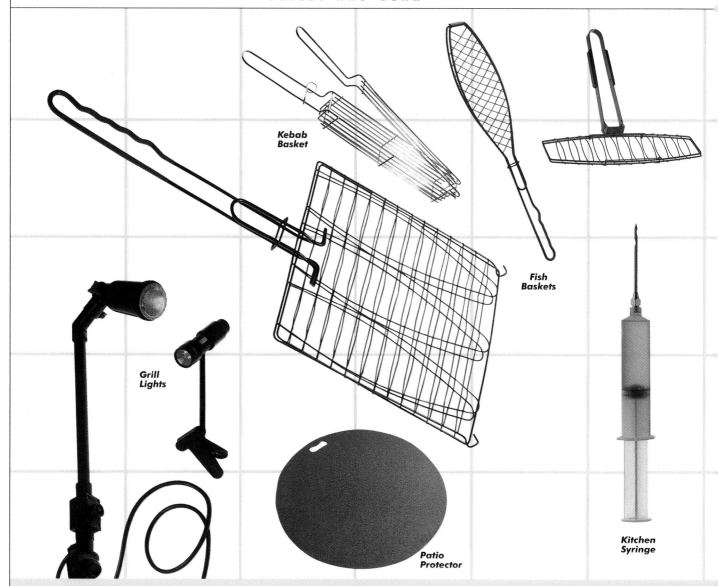

Kebab Basket

Fish Baskets

Grill Lights

Patio Protector

Kitchen Syringe

breaking, you turn the basket with the fish inside.

GRILL LIGHTS: These lamps clamp on to the side of your grill, shedding light on the food you're grilling. They are available in both plug-in and battery-powered versions. Avoid lights that clip on the lid of the grill. The heat will melt the plastic.

KEBAB BASKET: I wouldn't deem this essential, but in the event you should want to grill

vegetable pieces or cubes of fish that are too clumsy or fragile to skewer, this gadget is your ticket. To brown all sides you turn the basket.

KITCHEN SYRINGE: Also known as a barbecue injector. Shaped like an oversize hypodermic needle, the barbecue injector guarantees moistness by enabling you to inject melted butter, broth, or other liquid flavorings deep inside a turkey or roast. One good

brand is made by the Cajun Injector Company. Seen above is a kitchen syringe loaded and ready to go; to see it in action, see page 259.

MOPS: Mops are a must on the professional barbecue circuit, used for dabbing thin flavoring mixtures onto chickens, ribs, pork shoulders, and whole hogs. Professional barbecuers actually use full-size floor mops (brand-new ones, of course)— hence the name mop sauce. For

home grilling, buy a barbecue mop. You can wash mop heads in the dishwasher.

PATIO PROTECTOR: Diversi-Tech's fireproof patio protector, seen above, goes under your grill to shield your deck or patio from any falling sparks and dripping fat.

POULTRY ROASTER: A roaster enables you to barbecue a chicken in an upright position. This helps the fat drain off more

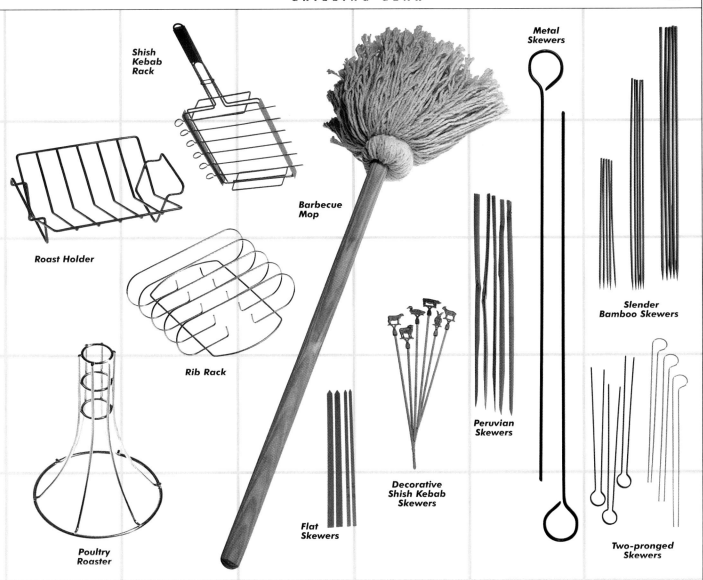

Shish Kebab Rack

Roast Holder

Rib Rack

Poultry Roaster

Barbecue Mop

Flat Skewers

Decorative Shish Kebab Skewers

Peruvian Skewers

Metal Skewers

Slender Bamboo Skewers

Two-pronged Skewers

efficiently, producing a crispier, juicier chicken.

RIB RACK: This elegantly simple device solves a problem that has bedeviled barbecuers for decades: how to cook a lot of ribs on a small grill. By standing the ribs on end in a rack, you can quadruple the capacity of your grill. Another advantage to using a rib rack: The vertical position helps the fat drain off, resulting in a lighter, crispier rib.

ROAST HOLDER: Using a roast holder helps a roast keep its cylindrical shape during indirect grilling.

SHISH KEBAB RACK: A metal rack that holds six or eight individual shish kebab skewers. The device is supposed to facilitate turning the kebabs and promote even cooking.

SKEWERS: Barbecue skewers come in all sizes and in a dazzling array of shapes, each

designed for a specific function. You're probably already familiar with the simple metal skewers shown above. Keep at least eight on hand. The flat blades of shish kebab skewers keep the chunks of meat from rotating. Two-pronged skewers are great for grilling slippery foods, like onions, tomatoes, and shrimp (the dual prongs keep the foods from slipping). Flat metal skewers from the Near East are designed for grilling ground meat kebabs and vegetables.

Ground meats cling to their broad surface area. Wet vegetables, like plum tomatoes, won't spin when you turn them over. Slender bamboo skewers—sold in all sizes—are the preferred kebab holder throughout Asia. Flat bamboo skewers from Peru are used for making Peru's beloved *anticuchos* (beef heart kebabs). Moroccan shish kebab skewers with slender blades, as seen on page 476, are perfect for skewering small cubes of meat. The curved skewers from

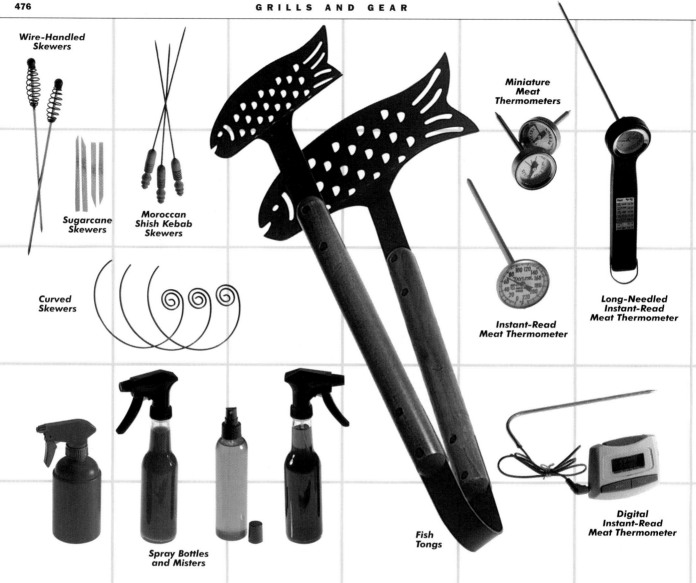

Wire-Handled Skewers

Sugarcane Skewers

Moroccan Shish Kebab Skewers

Curved Skewers

Miniature Meat Thermometers

Instant-Read Meat Thermometer

Long-Needled Instant-Read Meat Thermometer

Digital Instant-Read Meat Thermometer

Spray Bottles and Misters

Fish Tongs

Charcoal Companion, seen above, add a whimsical touch to a barbecue. In many parts of the world, grill meisters cook kebabs on lemongrass stalks, strips of sugarcane, rosemary sprigs, and other skewers you can actually eat or chew. The obvious advantage here is that you put flavor inside the meat, as well as on the surface.

SKILLETS AND WOKS: These ingenious baskets enable you to "stir-grill" vegetables, shrimp, and other small pieces of food the way you would stir-fry in a wok on the stove. The holes allow the smoke and flame flavors to reach the food. A long handle on a grill wok facilitates tossing, as you would when stir-frying. A short handle allows you to close the lid of the grill over the basket.

SPATULAS: Handy for turning flat foods, like burgers and fish fillets. Choose a spatula with a long, sturdy, angled handle (the angle keeps your hand away from the fire) and the widest blade possible. Holes in the blade prevent the buildup of steam, which could make your food soggy.

SPRAY BOTTLES AND MISTERS: One of the secrets of succulent barbecue is conscientiously spraying it with oil or a basting mixture. Spray bottles can be used for liquid flavorings, like apple cider or vinegar. Misters are designed for spraying thicker liquids, like olive oil.

THERMOMETERS: There's only one fail-safe way to tell when meat or poultry is ready to take off the grill—take its temperature. An instant-read meat thermometer with a long metal probe gives you the internal temperature as soon as you insert it. A long-handled, long-needled thermometer is useful for taking the temperature of

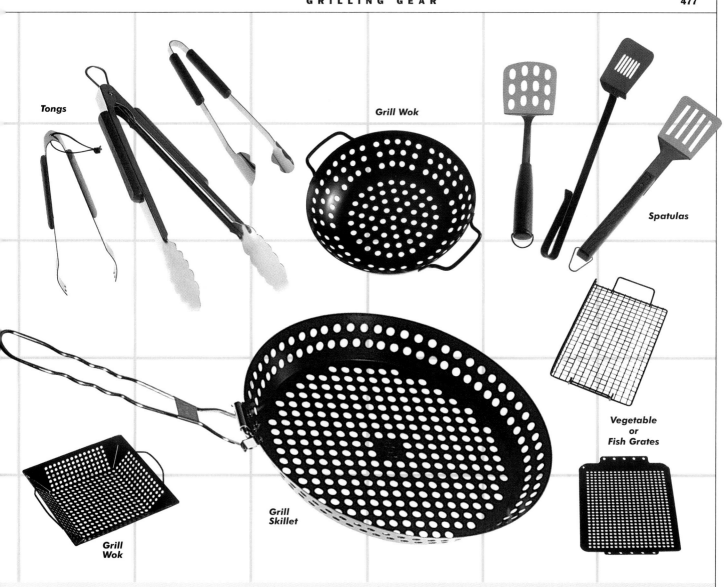

Tongs

Grill Wok

Spatulas

Vegetable or Fish Grates

Grill Wok

Grill Skillet

roasts, pork shoulders, and other large cuts of meat. Instant-read thermometers also come in digital models. And, you'll see a thermometer combined with a barbecue fork on page 473.

TONGS: The most important tool in a griller's workshop, tongs enable you to turn meat without stabbing it. When buying tongs, look for long, stiff arms (14 to 16 inches long), so you won't burn your-

self; stiff, so you can pick up a whole chicken without having the tongs bend. A lockable spring-loaded hinge enables you to secure your grip on a slippery or awkward piece of food. Scalloped ends give the tongs a surer hold. The wooden handles of the Grilla Gear tongs, in the center, above, act as insulators and are supposed to keep your hands from slipping. I also like spring-loaded restaurant tongs, available from restau-

rant supply houses. The slender metal arms of the other two tongs, seen above, may bend when you try to pick up heavy items.

VEGETABLE AND FISH GRATES: These wire or perforated metal plates are placed on top of the grill grate to hold small pieces of food (like mushrooms or okra) that would fall through the bars of a conventional grate. They're also good for fragile foods,

such as vegetable burgers and fish fillets. Wire vegetable grates allow fire and smoke to penetrate food easily, while perforated metal plates provide better support for fragile items. When using vegetable and fish grates, preheat them well and spray them with oil before placing the food on top.

STARTERS, FUELS, AND SMOKING MATERIALS

Lighter Fluid

Long-Stem Butane Lighter

Y ou can't start grilling until you light your fire. And once you've got your fire lit, you'll probably want to "season" it with the smoke from wood chips or dried herbs. For that matter, you may even want to grill on wood. Here's a guide to the fuels and smoking woods and fire starters essential to world-class barbecue.

Electric Starter

Chimney Starter

FIRE STARTERS

LIGHTER FLUID is something a lot of grill jockeys frown on, believing it may leave an oily residue on your food. But millions of people swear by it. For safety's sake, douse charcoal with lighter fluid first, close and remove the can, and then light the charcoal with a match.

LONG-STEM BUTANE LIGHTERS are ideal for lighting your chimney starter or a mound of self-lighting charcoal. A long lighting tube keeps your hands away from the mess of the charcoal.

ELECTRIC STARTERS have a metal loop that heats when you plug it in. To use it, bury it at the bottom of a mound of charcoal in your grill, then plug it in. You'll probably need a heavy-duty extension cord, as your grill should be well away from the side of your house. After 5 minutes or so the heat of the starter will ignite the coals. When the core of the mountain of coals glows red, you can remove the starter. Place it on a nonflammable surface (on concrete or a cinderblock, for example), and let it cool completely. Never leave a hot electric starter where someone can touch it.

CHIMNEY STARTERS are the ignition device preferred by ecologically minded grillers. Place the charcoal in the top, a crumpled sheet of newspaper in the bottom, and light. You'll have uniformly glowing coals in 15 to 25 minutes.

PARAFFIN STARTERS look like waxy white ice cubes. You light them with a match: 1 or 2 are enough to light a chimney starter full of coals without leaving a paraffin aftertaste.

SAWDUST STARTERS are similar to the pressed particle logs many of us burn in our fireplaces. Place them under a mound of charcoal or wood chunks and light.

Paraffin Starters

Sawdust Starters

Charcoal Briquettes

Lump Charcoal

Bag of Wood Chunks

Apple Wood Chunks

Oak Wood Chunks

Mesquite Wood Chunks

Wood Pellets

Dry Wood Chips

Soaking Wood Chips

CHARCOAL

CHARCOAL BRIQUETTES are the workhorse of backyard barbecues, but some brands contain coal dust, furniture trimmings, borax, and petroleum binders. (If you must use briquettes, try to find pure wood briquettes, which are sold at natural foods stores.)

LUMP CHARCOAL, also known as **CHARWOOD,** is made from whole logs that are burned in a kiln, then broken into chunks, but otherwise left in their natural state, with no binders or fillers. Most charcoal grill aficionados prefer the purity of lump charcoal.

WOODS

APPLE, OAK, AND MESQUITE CHUNKS are great for both grilling and smoking. To use chunks as fuel, light them in a chimney starter as you would charcoal. For smoking, soak them in water for 1 hour, drain, and toss on the coals, or if using a gas grill, place them in the smoker box or in a smoker pouch. You can also use hardwood logs for fuel. Oak, hickory, and mesquite are the most popular.

WOOD CHUNKS IN A BAG provide an easy-to-use fuel for grilling. The hickory chunks from W W Wood are coated with paraffin for quick ignition. Simply light the corners of the bag and you'll have a splendid bed of glowing wood embers in 15 to 20 minutes.

WOOD PELLETS are a convenient smoking fuel, available in a variety of flavors. Simply enclose them in a smoker pouch and place on the fire.

WOOD CHIPS FOR SMOKING will give the most smoke if you soak them for 1 hour in cold water, then drain them.

W W Wood makes a metal box that contains a premeasured quantity of wood chips—enough to smoke a chicken, turkey breast, or 4 racks of baby back ribs. Simply remove

Premeasured Wood Chips in a Box

Presoaked Wood Chips in a Can

Sawdust

Lava Stones

Diamond Shaped Ceramic Briquettes

Mesquite-Flavored Ceramic Briquettes

Grapevine Trimmings

Dried Sage Leaves

Dried Basil Stems

Sugarcane Trimmings

Pineapple Trimmings

the plastic wrapper and place the smoker box on the coals or over one of the gas burners. Wood chips also come presoaked in cans; Blue Moon Woods makes three flavors, mesquite, hickory, and wild cherry. Remove the lid and place the can on the fire; the can becomes the smoker box.

WOOD SAWDUST is too fine to go on the coals, but you can soak it and wrap it in aluminum foil to make a smoker pouch.

OTHER FUELS

LAVA STONES AND CERAMIC BRIQUETTES are the gas-heated cooking interfaces gas grills rely on to distribute their heat. Lightweight lava stones spread the heat evenly and, thanks to their porosity, they absorb lots of meat drippings. The gas burns these drippings, giving you a great smoke flavor but sometimes also flare-ups. Ceramic briquettes also spread the heat evenly and burn off the drippings. You can buy wood-

flavored ceramic briquettes that contain tiny pieces of hickory or mesquite. When heated they impart a wood smoke flavor.

GRAPEVINE TRIMMINGS are a popular fuel in France. Burn them as you would charcoal or soak them and toss on the coals.

DRIED SAGE LEAVES generate clouds of fragrant smoke when you toss them on the coals.

DRIED BASIL STEMS are another great herb for smoking.

Grapevine trimmings and dried herbs are available from Peoples Woods (see page 481).

UNUSUAL SMOKING MATERIALS, such as fruit and vegetable trimmings, can also be used for smoking. In the French West Indies, sugarcane trimmings are tossed on the coals to make *poulet boucanne* (buccaneer-style smoked chicken). Pineapple trimmings are a great fuel for smoking fish and chicken.

MAIL-ORDER SOURCES

GRILLS AND ACCESSORIES

Big Green Egg
3414 Clairmont Avenue
Atlanta, Georgia 30319
(800) 939-3447
www.BigGreenEgg.com
Ceramic cookers

Char-Broil
P.O. Box 1240
Columbus, Georgia 31902-1240
(800) 252-8248
www.charbroil.com
Gas and electric grills

Charcoal Companion
7955 Edgewater Drive
Oakland, California 94621-2003
(800) 521-0505
www.companion-group.com
Accessories

Chef Williams' Cajun Injector
P.O. Box 97
South Clinton, Louisiana 70722
(800) 221-8060
www.cajuninjector.com
Kitchen syringes

DCS
5800 Skylab Road
Huntington Beach, California 92647
(800) 433-8466
www.dcs-range.com
Gas grills

DiversiTech
2530 Lantrac Court
Decatur, Georgia 30035
(800) 397-4823
www.diversitech.com
Patio protectors

Ducane Gas Grills
800 Dutch Square Boulevard, Suite 200
Columbia, South Carolina 29210
(800) 382-2637
www.ducane.com
Gas grills

Grill Lover's Catalog
P.O. Box 1300
Columbus, Georgia 31902-1300
(800) 241-8981
www.grilllovers.com
Charcoal and gas grills; accessories

Grilla Gear
P.O. Box 7369
Endicott, New York 13760
(800) 545-4411
www.grillagear.com
Accessories

Jenn-Air
240 Edward Street
Cleveland, Tennessee 37311
(800) 536-6247
www.jenair.com
Gas and indoor grills

Pal Products
P.O. Box 905
Wisconsin Rapids, Wisconsin 54494-0905
(715) 421-0445
www.nu-temp.com
Instant-read thermometer forks

Viking Range Corporation
111 Front Street
Greenwood, Mississippi 38930
(888) 845-4641
www.vikingrange.com
Gas grills

Weber-Stephen Products Company
200 East Daniels Road
Palatine, Illinois 60067-6266
(800) 446-1071
www.weberbbq.com
Charcoal and gas grills; accessories

CHARCOAL AND WOOD

BBQr's Delight
P.O. Box 8727
Pine Bluff, Arkansas 71611
(877) 275-9591
www.BBQrsDelight.com
Wood grill pellets

Blue Moon Woods
P.O. Box 207
2350 Sopchoppy Highway
Sopchoppy, Florida 32358
(888) 959-9291
www.bluemoonwoods.com
Presoaked grilling woods

Peoples Woods
75 Mill Street
Cumberland, Rhode Island 02864
(800) 729-5800
www.peopleswoods.com
Natural lump charcoal and smoking woods

W W Wood, Inc.
P.O. Box 398
Pleasanton, Texas 78064
(830) 569-2501
Smoking and grilling woods

INGREDIENTS
GENERAL

American Spoon Foods
P.O. Box 566
Petoskey, Michigan 49770
(800) 222-5886
www.spoon.com
Dried fruits, barbecue sauces, chutney, and condiments

Brugger Brothers
3868 NE 169th Street, Suite 401
North Miami Beach, Florida 33160
(800) 949-2264
www.talamancapepper.com
Sells my favorite pepper, Talamanca white and black peppercorns (by mail, Web, or telephone only)

The Chile Shop
109 East Water Street
Santa Fe, New Mexico 87501
(505) 983-6080
www.thechileshop.com
Dried chiles, salsas, and sauces

Coyote Cafe General Store
132 West Water Street
Santa Fe, New Mexico 87501
(800) 866-4695
www.coyote-cafe.com
Dried chiles, salsas, and sauces

Dean & Deluca
2526 East 36 Circle North
Wichita, Kansas 67219
(800) 221-7714
www.dean-deluca.com
All manner of oils, vinegars, spices, condiments, hot sauces, and the like

El Paso Chile Company
909 Texas Avenue
El Paso, Texas 79901
(888) 472-5727
www.elpasochile.com
Salsas and condiments

Foodalicious
2035 NE 151st Street
North Miami Beach, Florida 33162
(305) 945-0502
Oils, vinegars, chiles, spices, and so on

Frieda's
4465 Corporate Center Drive
Los Alamitos, California 90720
(800) 241-1771
(714) 826-6100
www.friedas.com
Exotic produce

Jamison Farm
171 Jamison Lane
Latrobe, Pennsylvania 15650
(800) 237-5262
www.jamisonfarm.com
Lamb

Legal Sea Foods
33 Everett Street
Boston, Massachusetts
02134-1993
(800) 477-5342
www.sendlegal.com
Seafood

Marché aux Delices
P.O. Box 1164
New York, New York 10028
(888) 547-5471
www.auxdelices.com
Exotic mushrooms

Melissa's
P.O. Box 21127
Los Angeles, California
90021
(800) 588-0151
www.melissas.com
Exotic produce

Mo Hotta-Mo Betta
P.O. Box 1026
Savannah, Georgia 31402
(800) 462-3220
www.mohotta.com
Hot sauces and condiments

Nueske's Hillcrest Farm Meats
P.O. Box D
Wittenberg, Wisconsin
54499
(800) 392-2266
www.nueske.com
Bacon

Pendery's
1221 Manufacturing Street
Dallas, Texas 75207
(800) 533-1870
www.penderys.com
Spices

Peppers
2009 Highway One
Dewey Beach, Delaware
19971-2318
(800) 998-3473
www.peppers.com
Hot sauces and condiments

The Spice House
1031 North Old World
Third Street
Milwaukee, Wisconsin 53203
(414) 272-0977
www.thespicehouse.com
Spices

ETHNIC

Anzen Japenese Foods and Imports
736 Northeast Martin Luther
King Boulevard
Portland, Oregon 97232
(503) 233-5111
Asian

Aphrodisia Products
62 Kent Street
Brooklyn, New York 11222
(877) 274-3677
www.aphrodisiaproducts.com
Middle Eastern

Haji Baba Middle Eastern Food
1513 East Apache Boulevard
Tempe, Arizona 85281
(480) 894-1905
Middle Eastern

India Spice and Gift Shop
3295 Fairfield Avenue
Bridgeport, Connecticut 06605
(203) 384-0666
Indian

Indian Emporium
68-48 New Hampshire Avenue
Tacoma Park, Maryland
20012
(301) 270-3322
Indian

Jamaica Groceries & Spices
9587 S.W. 160th Street
Miami, Florida 33157
(305) 252-1197
Caribbean

Monterrey Food Products
3939 East Cesar E. Chavez
Avenue
Los Angeles, California
90063-1806
(323) 263-2143
www.monterreyfoods.com
Mexican

The Oriental Pantry
423 Great Road
Acton, Massachusetts
01720
(800) 828-0368
www.orientalpantry.com
Asian

Oriental Pastry and Grocery
170 Atlantic Avenue
Brooklyn, New York
11201
(718) 875-7687
Asian

Pars Market
9016 West Pico Boulevard
Los Angeles, California
90035
(310) 859-8125
Middle Eastern

Patel Brothers
18636 South Pioneer Boulevard
Artesia, California 90701
(562) 402-2953
Indian

Yekta Supermarket
1488A Rockville Pike
Rockville, Maryland 20852
(301) 984-1190
Middle Eastern; also carries
flat shish kebab skewers

BARBECUE BOOKS AND NEWSLETTERS

Barbecue Today
P.O. Box 9685
Kansas City, Missouri 64134
(816) 767-8311

The Kansas City Bullsheet
Kansas City Barbeque Society
11514 Hickman Mills Drive
Kansas City, Missouri
64134
(800) 963-5227
www.rbjb.com/rbjb/kcbs.htm

National Barbecue News
P.O. Box 981
Douglas, Georgia
31534-0981
(800) 385-0002
www.barbequenews.com

Pig Out Publications
4245 Walnut Street
Kansas City, Missouri 64111
(816) 531-3119
www.pigoutpublications.com

and don't forget my Web site
www.barbecuebible.com

GENERAL INDEX

(Page numbers in *italics* refer to illustrations.)

Gas grills, 15–18, 468–69
charcoal grills vs., 2, 8, 15, 464, 468
cleaning, 4
direct grilling on, 16
features to look for when buying, 467
heat control on, 20, 21
indirect grilling on, 16
lighting, 15–16
preheating, 5, 15, 21
preparing at beginning of barbecue season, 4
rotisserie cooking on, 23–24
shutting down, 3
smoking on, 16–18
time management with, 4–5
Glazes, making marinades into, 167
Gloves, 3, 473, *473*
Goat cheese, cutting thin, even slices of, 240
Grape leaves, grilling meats or fish in, 305, 308
Grapevine trimmings, as fuel, 480, *480*
Grate grabbers, 473, *473*
Grates:
fish, 295, 297, 477, *477*
vegetable, 381, 477, *477*
Grates, grill:
cleaning, 4, 5, 26
cooking fish fillets directly on, 297, 298
heat control and, 21
oiling, 5, 26, 27, 87, 297, 298
Grease collectors:
in gas grills, 16, 27
see also Drip pans
Grease fires, 3
see also Flare-ups
Greek-style lamb, grilling whole, 195–200
Green beans, grilling in raft, 356
Grilla Gear:
gloves, 473, *473*
tongs, 477, *477*
Grill baskets, 473, *473*
Grill cleansers, 4, 26
Grilling:
on charcoal grill, 8–14, 19–21
on electric grill, 22
on gas grill, 15–18, 20, 21
heat control in, 19–21
on rotisserie, 22–24
technical terms for, 6–7
timetable for, 4–5

use of term, 6
see also Direct grilling; Indirect grilling
Grilling gear, 472–77
mail-order sources for, 481
mise en place and, 3
storing, 3
Grill lights, 2–3, 474, *474*
Grill pans, 22, 470, *470*
Grills, 464–71
buying and assembling, 2
cleaning, 4, 5, 26, 472
covering, 21
determining needs and, 2
electric, 22, 470, *470*
features to look for when buying, 467
gas vs. charcoal, 2, 8, 15, 464, 468
large, renting, 195, 198
mail-order sources for, 481
placement of, 2–3
pseudogrills, 22, 470–71
see also Charcoal grills; Gas grills; Smokers
Grill skillets, 22, 476, *477*
Grill woks, 374, 476, *477*

Halibut fillets, grilling, 295–99
Hamburgers, 98–101
Harissa, 172
Hazelnut oil, 279
Heat control:
on charcoal or wood-burning grill, 13, 19–21
on gas grill, 20, 21
Herbes de Provence, 162
Herbs:
as basting brushes, 79, 80, 162, 472, *472–73*
as skewers, 345, 476
Hibachis, *464,* 464–65
heat control on, 21
Hickory, 12, 14, 479, *479,* 480
Horizontal barrel smokers, 471, *471*
Horseradish, fresh, grating, 455
Hot dogs, stuffing and grilling, 151–53
Hot pepper flakes, 29
Hot smoking, 7, 309

Indian-style:
chicken wings, grilling, 249
cilantro chutney, 460

rib lamb chops, grilling tandoori style, 82–85
tofu, grilling tandoori style, 417
tuna, grilling tandoori style, 303
Indirect grilling:
on gas grill, 16
setting up charcoal grill for, 12–13
use of term, 6–7
see also Barbecuing
Ingredients, 28–30
mail-order sources for, 481–82
mise en place and, 3
Injectors, barbecue, 474, *474*
injecting sauce into turkey with, 259–60
Italian-style:
asparagus, grilling, 356
chicken breasts, grilling under bricks, 244–46
eggplant slices, grilling, 367–69
lettuces, grilling, 370–72
pizza, grilling, 408–13
pork chop "calzones," grilling, 130–34
porterhouse steak, grilling, 56–59
Tuscan grills, 464, *464*
veal saltimbocca, 134

Jamaican jerk pork, 111–16
Japanese-style:
hibachis, 21, *464,* 464–65
tofu, grilling, 414–17
yakitori, grilling, 250–53
Jerk pork, 111–16
Juniper, marinating with, to give flavor of wild game, 69

Kebab baskets 474, *474*
Kebabs:
beef, 50, 327
beef satés, 78–81
chicken, 320, 327, 329
chicken satés, 81, 241, 254–57
cooking meat and vegetables separately on, 189
cutting onions and peppers for, 187, 319
flat skewers for, 188, 191

ground lamb, 190–94
marinating in coconut milk mixture, 320
mushroom, 374
shish, 186–89
shrimp, in shell, 325–29
shrimp, peeled, 316–20
on sugarcane, 328–29
tofu, 414–17
wrapped with basil and bacon, 326–27
yakitori, 250–53
Kettle grills, *465,* 465–66
adjusting vents on, 13
ash catchers on, 27
rotisserie attachments for, 23
Kitchen syringes, 474, *474*

Lamb, 159–200
burgers, 101
grilled, salad, 85
ground, kebabs, 190–94
internal temperature of, 12
jerk, 116
leg of, butterflied, grilling, 164–68
leg of, butterflied, stuffing and grilling, 121
leg of, butterflying, 165–66
leg of, rotisserie grilling, 23, 163
leg of, whole, grilling, 160–63
loin chops, grilling, 178–81
marinating to give flavor of wild game, 69
rack of, cutting into rib chops, 183–84
rack of, direct grilling, 169–73
rack of, indirect grilling, 174–77
rack of, removing fat flap from, 171
rib chops, grilling tandoori style, 182–85
riblets, rotisserie grilling, 147
satés, 81
shish kebabs, 186–89
whole, grilling, 195–200
see also Recipe Index for specific lamb dishes
Larding irons, 38
Latin American-style:
crosscut short ribs, grilling, 91–93

RECIPE INDEX

(Page numbers in *italics* refer to illustrations.)